W9-DGE-378

SIMPLE GUIDES

VERY SIMPLE FRENCH

COVER ILLUSTRATIONS

FRONT: Impressionist-style painting of the Champs
Elysées, Paris, at the turn of the century by contemporary
artist Christa Kieffer.
BACK: The Opera, Paris

ABOUT THE AUTHOR

MARIE-LUCE PUGH was born and educated in Paris and
is currently Lecturer in French at New College, Durham.
She has considerable experience in teaching adult
beginners courses on which this book is based.

ILLUSTRATED BY
PETER SEARLE

VERY SIMPLE

FRENCH

MARIE-LUCE PUGH

GLOBAL BOOKS LTD

Simple Guides • Series 2
VERY SIMPLE LANGUAGE

VERY SIMPLE FRENCH
By Marie-Luce Pugh
First published 1996 by
GLOBAL BOOKS LTD
PO Box 219, Folkestone, Kent, England CT20 3LZ

ISBN 1–86034–007–5

British Library Cataloguing in Publication Data
A CIP catalogue entry for this book
is available from the British Library

Distributed in the USA & Canada by:
The Talman Co. Inc. New York

PC
2121
.E5
P85
1995

Set in Futura 11 on 12 point by Bookman, Slough
Printed in Great Britain by
The Cromwell Press Ltd, Broughton Gifford, Wiltshire

Contents

Foreword

France is Europe's main tourist destination, but French is more than a European language and is spoken by up to 200 million people.

This 'very simple' guide provides ways of learning the basic skills needed to communicate with French people in France and French speakers in places as far apart as Senegal, Tahiti and Quebec.

Being able to converse in even very basic French will enable you to experience some of the great cultural riches of both mainland France and the French-speaking world.

Naturally, we provide a basic outline of French grammar, but to be understood in any language, you must be able to make the right sounds. This is why we give detailed tips on pronunciation, accompanied by equivalent or near-equivalent sounds in English in square brackets. French is not difficult to speak, but you may have to learn to make a few new vowel sounds so as to be more easily understood, some through the nose!

Above all, there are plenty of easy phrases to learn, all relating to typical situations. French people are very talkative – so now, whether you need to speak French for business or pleasure, you will be able to join in!

M-L.PUGH

1

A Quick Guide to Pronunciation
'Sounding French'

In French, all syllables have equal weight with a slight emphasis at the end of each word or group of words.

VOWELS

Vowels must be pronounced clearly and not be slurred.

The written vowels are **a e i o u y**. Sound:

a	as in **a**pple	= *Paris*
e*	as in th**e** (not thee)	= *le Havre*
i y	as in s**ee**	= *ici, Vichy*
o { as in d**o**g		= *poste*
{ as in **au**tumn		= *dos*
u	as in German **ü** or Scottish s**oo**n	= *tu*

1. ACCENTS

Accents can be written on top of *a e i o u*:

à â }	are sounded	= *là, château*
î }	exactly as	= *gîte*
û }	without accents	= *sûr*

ô is sounded as in **au**tumn = *côte d'Azur*

---

* In final position, **e** is only sounded in words of ONE syllable: *le Havre*. See also e+consonant in Pronunciation box p. 76

Accents on e change the pronunciation. Sound:

é	as in s**ay**	= *été*
è ê	as in **e**gg	= *très, fête*

2. COMBINATIONS OF VOWELS

eu { as in th**e** (not thee) but lips rounded and longer sound = *deux*
as in f**ur** = *heure*

ou   as in p**oo**l   = *route*

i/y + vowel as in **y**et   = *bière, Lyon*
ou + vowel } as in **we**   = *oui*
u + vowel }   = *nuit*

3. VOWELS + n*

Trying not to make a 'n' or 'm' sound, say:

an am en em	as in c**an't**	= *le Mans, en*
in yn im ym }	as in r**ung**	= *vin, timbre*
un um }		= *un, parfum*
on om	as in *bonbon*	= *bon, nom*

For more detail on how to go from letters to sounds, refer to Pronunciation boxes in the Vocabulary section.

4. VOWEL DELETION

When followed by a word starting with a vowel or 'h'*

De→D'	Je→J'	Le→L'	La→L'	Ne→N'
= of	= I	= the	= the	= not

---

* Except for some words starting with an 'h' marked with an * in dictionaries: *La Hollande*

2. CONSONANTS:

Most FINAL CONSONANTS are NOT SOUNDED.

croissant *baguettes* *camembert*

> To help you with your pronunciation, the silent final consonant in any word used for the first time in this text will be crossed out lightly, as above

However, the final consonant is SOUNDED:

1.   if it is followed by **e**:
vert (t NOT sounded) *verte* (t sounded) = green

2.   usually if it is **c f l r**:
lac = lake, *neuf* = nine, *ciel* = sky, *car* = coach

3.   if it is followed by a vowel or **h***:
très amusant   =   very funny
vous êtes   =   you are

> A line joining the words will remind you where to make such links

Note that **et** is NEVER linked to the next word:
train et ['ay'] *auto* = train and car

---

* Except for some words starting with 'h' marked with an * in dictionaries: *Les Hollandais*

Consonants are very similar to English. However, remember the following:

c	followed by *ieux/ial/ien* sounds like **ss** (never sh)	= *délicieux*, *spécial*
ç	sounds like **ss**	= *français*
ch	sounds like **sh** in shut	= *chambre*
h	is never sounded	= *heure*
g	followed by *i/e* sounds like **s** in pleasure	= *gîte, manger*
gu	followed by *i/e* sounds like **g** but u is silent	= *bourguignon*
gn	sounds like **ni** in onion	= *champagne*
j	sounds like **s** in pleasure	= *bonjour*
q	is always followed by u but this letter is silent	= *tranquillité*
r	is produced at the back of the throat. Make a gargling sound then practise	= *Paris, rose, route*
s	is sounded **z** between two vowels	= *désolé, vision*
	and **ss** in all other cases	= *pension*
ss	always sounds like **ss** (NOT z or sh)	= *possession*
t	followed by *-iel -ieux -ion* sounds like **ss** (NOT 'sh')	= *station*
th	sounds like **t** in table	= *théâtre*

Now for a little bit of practice. Pronounce each syllable very regularly, lingering slightly on the end, and say:

*un-**vin*** = a wine
*un-vin-**blanc*** = a white wine
*un-vin-blanc-in-té-re-**ssant*** = an interesting white wine

2

Very Simple Grammar

NOUNS

Nouns are either of masculine or feminine gender indicated by (m) or (f) in dictionaries and in this book.

    village (m)   =   village
    plage (f)   =   beach

They are usually preceded by an article (the French word for 'a', 'the', or 'some') in the singular as well as the plural.

SINGULAR

1. The article changes according to the gender of the noun. It is not (unfortunately!) usually possible to tell the gender of a noun by its ending. But you have a 50% chance of getting it right. And if you do not, no need to worry. People will still understand you.

A =
    UN   before (m) *un château*   = a castle
    UNE before (f) *une plage*   = a beach

THE =
    LE   before (m) *le château*   = the castle
    LA   before (f) *la plage*   = the beach

SOME (optional in English) =
    DU   before (m) *du pain*   = (some) bread
    DE LA before (f) *de la glace* = (some) ice

2. If the noun starts with a vowel or **h***, the SAME article is used for both (m) and (f):

THE = *L'*
  l'hôtel (m)   = the hotel
  l'auto (f)   = the car

SOME = *DE L'*
  de l'argent (m)   = (some) money
  de l'essence (f)   = (some) petrol

PLURAL

An **s** is added to the nouns** but NOT sounded [crossed out in this chapter only]:

  chambre ['shanbR']   = bedroom
  chambres ['shanbR']   = bedrooms
are sounded the same way. To indicate you are talking about more than one person or thing, you need to use a plural article.

In the plural the SAME article is used for both (m) and (f).

SOME (optional in English) = *DES* ['day']
  des timbres (m)   = (some) stamps
  des glaces (f)   = (some) ice-creams

THE   = *LES* ['lay']
  les timbres (m)   = the stamps
  les glaces (f)   = the ice-creams

ADJECTIVES

These words are used to describe things or people. Two important differences with English:

---

* See note p. 9
** Words ending in **s** or **x** do not change in the plural: *un repas* = a meal, *des repas* = meals. Words ending in **au eau eu** take **x**: *un château* = a castle, *des châteaux* = (some) castles

1. They usually FOLLOW the noun:
   *un touriste **anglais*** = an English tourist

But a few adjectives PRECEDE the noun such as:
   mauvais (bad), *petit* (small), *grand* (tall/big)
   jeune (young), *joli* (pretty) . . .
   *un **petit** village* = a small village

2. They AGREE with the noun. It means that:

● if the noun is masculine, the adjective is masculine:
   ***un** homme français* = a French man

● if the noun is feminine, the adjective is feminine. To make the adjective feminine, just add an **e** to the masculine adjective:
   ***une** femme française* = a French woman

Exceptions include:

Adjectives already ending in **e** which do not change:
un hôtel confortable   = a comfortable hotel
une chambre confortable = a comfortable bedroom

adjectives ending in **el er eux** or **n**:
see examples in the Vocabulary Section

● if the noun is plural, the adjective is plural: an **s*** is added to the adjective but NOT sounded (just like for the noun)

   des vins forts   = (some) strong wines
   des bières fortes = (some) strong beers

---

* Adjectives ending in **s** or **x** do not change:
   un touriste anglais = an English tourist
   des touristes anglais = English tourists
   un voyage merveilleux = a marvellous trip
   des voyages merveilleux = marvellous trips

PRONOUNS*

JE/J'	= I
TU/VOUS	= you (singular)
IL	= He/it
ELLE	= She/it
ON	= We
VOUS	= You (plural)

• *Je→J'* before a vowel or h**: *J'adore le Piat d'Or* (as in the famous advertisement).

• *TU* and *VOUS* = you (singular). So which pronoun will you choose?

In French, fairly strict rules govern the use of the familiar *TU* as opposed to the formal *VOUS*. For instance, within a French family, an in-law is addressed as 'vous'.

Apart from a child who can be addressed as *TU* up to the age of twelve, it is safer to use *VOUS*. The decision to switch to 'tu' will depend on gender and age: basically, a woman has the prerogative to decide over a man, an older person over a younger one. So if you are a younger man, you will have to be patient! These days, however, young people tend to be more casual about it and they address each other as 'tu' even when meeting for the first time.

> We will refer to *TU* as informal and *VOUS* as formal or plural.

• *IL* = he/it   *ELLE* = she/it

Il and Elle are used to refer to things (not just people). It is a bit similar to using 'she' when

---

* *NOUS* (another word for 'we') and *ILS/ELLES* ('they') can be found in a dictionary if needed.
** see note p.9

15

talking about a boat in English. But in French ALL objects are either (m) or (f).

● *ON* = we (also 'people': see ex. p.34)

On is very easy to use (see VERBS p.17) and the French generally prefer it to *NOUS* when they speak.

POSSESSION

To indicate that something belongs to somebody, you need the word *DE/D'*:
La chambre de Pierre = Peter's bedroom

Use the same order to express how a person is related to another:
La fille d' Henri = Henry's daughter

POSSESSIVE ADJECTIVES

Translating MY, YOUR (informal), HIS/HER:

In the singular, there are two words in French depending on the gender of the noun they refer to:

MY =
  MON before (m) *mon passeport* = my passport
  MA before (f)* *ma carte de visite* = my card
YOUR (informal) =
  TON before (m) *ton mari* = your husband
  TA before (f)* *ta femme* ['fam'] = your wife
HIS/HER =
  SON before (m) *son hôtel* = his/her hotel
  SA before (f)* *sa chambre* = his/her bedroom

In the plural, the SAME word is used for both (m) and (f). No need to worry about gender!

---

* Use *MON/TON/SON* before a feminine noun starting with a vowel or h: *Mon amie* = My (female) friend

MY = *MES* ['may']
  mes bagages = my luggage
  mes affaires = my belongings
YOUR = (informal) *TES* ['tay']
  tes enfants = your children
  tes amies = your friends
HIS/HER = *SES* ['say']
  ses sacs = his/her bags
  ses valises = his/her suitcases

Translating OUR, YOUR (formal or plural)

OUR =
NOTRE before (singular) *notre voyage* = our trip
NOS before (plural) *nos voitures* = our cars
YOUR (formal or plural) =
VOTRE before (singular) *votre hôtel* = your hotel
VOS before (plural) *vos photos* = your photos

VERBS

In French, there is a large category of verbs whose infinitive (the form given in dictionaries) ends in ER. Examples include:

  Aimer = to like   *Apporter* = to bring

They are easy to use because they are regular and all follow the same pattern.

REGULAR VERBS

The PRESENT tense of *ER* verbs is obtained by simply dropping the final 'r' of the infinitive.
Example: *Donner* = to give

je donne	= I give/am giving
tu donnes	= you give/are giving (informal)
il donne	= he/it gives/is giving
elle donne	= she/it gives/is giving
on donne	= we give/are giving
vous donnez	= you give/are giving
	(formal or plural)

For *TU* 's' is added but NOT sounded.

So the only form which sounds different is:
 vous donnez ['nay'] = you give/are giving

Note how the present tense expresses actions people do every day, in general, as well as actions in progress:

Il regarde la télé = he watches TV (every day. . .)
 = he is watching TV (now)

IRREGULAR VERBS

However, not all verbs are regular. the following very useful verbs are a bit more difficult. But they crop up all the time so you will get plenty of practice using them.

ETRE = to be
 Je suis = I am
 Tu es ['ay']   = you are (informal)
 Il/Elle est ['ay']   = he/she/it is
 On est   = we are
 Vous êtes   = you are (formal or plural)

AVOIR = to have
 J'ai   = I have
 Tu as   = you have
 Il/Elle a   = he/she/it has
 On a   = we have
 Vous avez ['vay']   = you have (formal or plural)

POUVOIR = to be able to
 Je peux   = I can
 Tu peux   = you can (informal)
 Il/Elle peut   = he/she can
 On peut   = we can
 Vous pouvez ['vay']   = you can (formal or plural)

VOULOIR = to want
 Je veux   = I want
 Tu veux   = you want (informal)
 Il/Elle veut   = he/she wants

On veut = we want
Vous voulez ['lay'] = you want (formal or plural)

NEGATIVE

To make a statement negative, use:
  NE/N' . . . PAS

*Elle **ne** parle **pas** anglais* = she doesn't speak English

Or: *NE/N' . . . JAMAIS* = never
      NE/N' . . . PERSONNE = nobody
      NE/N' . . . RIEN = nothing

*Tu **ne** téléphones **jamais*** = you never phone
*Il **n'**aime **personne*** = he likes nobody
*Elle **ne** mange **rien*** = she doesn't eat anything

QUESTIONS

The easiest ways to ask a question are:

1. RAISING YOUR VOICE

Elle parle français? (voice goes up)
              = Does she speak French?
Vous êtes anglais? (voice goes up)
              = Are you English?

2. Using QUESTION WORDS

  Qui?   = who?
  Où?   = where?
  Quand?   = when?
  Comment? = how?
  Combien? = how much/many?
  Pourquoi? = Why

Q'est-ce que/qu' . . .? ['kesker'] = What . . .?
Q'est-ce que vous voulez? = What do you want?
Q'est-ce qu'elle veut? = What does she want?

QUEL before (m) *Quel motel* = which hotel?
QUELLE before (f) *Quelle route?* = which road?
QUELS before (m) plural
        Quels motels = which hotels?
QUELLES before (f) plural
        Quelles routes? = which roads?

PREPOSITIONS

Placed before a noun, they indicate:

THE DIRECTION/LOCATION

sous	= under
de	= from/out of
devant	= in front of
derrière	= behind
sur	= onto, on
dans	= into, in

TO/AT/IN THE

AU	before (m) *au marché*	= to/at the market
A LA	before (f) *à la plage*	= to/at the beach
A L'	before (m) *à l'hôpital*	= to/at the hospital
	or before (f) *à l'auberge*	= to/at the inn
AUX	before plural *aux toilettes*	= to/in the toilets

THE TIME

avant	= before
après	= after
pendant	= during

THE MANNER

avec	= with
sans	= without
par	= by

3

Communicating With The French

'C'est ça!'

To help you UNDERSTAND and SPEAK French, here are some simple phrases which crop up all the time and are easy to memorize. Watch how the French use both intonation and body language to convey their messages and have fun imitating them. Remember, pronunciation 'sound alikes' are given in square brackets throughout.

PRESENTING SOMEBODY / SOMETHING

1. *VOILA/VOICI* = Here is/are

   Voilà / voici le guide ['geed']
   = Here is the guide
   Voilà / voici une carte = Here is a map

Voilà / voici un horaire = Here is a timetable
Voilà / voici les tickets ['tee-kay']
= Here are the tickets

2. *IL Y A* ['ee-lya']   = There is/are

Il y a une excursion = There is an excursion
Il y a un car = There is a coach
Il y a des places libres = There are some vacant
seats

3. *C'EST* ['say']   = This is/these are

C'est un ami = This is a friend
C'est la maison = This is the house
C'est les clés = These are the keys

GIVING A POSITIVE ANSWER

Oui ['wee']   = Yes
Tout à fait (meaning 'oui') = Quite (instead of yes)
This is used more and more commonly for 'yes'.

C'est exact = That's correct
C'est ça / cela! = That's it!

Oui, bien sûr! (stressing the ending 'üüR')
= Yes, of course!
Mais certainement! = Certainly!

D'accord! = Fine!
Je suis d'accord = I agree
Pas de problème! = No problem!
(hands spread and turned upwards, shrugging
one's shoulders)

Si (if the question is NEGATIVE)
    On ne visite pas le Louvre? = Aren't we visiting
the Louvre?
    Si, si. = Yes, we are.

GIVING A NEGATIVE ANSWER

Non   = No

Non, non et non!	= No, absolutely not

(accompanied by emphatic gestures of hands to punctuate each word)

Non, pas du tout	= No, not at all

(shaking your head)

Pas encore	= Not yet
Je ne suis pas d'accord	= I don't agree

GIVING A TENTATIVE ANSWER

Peut-être	= Maybe
Je ne sais pas	= I don't know
Je ne suis pas sûr(e)	= I am not sure
Pas exactement	= Not exactly

CHECKING YOU HAVE UNDERSTOOD

Vous pouvez répéter?	= Could you repeat?
Pardon?	= I beg your pardon?
Je ne comprends pas	= I don't understand

EXPRESSING A DESIRE

Je veux	= I want
Je voudrais	= I would like
Vous avez. . .?	= have you got. . . ?
Il y a . . . . .?	= Is/are there. . .?

OBTAINING ASSISTANCE:

Attracting people's attention on the street, in a café, a shop:

Pardon ⎫	
Excusez-moi ⎬	= Excuse me
S'il vous plaît	= Please

Add: Monsieur/Madame/Mademoiselle for greater formality.

Asking for a favour:

Tu peux . . .?	= Can you . . .? (informal)
Vous pouvez . . .?	= Can you . . .? (formal/plural)

SHOWING YOUR APPRECIATION

très ['tRe'] = very can be repeated for greater effect:

C'est très, très bon! = It's really very nice!

These expressions range from most to least formal to suit the occasion:

C'est très aimable	= This is most kind
gentil	= This is very nice
C'est très sympathique	= This is very pleasant
Merci beaucoup ['baukoo']	= Thank you very much

REACTING TO PEOPLE'S THANKS:

Je vous en prie	= My pleasure
De rien	= Don't mention it

BECOMING EMPHATIC

If you want to emphasize a word, clearly detach each syllable and use both arms held in front of you to punctuate each word:

c'est for-mi-dable	= It's absolutely
fan-tas-tique	Fantastic!
sen-sa-tion-nel	

Using *QUEL* (See Grammar section p.20) as an exclamation. You should linger on the last syllable.

Quel film! ['feelm']	= What a film!
Quelle vue splendide! [-'deed']	
	= What a splendid view!

MAKING SUGGESTIONS

Raise your voice to show you want an answer:

On mange?	= Shall we eat?
On danse?	= Shall we dance?

DECLINING A PROPOSITION

Désolé(e)	= Sorry
Je regrette	= I regret
Ah, non! Pas question	= It's out of the question

(Holding both hands in front of you as a barrier)

Je ne veux pas	= I don't want to
Je ne peux pas	= I can't
C'est impossible	= It's impossible
C'est interdit	= It's forbidden

ASKING FOR PERMISSION

On peut . . .?	= Can we . . .?
Je peux . . .?	= Can I . . .?
C'est permis?	= Is it allowed?
C'est possible?	= Is it possible

CHECKING WHETHER SOMETHING IS NECESSARY

Il faut réserver?	= Is it necessary
C'est nécessaire de réserver?	to book?

EXPRESSING YOUR FEELINGS

Je suis très content(e)	= I am very happy
Je suis furieux, furieuse	= I am furious
Je suis triste	= I am sad
Je suis déçu(e)	= I am disappointed

4

Personal Identification & Greetings

'Ça va?'

Verbs for this unit:

Habiter	(reg)	= to live
Parler	(reg)	= to speak
Travailler	(reg)	= to work
Etre	(irreg)	= to be

ALLER (irreg) = to go (in greetings: to be/feel)

Je vais	= I go
Tu vas	= you go (informal)
Il/Elle va	= he/she/it goes
On va	= we go
Vous allez	= you go (formal/plural)

GREETINGS

You can use the greeting expressions by themselves or add *Monsieur/Madame/Mademoiselle* when you want to be more formal.

SAYING HELLO

–   **Bonjour:** may be used throughout the day
    Bonjour   = Good morning/afternoon/evening

–   **Bonsoir:** is used from approx. 6.00 pm.
    Bonsoir   = Good evening

A handshake usually accompanies the greetings, which are followed by:

–   *Comment allez-vous?*   = How are you?
    Très bien, merci.   = Very well, thank you.

or less formally:
–   *Ça va?*   = You okay?
    Ça va , merci.   = Fine, thanks.

Because French people are frequently worried about their health, they may answer:

   Oh, ça ne va pas   = I am not (feeling) too good. . .

You can express your concern by saying:

Ah bon! Qu'est-ce qu'il y a? ['kes-kee-lya']
                        = Really! What's the matter?

SAYING GOODBYE

–   **Au revoir:** may be used any time of the day.
    Au revoir ['oRvwaR'] = Good bye/night

–   **Bonsoir:** is used from 6.00 pm
    Bonsoir   = Good bye/night

- *A tout à l'heure* = See you later (in the same day)
- *A bientôt* = See you soon
- *Bonne journée* = Have a nice day
- *Bonne nuit* = Sleep well!
- *Salut*: means both 'hello' and 'good bye' in an informal situation.

INTRODUCTIONS

To introduce your friends say:

Voici mon ami Pierre = Here is my friend Peter
Voici mon amie Jacqueline = Here is my friend Jacqueline

When introduced to someone, shake hands and say:

Enchanté(e)   = Pleased to meet you

TALKING ABOUT YOURSELF

A man will say:

Mon nom est John = My name is John
Je suis anglais = I am English
Je parle français = I speak French.
Je suis de Douvres = I am from Dover

A woman will say:

Mon nom est Marion = My name is Marion
Je suis anglaise ['anglez'] = I am English
Je parle français = I speak French
Je suis de Londres = I am from London

---

* For more nationalities see Reference Section

28

For foreign languages use the MASCULINE form of the adjective.

ASKING OTHERS ABOUT THEMSELVES

Quel est votre nom? = What is your name?
Quelle est votre nationalité? = What is your nationality?
Vous parlez anglais? = Do you speak English?
Vous habitez en France? = Do you live in France?
Vous travaillez ici? = Do you work here?
Votre ami parle français? = Does your friend speak French?

FILLING IN FORMS

Prénom = First Name
Nom de famille = Surname
Nom de jeune fille = Maiden name
Nationalité = Nationality
Date et lieu de naissance = Date and place of birth
Profession = Occupation
Numéro de pièce d'identité = Identity card number

USEFUL WORDS/EXPRESSIONS

marié(e) = married
divorcé(e) = divorced
célibataire = single
veuf/veuve = widower/widow
retraité(e) = retired
au chômage = unemployed
étudiant(e) = student

5

Numbers & Time, Seasons & Weather

'Quelle heure est-il?'

V erbs for this unit:

Arriver	(reg)	= to arrive
Travailler	(reg)	= to work
Avoir	(irreg)	= to have
FAIRE	(irreg)	= to do/make
Je fais		= I do/make
Tu fais		= You do/make (informal)
Il/Elle fait		= He/she/it does/makes
On fait		= We do/make
Vous faites ['fet']		= You do/make (formal or plural)

Firt, learn numbers 0 to 20:

0	*zéro*	10	*dix*
1	*un/une*	11	*onze*
2	*deux*	12	*douze*
3	*trois*	13	*treize*
4	*quatre*	14	*quatorze*
5	*cinq*	15	*quinze*
6	*six*	16	*seize*
7	*sept* ['set']	17	*dix-sept*
8	*huit*	18	*dix-huit*
9	*neuf*	19	*dix-neuf*

1: UN with a masculine word.
UNE with a feminine word
Vingt et UN dollars = 21 dollars
Vingt et UNE livres = 21 pounds

6 and 10: these numbers are sounded ['see'] and ['dee'] when followed by a noun:
Je voudrais 6 croissants = I'd like 6 croissants

They are sounded ['seess'] and ['deess'] when they are used on their own:
Combien de croissants? = How many croissants?
six! ['seess'] = Six!

8: silent 't' before a consonant

Now learn the multiples of tens:

20	*vingt*
30	*trente*
40	*quarante*
50	*cinquante*
60	*soixante* ('x' sounded 'ss')]
21	*vingt et un*
22	*vingt-deux* ['vintdeu']
23	*vingt-trois*
24	*vingt-quatre* etc. . . ['vintkatR']

Up to 69 (*soixante-neuf*), carry on as above.

THE TIME

– **Quelle heure est-il?** ['ay-teel']

= What time is it?

Or you can say:

– **Vous avez l'heure?** = Have you got the time?

You will hear first the hour figure, then the word *HEURE(S)* and finally the number of minutes as follows:

Il est neuf HEURES = it's nine
neuf HEURES cinq = it's five past nine
neuf HEURES dix = it's ten past nine

etc. . .

dix HEURES moins vingt = it's twenty to
ten etc. . .

Half past	= *et demie* ['ay-dmee']
A quarter past	= *et quart* ['ay-kaR']
A quarter to	= *moins le quart*
Midday	= *Midi*
Midnight	= *Minuit*

HEURES

Once used only in stations, airports . . . , the 24-hour clock is becoming more and more common. So when you ask the time, you are likely to get the answer:

vingt HEURES quarante = Twenty forty

– **A quelle heure . . .?** = (At) what time. . .?
A quelle heure on arrive à Nice?
= What time do we get to Nice?

SOME MORE NUMBERS

After the number 69, the system changes. Unlike the French-speaking Belgians or Swiss, the French have no specific words for 70, 80 and 90! So they make do with combining numbers. Here are some examples.

70: *soixante-dix* (sixty + ten)
71: *soixante ET onze* (sixty + eleven)
72: *soixante-douze* (sixty + twelve)
80: *quatre-vingt* (four twenties)
81: *quatre-vingt-un* (four twenties + one)
82: *quatre-vingt-deux* (four twenties + two)
90: *quatre-vingt-dix* (four twenties + ten)
91: *quatre-vingt-onze* (four twenties + eleven)
92: *quatre-vingt-douze* (four twenties + twelve)

100: *'cent* ['san']
1000: *'mille'* ['meel']

For multiples of hundreds or thousands, just add deux, trois etc in front:

200: *deux cents* ['san']
300: *trois cents*
4000: *quatre mille* (never takes an 's')

TIME EXPRESSIONS

Hier ['ee-yeR']	= yesterday
Aujourd'hui	= today
Demain	= tomorrow
Un jour	= one day
Une semaine	= one week
Huit jours (literally 8 days)	= one week
Quinze jours (literally 15 days)	= two weeks

Il arrive dans huit jours = He is arriving in a week
Un mois = one month
Un an = one year

The days of the week. (See Reference section)

Used on their own, they refer to a particular day:

> *On arrive jeudi* = We're arriving on Thursday
> *On visite le Louvre vendredi* = We're visiting the Louvre on Friday

Preceded by *LE*, they usually express a recurring event:

Tu travailles LE samedi? = Do you work on Saturdays?

Months. (See Reference section)

Vous êtes en vacances EN juillet?
= Are you on holiday in July?

Notice that days / months do not take a capital when inside a sentence.

Expressing the date:

Apart from the first of every month which is:
le premier = the first
Le premier mai, on ne travaille pas en France
= On the 1 May, people do not work in France

Use ordinary numbers for dates:

J'arrive le trois = I arrive on the third
le dix ['deess'] = tenth
le trente = thirtieth

Un jour férié = a bank holiday

SEASONS AND WEATHER

Le printemps ['-tan'] = spring
L'été = summer

L'automne = autumn
L'hiver ['ee-veR'] = winter

Quel temps ['tan'] fait-il?
= what's the weather like?

Il fait beau = The weather is nice
Il fait chaud = It's hot
Il fait mauvais = The weather is bad / It's not nice
Il fait froid = It's cold

Il pleut = It rains / it's raining

Quel temps fait-il à Nice l'hiver?
= What's the weather like in Nice in winter
En général, il fait assez doux
= In general, it's quite mild

If you want to say you are hot or cold:

J'ai chaud = I am hot
J'ai froid = I am cold

USEFUL WORDS/EXPRESSIONS:

trop = too
un peu = a little / a bit
Il fait trop chaud = it's too hot
Il fait un peu froid = it's a bit cold
Le matin = in the morning
L'après-midi = in the afternoon
Le soir = in the evening
La nuit = at night

6

Weights & Measures
Shopping & Money

'C'est combien?'

Verbs in this unit:

Changer	(reg)	= to change
Goûter	(reg)	= to taste
Vouloir	(irreg)	= to want
Je voudrais		= I'd like

MAIN MEASURES

un kilo (about 2 pounds)
une livre (half a kilo/a pound)
un litre (about 2 pints)
un kilomètre (5/8 of a mile)

MAIN CONTAINERS

un paquet ['pa-kay']   = a packet
une boîte   = a tin / a box
une bouteille ['boo-tei']   = a bottle

BUYING FOOD

Start with:
    Je voudrais   = I'd like

Add for example:
    deux kilos de pommes = 2 kilos of apples
    trois litres de lait   = 3 litres of milk
    quatre paquets de beurre = 4 packets of
                                   butter
    une boite de tomates   = a tin of tomatoes
    huit bouteilles de champagne = 8 bottles of
                                     champagne

And finish with:
    S'il vous plaît   = please

When the shop assistant asks:

    Et avec ça?   = anything else?

You might answer:
    C'est tout, merci = that's all, thanks

It is quite usual in shops, especially in open markets, to taste products:

    Vous voulez goûter? = Would you like to taste?
If you are not asked, do not hesitate to say:
    Je peux goûter? = Can I have a taste?

If you go to a good patisserie, you will see a large display of exquisite-looking gateaux. Prices may be steep, but on the whole they are certainly worth it. One of the larger cakes would be an ideal present if you are invited to an informal dinner. You can say to your friends:

On apporte le dessert, ['day-sseR'] *d'accord?*
= We're bringing the dessert, okay?

Y ou can say:

Je voudrais un gâteau comme ça = I'd like one of
those cakes
C'est pour combien de personnes? = How many
people is it for?
C'est pour dix! ['deess'] = It's for ten

BUYING CLOTHES

S tart with the item of clothing, then specify
the colour:
(For more colours, see Reference section)

je voudrais un T-shirt blanc = I'd like a white T-shirt

S ome items which are plural in English are
masculine singular in French.

un short blanc	= a pair of white shorts
un pantalon noir	= a pair of black trousers
un pyjama en coton	= a pair of cotton pyjamas
un jean bleu	= a pair of blue jeans

Y ou will probably be asked:

Quelle taille?	= What size? (for clothes)
Quelle pointure?	= What size? (for shoes)

CLOTHES		SHOES	
ENGLISH	FRENCH	ENGLISH	FRENCH
8	34	3	36
10	36	4	37
12	38	5	38
14	40	6	39
16	42	7	40
18	44	8	41

Clothes also come in: small / medium / large / extra-large. But be ready to recognize these words pronounced with a FRench accent!

MONEY

The easiest way to pay for goods in France is by credit card. Most shops and super-markets offer the facility. However, you will probably need cash in small food shops where you may be asked:

Vous avez la monnaie? = Have you got the right change?

Make sure you have a 10-franc coin for the trolley (*le chariot* – silent 't'). Or go to Reception and say:

Vous avez une pièce DE dix francs?
= Have you got a ten-franc coin?

For money, use *DE* before the value:

– *Je veux un billet DE cinquante francs*
= I want a 50-franc banknote

USEFUL WORDS/EXPRESSIONS

demi	= half
un demi-litre	= half a litre
une demi-livre	= half a pound
moins	= less
plus	= more
c'est assez	= that's enough
l'argent	= money
la monnaie	= change

7

Getting Around

'Allez tout droit!'

Verbs for this unit

Tourner	(reg)	= to turn
Continuer	(reg)	= to continue
Aller	(irreg)	= to go
Etre	(irreg)	= to be
PRENDRE	(irreg)	= to take

Je prends ['pRan']	= I take
Tu prends	= you take (informal)
Il/Elle prend	= he/she/it takes
On prend	= we take
Vous prenez	= you take (formal or plural)

ASKING WHERE THINGS ARE

If you ask:

Où est l'Office du tourisme?	= Where is the Tourist Office?
la gare?	= the station?
le camping ?	= the camp site?

The answer might be complicated. Have a street map or a road map ready. Hopefully, people will be able to direct you:

Vous êtes ici!	= You are here
La gare est là	= The station is there

They may add:

C'est à 3 km	= It is 3 km away
C'est à 10 minutes, environ	= It is about 10 minutes away

ASKING HOW TO GET THERE
(See Grammar Section p.20)

Pour aller à la piscine?	= to go to the swimming pool?
à l'hôtel?	= the hotel?
à l'auberge	= the inn
AU cinéma?	= the cinema?
AUX toilettes?	= the toilets?

Directions French people give you may include:

jusqu'à la mairie	= up to the town hall
jusqu'à l'hôpital	= up to the hospital
jusqu'AU rond-point	= up to the roundabout
jusqu'AUX magasins	= up to the shops
Allez tout droit ['dRwa']	= Go straight on
Tournez à gauche	= Turn on the left
Prenez la première à droite ['dRwat']	= Take the first on the right

Make sure you distinguish clearly *'tout droit'* ('t' is NOT sounded) from *'à droiTE'* ('t' is sounded)

To check that you have understood, say:

Il faut tourner à gauche après le pont?
= Do I have to turn left after the bridge?

Il faut continuer jusqu'au village?
= Do I have to go up to the village?

TRAVELLING BY TRAIN

Look out for the departure board (DEPARTS) indicating times, destinations and platform numbers. French railway stations are abundantly equipped with ticket machines, but ticket offices (*les guichets*) are also available if you do not mind queuing.

You might ask for:

Deux allers pour Cannes   = 2 singles to Cannes
Deux allers-retours pour Paris = 2 returns to Paris

For some trains, such as TGV or extra-fast trains, you may have to pay a surcharge or to book in advance. Say:

Il y a un supplément?   = Is there a surcharge?
Il faut réserver?   = Is it necessary to book?

Then specify:

Première	= first
Seconde	= second
Fumeurs	= smoking
Non fumeurs	= non smoking
Dans le sens ['sans'] *de la marche*	
	= facing the engine

Finally ask:

C'est combien?   = How much is it?

NOTE: Visa cards can be used for sums over 100F.

Once you have your ticket, you must not forget to stamp it (*composter*) before boarding the train or you will be fined. The stamping machines (*composteurs*) are orange pillars situated next to the platforms. If you miss them, ask:

> *Où est le composteur?* = Where is the stamping machine?

Insert your ticket in the slot. It will be stamped for that particular day.

TRAVELLING BY CAR

The road network in France is extensive. The choice ranges from small roads (*départementales*), indicated by the letter 'D' on the road map, which wind their way through the countryside to modern motorways (*autoroutes*) indicated by the letter 'A'.

If you have the time, take a secondary road to your destination. Ask for a map showing alternative itineraries. They are given out free at Information Points along the road and major petrol stations. Say:

Vous avez la carte Bison ['bee-zon'] *Fûté?*
    = Have you got the map of alternative routes?

'Bison Fûté' (literally: Willy Bison, an Indian boy) is a cartoon character invented by the Ministry of Transport to encourage drivers to opt for unbeaten tracks.

These alternative roads (*itinéraire bis*) are signposted in green all over the country. If you use them, you should have peace and quiet away from the rush of HGVs and holiday-makers.

If you are in a hurry, use the motorways. You will find that they are usually fairly quiet except near major cities, a zone left free of charge for city-dwellers. You can use your credit card to pay at the toll (*le péage*). Complimentary up-to-date maps of French motorways indicating rates are available at the toll. Say:

Vous avez la carte des autoroutes svp?
    = Have you got a motorway map please?

It is recommended to avoid 'RED DAYS' (*les jours rouges*) of major departures to or from holiday places.

'RED DAYS' occur on: 1   July
                        1   August
                        14 July
                        15 August
                        31 August

Allow one day on each side of these dates before you start travelling.

Many petrol stations offer customer service. Ask for:

Le plein svp   = Fill it up, please

Strong, good quality expresso coffee is often available from machines for 4-5 francs.

Je voudrais 2 pièces de 5 francs pour le café
    = I'd like two 5 franc coins for the coffee

TRAVELLING BY PLANE

Check how to get to the airport:

Il y a un bus pour l'aéroport ['-poR']?
    = Is there a bus to the airport?

Où est l'arrêt? = where is the stop?
A quelle heure il arrive? = what time does it come?

At the check-in, say:

Voilà mon passeport ['pass-poR']
= Here is my passport
Voilà mon billet ['bee-ay'] = Here is my ticket
Quand est le départ? = When is the departure?

USEFUL WORDS/EXPRESSIONS

le péage	= toll
environ	= approximately, about
les bagages	= the luggage
l'enregistrement	= the check-in
la porte	= the gate

Accommodation: Hotels & Camp-sites

'Vous avez une chambre?'

Verbs for this unit:

Chercher	(reg)	= to look for
Rester	(reg)	= to stay
Passer	(reg)	= to spend
Avoir l'intention de + Verb		= to intend to

WRITING FOR INFORMATION

When you plan a holiday, write to the French Tourist Office in your country. They will supply you with plenty of general information on the area of your choice, including the addresses of local Tourist Offices, which you can contact for additional information. For example, you might address your letter to:

> OFFICE DU TOURISME
> 06150 CANNES
> FRANCE

The first two digits represent the number of the département (Here: 06 = Alpes Maritimes). The last three represent each individual town in the département (Here: 150 = Cannes).

Monsieur,

J'ai l'intention de passer . . . jours/semaines à Grasse en juillet. Je voudrais des brochures (en anglais si possible) sur la ville et la région.

Veuillez agréer, Monsieur, l'expression de mes sentiments distingués

This translates as:

Dear Sir,

I intend to spend . . . days/weeks in Grasse in July. I would like some brochures (in English if possible) on the town and the region.

Yours faithfully

ASKING FOR INFORMATION

Vous avez une brochure sur la ville/région?
    = Have you got a brochure on the town/region?
Vous avez un plan de la ville? = Have you got a
                                    street map?
Qu'est-ce qu'on peut visiter?   = What is there to
                                      see?
C'est où ['say-oo'] exactement?
                          = Where is it exactly?
Il y a une réduction pour les enfants?
    = Is there a reduction for children?

Eating Out: Restaurants & Cafes

'C'est un fromage fort?'

V erbs for this unit:

Manger	(reg)	= to eat
Proposer	(reg)	= to propose/offer
Recommander	(reg)	= to recommend

Prendre (irreg) = to take / to have (a drink. . .)
Pouvoir (irreg) = To be able to

BREAKFAST

B reakfast (*le petit-déjeuner*) is served any time between 7.30 and 10.00 in hotels. If you are driving, you can also enjoy breakfast in cafes or restaurants along the road. Say:

On peut prendre le petit-déjeuner?
                          = Can we have breakfast?
The answer is likely to be:
Bien sûr! Combien de personnes? = Of course!
                                How many people?
Pour trois personnes = Breakfast for three

A continental breakfast will automatically include bread and croissants, both fresh from the nearby baker's, with butter and jam as well as a drink. You will be charged for everything unless you specify:

sans croissants   = without croissants

The waiter will take the orders for the drinks. Say what you would like:

un café noir	= one black coffee
un café au lait	= one coffee with milk
un thé	= one tea
un chocolat chaud	= one hot chocolate
un jus d'orange	= an orange juice

In modern hotels, however, the trend is very much towards the buffet-type of breakfast where you may have to specify how you would like your egg:

Un oeuf à la coque	= soft-boiled egg
Un oeuf sur le plat	= a fried egg

LUNCH & DINNER

Customers are usually expected to start on their lunch (*le déjeuner*) between 12.00 and 1.00 o'clock and their dinner (*le dîner*) between 7.00 and 8.00 o'clock.

As before, be ready to say:

On peut déjeuner?	= Can we have lunch?
Cinq personnes	= five people

You are likely to be asked:

Vous désirez: = Would you like
Fumeurs? / Non fumeurs? = (Smoking/non smoking?)
Une table à l'extérieur/à l'intérieur?
= a table outside/ inside?

You will be given the menu (*la carte*) which displays a range of fixed-price menus, each including a minimum of 3-4 courses. If nothing takes your fancy, look at the '*à la carte*' section. Each dish being priced individually, the total will be quite a lot higher.

Now you are ready to order. Say:

Trois menus à cent-trente francs
= Three 130-franc menus
deux menus à cent-dix francs
= two 110-franc menus
et un repas à la carte = and one meal à-la-carte

If the busy waiter/waitress does not notice your empty bread basket, raise your arm and call out for attention:

(Monsieur/Madame/mademoiselle) S'il vous plait? = Please?
je voudrais DU pain = I'd like some bread

If you ask for water, s/he will encourage you to order mineral water by saying:

Vous voulez de l'eau minérale?
= Would you like some mineral water?

Either say:

Oui, merci. De l'eau minérale plate/gazeuse
= Yes, thank you. Some still/sparkling water

Or:

Non merci, une carafe d'eau
= No thanks, a jug of water

The main categories are : (silent final 's' for all)

entrées	= starters
viandes	= meats
poissons	= fish
légumes	= vegetables
fromages	= cheeses
desserts ['daysseR']	= desserts

Grilled meats tend to be cooked rare. If you usually ask for your steak to be 'medium', say:

'bien cuit' ['kwee'] = well done
'à point' which, strictly speaking, is 'medium' would be too red for most British and American people.

If you have any queries, involving choice, use:

QU'EST-CE QUE/QU' . . . COMME . . .?

qu'est-ce que vous recommandez comme vin?
= What sort of wine do you recommend?

Cheeses come before the dessert. In more up-market establishments, the waiter/waitress will bring a tray of cheeses selected from the 340 different kinds available in France. These are likely to include the specialities of the region. S/he will either leave the tray with you or help you to the ones you want to sample. Do not hesitate to point out and ask:

Qu'est-ce que c'est? = What is this?
C'est un fromage fort?
= Is this a strong cheese?
C'est un fromage doux?
= Is this a mild cheese?
C'est un fromage de la région?
= Is this a regional cheese?

When s/he comes back to take the order for the desserts, ask:

Qu'est-ce qu'il y a comme desserts?
  = What sort of desserts are there?

Finally ask for:

  L'addition, svp! = the bill please!

Service is included. You do not have to leave a tip in cafes, restaurants, hotels etc. . .although you may want to leave something to show your appreciation.

CAFES, BRASSERIES

You will be able to get a drink, a sandwich or a single dish practically any time of the day. A good example of local enterprise was the following note seen posted in a Breton cafe's window:

```
ICI
FIVE O'CLOCK
A TOUTE HEURE
```

(Here, five o'clock any time of the day!)

You might have to attract the waiter's attention.

On peut manger? = Can we eat?
Qu'est-ce que vous avez comme sandwichs?
  = What sort of sandwiches have you got?

USEFUL WORDS/EXPRESSIONS	
j'ai faim	= I am hungry
j'ai soif	= I am thirsty
adorer	= to love
être végétarien(ne)	= to be a vegetarian

54

Banks & Services
Phoning

'C'est de la part de qui?'

Verbs for this unit:

Appeler	(reg)	= to call (on the phone)
Rappeler	(reg)	= to call back
Laisser	(reg)	= to leave
Pouvoir	(irreg)	= to be able to

Banks are open five days a week, including either Mondays or Saturdays. The opening times (*heures d'ouverture*) are usually:

9.00–12.30
14.00–16.30

But watch out for long weekends when banks are usually closed from the Friday evening to the following Tuesday morning.

At the bank, say:

Je voudrais changer des chèques de voyage
= I'd like to change some traveller's cheques
Je voudrais changer des livres/des dollars
= I'd like to change pounds/dollars
En billets de cent francs = To 100-franc notes.

Post offices are indicated by a blue and yellow sign. They offer a wide range of services including the MINITEL, which can give anybody's telephone number and address from just their name, as well as machines for franking your own parcels.

At the window (*le guichet*), say:

Une lettre pour l'Amérique, c'est combien?
= How much is it for a letter to America?
Et pour une carte? = What about a postcard?
Je voudrais deux timbres pour des lettres
= I'd like two stamps for letters
et dix ['dee'] *timbres pour des cartes*
= and 10 stamps for cards

Tobacconists (*le tabac*) also sell stamps for letters to Europe. Say:

Je voudrais deux timbres pour l'Angleterre
= I'd like two stamps for England

Post your letters in the *'boîtes aux lettres'*, yellow boxes fixed to buildings.

PHONING

It is possible, even with only a basic knowledge of French, to establish contact by telephone as long as you recognize a few simple phrases such as:

à l'appareil ['a-la–pa-Rei'] = speaking
c'est de la part ['paR'] *de qui?* = who is calling?

Here is a typical telephone conversation:

Allô, bonjour! = Hello, good morning!
Je voudrais parler à monsieur Dupont
   = I'd like to speak to M.Dupont

– *C'est de la part de qui?* = Who is calling?

Madame Jones à l'appareil = Mrs Jones speaking

– *Un instant svp* = Just a moment please

If the person you want to speak to is not available:

– *Je regrette, monsieur Dupont n'est pas là*
   = I am sorry. Mr Dupont is not in.

– *Vous pouvez rappeler?* = Can you call back?

A quelle heure svp? = At what time, please?

– *A dix heures* = at ten

Très bien, merci = Very good, thanks

USEFUL WORDS/EXPRESSIONS

laisser un message	= to leave a message
le mauvais numéro	= the wrong number
plus fort!	= louder!
ne quittez pas	= hold on
affranchissement	= franking

Leisure

'On va au cinéma?'

Verbs for this unit:

Aimer	(reg)	= to like/love
Adorer	(reg)	= to love
Détester	(reg)	= to hate
Terminer	(reg)	= to finish
Commencer	(reg)	= to start
Faire	(irreg)	= to do/make

LIKES & DISLIKES

Verbs expressing likes/dislikes are followed by *LE / LA / L'* when talking about the activity and by the INFINITIVE when talking about doing the activity

*Il aime **le** tennis, **la** natation, **l'**équitation*
    = he likes tennis, swimming, horseriding
*Elle déteste **le** football, **la** gymnastique*
    = she hates football, gymnastics

Tu aimes danser? = Do you like dancing?
Vous aimez regarder la télévision? = Do you like watching television?
Qu'est-ce que vous aimez faire? = What do you like doing? (formal)
Qu'est-ce que tu fais le weekend? = What do you do on weekends?

PLANNING ENTERTAINMENT:

First, find out what is available by asking:

Il y a un théâtre? = Is there a theater?
Il y a un stade? = Is there a sports stadium?
Qu'est-ce qu'on peut faire le soir? = What can we do in the evening?

Then make suggestions:

On va au cinéma? = Shall we go to the cinema?
au théâtre? . . .to the theatre?
à la discothèque . . .to the discotheque?

Ask how people feel about it:

Vous êtes d'accord? = Do you agree?

React to other people's suggestions:

D'accord. C'est une bonne idée = OK. It's a good idea.
Alors, on va au cinéma = Alright, then. Let's go to the cinema
Le film commence à quelle heure? = What time does the film start?
Il termine à quelle heure? = What time does it finish?
Qu'est-ce que c'est comme film? = What kind of film is it?
Deux places pour (title of the film) = Two seats for (title)

59

Business Matters

'On peut fixer un rendez-vous?'

Verbs for this unit:

Exporter	(reg)	= to export
Fixer	(reg)	= to fix / arrange (a meeting)
Fermer	(reg)	= to close
Regretter	(reg)	= to be sorry

In small provincial cities, businesses usually open from 8.30 until noon and from 1.30 until 6.00. In the capital or major cities, many offices have a continuous working day (*la journée continue*) from 8.30 until 4.30 with just a short break between the morning and the afternoon sessions. It is worth checking opening hours (*les horaires d'ouverture*):

Vous fermez à midi? = Do you close at midday?
Vous fermez à quelle heure? = At what time do you close?

It is quite common to be invited to a business lunch in a restaurant and your ability to demonstrate some knowledge of French will be much appreciated by your French counterparts.

Note the two words for director:

un directeur (m)
une directrice (f)

Je suis directrice de la société X
  = I am the director of company X
Je suis dans la société X depuis dix ans
  = I have been at X for ten years
La société X exporte en Amérique, en Espagne, en Italie, au Japon, au Brésil, au Canada
  = The company exports to America, Spain, Italy, Japan, Brazil, Canada

To translate 'to'/'in' before a country:*

–   use *EN* when the country ends in 'e':

  En France   = to/in France

–   use *AU* (*AUX* if the country is plural) with any other ending:

  Au Portugal   = to/in Portugal
  Aux Etats-Unis   = to/in the United States

Exception: *AU Mexique* = to/in Mexico

– *Voici ma carte de visite* = Here is my card
– *On peut fixer un rendez-vous?* = Can we fix an
                                     appointment?
Je regrette. Pas mercredi. J'ai une réunion
  = Sorry. Not on Wednesday. I have a meeting

– *Jeudi? C'est possible?*   = Is Thursday possible?
D'accord, à jeudi!   = Agreed. See you on
                                Thursday!

---

* For more countries, see Reference Section

61

Many words referring to technology are similar to English. So *'un fax'* and *'faxer'* (to send a fax) are commonly used. Note, however, that *'une télécopie' et 'télécopier'* are the terms recommended by the French Academy. (Academie Française – the institution closely monitoring the evolution of the French language.)

USEFUL WORDS/EXPRESSIONS

un congrès	= a conference
un ordinateur	= a computer
un logiciel	= software
le matériel	= hardware

Health Matters
'J'ai mal!'

Verbs for this unit:

Avoir mal = to have an ache / a pain

HEALTH PROBLEMS

To describe a pain, use: *'avoir mal'* followed by *'à'* and any part of the body

- the part of the body is feminine:
  avoir mal à la
  J'ai mal à la tête = I have a headache

- the part of the body starts with a vowel or 'h':
  avoir mal à l'
  J'ai mal à l'oreille = I have an earache

- the part of the body is masculine:
  avoir mal au
  J'ai mal au dos = I have a backache

- the part of the body is plural:
  avoir mal aux
  J'ai mal aux dents = I have a toothache

For a minor ailment, do not hesitate to go to the chemist's first.

AT THE CHEMIST'S

Vous avez quelque chose pour l'estomac?
    = Have you got something for the stomach?

Be ready to answer some questions such as:

– *Vous avez mal depuis longtemps?*
        = Have you been in pain for long?
Depuis trois heures, deux jours, hier soir
        = For three hours, two days, since last night

– *Vous avez de la fièvre?* = Have you got a
                temperature?
Oui, un peu/beaucoup = Yes, a little/a lot

If the pain is too acute, say:

Je veux un docteur/un dentiste = I want a doctor/
                a dentist

AT THE DOCTOR'S

As well as the preceding questions, you may have to answer:

– *Vous avez mal souvent?* = Do you often get this
                pain?
– *Non, c'est la première fois* ['fwa']
        = No, it's the first time
– *Vous avez mal ici?* = Does it hurt here?
Oui, beaucoup / un peu = Yes, a lot / a little
– *Vous êtes allergique à. . . ?* = Are you allergic
                to . . .?

– *Il faut prendre ça trois fois par jour*
   = You must take this three times a day

In France, you pay the doctor for his services. Say:

C'est combien, docteur? = How much is it, Doctor?

The cost of a visit to a GP in France is 110 F. If you are a EU national, a percentage of the amount spent will be reimbursed to you. Do not forget to fill in the medical form (*feuille de maladie*) which the doctor will give you. Then send it to the nearest CPAM (*Centre Primaire d'Assurance Maladie*). The doctor or chemist will give you the address.

ACCIDENT

Il faut appeler un docteur	= It's necessary to call a doctor
une ambulance	= an ambulance
la police	= the police
C'est de ma faute	= It's my fault
Ce n'est pas de ma faute	= It's not my fault

USEFUL WORDS/EXPRESSIONS

gauche	= left
droit(e)	= right
souvent	= often
une fois	= once
deux fois ['fwa']	= twice
premier, première	= first
deuxième ['deuzyem']	= second
troisième	= third
un médicament	= a medicine

Talking About the Past

'Vous êtes arrivé hier?'

For the past tense, we'll consider only verbs ending in 'er'. When talking about a PAST event, use two parts:

1 the present of *AVOIR* or *ETRE*	+	2 the chosen verb ending in **-é**

Parler (to speak)
J'ai parlé   = I spoke
Tu as parlé   = you spoke
Il/elle a parlé   = he/she spoke
On a parlé   = we spoke
Vous avez parlé   = you spoke

Useful vocabulary for talking about the past:

Il y a dix minutes	= ten minutes ago
Il y a deux heures	= two hours ago
Hier ['ee-yeR']	= yesterday
La semaine dernière	= last week
Le mois dernier	= last month
L'année dernière	= last year
Déjà	= already

Vous avez téléphoné hier? = Did you phone
yesterday?

J'ai acheté deux billets la semaine dernière
= I bought two tickets last week

On a réservé une chambre il y a deux jours
= We booked a room two days ago

A limited number of verbs require the verb *ETRE* as the first part (instead of *AVOIR*). They are:

rester	= to stay
aller	= to go
arriver	= to arrive
entrer	= to go in
monter	= to go up

Note that when used with *ETRE*, the verb agrees with the person: add 'e' for the feminine form, 's' for the plural. This ending does NOT affect the way the word is sounded.

The question: 'Did you arrive yesterday?' can be written in FOUR different ways depending on whether you ask:

– a man:	*Tu es arrivé hier?*
– a woman:	*Tu es arrivée hier?*
– several men:	*Vous êtes arrivés hier?*
– several women:	*Vous êtes arivées hier?*

67

When Things Go Wrong

'Elle ne marche pas!'

Verbs for this unit:

Changer	(reg)	= to change
Laisser	(reg)	= to leave
Marcher	(reg)	= to work/function
Réparer	(reg)	= to repair
Trouver	(reg)	= to find

BREAKDOWN

At the garage's, say:

La voiture ne marche pas bien
    = the car is not working properly

.

Ask:

Vous pouvez réparer la voiture? = Can you repair the car?

Quand? = When?

Combien de temps il faut? = How long do you need?

COMPLAINTS

Written on a notice:

'*Hors service*' or '*en dérangement*' means: 'out of order'

<u>At the hotel:</u>

La douche ne marche pas = The shower is not working properly

La chambre est trop petite = The room is too small

Le lit est trop mou = The bed is too soft

Je ne suis pas satisfait(e) = I am not satisfied

<u>In a shop:</u>

Je voudrais changer le T-shirt = I'd like to change the T-shirt

Il est trop grand/petit = It's too big/small

J'ai acheté ça il y a deux jours = I bought this two days ago

Ça ne marche pas = It's not working properly

Voici le reçu = Here's the receipt

LOST PROPERTY

Il y a un bureau des objets trouvés? (literally = 'found objects') = Is there a lost property office?

To claim from your insurance policy, you will have to sign an oficial statement (*une déclaration de perte*) at the police station.

Ask:

Où est le commissariat? = Where is the police
station?

Y ou will be asked to identify yourself by filling
in a form (See Ch. 4). Then you will have to
give details about the incident:

Say what you lost:

J'ai perdu mon sac	= I lost my bag
– Quand?	= When?
Hier soir	= Yesterday evening
– Où?	= Where?
Dans le train	= In the train
– Comment est votre sac?	= What is your bag like?

D escribe the object by looking up COLOURS
and SHAPES in the Reference Section.

– On a trouvé votre sac	= We found your bag
Vous avez trouvé mon sac?	= You found my bag?
C'est formidable!	= That's great!

Talking About the Future

'Vous allez arriver demain'

The easiest way to talk about future events is to use the present tense of the verb *ALLER* (to go) followed by the infinitive. This is very similar to what happens in English.

*Je **vais changer** des chèques de voyage*
= I am going to change some traveller's cheques
*Tu **vas téléphoner** à l'hôtel*
= You are going to phone the hotel
*Elle **va réserver** des places*
= She is going to book seats
*On **va acheter** des billets*
= We are going to buy tickets
*Vous **allez commander** le repas*
= You are going to order the meal

USEFUL WORDS/EXPRESSIONS

dans 10 minutes = in ten minutes
dans trois jours = in three days
demain = tomorrow
la semaine prochaine = next week
le mois prochain = next month
l'année prochaine = next year
plus tard = later
Elle va rappeler plus tard = She is going to call back later
Vous allez arriver demain? = Are you arriving tomorrow?

Reference Section

DAYS & MONTHS

Note that days / months do NOT take a capital when inside a sentence.

Lundi ['dee']	= Monday
Mardi	= Tuesday
Mercredi	= Wednesday
Jeudi	= Thursday
Vendredi	= Friday
Samedi	= Saturday
Dimanche	= Sunday

Janvier	*Juillet*
Février	*Août* ['oot']
Mars ['maRss']	*Septembre*
Avril	*Octobre*
Mai	*Novembre*
Juin	*Décembre*

COLOURS

Blanc, blanche	= white
Bleu(e)	= blue
Gris(e)	= grey
Jaune	= yellow
*Marron***	= brown
Noir(e)	= black
*Orange***	= orange
Rose	= pink
Rouge	= red
Vert(e)	= green

* Are invariable. Do NOT agree with the noun.

SHAPES

Carré(e)	= square
Ovale	= oval
Rectangulaire	= rectangular/oblong
Rond(e)	= round
Triangulaire	= triangular

COUNTRIES & NATIONALITIES*

Notice that adjectives used for nationalities and languages do NOT take a capital

L'Amérique / Les Etats-Unis	*américain(e)*
L'Angleterre	*anglais(e)*
L'Australie	*australien(ne)*
Le Canada	*canadien(ne)*
L'Ecosse	*écossais(e)*
L'Europe	*européen(ne)*
La France	*français(e)*
La Grande-Bretagne	*britannique*
L'Irlande	*irlandais(e)*
La Nouvelle-Zélande	*néo-zélandais(e)*
Le Pays de Galles ['pay-ee-dgal']	*gallois(e)*

---

* For languages, use the masculine adjective:
Ex: *le gallois* = the Welsh language
   il parle gallois = he speaks Welsh.

73

Vocabulary

The following abbreviations apply:

adj = adjective
adv = adverb
nf   = noun, feminine
nm   = noun, masculine
prep = preposition
pron = pronoun
v   = verb

PRONUNCIATION		
ai ay	as in egg	= aimable, Vouvray
ain	as in rung	= train
au	as in autumn	= automne

à (prep) – to, in
acheter (v) – to buy
addition (nf) – bill
adorer (v) – to love
aéroport (nm) – airport
aimable (adj) – kind
aimer (v) – to like, to love
aller (nm) – single (ticket)
aller-retour (nm) – return ticket
ami(e) (nm/f) – friend
an (nm) – year
apporter (v) – to bring
après (adv) – after
assez (adv) – enough, rather
aujourd'hui (adv) – today
autoroute (nf) – motorway
avoir faim (v) – to be hungry
avoir mal (v) – to be in pain

avoir soif (v) – to be thirsty

bagages (nm) – luggage
bain (nm) – bath, swim
beau, belle (adj) – beautiful
beaucoup (adv) – a lot
billet (nm) – ticket (airplane/train/theatre)
bière (nf) – beer
boîte (nf) – box, tin, carton
bon, bonne (adj) – good
bouteille (nf) – bottle
bureau (nm) – office, study

car (nm) – coach
carte (nf) – map
certainement (adv) – certainly
changer (v) – to change
château (nm) – castle
chaud(e) (adj) – hot, warm
chèque de voyage (nm) – traveller's cheque
chercher (v) – to look for
commencer (v) – to start
comprendre (v) – to understand
content(e) (adj) – pleased, happy
continuer (v) – to carry on, continue

dans (prep) – in, inside
de, d' (prep) – of, from, out of
déçu(e) (adj) – disappointed
déjeuner (nm) – lunch
délicieux, délicieuse (adj) – delicious
demain (adv) – tomorrow
demi(e) (adj) – half
départ (nm) – departure
depuis (prep) – since, for
désolé(e) (adj) – sorry
détester (v) – to hate
devant (prep) – in front of
dîner (nm) – dinner
docteur (nmf) – doctor
donner (v) – to give
dos (nm) – back

douche (nf) – shower
doux, douce (adj) – mild, sweet, gentle
droit (adv) – straight
droit(e) (adj) – right

eau (nf) – water
elle (pron) – she, it
en (prep) – in, to
enfant (nmf) – child
enregistrement (nm) – check-in
entrer (v) – to go in, enter
environ (adv) – about, approximately
essence (nf) – petrol
été (nm) – summer
étoile (nf) – star
étranger, étrangère (adj) – foreign
être d'accord (v) – to agree
exporter (v) – export
extérieur (nm) – outside

faire (v) – to do, make
famille (nf) – family
fantastique (adj) – marvellous
femme (nf) – woman, wife
fermer (v) – to close, shut
fille (nf) – daughter, girl
fois (nf) – time

formidable (adj) – fantastic, marvellous
fort(e) (adj) – strong
froid(e) (adj) – cold
fromage (nm) – cheese

gare (nf) – station
gauche (adj) – left
gazeux, gazeuse (adj) – sparkling, fizzy
glace (nf) – ice, icecream
goûter (v) – to taste
grand(e) (adj) – tall, large
gros, grosse (adj) – fat, large

habiter (v) – to live
heure (nf) – hour
hier (adv) – yesterday
hiver (nm) – winter
homme (nm) – man
horaire (nm) – timetable

PRONUNCIATION

il(l)   as in <u>y</u>et   = *taille, fille*

ici (adv) – here
intéressant(e) (adj) – interesting
intérieur (nm) – inside
itinéraire (nm) – itinerary

jamais (adv) – never
je (pron) – I
jean (nm) – jeans
jeune (adj) – young
joli(e) (adj) – pretty
jus (nm) – juice

là (adv) – there
laisser (v) – to leave
lait (nm) – milk
légume (nm) – vegetable
libre (adj) – free, vacant
lit (nm) – bed

livre (nf) – pound (sterling, weight)
loin (adv) – far

maintenant (adv) – now
mairie (nf) – town-hall
maison (nf) – house
mal (adv) – badly
manger (v) – to eat
marcher (v) – to function/to walk
mari (nm) – husband
matin (nm) – morning
mauvais(e) (adj) – bad
moins (adv) – less
mois (nm) – month

nom (nm) – name
numéro (nm) – number
nuit (nf) – night

PRONUNCIATION

oeu	as in f<u>ur</u>	=	*soeur*
oi oî	as in w<u>a</u>ggon	=	*droite, boîte*
ou où oû	as in p<u>oo</u>l	=	*route, où, coût*

oeuf (nm) – egg
on (pron) – we
oreille (nf) – ear
ou (conj) – or
où (adv) – where

pantalon (nm) – trousers
paquet (nm) – packet, parcel
par (prep) – by
parler (v) – to speak, talk
passer (v) – to spend (time)
perdre (v) – to lose
petit(e) (adj) – small
petit-déjeuner (nm) – breakfast
peu (adv) – little
peut-être (adv) – perhaps
pièce (nf) – coin, play

piscine (nf) – swimming-pool
place (nf) – seat, site (tent)
plan (nm) – street map
plat(e) (adj) – flat, still (water)
plein (nm) – full tank
plus (adv) – more
pointure (nf) – shoe size
poisson (nm) – fish
pont (nm) – bridge
pour (prep) – for
pouvoir (v) – to be able to
premier, première (adj) – first
prendre (v) – to take
printemps (nm) – spring
prix (nm) – price
problème (nm) – problem
profession (nnf) – occupation
proposer (v) – to suggest
pyjama (nm) – pyjamas

quand (adv) – when
quart (nm) – quarter
quel, quelle (adj) – which
qui (pron) – who
qu'est-ce que (pron) – what

rappeler (v) – to call back
recommander (v) – to recommend
reçu (nm) – receipt
regretter (v) – to be sorry
rendez-vous (nm) – appointment
réparer (v) – to repair
repas (nm) – meal
réservation (nf) – booking
réserver (v) – to book
rester (v) – to stay
réunion (nf) – meeting
rond-point (nm) – roundabout
route (nf) – road

sac (nm) – bag
sans (adv) – without

semaine (nf) – week
sensationnel, sensationnelle (adj) – marvellous
short (nm) – shorts
si (adv) – yes
société (nf) – company
soir (nm) – evening
sous (prep) – under
souvent (adv) – often
stade (nm) – stadium
supplément (nm) – surcharge
sur (prep) – on

taille (nf) – clothes size
tard (adv) – late
temps (nm) – weather, time
terminer (v) – to finish
tête (nf) – head
thé (nm) – tea
théâtre (nm) – theatre
ticket (nm) – ticket (metro/bus)
timbre (nm) – stamp
ton, ta, tes (adj) – your (informal)
tourner (v) – to turn
tout à l'heure (adv) – later
travailler (v) – to work
très (adv) – very
triste (adj) – sad
trouver (v) – to find

vacances (nf) – holiday
viande (nf) – meat
ville (nf) – town, city
village (nm) – village
vin (nm) – wine
voici/voilà (prep) – here is
voiture (nf) – car
votre, vos (adj) – your (formal or plural)
vouloir (v) – to want, wish
vous (pron) – you (formal/plural)
voyage (nm) – trip

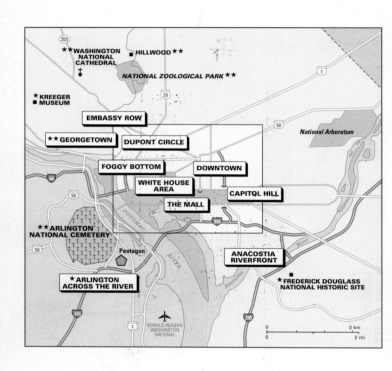

★★WASHINGTON
NATIONAL
CATHEDRAL
■ HILLWOOD ★★

NATIONAL ZOOLOGICAL PARK ★★

★ KREEGER
■ MUSEUM

National Arboretum

EMBASSY ROW

★★ GEORGETOWN
DUPONT CIRCLE

FOGGY BOTTOM
DOWNTOWN

WHITE HOUSE
AREA

CAPITOL HILL

THE MALL

★★ ARLINGTON
NATIONAL CEMETERY

Pentagon

ANACOSTIA
RIVERFRONT

★ ARLINGTON
ACROSS THE RIVER

★ FREDERICK DOUGLASS
NATIONAL HISTORIC SITE

POTOMAC

RIVER

Anacostia

River

RONALD REAGAN
WASHINGTON
NATIONAL

0   3 km
0   2 mi

WASHINGTON, DC

Chief Editor   Cynthia Clayton Ochterbeck

THE GREEN GUIDE WASHINGTON, DC

Editor   Gaven R. Watkins
Contributing Writers   Gwen Cannon and Sean Cannon
Production Coordinator   Natasha G. George
Cartography   Peter Wrenn
Photo Editor   Lydia Strong
Proofreader   Gwen Cannon
Layout & Design   Therese Schneider and Franz Pinga
Cover Design   Laurent Muller and Ute Weber
Interior Design   Agence Rampazzo

Contact Us: The Green Guide
                                                    Michelin Maps and Guides
                                                    way South
                                                    e, SC 29615

                                                    423-0485
                                                    chelintravel.com
                                                    .guides@us.michelin.com

                                                    Maps and Guides
                                                    House
                                                    don Road
                                                    Herts WD17 1JA

                                                    UK
                                                    ☎01923 205240
                                                    www.ViaMichelin.com
                                                    travelpubsales@uk.michelin.com

Special Sales: For information regarding bulk sales,
                                                    customized editions and premium sales,
                                                    please contact our Customer Service
                                                    Departments:
                                                    USA   1-800-432-6277
                                                    UK   01923 205240
                                                    Canada 1-800-361-8236

Note to the Reader
While every effort is made to ensure that all information printed in this guide is
correct and up-to-date, Michelin Apa Publications Ltd. accepts no liability for
any direct, indirect or consequential losses howsoever caused so far as such
can be excluded by law.

One Team …
A Commitment to Quality

There's just one reason our team is dedicated to producing quality travel publications—you, our reader.

Throughout our guides we offer **practical information**, **touring tips** and **suggestions** for finding the best places for a break.

Michelin driving tours help you hit the highlights and quickly absorb the best of the region. Our descriptive **walking tours** make you your own guide, armed with directions, maps and expert information.

We scout out the attractions, classify them with **star ratings**, and describe in detail what you will find when you visit them.

Michelin maps featured throughout the guide offer vibrant, detailed and easy-to-follow outlines of everything from close-up museum plans to international maps.

Places to stay and eat are always a big part of travel, so we research **hotels and restaurants** that we think convey the essence of the destination and arrange them by geographic area and price. We walk you through the best shopping districts and point you towards the host of entertainment and recreation possibilities available.

We **test**, **retest**, **check and recheck** to make sure that our guidebooks are truly just that: a personalized guide to help you make the most of your visit. And if you still want a speaking guide, we list local tour guides who will lead you on all the boat, bus, guided, historical, culinary, and other tours you shouldn't miss.

In short, we remove the guesswork involved with travel. After all, we want you to enjoy exploring with Michelin as much as we do.

The Michelin Green Guide Team

PLANNING YOUR TRIP

WELCOME TO WASHINGTON, DC

SYMBOLS

🛈	**Tourist Information**
🕐	**Hours of Operation**
🕐	**Periods of Closure**
☺	**A Bit of Advice**
☺	**Details to Consider**
☞	**Entry Fees**
👶	**Especially for Children**
☞	**Tours**
♿	**Wheelchair Accessible**

CONTENTS

DISCOVERING WASHINGTON, DC

EXCURSIONS

YOUR STAY IN WASHINGTON, DC

HOW TO USE THIS GUIDE

Orientation

To help you grasp the "lay of the land" quickly and easily, so you'll feel confident and comfortable finding your way around the city, we offer the following tools in this guide:

- Detailed table of contents for an overview of what'll you find in the guide, and how it is organized.
- Map of Principal Sights showing the starred places of interest at a glance.
- Detailed maps of some of the city's neighborhoods.
- Floor plans of the Capitol and some of the major museums.
- Metro map of Washington, DC on the inside back cover, showing the metro lines by color.
- The capital city's attractions described by neighborhoods, which are organized by descending star ratings.

Practicalities

At the front of the guide, you'll see a section called "Planning Your Trip" that contains information about planning your trip, the best time to go, getting to the city and getting around, basic facts, tips for making the most of your visit, and more. It includes suggested itineraries for two and four days, and a calendar of popular annual events in the city. Then comes information on sightseeing, kids' activities, and sports and recreational opportunities.

WHERE TO STAY

We've made a selection of hotels and arranged them within the city by neighborhood and by price category to fit all budgets (*see the Legend on the cover flap for an explanation of the price categories*). For the most part, we've selected accommodations based on their unique urban quality, their DC feel, as it were. So, unless the individual hotel embodies local ambience, it's rare that we include chain properties, which typically have their own imprint.

WHERE TO EAT

We thought you'd like to know the popular eating spots in Washington, DC. So we selected restaurants that capture the capital city experience—those that have a unique DC flavor and local atmosphere. We're not rating the quality of the food per se. As we did with the hotels, we selected restaurants by neighborhood, and categorized them by price to appeal to all wallets (*see the Legend on the cover flap for an explanation of the price categories*).

Attractions

Principal Sights are arranged geographically by neighborhood or area. Within the neighborhood, sights are ordered by descending stars or by walking tours. Nearby Excursions have been added for seeing several attractions outside the District. Contact information, admission charges and hours of operation are given for the majority of attractions. Unless otherwise noted, admission prices shown are for a single adult only. Discounts for seniors, students, teachers, etc. may be available; be sure to ask. If no admission charge is shown, entrance to the attraction is free.

If you're pressed for time, we recommend you visit the three- and two-star sights first: the stars are your guide.

STAR RATINGS

Michelin has used stars as a rating tool for more than 100 years:

★★★ Highly recommended
★★ Recommended
★ Interesting

SYMBOLS IN THE TEXT

Besides the stars, other symbols in the text indicate sights that are closed to the public ☞; on-site eating facilities ✕; also see ☞; breakfast included in the nightly rate ☞; on-site parking 🅿; spa facilities Spa; camping facilities △; swimming pool ☞; beaches ☞; and expect long lines/queues ▥▥▥.

See the box appearing on the Contents page and the Legend on the cover flap for other symbols used in the text.

See the Maps explanation below for symbols appearing on the maps.

Throughout the guide you will find peach-colored text boxes or sidebars containing anecdotal or background information. Green-colored boxes contain information to help you save time or money.

Maps

All maps in this guide are oriented north, unless otherwise indicated by a directional arrow. The term "Local Map" refers to a map within the chapter or Tourism Region. See the map Legend at the back of the guide for an explanation of other map symbols. A complete list of the maps found in the guide appears at the back of this book.

Addresses, phone numbers, opening hours and prices published in this guide are accurate at press time. We welcome corrections and suggestions that may assist us in preparing the next edition. Please send your comments to:

Michelin Maps and Guides
Hannay House
39 Clarendon Road
Watford, Herts WD17 1JA
UK
travelpubsales@uk.michelin.com
www.michelin.co.uk

Michelin Maps and Guides
Editorial Department
P.O. Box 19001
Greenville, SC 29602-9001
USA
michelin.guides@us.michelin.com
www.michelintravel.com

Pennsylvania Avenue and the Capitol
DC Convention & Tourism Corp.

WHEN AND WHERE TO GO

When to Go

CLIMATE

Generally speaking, there is rarely a season of the year when the weather is too inclement to see the sights of Washington, DC. The capital city enjoys a mild climate pretty much year-round. Along with Maryland and Virginia, the city falls into the **humid subtropical** climatic zone that defines the lower half of the eastern US. In summer DC is subject to high humidity and temperatures of at least 75°F (24°C). The average high in July in DC is 88°F (31°C), while the average low is 70°F (21°C). Precipitation is typically highest in summer (July averages 3.9in/10cm). The winter months, especially January and February, can witness ups and downs in terms of temperatures. January's average high is 43°F (6°C), and the average low is 28°F (-2°C). The District on the whole experiences little snowfall, so when it does snow, even a modest snowstorm can bring the capital to a virtual standstill. Severe snowstorms are infrequent in Washington.

SEASONS

Spring is Washington's **peak tourist season**. The mild temperatures and the blossoming of the famous cherry trees *(late Mar–early Apr)* attract the greater part of the capital's 15 million annual visitors. Hotel reservations should be made well in advance, and long lines are to be expected at the main sights. The hot and humid **summer** weather can make touring uncomfortable and tiring, but the season's long days, extended operating hours for some sights and numerous outdoor events are a major draw. **Fall** is a very pleasant season to visit Washington. Temperatures are moderate, the summer crowds have thinned out and the display of autumn foliage is often spectacular. **Winter** months are unpredictable, with temperatures

ranging from the high 40s (up to 9°C) to well below freezing.

WEATHER FORECASTS

The website of *The Washington Post* newspaper *(www.washingtonpost.com)* shows (under Local) the current weather and the 6-day outlook for the capital. The DC Visitor Center's website provides local weather and a 10-day projection *(www.dcvisit.com)*. The Weather Channel *(www.weather.com)* gives current conditions, a 10-day forecast and other types of outlooks, such as hourly.

WHAT TO PACK

Pack as little as possible. But always take an umbrella or hooded jacket for protection against rain. A hat with a brim is handy to ward off the sun on summer days. It is advisable to carry a lightweight jacket, since most buildings are chilly due to air-conditioning. Sunglasses and sunscreen are also recommended for the warmer months. A sweater or light jacket is useful for possible cooler evenings, even when the day temperatures are hot. Some dressier clothes (a coat and tie for men) are suggested for evening activities. Take a tote bag for a picnic lunch, a shopping spree or as an extra carry-on to hold your souvenirs. A good pair of comfortable walking shoes will be needed for getting to and from the Mall's many museums, as well as touring inside them.

Two- and Four-Day Itineraries

Especially if you are pressed for time, use the Itineraries for two days and four days outlined on the page following the itinerary map. You'll find planning tips and suggestions for where to eat based on the type of dining experience you are seeking.

Two- and Four-Day Itineraries

Starting point and path of itinerary:

1 ━━ **First Day**

2 ━━ **Second Day**

3 ━━ **Third Day**

Fourth Day (see Excursions)

○━━▶ Tourmobile route
(with stop and direction of tour)

WHITE HOUSE   Sight illuminated at night

✗ K Street   Principal restaurant district

0   500m
0   1500ft

Two- and Four-Day Itineraries

Planning Tips

The fast-paced itineraries mentioned below and shown on the map on pp13–15 are designed for visitors pressed for time and are best suited to the period from April to September, when daylight is more plentiful. To avoid long lines, it is best to reserve some of the more popular tours in advance (see Reservations for Sights). Purchasing advance tickets for the Holocaust and Spy museums is also strongly advised. **Shuttle buses** – Travel by **Tourmobile** shuttle bus is incorporated into the second day.

Old Town Trolley also serves some of the sights below. **Eating** – On-site eating facilities are indicated in the individual sight descriptions in this guide by the symbol ✕. In warm seasons snacks are available from kiosks on the Mall or from street vendors along Independence Avenue. Picnicking is permitted on the Mall. Union Station, the Old Post Office (Pennsylvania Ave. & 12th St. NW) and the Shops at National Place (Pennsylvania Ave. & 13th St. NW) house a multitude of eateries for all tastes and budgets. Upscale establishments on K Street and Connecticut Avenue offer formal dining, while the large waterfront restaurants on Maine Avenue SW specialize in seafood. Many Asian eateries are located in the Arlington–Clarendon area, while the vibrant **Adams Morgan** neighborhood in the vicinity of Columbia Road and 18th Street NW, known mainly for its Hispanic and Ethiopian cuisine, hosts a wide variety of ethnic restaurants. Historic **Georgetown** and **Alexandria,** each with a large concentration of restaurants, offer a full range of dining experiences.

Two-Day Itinerary

First Day	Itinerary in red 1➡
Morning	The Capitol★★★, Library of Congress★★, Supreme Court★★
Lunch	Supreme Court★★ or National Air and Space Museum★★★
Afternoon	National Air and Space Museum★★★, National Gallery of Art★★★
Evening	Kennedy Center★★

Second Day	Itinerary in purple (with Tourmobile) 2➡
Morning	White House★★★ (reservations required), National Museum of American History (closed until mid-2008)
Lunch	National Museum of American History★★★ or picnic on the Mall
Afternoon	US Holocaust Memorial Museum★★, Jefferson Memorial★★★ Lincoln Memorial★★★, Vietnam Veterans Memorial★★★, Arlington National Cemetery★★ (open until 7pm Apr–Sept)
Evening	City lights. Tour by car the illuminated sights shown on the map.

Four-Day Itinerary

(For the first two days, follow the itinerary described above.)

Third Day	Itinerary in green 3➡
Morning	National Museum of Natural History★★, Arthur M. Sackler Gallery★★, Freer Gallery of Art★★, National Museum of African Art★★, or Hirshhorn Museum and Sculpture Garden★★
Lunch	On the Mall (see Eating above)
Afternoon	National Archives★★, FBI★, Ford's Theatre and Petersen House★, International Spy Museum★★ (return to Pennsylvania Ave. and take any no.30s bus to Georgetown)
Late Afternoon/ Evening	Georgetown Walking Tour and dinner In Georgetown

Fourth Day	Excursions Map
Morning	Mount Vernon★★★, Woodlawn★
Lunch	Mount Vernon★★★
Afternoon/Evening	Gunston Hall★, Alexandria Walking Tour of Old Town★★ and dinner in Alexandria

KNOW BEFORE YOU GO

Useful Websites

Here are several websites to help you plan your trip or find out information once you get to Washington, DC:

www.thecapitol.net – A good resource for business professionals visiting the DC area. Includes a legislative glossary.

www.culturaldc.org – Information on the DC area's art exhibits, cultural events and activities. Festivals and little-known treasures can be found on this online "Insider's Arts Guide."

www.dcchamber.org – The DC's Chamber of Commerce informational site. Business-oriented events and topics.

www.dc.gov – The government of DC's official website, including city services, and resources for visitors.

www.dcvisit.com – The DC Visitor Information Center website. Tells what services the center provides to visitors.

www.downtowndc.org – What to do and how to get there for Downtown DC, provided by the Business Improvement District.

www.firstgov.gov – All you need to know about our nation's government.

www.washingtonian.com – The magazine's online version, with restaurant and theater reviews, events and more.

www.washington.org – Official visitors guide for Washington, DC.

www.washingtonpost.com – Current events from what's in the news to where to see your favorite band in DC.

www.where-events.com – *Where* magazine online: dining, entertainment, etc.

www.whitehouse.gov – Information on White House events, history, past and present residents.

www.dccirculator.com – About bus travel within the city's central core.

www.fly2dc.com – *Washington Flyer* magazine online, a free publication.

www.wmata.com – Official site of Washington Metropolitan Area Transit Authority, including bus and Metro travel

Tourist Offices

LOCAL

Visitors may contact the following agencies to obtain maps and information on points of interest, accommodations and seasonal events:

Washington, DC Convention and Tourism Corp.
901 7th St. NW, Fourth Floor
Washington, DC 20001. ☎202-789-7000.
www.washington.org

Washington, DC Visitor Information Center
Ronald Reagan International Trade-Center Building, 1300 Pennsylvania Ave. NW, Washington, DC 20004.
☎866-324-7386. www.dcvisit.com

Alexandria Convention and Visitors Association
421 King St., Suite 300
Alexandria VA 22314.
☎703-838-4200. www.funside.com

Arlington Visitors Center
1301 S. Joyce St., Arlington VA 22202
☎800-677-6267.
www.stayarlington.com

OTHER

Annapolis Visitors Bureau
Annapolis and Anne Arundel County Conference and Visitors Bureau
26 West St. Annapolis, MD 21401
☎888.302.2852.
www.visitannapolis.org

International Visitors

For tourist information, visitors from outside the US can contact the **Meridian International Center** (*☎202-667-6800; www.meridian.org*), the US embassy in their country and the organizations listed under Tourist Offices above.

EMBASSIES AND CONSULATES

Since Washington, DC is the nation's capital, all embassies and many consulates are located here. International visitors may contact the consulate or embassy of their country of residence for information. Below are addresses and phone numbers of several. To obtain the phone numbers of others, call the information line for Washington, DC (☎202-555-1212) or go online to www.embassy.org.

ENTRY REQUIREMENTS

Citizens of countries participating in the Visa Waiver Pilot Program (VWPP) are not required to obtain a visa to enter the US for visits of fewer than 90 days. For more information contact the US consulate in your country of residence. Citizens of nonparticipating countries must have a visitor's visa. Upon entry, nonresident foreign visitors must present a valid passport and round-trip transportation ticket. Under a new law, effective December 31, 2006, Canadian citizens need a passport to enter the US. Inoculations are generally not required, but check with the US embassy or consulate before departing.

HEALTH

The US does not have a national health program. Before departing, visitors from abroad should check their health care insurance to determine if doctors' visits, medication and hospitalization in the US are covered. Prescription drugs should be properly identified, and accompanied by a copy of the prescription.

Embassies and Consulates			
Country	**Address**	**☎**	**Website**
Australia	601 Massachusetts Ave. 1 NW	202-797-3000	www.austemb.org
Belgium	3330 Garfield St. NW	202-333-6900	www.diplobel.us
Britain	3100 Massachusetts Ave. NW	202-588-7800	www.britainusa. com
Canada	501 Pennsylvania Ave. NW	202-682-1740	www.canadaembassy.org
China	Van Ness St. at International Dr. NW *(opens 2008)*	202-328-2500	www.china-embassy.org
France	4101 Reservoir Rd. NW	202-944-6000	www.info-france-usa.org
Germany	4645 Reservoir Rd. NW	202-298-4000	www.germany-info.org
India	2107 Massachusetts Ave. NW	202-939-7000	www.indianembassy.org
Ireland	2234 Massachusetts Ave. NW	202-462-3939	www.irelandemb.org
Italy	3000 Whitehaven St. NW	202-612-4400	www.italyemb.org
Japan	2520 Massachusetts Ave. NW	202-238-6700	www.embjapan.org
Mexico	1911 Pennsylvania Ave. NW	202-728-1600	www.sre.gob.mx
Netherlands	4200 Linnean Ave. NW	202-244-5300	www.netherlands-embassy.org
Spain	2375 Pennsylvania Ave. NW	202-452-0100	www.spainemb.org
Switzerland	2900 Cathedral Ave. NW	202-745-7900	www.swissemb.org

CUSTOMS

All articles brought into the US must be declared at the time of entry. **Exempt** from customs regulations: personal effects; one liter (33.8 fl oz) of alcoholic beverages (providing visitor is at least 21 years old); 200 cigarettes or 100 cigars or 2 kilograms (4.4 lbs.) of smoking tobacco; and gifts (to persons in the US) that do not exceed $100 in value. **Prohibited items** are plant material, firearms and ammunition (if not intended for sporting purposes) and meat and poultry products. For further information, contact the US embassy or consulate before departing, or the US Customs Service and Border Patrol, 1300 Pennsylvania Ave. NW, Washington, DC 20229 (☎202-354-1000; www.customs.treas.gov).

DRIVING IN THE US

Visitors bearing valid driver's licenses issued by their country of residence are not required to obtain an International Driver's License to drive in the US. Drivers must carry vehicle registration, or rental contract, and proof of automobile insurance at all times. Rental cars in the US are usually equipped with automatic transmission, and rental rates tend to be less expensive than overseas. Gasoline is sold by the gallon (1 gallon = 3.8 liters) and is cheaper than in many other countries. Most self-service gas stations do not offer car repair, although many sell standard maintenance items. Road regulations in the US require that vehicles be driven on the right side of the road. Distances are posted in miles (1 mile = 1.6 kilometers).

Accessibility

Throughout this guide, wheelchair access is indicated on floor plans and in the admission information that accompanies sight descriptions by means of the ♿ symbol. Handicap parking is available at most of the National Park Service sights in the city. The Smithsonian offers numerous services for visitors with disabilities. To obtain a copy of Smithsonian Access (large-type edition available), call or write Smithsonian Institution, SI Building, Room 153, Washington, DC 20560 ☎202-633-1000, TTY ☎202-357-1729 (open year-round Mon–Fri 9am–5pm, weekends 10am–4pm; closed Dec 25).
The Washington Metropolitan Area Transit Authority has facilities and reduced fares for disabled riders on the Metro and public buses. For information and free publications, call ☎301-562-5360, TTY ☎301-588-7535; www.wmata.com.

© Brigitta L. House/MICHELIN

Washington Monument

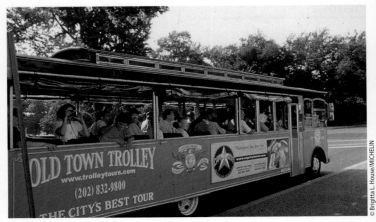

Sightseeing Tour Bus

Wheelchair Mobile Transport provides transportation for disabled individuals in the DC area. For more information or reservations, contact Wheelchair Mobile Transport, 1119 Taft St., Rockville, MD 20850; ☎301-294-0600. Disabled travelers using **Amtrak** and **Greyhound** should contact these companies prior to their trip to make special arrangements and to receive useful brochures. For information about travel for individuals or groups, contact the Society for Accessible Travel & Hospitality, 347 Fifth Ave., Suite 605, New York NY 10016; ☎212-447-7284; www.sath.org.

SENIOR CITIZENS

Most attractions, cinemas, hotels and restaurants offer discounts to visitors age 62 and older (proof of age may be required). Discounts on lodging, car rentals and other travel-related items may be available to members of AARP, 601 E St. NW, Washington, DC 20049; ☎202-434-2277 or 888-687-2277; www.aarp.org.

GETTING THERE

By Plane

Washington is served by three major airports (☞ *map in Welcome to Washington, DC*).

RONALD REAGAN WASHINGTON NATIONAL AIRPORT (DCA)

☎703-417-8000 *(information)*, ☎703-417-8600 *(corporate offices)*. *www.metwashairports.com. 4.5mi south of downtown DC, across the Potomac in Virginia.*

Domestic and commuter flights arrive at and depart from National. **Traveler's Aid Booths** *(open Mon–Fri 9am–9pm, weekends 9am–6pm)* are located near the baggage claim of each terminal. **Smoking** is prohibited in the airport except in designated restaurants. **Restaurants** with sit-down service are located in all terminals. Free airport shuttle buses provide transportation *(daily 6am–1am)* to and from all terminals, the satellite parking lots and garages, and the Metro station. Most **public transportation** departs from the curbside in front of each terminal.

Taxis

Taxis are available at the exits of Terminal A and the baggage-claim levels of Terminals B and C. Passengers are obligated to wait in line and take the dispatched cab. Taxi service to downtown DC takes approximately 15min and costs on average $20, plus an airport fee of $1.75.

Shuttles

For transport to residences, businesses and hotels throughout the greater DC area, **SuperShuttle** provides shared-ride, door-to-door service year-round 24hrs daily *(☎800-258-3826; www.supershuttle.com)*. Telephones for hotel/motel courtesy shuttles are located on the baggage-claim levels of the terminals.

Rental Cars

Rental-car company service counters are located on the lower level of Parking Garage A opposite Terminal A *(free airport shuttle buses stop at the garage)*. At the airport, a sales tax of 10% plus an airport fee of $2.50 per day are added to the rental rate.

Public Transportation

The airport is served by the Blue and Yellow **Metrorail** lines. The Metro station is adjacent to Terminals B & C. Public bus service is available to areas not served by Metrorail. The **Metrobus** stop is located at the base of the Metrorail station *(☎202-637-7000; www.wmata.com)*.

DULLES INTERNATIONAL AIRPORT (IAD)

☎703-572-2700. *www.metwashairports.com. 26mi west of downtown DC, in Loudoun County, VA.* International flights and domestic flights arrive at and depart from Dulles. A **Traveler's Aid Booth** *(open Mon–Fri 8am–9pm, weekends 8am–7pm)* is located on the lower level of the Main Terminal. Smoking is prohibited in the airport except in **smoking rooms** located in each of the concourses *(open 24hrs daily)*. **Restaurants** with sit-down service are located on the upper level of the Main Terminal and in the concourses. **Public transportation** departs from the lower level of the Main Terminal.

Taxis

Taxis are available at the exits of the baggage-claim level of the Main Terminal. Passengers are obligated to wait in line and take the dispatched cab. Taxi service to downtown DC takes about 30min and costs on average between $51–$58 *(Washington Flyer Taxicabs; ☎703-661-6655)*.

Shuttles

For transport to residences, businesses and hotels throughout the greater DC area, **SuperShuttle** provides shared-ride, door-to-door service year-round, 24hrs daily (*☎800-258-3826*). Telephones for hotel/motel courtesy shuttles are located on the lower level of the Main Terminal in the ground-transportation centers.

Rental Cars

Rental-car company courtesy telephones are located on the lower level of the Main Terminal. A 9% sales tax is added to the rental rate; some car companies add a 10% airport access fee or a daily surcharge.

Public Transportation

An airport–Metro shuttle operates between Dulles and West Falls Church **Metro** station (Orange line). *Shuttles run daily 5:45am–10:15pm, weekends 7:45am–10:15pm; every half hour; 25min; $9 one way/$16 round-trip; ☎888-927-4359.* Public bus service is available to areas not served by Metrorail. The **Metrobus** stop is located at the base of the Metro station.

BALTIMORE-WASHINGTON INTERNATIONAL AIRPORT (BWI)

☎ 800-I FLY BWI. www.bwiairport. com. 28mi north of Washington and 8mi south of Baltimore. Domestic, commuter and international flights arrive at and depart from BWI. **Airport Information Booth** (*open daily 9am–9pm*) is located at the entrance to Pier C on the upper level of the terminal building. Smoking is prohibited in the airport except in **smoking areas** located in designated restaurants. **Restaurants** with sit-down service can be found on the upper level of the terminal. Free airport shuttle buses operate 24hrs daily to and from the short-term parking lots and the BWI rail station. **Public transportation** departs from the lower level of the terminal.

Taxis

Taxis are available at the exits of the lower level of the terminal. Taxi service to downtown DC takes about 50min and costs on average $63 (*BMI Airport Taxi Management; ☎410-859-1100*).

Shuttles

SuperShuttle is available from BMI to the downtown DC area. From 9am-2pm, go to the Guest Services Desk in the Ground Transportation area to request the service, or call ☎800-258-3826.

Rental Cars

Rental-car company service counters are located at Stony Ridge Rd. and New Ridge Rd. Free shuttles take pas-

Departure Hall, Ronald Reagan Washington National Airport

© Brionna L. House/MICHELIN

sengers to and from the rental area. An 11.5% sales tax is added to the rental rate; some car companies add a 10% airport access fee as well as a $3 daily facility charge.

Trains

See below. Maryland Rail Commuter Service, known as **MARC**, provides commuter service between the airport and Union Station in DC Mon–Fri 5:30am–10:30pm *(1hr; $6 one way; ☎800-325-7245)*. **Amtrak** offers daily service between Baltimore and DC *(45min)*. For fares and schedules: ☎800-USA-RAIL; www.amtrak.com.

By Train

Union Station is Washington's only railroad station and offers **Amtrak** and other rail service. Located near Capitol Hill at Massachusetts and Delaware Aves. NE, the station is accessible by Metrorail (Red line). Amtrak's Metroliner and Acela Express provide direct daily service between the nation's capital and major destinations throughout the Northeast (from DC to Boston via Philadelphia and New York), the Midwest and the South. Advance reservations are recommended to ensure the best fares and desired accommodations. Major short-distance routes to DC are from Philadelphia *(1hr 30min)*, New York *(3 hrs 30min)* and Boston *(8hrs)*. Amtrak also offers daily service between Baltimore and DC. Maryland Rail Commuter Service (**MARC**) operates trains between the two cities weekdays. Amtrak's longer routes include those from Atlanta *(13hrs 30min)*, Chicago *(20hrs)* and Miami *(22hrs)*. Travelers from Canada should ask their local

travel agents about Amtrak/VIARail connections. The **North America Rail Pass** allows up to 30 days of travel throughout the US and Canada. The **USA RailPass** *(not available to US or Canadian citizens or legal residents)* offers unlimited travel within Amtrak-designated regions at discounted rates: 15- and 30-day passes are available. For schedules and routes, call ☎800-872-7245 *(toll-free in North America only; outside North America, contact your local travel agent)* or visit www.amtrak.com.

By Bus/Coach

Greyhound provides access to Washington, DC at fares that are generally lower than air or rail rates. However, some travelers may find long-distance bus travel uncomfortable due to the lack of sleeping accommodations. The **Discovery Pass** allows unlimited travel for anywhere from 4 to 60 days. Advance reservations are suggested. For fares, schedules and routes, call ☎800-231-2222 or visit www.greyhound.com. The capital's main bus terminal *(☎202-289-5160)* is located at 1005 1st St. NE, a short walk from Union Station.

By Car

Map below. Washington is situated at the crossroads of several major interstate routes: I-95 (north–south), I-66 (east), Rte. 50 (west) and I-270 (north–west). These and other roads leading to the capital connect with the Capital Beltway (I-495), which encircles the city at a distance of about 12mi from the center.

BALTIMORE

B

BALTIMORE-WASHINGTON INTL. AIRPORT

Beaverdam Creek

Baltimore-Washington Pkwy.

M A R Y L A N D

GREENBELT

Goddard Space Flight Center

SILVER SPRING

COLLEGE PARK

Greenbelt Park

Y

TAKOMA PARK

BERWYN HEIGHTS

NEW CARROLLTON

RIVERDALE

Annapolis ★

MT. RAINIER

HYATTSVILLE

BRENTWOOD

BLADENSBURG

Hwy.

Glenarden

e John Paul II ltural Center

National Shrine of the Immaculate Conception

CHEVERLY

J. Hanson

Beaverdam Branch

Village Green

Fed Ex Field

National Arboretum

Kenilworth Aquatic Gardens

FAIRMOUNT HEIGHTS

RFK Stadium

SEAT PLEASANT

East Capitol St.

Central   Ave.

Millwood

Congressional Cemetery

CAPITOL HEIGHTS

Fort Dupont Park

Pennsylvania

River

★ F. Douglass ■ National Hist. Site

DISTRICT HEIGHTS

Capital Beltway

Anacostia

Anacostia ■ Museum

Suitland

SUITLAND

Ave.

HILLCREST HEIGHTS

Pkwy.

Branch

MORNINGSIDE

Z

FOREST HEIGHTS

Creek

Camp Springs

ANDREWS

UPPER MARLBORO

Oxon Hill

Henson

AIR FORCE BASE

WASHINGTON DC

0 ——— 4km
0 ——— 2mi

INDIAN HEAD

B

GETTING AROUND

Lay of the Land

DC STREET SYSTEM

Based on L'Enfant's design, the layout of DC's streets is logical. The focal point of Washington's street system is the US Capitol building. From this prominent landmark, the two cardinal axes—North Capitol and South Capitol streets, and East Capitol Street and the Mall—divide the city into four quadrants: Northwest, Northeast, Southeast and Southwest.
Numbered streets running north-south are laid out in ascending order on either side of North and South Capitol streets, while **lettered streets** running east-west begin on either side of the Mall/East Capitol axis. This arrangement gives rise to two sets of numbered streets and two sets of lettered streets. For example, the street one block east of the Capitol and the street one block west of the Capitol are both named 1st Street; similarly there is a C Street three blocks north and three blocks south of the Capitol. Since the same address may be found in each of the four quadrants, it is imperative that the appropriate designation (NE, SE, SW, NW) be attached to the address to avoid confusion. **Avenues** bearing the names of the states of the Union run diagonally across the grid pattern and generally radiate from **circles** named after prominent Americans such as Washington, Sheridan and Dupont. Note the following particularities: in the NW and SW quadrants there is no A Street owing to the location of the Mall; B Street is replaced by Constitution Avenue (NE and NW) and Independence Avenue (SE and SW); there is no J Street; and I Street is commonly spelled Eye Street. The lettered streets end at W Street, beyond which a new alphabetical series begins with two-syllable names (Adams, Bryant, Channing, etc.).

HOW TO FIND AN ADDRESS

Once you understand the city's rational street layout, you should be able to locate an address in central DC with ease. Bear in mind that the quadrant designation (NW, NE, SE, SW) indicates the location in relation to the Capitol and that building numbers run in series of 100 per block. The odd-even numbering of buildings in each of the four quadrants follows a distinct pattern according to the street's orientation in relation to the Capitol. As a general rule, in the **Northwest quadrant**, the north and east sides of streets and avenues are odd-numbered, while the south and west sides are even-numbered. Some examples:

1 The intersection of 2nd and C streets SE is two streets east of the Capitol and (C being the 3rd letter of the alphabet) three streets south of East Capitol Street.

2 The Hart Senate Office Building, located at the intersection of 2nd and C streets NE, is two streets east of the Capitol and three streets north of East Capitol Street.

3 Ford's Theatre at 511 10th Street NW is ten numbered streets west of the Capitol and five lettered streets north of the Mall between E (the 5th letter of the alphabet) and F streets. The number 511 indicates that the theater is located on the east side of 10th Street.

4 The Martin Luther King Library at 901 G Street NW is located on G Street in the northwest quadrant between 9th and 10th streets. The odd-numbered street address (901) indicates that the library stands on the north side of G Street.

A CITY FOR WALKERS

The principal sights, government buildings, and entertainment and business centers are concentrated in the northwest quadrant and on Capitol Hill. The logical street layout, the well-manicured appearance and the abundant greenery of this quadrant make orientation easy and walking a pleasure. The city's most heavily visited areas, such as the Mall, Capitol Hill and Georgetown, where parking is limited, are best visited on foot. However, most visitors will find walking uncomfortable and tiring during the summer months, when temperatures and humidity are high. 🖐*It is advisable to remain in the northwest quadrant of the city after nightfall.*

During **rush hours**—the peak transit times for business commuters *(7am–9:30am and 4pm–6:30pm)*—when no street parking is permitted, visitors should be aware of fast-moving vehicles in traffic lanes close to the sidewalks. Compliance with pedestrian walking signs is expected. Violators may be fined for crossing in the middle of the block rather than at corners.

By Public Transportation

The **Washington Metropolitan Area Transit Authority** *(☎202-637-7000; www.wmata.com)* operates a public rapid transit (Metrorail) and bus system (Metrobus) that links Washington, DC and areas of Maryland and northern Virginia. Other bus service is provided by Alexandria's **DASH** buses *(☎703-370-3274; www.dashbus.com)* and Fairfax County's Fairfax Connector buses *(☎703-339-7200; www.fairfaxconnector.com)*, both of which join with Metrobuses and Metrorail *(🖐service to Mount Vernon, see Sightseeing Tours).* Montgomery County's **Ride On** buses also connect to Metrorail and Metrobuses *(☎240-777-7433; www.montgomerycountymd.gov).*

RAPID TRANSIT SYSTEM

The Metrorail subway system, known locally as the **Metro**, provides an efficient, dependable means of transportation. The Metro carries commuters to and from the suburbs during peak commuting hours *(7am–9:30am and 4pm–6:30pm)* and is convenient and inexpensive for sightseeing in the city. Stations are open Mon–Thu 5:30am–midnight, Fri 5:30am–3am, Sat 7am 3am, Sun 7am–midnight. *For easy reference,*

© Brigitta L. House/MICHELIN

you'll find a Metro system map and information about fares, ticket purchase and transit lines inside the back cover of this guide.

CITY BUSES

Metrobuses – These buses operate daily; hours of operation differ by route, please contact the information line (☎202-637-7000) or the website *(www.wmata.com)* for more detailed information. Bus stops are indicated by red, white and blue signs. The buses display the route number and final destination above the windshield. **Fares** are determined by the time of day and length of trip; fares are higher during peak commuting hours *(5:30am–9:30am and 3pm–7pm)*. The base fare for most rides is $1.35. Exact fare is required. Some surcharges and transfer fees may apply. Bus-to-bus transfer is free within a two-hour period. If a bus trip follows a ride on the Metro, transfers for the bus are free providing you collect the transfer at the originating station (machines distributing transfers are located at the escalators descending to rail level). There is no free transfer from buses to the Metro. Many routes are accessible to riders with disabilities.
To request a *Metro Visitor's Kit*, call ☎202-962-2733 or consult the website www.mwmta.com.
DC Circulator – Buses operate daily within DC's central core every 10min along three main routes: Smithsonian/National Gallery of Art loop; Convention Center/SW Waterfront; Georgetown/Union Station. For fares and schedules: ☎202-962-1423 or www.dccirculator.com.

By Taxi

Within the District of Columbia, you can hail a taxi on the street or at taxi stands at hotels and transportation terminals. Numerous taxi companies operate under the supervision of the DC Taxicab Commission (☎202-645-6018 or www.dctaxi.dc.gov). When the "TAXI" sign on the roof of the cab is lit, the vehicle is available for hire. DC taxis do not have meters; instead, the fare is calculated according to a **zone system**. The District is divided by a zone system that approximates concentric circles radiating from the Capitol. A ride within one zone is $6.50. The fare increases to $8.80 if crossing into a second zone, $11 if crossing into a third zone, etc. as described in the chart below:
A zone map with charges is displayed in the taxi, along with a list of passenger rights. It is not unusual for the driver to request payment before setting out or to pick up another passenger en route.
A rider can expect additional charges for radio-dispatched telephone requests, multiple stops, waiting time, rush-hour travel, more than one piece of luggage, special assistance, or service during official snow emergencies. If traveling to the suburbs from the District, fares are based on mileage.

CHARGE FOR NUMBER OF ZONES/ SUBZONES TRAVELED

1 = $6.50	5 = $14.00
2 = $8.80	6 = $15.50
3 =$11.00	7 = $17.80
4 =$12.60	8 = $18.90

By Car

Given the efficiency of the public transportation system, the availability of taxis and the ease with which many sights can be reached on foot, a car is not necessary to visit central Washington. Keep in mind that street parking is limited and rush-hour traffic jams are frequent. If you are staying outside the District, consider leaving your car at the parking facilities of one of the fringe Metro stations (☞*see Metro map on the inside back cover*) and riding the Metro into the city (it is advisable to arrive early on weekdays, as these lots are often filled with commuters' vehicles). For excursions outside the city, a vehicle is recommended. Visitors are encouraged to avoid driving during **rush hours**: 7am–9:30am and 4pm–6:30pm.

ROAD REGULATIONS

Effective July, 2004, talking on a hand-held cell phone while driving in DC is punishable by a $100 fine. The maximum **speed limit** on major expressways is 55mph in rural areas and 55mph in and around cities. The speed limit within the city is 25mph unless otherwise posted. The use of **seat belts** is mandatory for driver and passengers. Child safety seats are required for children under four years or weighing less than 40 pounds (seats available from most rental-car agencies). Drivers must always yield the **right of way** to pedestrians. DC school-bus law requires motorists to bring vehicles to a full stop when warning signals on a school bus are flashing. Unless otherwise posted, drivers may turn right at a red traffic light after coming to a complete stop.

PARKING

In the city, parking space on the street is limited and parking regulations are strictly enforced. Some metered parking is available. Arterial streets in the District have posted **rush-hour restrictions** that generally prohibit parking from 7am–9:30am and 4pm–6:30pm. Parking in some residential areas is by permit only (restricted to area residents). Nonresidents are allowed to park in these areas for a maximum of two hours between 7am and 8:30pm. Parking signs are color-coded: **green and white** signs indicate hours when parking is allowed; **red and white** signs indicate hours when parking is not allowed. Parking spaces reserved for specific use by permit only (e.g., diplomatic or government vehicles) are reserved 24hrs daily unless otherwise specified. Parking spaces identified with ♿ are reserved for people with disabilities; anyone parking in these spaces without proper identification is subject to a heavy fine. Private parking garages are easy to find throughout the central sections of the city.

RENTAL CARS

Major rental-car agencies have offices downtown and at the airports serving the metropolitan area. Most agencies will rent only to persons at least 25 years old, although some will rent to younger drivers for a daily surcharge. A major credit card and a valid driver's license are required for rental (some agencies also require proof of insurance). The daily rate for a compact car when renting for 5–7 days averages $58. Note that a 10% sales tax and a 11.10% concession recoup fee are added to the daily rate in DC. Also, be aware when renting from airports that in addition to the sales tax and recoup fee, there is also a $2.81 per-day contract fee.
⏱ See the chart of rental companies below *(toll-free numbers may not be accessible outside North America)*.

Rental Company	☎ Reservations	Website
Alamo	800-462-5266	www.alamo.com
Avis	800-331-1212	www.avis.com
Budget	800-527-0700	www.budget.com
Dollar	866-434-2226	www.dollar.com
Enterprise	800-264-6350	www.enterprise.com
Hertz	800-654-3131	www.hertz.com
National	800-227-7368	www.nationalcar.com
Thrifty	800-847-4389	www.thrifty.com

WHAT TO SEE AND DO

Sightseeing

GENERAL INFORMATION

Free publications such as *Where Washington* and the *Washington Flyer* magazine (the latter available at local airports) offering information on events, attractions, shopping and dining can be found at hotels and visitor information kiosks. Contact the **Washington, DC Convention and Tourism Corp.**, 901 7th St. NW, Fourth Floor, Washington, DC 20001 *(☎202-789-7000; www.washington. org)* to obtain a free *Official Visitors Guide (☎800-422-8644)* or visit the **DC Visitor Information Center** *(☎202-328-4748; www.dcvisit.com)* in the Ronald Reagan International Trade Center Building, 1300 Pennsylvania Ave. The **Smithsonian Information Center** is located at 1000 Jefferson Dr. SW in the Castle *(open year-round daily 8:30am–5:30pm; ☎202-633-1000; www.si.edu)*. This state-of-the-art visitor center (interactive touch screens, video disks, electronic wall maps) is the place to plan your visit to Smithsonian attractions. The **White House Visitor Center** on Pennsylvania Ave. between 14th and 15th Sts. provides information about White House tours *(open year-round daily 7:30am–4pm; ☎202-208-1631; www.whitehouse.gov)*.

For visitors with little time at their disposal, we recommend following the two- or four-day itineraries on pp13-16. Addresses, opening hours, admission charges and other useful information designed to help you organize your visit are included with each of the sight descriptions in this guide. A variety of guided tours (sightseeing buses, walking tours, cruises and special tours) are available to the visitor. For principal tours, see Sightseeing Tours and Cruises.

🚌 **Be aware:** Security has tightened at many tourist attractions in recent years. As a result, many attractions now require visitors to pass through metal detectors and to submit to searches of large bags prior to admission.

RESERVATION FOR SIGHTS

It is wise to make reservations in advance for guided tours of certain Washington sights (Diplomatic Reception Rooms and Hillwood, for example). Due to increased security in the capital city, several sights, like the Pentagon and the Washington Navy Yard, require advance reservations. Consult the admission information that accompanies the sight descriptions in this guide for details on the attractions you intend to visit. Tickets for **congressional visits** (special tours of some of the more popular sights, such as the White House, Capitol, and the Bureau of Engraving and Printing) may be obtained by writing to your senators or representative *(below)*. As each member of Congress is allotted a limited number of tickets, requests should be made several months in advance. These visits, which are generally scheduled early in the morning, are sometimes more extensive than the standard tours and, best of all, you avoid the long lines.

VISITING YOUR SENATORS OR REPRESENTATIVES

If you would like to meet the elected officials who represent you in Congress, you should write two to three months in advance to request an appointment. Call the Capitol *(☎202-224-8601)* or write:
US Senate
Washington, DC 20510
US House
Washington, DC 20515

SIGHTSEEING TOURS

Tourmobile – *☎202-554-5100; www. tourmobile.com*. One bus route is indicated on the itinerary map in this chapter. Operating a concession authorized by the National Park Service, this company is the only sightseeing service allowed to take visitors up to the monuments and through Arlington National Cemetery. Tourmobile offers shuttle-bus service to the principal Mall and Capitol Hill sights, as well as to the White House, Kennedy Center, Arlington National Cemetery, Frederick Douglass National Historic Site and Mount Vernon. Daily tours *(except Jan 1 & Dec 25)* are offered daily 9:40am–4:30pm. Tickets *($25)* can be purchased from Tourmobile ticket booths located near many of the sights or from the driver of any of the blue and white buses; tickets are valid all day and entitle you to unlimited reboarding at any of the stops indicated with a blue and white Tourmobile sign. Tickets may also be purchased from Ticketmaster *(☎202-432-7328 or 800-551-7328; www.ticket-master.com)*. On-board commentary is provided by trained guides. Twilight Tours *($25)* are offered mid-Mar–mid-Nov daily 7pm. Tours are available to Mount Vernon *(mid-Jun–Labor Day daily; $30)* and to Frederick Douglass National Historic Site *(mid-Jun–Labor Day daily; $7)*.

Old Town Trolley – *☎202-832-9800; www.trolleytours.com.* Tours of Washington operate daily 9am–5:30pm (4:30pm in winter), except Marine Corps. Marathon day, Thanksgiving Day, Sun before Memorial Day, Jul 4 and Dec 25. Visitors can board the orange and green trolleys every 30min at any of 16 locations. The complete itinerary lasts about 3hrs and the same ticket *($32)* allows free reboarding the entire day. After-hours tours (2hrs 30min) depart from Union Station *(Mar–Oct 7:30pm, rest of the year 6:30pm; $28)*.

Martz Gold Line/Gray Line – *☎301-386-8300 or 800-862-1400; www.graylinedc.com.* This company offers a variety of tours year-round in and around Washington. Fares range from $38 for a 4hr tour of Arlington,

Embassy Row and Capitol Hill to $95 for a 2-day "grand tour" of the principal sights. Excursions to Alexandria, Mount Vernon, Williamsburg, VA, Civil War battle sites, Charlottesville, VA and Atlantic City, NJ are also available.

SIGHTSEEING CRUISES

Departing from DC
Tours along the Potomac River offer views of the capital city by day and by night, when many sights are illuminated. Some companies offer dinner/dance cruises in addition to lunch and party tours. All cruises are round-trip. Below are the principal boat cruises operating on the river.

DC Ducks takes occupants in amphibious open-air "boats" on a land tour of major sights, followed by a half-hour cruise on the Potomac *(departs from Union Station Mar–Nov daily 10am–4pm on the hour; 1hr 30min; $29; ☎202-832-9800; www.dcducks.com)*. **Spirit Cruises** offers lunch, dinner and party cruises: dinner cruises aboard the *Spirit of Washington* head south beyond Alexandria before returning to DC *(depart from Pier 4, 6th & Water Sts. SW; year-round daily 6:30pm; 3hrs; $61–$105)*. The *Spirit of Mount Vernon* cruises to **Mount Vernon** *(departs from Pier 4 mid-Mar–Oct, day vary 8am; $39)*. Reservations recommended for both cruise boats *(♿🅿 ☎866-302-2469; www.spiritcitycruises.com)*. **Odyssey** offers year-round dinner cruises to Georgetown aboard the glass-atrium yacht **Odyssey III** *(departs from Gangplank Marina, 6th & Water Sts. SW; year-round Mon–Thu 6pm, Sun 5pm, $84, Fri 7pm, $92, Sat 7pm, $101; 3hrs; coat & tie recommended; board 1hr before departure time)*. Lunch and brunch cruises are also available. Reservations required for all cruises *(♿🅿 ☎866-306-2469; www.odysseycruises.com)*.

Departing from Alexandria
🌿*see Excursions map.* **Potomac Party Cruises, Inc.** offers dining cruises to DC aboard the **Dandy** *(departs from Prince St. year-round daily 12:30am;*

2hrs 30min; $34-$41; dinner cruises 7:30pm; 3hrs; $72–$80; board 1hr before departure time). Reservations & dinner jackets required for all cruises (♿🅿 ☎703-683-6076; www.dandydinner-boat.com). The **Potomac Riverboat Co.** features a narrated sightseeing cruise along Old Town's waterfront aboard the *Admiral Tilp (departs from Cameron St. year-round Tue–Sun; 40min; $12; phone for departure times* ☎703-548-9000; www.potomacriver boatco.com).

WALKING TOURS

DC Sightseeing – Interesting, informative and fun summarizes these five area tours led by author and former editor for the Associated Press, Anthony Pitch. Visitors walk the streets of Georgetown, Adams Morgan or Capitol Hill, visit historically significant or insignificant sights, learn fun facts and explore the secrets of our nation's capital. (*Tours suspended indefinitely; check website for tours by appointment; $15;* ☎301-294-9514; www.dcsightseeing.com.)

Washington Walks – Licensed guides walk you through the DC area while sharing anecdotes and ghost stories: what skeletons are in whose DC closet and what past DC residents still linger in the present. Regularly scheduled

tours are available throughout the week; other tours are available by reservation *(call for tour times and departure locations; $10;* ☎202-484-1565; www.washingtonwalks.com).

OTHER TOURS

Bike the Sites, Inc. – Guided tours offered through Downtown, George-town, Mount Vernon and other DC-area points of interest. Bicycles, hel-mets, water and a snack are included in the cost of the guided tour *(call for tour availability; $30–$40;* ☎202-842-2453; www.bikethesites.com).

Spy City Tours – Sponsored by the International Spy Museum and Gray-line, these 2hr tours visit more than 25 of downtown Washington's notable espionage sites and include an inter-active "mission" for each participant. The tour is held Saturdays at 10am. Ticket includes same-day admission to the International Spy Museum *($79;* ☎800-GRAYLINE; www.grayline.com).

Outdoor Fun

The District's two main recreational areas are the Mall and Rock Creek Park, both situated in the northwest quadrant and administered by the National Park Service. The **Mall**, with

C&O Canal

its sprawling lawns, planted gardens and waterfront parks, is well suited to outdoor activities such as jogging, biking, picnicking, paddleboating and a variety of sports (tennis, baseball, football, soccer and polo).

Covering some 2,100 acres astride scenic Rock Creek in the heart of the northwest quadrant, the rugged terrain of **Rock Creek Park** is crossed by an extensive network of paved roads, trails, and bicycle and bridle paths. Facilities include picnic groves, playgrounds, tennis courts, a golf course and stables.

BIKING ⚲

There are many bike routes in and around Washington. Parts of **Potomac Park** are designated for cyclists. The picturesque **Chesapeake and Ohio Canal towpath,** which meanders 184mi from Georgetown to Cumberland, Maryland, is very popular with cyclists and hikers. Extending 17mi from the Arlington Bridge to George Washington's estate in Virginia, the **Mount Vernon Trail** borders the western shore of the Potomac River alongside the George Washington Memorial Parkway.

Bike Rentals

Bike shops and boating centers offering bike rentals and trail information include:

⚲ **Big Wheel Bikes**
road, hybrid, mountain
1034 33rd St. NW
☎202-337-0254
www.bigwheelbikes.com

⚲ **Bike the Sites, Inc**
mountain, tandem, trailer tandems, landcruisers
1100 Pennsylvania Ave. NW
☎202-842-2453
www.bikethesites.com.

⚲ **City Bikes**
hybrid, mountain
2501 Champlain St. NW
☎202-265-1564
www.citybikes.com

⚲ **Fletcher's Boat House**
landcruisers
4940 Canal Rd. NW

☎202-244-0461
www.fletchersboathouse.com

⚲ **Thompson's Boat Center**
hybrid, mountain, landcruisers
Rock Creek Parkway & Virginia Ave.
☎202-333-9543
www.thompsonboatcenter.com

⚲ **Washington Sailing Marina**
landcruisers, mountain
One Marina Dr., Alexandria, VA
☎703-548-9027
www.washingtonsailingmarina.com

Cycling Events

For information concerning cycling events and bike routes, contact:

⚲ **National Park Service**
(bike-route maps)
☎202-619-7222
www.nps.gov

⚲ **Potomac Pedalers Touring Club**
☎202-363-8687
www.bikepptc.org

⚲ **Washington Area Bicyclist Assn.**
☎202-518-0524
www.waba.org

⚲ **Maryland National Capital Parks & Planning Commission**
☎301-454-1740
www.mncppc.org

⚲ **Alexandria Department of Recreation & Parks**
☎703-838-4343
http://alexandria.gov/recreation

⚲ **Arlington County Department of Parks & Recreation**
☎703-228-3323
www.co.arlington.va.us

BOATING 🚤

For sightseeing and dining cruises on the **Potomac** 🄲 *see Sightseeing Cruises, above.* Because of its location on the Potomac River and its proximity to the Chesapeake Bay, Washington offers a range of activities for boating enthusiasts. Renting a paddleboat on the Tidal Basin is a classic DC activity and a favorite with children. Boats can be rented by the hour from Tidal Basin Paddleboats *(photo ID required; 1501 Maine Ave. SW; ☎202-479-2426; www. tidalbasinpaddleboats.com).* Boating

Great Falls Park

Gwen Cannon/MICHELIN

on the **Chesapeake and Ohio Canal** between Georgetown and Violettes Lock can be a delightful excursion. Mule-drawn barge trips depart from the towpath in Georgetown Jun–Oct (☎202-653-5190; www.nps.gov/choh). Canoes and rowboats can be rented from **Fletcher's Boat House or Thompson's Boat Center** (✆ see Bike Rentals above). Sailboats can be rented from **Washington Sailing Marina** (Alexandria, VA ☎703-548-9027). For information on sailing and boating events on Chesapeake Bay, contact the **Chesapeake Bay Yacht Racing Assn.,** 612 Third St., Suite 401, Annapolis MD 21403; ☎410-269-1194; www.cbyra.org.

Marinas
(docking facilities only – no rentals)
Buzzard Point Boat Marina
Half & V Sts. SW
☎202-488-8400
Capital Yacht Club
1000 Water St. SW
☎202-488-8110
www.capitalyachtclub.net
Washington Marina
1300 Maine Ave. SW
☎202-554-0222
www.washingtonmarina.com

GOLF

The following public golf courses are maintained by the **National Park Service** (www.nps.gov); all of them rent clubs and other equipment.

Pros N Hackers
Provides information on over 100 public golf courses in DC, Virginia and Maryland. Available information on each course includes course details, cost, location, contact information, local pro and course reviews by other golfers (☎703-866-9646; www.prosnhackers.com).
In addition, numerous country-club courses in the District welcome only members or guests of members to play, including the well-known **Congressional Country Club** in Bethesda, MD.

East Potomac Park (par 65)
Hains Point SW   ☎202-554-7660
Langston Park (par 72)
28th St. & Benning Rd. NE
☎202-397-8638
Rock Creek Park (par 71)
16th & Rittenhouse Sts. NW
☎202-882-7332

HIKING

Rock Creek Park offers year-round hikes and nature walks guided by US park rangers. Favorite walks within the District include a 5mi loop around Hains Point and the Tidal Basin, especially when the famous Japanese cherry trees are in bloom. For information: ☎202-895-6070. **Theodore**

Roosevelt Island, located off the banks of Foggy Bottom, has 2.5mi of footpaths through woods, swamp and marshland with a variety of native plants and animals. The only access to the island is provided by a footbridge on the Virginia side. Free parking is available. For information: ☎703-619-7222; www.nps.gov.

For a hike outside the city limits, take the Chesapeake and Ohio Canal towpath to Old Anglers Inn (12.5mi), Great Falls Park (14mi), or Violettes Lock (22mi). Hikers to Glen Echo Park (7mi) have the option of returning to Washington by Metrobus. The trail system provides scenic but sometimes rugged hiking terrain. Maps and books about the canal are sold at some visitor centers along the trail. For further information, call the C&O Canal National Historical Park (☎301-739-4200). The Mount Vernon Trail is also designed for bikers.

For further information on hiking in the metropolitan area:

- **National Park Service**
  ☎202-619-7222
  www.nps.gov
- **Sierra Club**
  ☎202-547-2326
  www.mwrop.org
- **Maryland National Capital Parks & Planning Commission**
  ☎301-699-2407
  www.mncppc.org

HORSEBACK RIDING

There are numerous stables in and near the metropolitan area that provide mounts and riding instruction. Rock Creek Park has miles of designated bridle paths. **Rock Creek Park Horse Center**, managed by the National Park Service, offers trail rides, lessons and boarding year-round (☎202-362-0117; www.rockcreekhorse-center.com). Full riding and horse-care facilities are offered by **Meadowbrook Stables**, 8200 Meadowbrook Lane, Chevy Chase MD; ☎301-589-9026; www.meadowbrookstables.com. The city's main equestrian event is the Washington International Horse Show held yearly at the end of October at the Verizon Center; ☎301-987-9400; www.wihs.org).

ICE-SKATING

There are two major outdoor skating rinks in Washington *(skates are available to rent)*:

National Sculpture Garden & Ice Rink
On the Mall at Madison Dr. & 9th St. NW
☎202-289-3361

Pershing Park Ice Rink
Pennsylvania Ave. & 14th St. NW
☎202-737-6938
www.pershingparkicerink.com

TENNIS

About 150 public courts are available on a first-come, first-served basis at no charge. For information and a list of court locations and schedules, contact the DC Department of Recreation *(open year-round Mon–Fri 8:30am–6:30pm ☎202-673-7647; www.dpr.dc.gov).* The National Park Service maintains the following courts:

- **East Potomac courts**
  (indoor and outdoor courts)
  Hains Point SW
  ☎202-554-5962
- **Rock Creek Park courts**
  (outdoor)
  16th & Kennedy Sts. NW
  ☎ 202-722-5949
- **Montrose Park court**
  (outdoor)
  R St. between 30th & 31st Sts. NW, Georgetown

SWIMMING

In general, hotel pools are reserved for guests only. Some private clubs with pools offer short-term memberships. The DC Department of Recreation operates several outdoor pools in the summer *(open mid-Jun–Labor Day).* For locations and opening hours, call the DC Department of Recreation's Aquatics Division *(☎202-673-7647; www.dpr.dc.gov).*

DC for Kids

Where to eat

ESPN Zone ☎202-783-3776
Hamburgers and games in one place!
555 12th St. NW; www.espnzone.com

Air and Space Museum Shop ☎202-633-1000
Astronaut Food
On the Mall

Hard Rock Cafe ☎202-737-7625
Rockin' hamburgers and ribs.
999 E St. NW; www.hardrock.com

Mitsitam Cafe ☎202-633-1000
Buffalo burgers and other Native American food.
National Museum of American Indian (on the Mall)

Supreme Court Cafeteria ☎202-479-3246
Soup and sandwiches where history is made.
1st & E. Capitol Sts. NE

What to see

Bureau of Engraving and Printing – Watch money being made.

Mount Vernon – Dress up in colonial clothes, and hang out in a Revolutionary soldier's tent.

National Air and Space Museum – Gaze at the stars in the Einstein Planetarium and take a ride in a flight simulator.

National Archives' Charters of Freedom - See the original copies of the Declaration of Independence, Constitution and the Bill of Rights.

National Aquarium – Meet a sea urchin and his friends at the Touch Tank.

National Gallery of Art – See a free film in the East Building *(ages 4 and older)*.

National Museum of Natural History – Have you ever seen a tarantula eat?

National Postal Museum – Make a postcard and send yourself some junk mail.

National Zoological Park – Visit the pandas, learn about a rainforest in Amazonia and check out an orangutan using a computer!

Navy Museum – Look at the world through a real submarine periscope.

The Castle – Explore the Haupt Garden—and on a hot day the Persian-style *chadar* (water chute) is a great way to cool off.

Planning your trip

Children's Concierge – Consultants help you organize your trip from where to stay and where to go to how to ensure your children fully enjoy their trip. They even provide a Kidspack with age-appropriate supplies to enhance your children's visit. *($120/hr; ☎877-888-5462; www.childrensconcierge.com)*

What to do

"Goodnight Mr. Lincoln" – Put on your PJs and go to the Lincoln Memorial. Parents and children experience the life of Abraham Lincoln through stories, games and music *($10; ☎202-484-1565; www.washingtonwalks.com)*.

Carousel Ride – Ride an old-fashioned carousel on the Mall.

Online Information

www.nga.gov/kids

www.whitehousekids.gov

www.our-kids.com

Activities for Children

Kids

Throughout this guide, sights of particular interest to children are indicated with a Kids symbol. Many museums and other attractions offer special children's programs and resource centers. Most attractions in Washington offer discounted admission to visitors under 18 years of age. In addition, many hotels offer family discount packages, and some restaurants provide a children's menu. ⟲ *See the* **DC for Kids** *sidebar opposite for specific sightseeing activities and places to eat for chlldren in Washington, DC.*

Calendar of Events

Listed below is a selection of Washington, DC's popular annual events; some dates may vary from year to year. For more information, consult the quarterly Calendar of Events available from the Washington, DC Convention and Tourism Corp. *(☎202-789-7000; www. washington.org).* Events for Alexandria are listed under that city. Unless otherwise specified, the area code for all telephone numbers is 202.

SPRING

mid-Mar
St. Patrick's Day Parade — Constitution Ave. NW. ☎637-2474. www.dcstpatsparade.com
Washington Home and Garden Show — Washington Convention Center. ☎703-823-7960. www. washingtonhomeandgardenshow. com

late Mar–Apr
National Cherry Blossom Festival — Tidal Basin. ☎661-7584. www. nationalcherryblossomfestival.org
Easter Sun
Easter Sunrise Service — Arlington National Cemetery. ☎703-607-8000. www.arlingtoncemetery.org

Kids and Cats at the Zoo

© Brigitta L. House/MICHELIN-

Easter Mon
Easter Egg Roll and Egg Hunt — White House. ☎456-7041. www.whitehouse.gov

early Apr
Spring Garden Tours — White House. ☎456-7041. www.whitehouse.gov
Apr 13
Thomas Jefferson's Birthday — Jefferson Memorial. ☎426-6841. www.nps.gov/thje

late Apr
Shakespeare's Birthday — Folger Shakespeare Library. ☎544-4600. www.folger.edu
Georgetown House Tour — Georgetown. ☎338-2287. www.georgetownhousetour.com

early May
Flower Mart — Washington National Cathedral. ☎537-3185. www.cathedral.org

mid-May
Spring Wine Festival — Mt. Vernon, VA. ☎703-780-2000. www.mountvernon.org

37

late May
Memorial Day Weekend Concert — US Navy Memorial. ☎737-2300. www.lonesailor.org

May–Jun
Twilight Tattoo — (military parade/show). Washington Monument. ☎685-2888. www.mdw.army.mil/tlt

SUMMER

early Jun
Dupont-Kalorama Museum Walk — Dupont Circle. ☎785-2040, ext. 428. www.dkmuseums.com
Dance Africa DC — Dance Place, 3225 8th St. NE, ☎269-1600. www.danceplace.org

late Jun
National Capital Barbecue Battle — Pennsylvania Ave. NW at 9th St. NW. ☎301-860-0630. www.bbqusa.us

late Jun–early Jul
Smithsonian Folklife Festival — Mall. ☎633-6440. www.folklife.si.edu

Jul 4
National Independence Day Celebrations — Mall. ☎619-7222. www.nps.gov.

mid-Jul
Capital Fringe Festival — Downtown. ☎703-395-6334. www.capfringe.org

Eastern Market

DC Convention & Tourism Corp.

mid-Aug
US Army Band's 1812 Overture Concert — Sylvan Theatre, Mall. ☎703-696-3399. www.usarmyband.com

FALL

early Sept
National Symphony Orchestra Labor Day Concert — Capitol (west lawn). ☎467-4600. www.kenney-center.org
Adams Morgan Day Festival — Between Columbia Rd. & Florida Ave. NW. ☎232-1978. www.adamsmorgandayfestival. com

mid-Sept
Arts on Foot Festival — Downtown, Pennsylvania Ave. & L St. NW. www.artsonfoot.org

late Sept
Annual Open House — Washington National Cathedral. ☎537-6200. www.cathedral.org
International Children's Festival — Wolf Trap, Vienna, VA. ☎703-642-0862. www.international childrensfestival.org

Oct–Dec
US Army Band Fall Concert Series — Brucker Hall, Fort Myer, Arlington. ☎703-696-3399. www.usarmyband.com

mid-Oct
Fall Garden Tours — White House. ☎208-1631. www.whitehouse.gov
Washington International Horse Show — Verizon Center, Downtown. ☎301-987-9400. www.wihs.org

late Oct
Marine Corps Marathon — Marine Corps War Memorial, Downtown DC, and northern VA. ☎800-786-8762. www.marinemarathon.com

mid-Nov
Veterans Day Ceremonies —
Arlington National Cemetery
☎703-607-8000
www.arlingtoncemetery.org
Vietnam Veterans Memorial
☎619-7222. www.nps.gov/vive
US Navy Memorial
☎737-2300
www.navymemorial.org

WINTER

Dec–Jan 1
**National Christmas Tree Lighting
& The Christmas Pageant of
Peace** — The Ellipse.
☎208-1631.
www.nps.gov/whho/pageant

early Dec
Wolf Trap Holiday Sing-A-Long —
Filene Center. ☎703-255-1902.
www.wolftrap.org
US Army Band Holiday Festival —
DAR Constitution Hall.
☎703-696-3399.
www.usarmyband.com

mid-Dec
People's Christmas Tree Lighting —
Capitol (west lawn).
☎225-6827.

Dec 24, 25
Christmas Celebration Services —
Washington National Cathedral.
☎537-6200. www.cathedral.org

late Dec
Christmas Candlelight Tours
— White House.
☎456-7041. www.whitehouse.gov

1st week Jan
Congress convenes — Capitol.
www.senate.gov, www.house.gov

mid-Jan
**Martin Luther King Jr. Birthday
Observance** — Mall.
☎426-6841. www.nps.gov

early Feb
Chinese New Year Celebration —
Chinatown. ☎633-1000.
www.nps.gov

February 12
Abraham Lincoln Birthday Celebration — Lincoln Memorial.
☎426-6841. www.nps.gov

mid-Feb
Washington Boat Show — Convention Center. ☎703-823-7960.
www.washingtonboatshow.com

Books

REFERENCE
Above Washington. Robert Cameron.
(1989). This coffee-table-size book
features full-color aerial photos of
major DC sights and areas.
AIA Guide to the Architecture of Washington, D.C. G. Martin Moeller Jr.
(2006). Historical and architectural
descriptions of DC's famous and
less-known landmarks.
Washington, DC: Then and Now.
Alexander D. Mitchell IV. (1999).
A collection of black-and-white
photographs of the capital city,
some dating to the mid-19C.
BIOGRAPHY
*Grand Avenues: The Story of Pierre
Charles L'Enfant.* Scott W. Berg.
(2008). The story of the Frenchman
whose visionary design made DC
the grand city that it is today.
Narrative of the Life of Frederick Douglass. Frederick Douglass. (2004).
The autobiography of America's
famous orator and abolitionist, a
former slave himself.
Personal History. Katharine Graham.
(1998). The author's memoirs
detailing her stint as head of the
Washington Post amid a background of personal tragedy.
FICTION
Clear and Present Danger. Tom Clancy.
(1989). The presidency, politics,
drugs and covert CIA operations
steer this fast-paced thriller.
Murder at the Watergate. Margaret
Truman. (1999). One of President

US Military Band Summer Concerts are usually held at 8pm from **Memorial Day to Labor Day**. For information contact: US Army Band (☎703-696-3399; www.usarmyband.com); US Marine Band (☎202-433-4011; www.marineband.usmc.mil); US Navy Band (☎202-433-2525; www.navyband.navy.mil); US Air Force Band (☎202-767-4310; www.usafband.com).

US Army's **Twilight Tattoo Sunset Parade** is held at the Washington Monument May–late July, Wed at 7pm (www.mdw.army.mil./tlt). **Marine Corps Evening Parade** (1hr 15min) takes place at the Marine Barracks (8th & Eye Sts. SE, May–Aug, Fri 8:45pm; : ☎202-433-6060; www.marineband.usmc.mil).

Mon	Navy Band	Capitol (west side)
Tue	Army Band	various locations
	Air Force Band	Capitol
7pm	Marine Corps Sunset Parade	Iwo Jima Memorial
Wed	Marine Band	Capitol (lower west terrace)
Thu	Navy Band	US Navy Memorial
	Marine Band	Iwo Jima Memorial
Fri	Air Force Band	Sylvan Theatre, Mall
	Army Band	Capitol (west steps)

Truman's daughter's many Capital Crimes Mysteries spotlighting familiar DC locales.

FOR CHILDREN

Good Night Washington, DC. Adam Gamble (2006). One in a series of educational bedtime stories, surveying the best-known attractions of each destination.

We're There! Washington, DC. Elizabeth Skinner Grumbach. (2005). A fun, interactive guide to the major sights of the capital, in which kids can write their reactions.

Films

Mr. Smith Goes to Washington (1939). Frank Capra's classic film starring Jimmy Stewart defending his ideals among DC's corrupt politicians.

Advise and Consent (1962). Based on Allen Drury's novel about the unpleasant political consequences of a presidential appointment.

All the President's Men (1976). Timeless thriller about the two *Washington Post* reporters who probed the Watergate break-in.

First Monday in October (1981). The first appointment of a woman to the US Supreme Court sparks a liberal vs. conservative standoff.

The Distinguished Gentleman (1992). Comedy starring Eddie Murphy about a petty swindler who cons his way to a seat in Congress.

In the Line of Fire (1993). Clint Eastwood is an aging Secret Service presidential bodyguard facing a would-be assassin, again.

The American President (1995). The pitfalls of a widowed president's mating game under public and political scrutiny.

Along Came a Spider (2001). Morgan Freeman plays an embittered detective involved in a case of a kidnapped senator's daughter.

Legally Blonde 2 (2003). Audacious yet endearing postgrad learns DC's inner workings from a doorman in her novice attempt to legislate a bill.

Chasing Liberty (2004). Washington is just one locale in this escapade, mainly through Europe, by the daughter of an overly protective father who happens to be president of the US.

The Good Shepherd (2006). The personal toll of the nascent CIA's covert missions on the life of a dedicated American agent.

Breach (2007). True story of long-time CIA agent Robert Hanssen's deadly betrayal of his country for personal gain.

BASIC INFORMATION

Business Hours

Most businesses operate Monday to Friday 9am–5pm. Banks are generally open Monday to Thursday 9am–3pm with longer hours on Friday; some banks offer limited Saturday service. Department stores and shopping centers operate Monday to Saturday 10am–9pm, and many are open Sunday noon–5pm or 6pm; some extend their hours on Saturday.

Communications

A local call generally costs 35¢ from a pay phone. Most calls within a distance of 12mi from the Capital Beltway (Interstate 495) are charged as local calls but require dialing 1 and the area code. Talking on a hand-held cell phone while driving in DC is punishable by a $100 fine.

AREA CODES

Washington, DC	202
Suburban Virginia	703, 571
Eastern Maryland	410, 443
Suburban Maryland	301, 240

Instructions for using public telephones are listed on or near the telephone. Some **public telephones** accept credit cards, and all will accept **long-distance** calling cards. Post offices, convenience stores and supermarkets sell pre-paid phone cards for long-distance and international calls. For long-distance calls in the US and Canada, dial 1+area code+number. To place an **international call**, dial **011**+country code+number. A list of country codes can be found in the Yellow Pages. To place a **collect call** (person receiving call pays charges) dial 0+area code+number and tell the operator you are calling collect. If it is an international call, ask for the overseas operator.

The cost for a local call from a pay phone is generally 35¢ or 50¢ (any combination of nickels, dimes or quarters is accepted). Most phone numbers in this guide that start with **800**, **866**, **877** or **888** are toll-free (no charge) in the US only and may not be accessible outside of North America. Dial 1 before dialing an 800 or 888 number in the US. The charge for numbers preceded by **900** can range from 50¢ to $15 per minute. Most hotels add a surcharge for local and long-distance calls. For further information dial 0 for operator assistance.

TELEGRAMS

You can send a **telegram** or money, or have money telegraphed to you, via the Western Union system ☎800-325-6000 or www.westernunion.com.

Electricity

The voltage in the US is 110 volts AC, 60 Hz. Foreign-made appliances may need voltage transformers and North American flat-blade adapter plugs (available at specialty travel and electronics stores).

Emergencies

In all major US cities you can call the police, ambulance or fire service by dialing **911**. Another way to report an emergency is to dial **0** for the operator.

IMPORTANT NUMBERS

✚ Emergency Police/Ambulance/
   Fire Department (24hrs)   911
✚ Police (nonemergency)   311
✚ Hotel Docs (24hrs)
   ☎877-244-7362
✚ Dental Referral
   (Mon–Fri 8am–4pm)
   ☎202-547-7615
✚ Pharmacies (24hrs):

CVS, 6 Dupont Cir. NW
☎202-785-1466
CVS, 2240 M St. NW
☎202-296-9876
✚ Poison Control Center *(24hrs)*
☎800-222-122

Liquor Law

The legal minimum age for purchase and consumption of alcoholic beverages is 21. Proof of age is normally required. Establishments can serve alcoholic beverages Monday to Thursday 8am–2am, Friday to Saturday 8am–3am and Sunday 10am–2am. Beer and wine can be purchased in some convenience stores seven days a week. Liquor stores are closed on Sunday.

Major Holidays

Most banks and government offices in the District are closed on the following legal holidays:

New Year's Day
    January 1
Martin Luther King Jr.'s Birthday
    3rd Monday in January
Presidents' Day
    3rd Monday in February
Memorial Day
    Last Monday in May
Independence Day
    July 4
Labor Day
    1st Monday in September
Columbus Day
    2nd Monday in October
Veterans Day
    November 11
Thanksgiving
    4th Thursday in November
Christmas
    December 25

Mail/ Post

National Capitol Station Post Office, at Capitol St. and Massachusetts Ave. NE (next to Union Station) is open Monday to Friday 7am–midnight and weekends 7am–8pm. For location and hours of local post offices and other information, contact the Postal Service Customer Call Center *(Mon–Fri 8am–8:30pm, Sat 8am–6pm* ☎800-275-8777; www.usps.com). First-class rates within the US: letter 41¢ (1oz), postcard 26¢. Overseas: letter 90¢ (1/2oz), postcard 90¢. Letters can be mailed from most hotels. Stamps and packing material may be purchased at post offices, grocery stores and businesses offering postal and express shipping services located throughout the city (*see the Yellow Pages of the telephone directory under "Mailing Services" or "Post Offices"*).

Money

Most banks are members of the network of Automatic Teller Machines (ATMs), which allows visitors from around the world to withdraw cash using bank cards and major credit cards 24hrs a day. ATMs can usually be found in banks, airports, grocery stores and shopping malls. Networks (Cirrus, Honor, Plus) serviced by the ATM are indicated on the machine. To inquire about ATM service, locations and transaction fees, contact your local bank, Cirrus ☎800-424-7787 or Plus ☎800-843-7587. Traveler's checks are accepted in banks, most stores, restaurants and hotels. To report a lost or stolen credit card: American Express ☎800-528-4800; Diners' Club ☎800-234-6377; MasterCard ☎800-307-7309 or the issuing bank; Visa ☎800-336-8472. American Express Travel Service offices are 1501 K St. NW ☎202-457-1300.

CREDIT CARDS AND TRAVELER'S CHECKS

Rental-car agencies and many hotels require credit cards. Most banks will cash brand-name traveler's checks and give cash advances on major credit cards (American Express, Visa, MasterCard/Eurocard) with proper identification.

CURRENCY EXCHANGE

Foreign currency exchange, traveler's checks and wire transfers are available through many banks in central DC, including **PNC Bank**, 1919 Pennsylvania Ave. NW (and other branch locations); ☎800-368-5800; www. pnc.com. Private companies offering exchange services include **American Express Travel Service**, 1501 K St. NW; ☎202-457-1300 or www. amercanexpress.com. Visitors can also exchange currency at Reagan National Airport (Main Terminal, upper level, near Travelers Aid booth); Dulles International Airport (Main Terminal, upper level east end and west end; Midfield Concourses, upper levels of C & D concourses); and BWI (in the business center, upper level of the Terminal).

Newspapers and Magazines

The city's leading daily paper, the *Washington Post* (established 1877), known for its investigative reporting, is one of the country's most influential newspapers, providing national and international coverage. The weekend section in the Friday edition lists entertainment, special events, and attractions for children. The Sunday edition contains a section highlighting the performing arts. *The Post* also publishes the day's congressional and Supreme Court schedules. The *Washington Post* is also accessible online: www.washingtonpost.com. Another daily, the *Washington Times*, was established in 1982 *(www.washingtontimes.com)*. The *Washingtonian*, a monthly magazine, features listings of restaurants, upcoming events and stories about the city *(www.washingtonian.com)*. Free alternative papers include *City Paper*, a weekly publica-

tion *(distributed Thursday)* covering the local entertainment scene *(www. washingtoncitypaper.com)*, and *Washington Blade*, a weekly publication *(distributed Friday)* focusing on the gay and lesbian community. Several free publications found at hotels (such as *This Week in the Nation's Capital, The InTowner* and *Where Washington*) feature practical information and listings of cultural events, restaurants, nightspots and shops. *Sports Focus* and *Recreation News*, sports and recreation monthlies for the DC area, are available free at workout facilities, some stores and newspaper stands.

Taxes and Tipping

In Washington, DC the general sales tax is 5.75%. The hotel tax is 14.5%. Rental-car tax is 10% in DC. The food and beverage tax (restaurants) is 10%. Sales taxes in neighboring areas outside DC vary depending on the state and city.

In restaurants it is customary to tip the server 15-20% of the bill. Taxi drivers usually receive 15% of the fare. Skycaps and porters are generally tipped $1 per bag and hotel maids $1 per night.

Temperature and Measurement

In the US temperatures are measured in degrees Fahrenheit and measurements are expressed according to the US Customary System of weights and measures.

Time

Washington, DC is located in the Eastern Standard Time (EST) zone, which is five hours behind Greenwich Mean Time. Daylight Saving Time *(clocks advanced 1hr)* is in effect for most of the US from the second Sunday in March until the first Sunday in November, beginning in 2007.

The Capitol
Jake McGuire/Courtesy Washington Convention
& Tourism Corp.

THE DISTRICT OF COLUMBIA

The seat of the nation's government occupies a relatively small amount of real estate, yet, with its height restrictions and well-planned development, the capital, for the most part, does not feel crowded. Yes, there is traffic, but sweeping green spaces, monumental buildings, parks and two water bodies make the city a desirable, if costly, place to live. An international populace peppers the mix of neighborhoods.

Location and Climate

Washington, DC lies approximately in the middle of the eastern seaboard of the US, about 90 miles inland from the Atlantic Ocean. Situated on the northern banks of the Potomac River, the city rises from low bottomland along the riverfront to a series of hills in the north. At its highest elevation in the Northwest quadrant of the city, it is 390ft above sea level. Rock Creek, a tributary of the Potomac, follows a shallow, wooded valley extending through the heart of the city from north to south. Located at 39° north latitude and 77° west longitude, the city has a temperately continental climate. Winds are generally from the west, and humidity is often high because of proximity to the ocean and the Chesapeake Bay, 25 miles east of the city. In the vicinity of Washington, the Potomac River has an average channel depth of about 14ft, making it unnavigable for large cargo-carrying vessels.

Size and Population

Shaped like a truncated diamond, each side measuring 10 miles, the city is carved out of Maryland and separated from Virginia by the Potomac. It covers 67 square miles and is divided into four quadrants: **Northwest** (NW), **Northeast** (NE), **Southeast** (SE) and **Southwest** (SW). The longest distance from its southern to its northern tip is 12 miles. The official 2000 census count of 572,059 was a population decrease of about 35,000 from 1990, making Washington the 21st-largest city in the US. The decline was attributed to an exodus of blacks from the district, which is now 57 percent black and 32 percent white. DC's

former mayor Anthony A. Williams successfully challenged the Census Bureau's 2005 population estimate of 550,521. As a result, the bureau revised its number upward to 582,049, a figure that represents the largest increase in the city's population since 1950.

In the Northeast, Southeast and Southwest quadrants, blacks predominate; the Northwest quadrant is largely white. The neighborhood known as Adams Morgan, concentrated mainly in the area of Columbia Road and 18th Street NW, has been the hub of Washington's growing Hispanic community, which constitutes nearly nine percent of the population. Since 1990 a quarter of a million immigrants, primarily Asians—now composing 3 percent of the population—have settled in the metropolitan area, mainly in the suburbs. The region's Indian immigrant community has doubled in the last decade, to 80,000, among them many engineers attracted by Northern Virginia's booming high-tech economy.

The District Government

After a century of congressional rule, Washington was given the federally mandated authority to govern itself under the Home Rule Act of 1973. Headed by an elected mayor and a 13-member legislative council, the city government, by merit of the District's unique status, undertakes all local, county, and state government responsibilities—the schools, the police, the courts, the department of motor vehicles, etc. Though the city functions somewhat independently of the federal legislature, Congress retains veto power over bills passed by the District

Washington DC
METROPOLITAN AREA

Suburban Ring   Metropolitan Periphery

Boundaries of the metropolitan area and its counties as defined by the Office of Management and Budget (30 June 1990) council. In addition, many federal agencies and commissions exercise oversight jurisdiction in District matters. The National Capital Planning Commission, a 12-member body appointed by the president and the mayor, reviews city development plans, while the Commission of Fine Arts oversees the design of buildings, parks and monuments. Congress itself sets height restrictions on all District buildings, and the president's Office of Management and Budget establishes limits for the city budget.

Historically, suffrage has been a matter of concern to the citizens of Washington. In 1964 they were allowed to vote in the presidential election for the first time. As part of the 1973 Home Rule Act, they were also allowed to elect one delegate to the House of Representatives. The delegate serves a two-year term and, though not granted a vote on the floor of Congress, is allowed to vote on issues within the congressional committees on which he or she serves. Unbowed by the failure of a proposed constitutional amendment in 1978, the defeat in the House of DC statehood legislation in 1993, and the denial of a voting-rights lawsuit by the Supreme Court in 2000, DC residents continue to push for a voice in Congress. Recently the city government showed its support, offering license plates with the slogan "Taxation Without Representation."

The Metropolitan Area

The Washington, DC metropolitan area comprises 18 counties in Maryland, Virginia and West Virginia, and the District of Columbia itself. The total metropolitan area encompasses 6,510 square miles. With a population of 5,290,400, it ranks eighth among the nation's 361 metropolitan areas.

Continued growth has drawn many of the outlying towns and villages into a steadily expanding ring of suburban settlements. The municipalities bordering the Capital Beltway (Interstate 495), which encircles the District at a distance of approximately 12 miles from the center, tend to be suburban "bedroom" communities closely attached to Washington culturally and economically. As the suburban reach of Washington extends farther west and south into the hinterland, more distant and traditionally more rural counties in Virginia and West Virginia—as well as independent cities of Virginia, such as Fairfax, Manassas and even more remote Fredericksburg—serve as commuter communities as well.

National Capital Planning Commission

The National Capital Region covers the District of Columbia, the city of Alexandria and Maryland's Prince George's and Montgomery counties as well as Virginia's Arlington, Fairfax, Prince William and Loudoun counties. It is the central planning agency of the federal government in the Capital Region.

First established in 1924 by Congress, the National Capital Planning Commission (NCPC) was authorized to acquire land for a park and recreation system for the nation's capital. Major federal laws underpinning the commission's decisions include the Height of Buildings Act of 1910, the Commission of Fine Arts Act of 1910 and the Commemorative Works Act of 1986.

Responsibiilties include approving new federal building plans in the District, reviewing plans for federal structures and preparing a yearly analysis of all federal agency capital project proposals in the Region.

In 1997 NCPC released its Extending the Legacy plan—measures for preserving and enhancing the city's Monumental Core, from the Mall to the Potomac and Anacostia rivers, as well as 22 miles of waterfront from Georgetown to the National Arboretum.

More recently, NCPC and the Commission of Fine Arts launched the National Capital Framework Plan, an initiative to relieve pressure on the Mall by enhancing its surroundings. More detailed than the Legacy plan, it seeks to focus on underused federal lands. The first meeting for public comment was held mid-2006; a second meeting took place in January 2007.

HISTORY

The history of the capital city is one of setbacks: delayed site selection, sluggish lot sales, L'Enfant's dismissal, Britain's torching of the White House, the Washington Canal boondoggle, Alexandria's retrocession, and the Civil War, to name a few. Compromise, self-interest or forbearance prevailed, as they continue to do in this epicenter of politics and power. The new millennium, however, is witnessing a boom in new construction, the reversal of the city's long-standing population decline, and the addition of cultural and recreational venues.

200 Years of Growth

SELECTING A SITE

After the Revolutionary War the delegates of the newly formed government expressed interest in designating a federal district to be the seat of power for the new country. A number of existing cities, including New York and Philadelphia, vied to be selected, offering money and land as incentives. Rivalry between the northern and southern states concerning the site of the new capital was resolved through a political compromise: In exchange for agreeing to locate the city in the "southern" precinct, the northern states would be relieved of the heavy debts they had incurred during the Revolution.

In July 1790 Congress passed the Residence Act empowering President George Washington to select a site for the new federal district. Ultimately Washington designated a tract on the Potomac River in the vicinity of Georgetown, though he left its exact boundaries and size undefined. Washington was well acquainted with this area, as his own plantation, Mount Vernon, was 16 miles down the Potomac, and he believed that the site had great commercial potential as a port

L'Enfant Plan for the Federal City Adapted from Thackara & Vallance plan, 1792. Silhouette redrawn from a work in the collection of the Diplomatic Reception Rooms, Department of State

if it were linked by canal to the productive lands of the Western frontier. To facilitate its development, Washington convinced major landholders in the area to give portions of their land to the new capital.

L'ENFANT'S "CITY OF MAGNIFICENT DISTANCES"

In 1789, even before Congress voted to create a federal district, the French Maj. **Pierre Charles L'Enfant** (1754-1825) expressed to President Washington his eagerness to draw up the plans for the new capital. Trained at the Royal Academy of Painting and Sculpture in Paris, L'Enfant arrived in the US in 1777 at the age of 22 and fought under General Washington in the American Revolution. After the war L'Enfant established himself in American social circles and enjoyed a fine reputation as a designer and architect, particularly for his work in remodeling Federal Hall in New York City. Impressed with L'Enfant's ideas, and realizing that there were few trained engineers from which to choose, Washington eventually appointed him to design the city and its public buildings.

Following his appointment by Washington, L'Enfant traveled to Georgetown, arriving in March 1791. He had in hand a city layout sketched by Thomas Jefferson, who, along with Washington,

was instrumental in fostering the early development of the federal city. L'Enfant immediately began reconnoitering the area, which at that time had been settled by several landowners and contained three settlements: the well-established Georgetown and the fledgling towns of Carrollsburg (adjacent to present-day Fort Lesley J. McNair) and Hamburg (now the site of the State Department Building in Foggy Bottom).

One of L'Enfant's first decisions was to situate the future "Congress house" on Jenkins Hill, which had a commanding view of the Potomac River. Along this east-west axis, L'Enfant planned a 400ft-wide "Grand Avenue" (now the Mall) to be lined by foreign ministries and cultural institutions. The avenue would culminate in an equestrian statue of George Washington, connected on a north-south axis with the "president's house." This mansion in turn would be linked back to the Capitol via a mile-long commercial corridor (present-day Pennsylvania Avenue). Tiber Creek, a tributary of the Potomac situated south of this projected corridor, would be transformed into a city canal that would run along the northern side of the Grand Avenue, turning south at the foot of Jenkins Hill before emptying into the eastern branch. The watercourse was to be decorative as well as functional, punctuated by reflecting pools and fountains.

The District:
TAKING SHAPE IN THE 19C

Georgetown (consolidated with the District in 1871)

City of Washington

Arlington

Alexandria

10 miles

VIRGINIA MARYLAND

MARYLAND

VIRGINIA

Potomac River

Boundary markers along the original borders of the District

City of Washington as planned by L'Enfant (1791)

Retroceded to Virginia in 1846

Built-up areas in late 19C

Rock Creek Park (est. 1890)

Swampland reclaimed (late 19C– early 20C) for extension of the Mall and creation of Potomac Parks

Pennsylvania Avenue and 15th Street (c.1900)

Kiplinger Washington Collection

L'Enfant laid out the remainder of the city in a grid pattern of streets intersected by broad diagonal avenues at "round-points," each intended to serve as the focus of a neighborhood area. In emphasizing monumental buildings, grand perspectives, gracious circles, wide avenues and expansive views, the Frenchman was influenced by the Baroque notions of urban planning then prevalent in Europe. L'Enfant's widely dispersed, multicentered city, which later earned the sobriquet "the City of Magnificent Distances," anticipated a population of approximately 800,000 people and extended north to the present Florida Avenue escarpment, encompassing an estimated 6,000 acres.

DREAMS AND REALITIES

Once Washington had approved the expanded city plan, L'Enfant directed his energies toward implementing his grand scheme. Refusing to divert his attention to practicalities, L'Enfant was seen as uncooperative and peremptory by the city surveyor, **Andrew Ellicott**, by Jefferson and by the three city commissioners appointed by Washington to oversee the capital's development.

In September 1791 the commissioners named the new diamond-shaped federal district the "Territory of Columbia" (the current designation, "District of Columbia," came into use in the 19C).

Ten miles long on each side, the territory encompassed the County of Alexandria on the Virginia shore of the Potomac and portions of Maryland on the northern shore. The commissioners named the capital itself the City of Washington and stipulated that its street grid be designated by numbers and letters.

To generate revenue for public works and buildings, the commissioners held an auction of lots in October 1791, but only 35 parcels in the as-yet-undeveloped city were sold. Before long, a series of conflicts arose between L'Enfant and the commissioners. Finally, in February 1792, unable to defend the designer's recalcitrance any longer, Washington dismissed him. Gathering up most of his plans and drawings, L'Enfant left the town he had conceptualized. Thirty-three years later the talented Frenchman died penniless and forgotten in nearby Maryland, having never received just compensation or recognition during his lifetime. (In 1909 L'Enfant's remains were transferred to Arlington National Cemetery. The L'Enfant Plan of 1791, restored in 1991, is now in the custody of the Library of Congress.)

Andrew Ellicott took over where L'Enfant left off, reconstructing the Frenchman's original plan from preparatory sketches. Ellicott recruited the gifted, self-taught mathematician Benjamin Banneker, a free black, to assist with the surveying, and proceeded to lay out streets and avenues. On instructions from Jefferson and Washington, Ellicott named the latter after states of the Union.

During the same period, competitions were held to design the president's house and a home for Congress, but even after architects were chosen, work proceeded slowly because the lot sales needed to finance construction continued to lag. A syndicate of private financiers was formed in the late 1790s to act as a real-estate development company for Washington, but the syndicate's bankruptcy in 1797 curtailed further growth. In addition to the lack of an economic base, the city suffered from a critical shortage of stonemasons and other skilled laborers.

"CITY OF MAGNIFICENT INTENTIONS"

When Congress and President John Adams relocated from Philadelphia to Washington in November 1800, they found the skeleton of the nascent city etched into the wilderness. Both the Capitol and White House were incomplete; Pennsylvania Avenue was a rutted, marshy thoroughfare; and the town was bereft of finesse or comfort. In August 1814 the fledgling capital suffered a major setback when the British invaded the town and set fire to the Capitol, the White House and other public buildings.

After the war a contingent of federal officials, despairing that the town would ever become a capital, lobbied to desert Washington and move the federal government to a more established city. A group of local entrepreneurs put up their own funds as loans for rebuilding, thereby persuading the lawmakers to remain in Washington. Congress appropriated additional monies to repair the damaged Capitol and Executive Mansion, and development continued as before, slowly but a little more surely.

In 1815 the Washington Canal opened along Pennsylvania Avenue. Unfortunately, the canal provided neither the decorative element intended by L'Enfant nor the commercial boon that had been hoped for by George Washington and others. In 1835 the Baltimore and Ohio Railroad reached Washington, signaling the age of rail transport and the doom of the canal trade so necessary to the prosperity of Alexandria and Georgetown. Alexandrians, feeling they had suffered economically and politically by their integration into the federal district, petitioned for retrocession to Virginia. Their petition was granted in 1846.

In spite of numerous setbacks, by the mid-19C Washington was on its way to becoming a city, and its prevailing Neoclassical flavor had been established, thanks to such monumental structures as the Old City Hall, the Treasury Building and the Old Patent Office Building. Impressive Federal-style residences were also scattered throughout the burgeoning city. Washington had newspapers, theaters and, if not a rich, at least a respectable cultural life.

In 1850 President Millard Fillmore commissioned **Andrew Jackson Downing** to devise a major landscape plan for Washington's central quarters, particularly Lafayette Square and the present-day Mall. Although Downing's plans were never funded, they represented an early and instrumental effort to unify the green spaces of the "monumental city." In 1855 the newly created Smithsonian Institution opened its brick Castle on the Mall.

During the Civil War, development in Washington came to a halt as the city turned its attention to national and local defense. A ring of forts was built along the Potomac, and several of the city's grand public structures became hospitals for the Union wounded.

The brief period of territorial government that began in 1871 was dominated by **Alexander "Boss" Shepherd**, the driving force behind a citywide public works program that resulted in the development of such outlying areas as Dupont Circle; the alteration of street levels to improve drainage; the paving over of the old, unsanitary canal; and the planting of thousands of trees. Shepherd's grand plan also bankrupted the city, which, as always, relied on federal coffers for support. A disgruntled Congress revoked territorial government and returned the city to district status in 1874. In 1871 Washington was significantly enlarged by the incorporation of

Georgetown. As the century drew to a close, railroad, streetcar and trolley lines led to the growth in nearby Virginia and Maryland of suburban communities that were linked economically and culturally to the city.

"THE CITY BEAUTIFUL"

In 1901 the US Senate appointed the four-member **McMillan Commission** to recommend an overall building and landscape plan for the Mall area, which was then an unsightly hodgepodge. The commission's report, inspired by L'Enfant's original plan, established an 800ft greensward for the Mall and extended it west and south along the reclaimed Potomac flats, where the grand monuments to Lincoln and Jefferson were subsequently positioned. To oversee all future planning for and building in the capital, the Commission of Fine Arts was created in 1910. In the same year, the Height of Buildings Act stipulated that no structures exceed 15 stories, thus ensuring that Washington would remain a horizontal and spacious city. Another law, the Public Buildings Act of 1926, resulted in the construction of a number of the city's monumental Classical Revival buildings, including those on the Federal Triangle and the structures housing the National Archives and the Supreme Court.

During the first half of the 20C, Washington's population increased from 278,000 to 800,000. The two world wars and the 1930s Works Progress Administration attracted an influx of workers to the city and its suburbs. To meet the administrative needs of the war efforts, a number of temporary buildings were constructed in the Mall area. In the postwar decades, Washington became a decentralized city with a decaying central core and an ever-increasing dependence on the automobile. While a system of expressways was built around the periphery of the District, traffic remained a critical problem. To alleviate congestion, a subway system, the Metrorail, began operations in 1976 and has since continually expanded its intercity and suburban service. The system's efficiency and elegant, albeit stark,

design by the architect Harry Weese has won national acclaim.

THE CONTEMPORARY CITY

In the 1960s and 70s, tax laws favored the demolition of the city's old structures, and many charming architectural features were removed forever from the cityscape. At the same time, however, an awareness of historic preservation was burgeoning. The Kennedy administration (1961-63) began efforts to rejuvenate and restore historic Pennsylvania Avenue. In 1978 the city passed the Historic Landmark and Historic District Protection Act, which set guidelines for the designation and protection of historic structures and districts. By the 1980s the growing awareness of Washington's architectural heritage was reflected in commercial, as well as public, endeavors. Old buildings were renovated rather than demolished, new buildings were designed to interface with traditional architecture and the resuscitation of historic Downtown was well under way.

In addition to this architectural awareness, increasing focus was placed on developing and maintaining the parks and green spaces for which the city is famous. During her tenure as First Lady, **Ladybird Johnson** was instrumental in a city beautification process that led to the landscaping of park areas and public squares. In the late 1960s and 70s, the National Capital Planning Commission instituted long-range plans that strove to achieve an integrated look for the city and its natural areas. The commission's

Metro Station

Extending the Legacy plan (1997) and the National Capital Framework Plan (2006) are further attempts to develop and maximize the city's physical assets over time. The District's public parkland, some 7,000 acres that include the elm-lined lawns of the Mall and the hilly, forested terrain of Rock Creek Park, is administered and maintained by the National Park Service.

Time Line

THE COLONIAL PERIOD

1608 — Capt. John Smith sails up the Potomac.

1662 — The first land patent on the future site of the District is granted.

1749 — Alexandria is laid out.

1751 — Georgetown is established.

1763 — The French and Indian War ends, affirming British supremacy in eastern North America.

1775–83 — The American Revolution takes place.

1776 — The Continental Congress sign the Declaration of Independence in Philadelphia.

1783 — Britain recognizes the independence of the 13 colonies.

1788 — Maryland cedes territory on the Potomac for the establishment of a federal city.

1789 — The US Constitution is ratified. New York is designated capital. George Washington is elected first US president.

1790 — The nation's capital is moved to Philadelphia. Congress passes the Residence Act, giving George Washington the power to choose the site for the new capital and 10 years to create a federal city.

BUILDING A CAPITOL

1791 — President Washington selects a site for the federal district and authorizes Pierre Charles L'Enfant to draft city plans.

Congress appoints three commissioners, who name the 10sq mi diamond-shaped area the Territory of Columbia (later known as the District of Columbia) and the capital the City of Washington.

1792 — L'Enfant is dismissed by President Washington.

The cornerstone is laid for the White House.

1793 — The cornerstone is laid for the Capitol.

1800 — President John Adams is the first occupant of the White House.

Congress convenes for the first time in the unfinished Capitol building.

1801 — Thomas Jefferson is the first president to be inaugurated in Washington.

1802 — Under congressional jurisdiction, the City of Washington is chartered.

The first district government buildings are erected.

City population: 3,000.

1808 — Construction begins on the Washington Canal along present-day Constitution Avenue.

1812 — War of 1812 begins. The US declares war on Britain.

1814 — The British invade Washington and burn the Capitol, the White House and other public buildings. Washington banks offer $500,000 in loans to help rebuild the city and to quell a movement to abandon the capital.

1815 — President James Madison signs the Treaty of Ghent, ending the War of 1812.

A CENTURY OF GROWTH

1824 — Citywide celebrations take place on the occasion of the second visit of the Marquis de Lafayette, America's Revolutionary ally.

1832 — A severe cholera epidemic sweeps the city.

1835 — The Baltimore and Ohio Railroad reaches the District, initiating the eventual decline of canal traffic through Georgetown and Washington.

1836 — Construction of the Treasury and Patent Office buildings gets under way.

1846 — Congress establishes the Smithsonian Institution. District territory south of the Potomac is retroceded to Virginia, reducing the District by one-third of its original size.

1850 — Chesapeake and Ohio Canal is completed.

1855 — The Castle, the Smithsonian's first building, opens on the Mall.

1861 — Beginning of the Civil War. Many public buildings in the District become hospitals and barracks for Union soldiers. Forts are erected around the city's southern edge.

1862 — Congress grants compensatory emancipation of all slaves in the District.

1863 — President Abraham Lincoln issues the Emancipation Proclamation.

1864 — Confederate Gen. Jubal Early is repulsed at nearby Fort Stevens, saving the capital from capture by the South.

1865 — End of the Civil War. Gen. Robert E. Lee surrenders to Gen. Ulysses S. Grant at Appomattox. President Lincoln is assassinated five days later at Ford's Theatre.

1867 — DC citizens are granted suffrage. Howard University, the capital's first black university, is chartered by Congress.

1871 — DC population has doubled since the beginning of the decade due largely to the influx of former slaves. Georgetown is incorporated with Washington.

1871–74 — An act of Congress establishes a brief period of territorial government for the District.

Alexander "Boss" Shepherd begins a citywide public works project that results in a beautified but near-bankrupt city.

1874 — The city's first art museum, the Corcoran Gallery of Art, opens on Pennsylvania Ave.

1880s — Establishment of streetcar lines leads to the growth of outlying areas.

1884 — The Washington Monument, begun in 1848, is completed.

1897 — The first Library of Congress building opens.

"THE CITY BEAUTIFUL"

1900 — Washington celebrates its centennial.

1901 — The McMillan Commission is established to beautify the Mall.

1908 — Union Station is completed.

1914 — The Lincoln Memorial is begun in the reclaimed West Potomac Park.

1917 — US enters World War I. Washington experiences a wartime boom. Rows of temporary war buildings, or "tempos," are erected around the Mall.

1918 — Armistice ends World War I. DC population has risen to nearly 440,000.

1926 — National Capital Park and Planning Commission is established. The Public Buildings Act leads to construction of many federal edifices.

1931–32 — Hunger marchers demonstrate in Washington.

1941 — US enters World War II. DC experiences another wartime boom. The National Gallery of Art opens on the Mall.

1945 — World War II ends in victory for the US and Allied forces.

1950–53 — Korean War takes place. DC population peaks at 800,000.

1961 — John F. Kennedy is inaugurated 35th US president and appoints a committee to study the rejuvenation of Pennsylvania Ave.

Congress ratifies the 23rd Amendment to the Constitution, giving District residents the right to vote in presidential elections.

1963 — Martin Luther King Jr. leads 200,000 in the March on Washington for Jobs and Freedom. King delivers his "I Have a Dream" speech from the Lincoln Memorial.

President Kennedy is assassinated in Dallas and buried in Arlington National Cemetery.

Late 60s — Racial riots erupt in the capital. Areas of the city are looted and burned.

Early 70s — Anti-Vietnam War demonstrations are staged on the Mall.

District residents are allowed to elect one nonvoting delegate to the House of Representatives.

TOWARD THE 21C

1973 — Congress passes the Home Rule Act, establishing self-government for DC.

US troops are withdrawn from Vietnam.

1974 — President Richard Nixon resigns in the wake of the Watergate scandal.

1976 — US bicentennial celebrations.

Metrorail, the city's first subway system, begins operations.

The Cooperative Use Act is passed, allowing commercial activities in federal buildings and encouraging restoration of historic structures.

1979 — Farmers' Tractorcade invades Washington; protesters camp on the Mall.

Pope John Paul II delivers a mass on the Mall.

1982 — The Washington Convention Center opens, spurring downtown development.

1983 — The renovated Old Post Office opens.

1987 — The Smithsonian Quadrangle opens.

1990 — The Washington National Cathedral, begun in 1907, is completed.

1993 — The US Holocaust Memorial Museum and the Smithsonian Institution's National Postal Museum open.

The Vietnam Women's Memorial is dedicated.

Bill proposing DC statehood is defeated in Congress.

1995 — Million Man March terminates at the Lincoln Memorial.

Korean War Veterans Memorial is dedicated.

1996 — Last Washington Redskins football game is played in RFK Stadium. New stadium to be built outside DC by 1997.

1997 — Memorial to President Franklin D. Roosevelt opens to the public. The Ronald Reagan Building completes the Federal Triangle complex.

1998 — National Airport officially named in honor of President Ronald Reagan. President Bill Clinton is impeached by the House of Representatives. He is acquitted by the Senate.

THE NEW MILLENNIUM

2000 — After weeks of recounts and lawsuits, the battle to determine the winner of the presidential election moves to the capital, where a Supreme Court decision gives the victory to George W. Bush.

2001 — As part of the worst terrorist attack in US history, the Pentagon suffers severe damage, resulting in 184 fatalities.

2003 — The new Steven F. Udvar-Hazy Center opens near Dulles International Airport.

2004 — Ronald Reagan, the 40th US president, dies. His body lies in state at the Capitol, before burial in California.

2005 — The Washington Nationals return professional baseball to DC after a 34-year hiatus.

2006 — The Smithsonian American Art Museum and the National Portrait Gallery reopen after a six-year renovation.

2007 — The National Capital Planning Commission issues its findings and solutions after studying the 2006 flooding of the Federal Triangle.

2008 — New baseball stadium for Washington Nationals to be completed in April on Anacostia River, south of the Capitol.

ART AND CULTURE

Conceived as a national showplace. Washington, DC embodies the spirit of American idealism in its Neoclassical monuments and grand museums. Rich in cultural offerings, the capital is truly an international city, with a world-class performing arts complex, fine restaurants, shops and art galleries, and a mixed population of foreign nationals.

Architecture

From its inception Washington has attracted the talents of nationally prominent architects whose skills and vision are reflected in the city's many historic buildings. Because of the dominance of the Neoclassical style within the city and the strict building codes that set a 15-story height limit, modern Washington never developed as a center of innovative, high-rise architecture. Designed as a showcase for the new democracy, it remains in appearance a city of government, featuring massive, columned buildings adorned with allegorical motifs that recall the democratic and aesthetic ideals of ancient Greece and Rome. The District inventory of historic sites currently lists some 396 buildings, parks and historic districts, including lesser-known treasures such as the Classical Revival-style Embassy Gulf Service Station, a less prominent but enduring symbol of the capital.

18C

Washington preserves few vestiges from the 18C, since the city's foundation dates back to the 1790s. During the colonial period, the **Georgian** style, so named because it was popular in England under kings George I-IV (1714-1830), predominated in the design of brick and stone plantations and manor houses in nearby Virginia and Maryland. Existing examples of this style, which is typified by porticoes, cornices, quoins (prominent corner masonry) and hipped roofs, include Carlyle House, and Gunston Hall in Virginia.

In Georgetown the simple Old Stone House is one of the few extant buildings that reflect colonial vernacular architecture prior to the Revolution. Following independence, the influence of the successful English architects the **Adam brothers** was seen in the work of colonial designers who adapted the Adam style to an American idiom that became known as **Federal** architecture. This style relies on symmetry and decorative elegance, often integrating such adornments as delicate columns, rosettes, urns and swags. The circular and oval-shaped rooms that characterize this style were used to great effect in The Octagon and Tudor Place, both private residences designed by **Dr. William Thornton** (1759-1828), the first architect of the Capitol. Many of the late-18C and early-19C row houses in Georgetown and Old Town Alexandria also exemplify the Federal style.

19C

In America as in Europe, the 19C gave rise to an eclectic mix of revival styles.

In Washington, however, the prevailing taste for Neoclassical style frequently led to criticism of buildings that broke with this tradition. Some fine 19C structures that did not adhere to classical principles, such as the Old Post Office, the Old Executive Office Building and the Pension Building, were little appreciated, neglected and even threatened with demolition.

The **Greek Revival** style, modeled on the Doric temple, gained prominence in the 1800s under the talented hands of **Benjamin H. Latrobe** (1764-1820), who modified the original White House design and was responsible for many small architectural gems, such as Decatur House and St. John's Church. Another proponent of this style, **Robert Mills** (1781-1855) created the Treasury Building, the Old Patent Office Building and the original design of the Washington Monument. By midcentury a few architects began experimenting with the **Romanesque Revival** style, as exemplified in the turrets and battlemented cornices of the Smithsonian Castle, designed by **James Renwick** (1818-95). In the 1870s and 80s, Henry Hobson Richardson (1838-86) modified this approach into the popular Richardsonian Romanesque. Distinctive for its massive stone constructions that feature arched windows, doorways and turrets, this style can be found in the Old Post Office and in private residences in the Northwest quadrant, such as the Heurich Mansion.

The **Italianate**, a simpler residential style, can be seen in several of the 19C brick row houses in Georgetown, the Dupont Circle area and Foggy Bottom. One of many versions of what is popularly called Victorian architecture, the Italianate employs overhanging cornices, decorative brackets, bow windows and porches.

The **Second Empire** style, a mid-19C French innovation, first made its appearance in America in the early 1860s, with the building that now houses the Renwick Gallery. Named after its architect, James Renwick, this building features the characteristic Second Empire mansard roof—a dual-pitched roof pierced with dormer windows on the steep lower slope. During the Grant administration (1869-77), the style became so prevalent that it was known as the General Grant style. The massive Old Executive Office Building is one of the nation's finest examples of the style.

At the turn of the century, the exuberant **Beaux-Arts** style dominated the new buildings of Washington. Developed in France's famous École des Beaux-Arts, where many prominent American architects studied, this style was typified by a monumentality that reflected the optimistic spirit of the nation in the late 19C and early 20C. Its eclecticism combines classical elements with elaborate detailing, as seen in such public buildings as Union Station by **Daniel H. Burnham** (1846-1912), one of the leading advocates of Beaux-Arts, and the Library of Congress. In residential architecture, Waddy B. Wood and Jules Henri de Sibour designed a number of the palatial homes along Embassy Row in the Beaux-Arts manner.

20C

In the 1920s Beaux-Arts enthusiasm gradually became restrained, evolving into the more formal **Classical Revival** architecture that again dominated Washington from the 1920s through World War II. The Federal Triangle complex, built in the 1930s, includes seven buildings designed in the Classical Revival style by seven different architects, one of whom was **John Russell Pope** (1874-1937). The most prolific proponent of this style, Pope is responsible for such grand public buildings as the National Gallery of Art, the National Archives, the Scottish Rite House of the Temple (1733 16th St. at S St. NW) and

The Octagon

R. Corbel/MICHELIN

the Jefferson Memorial. Sweeping staircases, pedimented porticoes, domes, and unadorned surfaces are all hallmarks of Pope's edifices.

Post-World War II Modernism has had little impact on Washington architecture. Rather than producing innovative architectural design, the 1950s, 60s and 70s saw the loss of many fine 19C structures, as undistinguished boxlike office buildings proliferated throughout the city. It was during this uninspired period that the Kennedy Center and the National Geographic Society building, both by **Edward Durell Stone**, were erected. Washington does, however, possess a few exceptional examples of modern architecture: Dulles International Airport (1962, Eero Saarinen), the Martin Luther King Memorial Library (1972, Mies van der Rohe) and the East Building of the National Gallery of Art (1978, I.M. Pei). In recent years the currents of **post-Modernism** have resurrected the use of columns, arches and other embellishments that had been banished during the austere Modernist period. Washington Harbour, designed by Arthur Cotton Moore, embodies the extravagances of the 1980s, while a more restrained and academic approach can be seen in the newer structures along the historic Pennsylvania Avenue corridor, where classical elements are used in an attempt to integrate new architecture with the existing building stock. The Market Square complex (between 6th and 7th Sts.) by Hartman-Cox exemplifies this trend. A decidedly post-Modern influence is apparent in the architecture of the US Holocaust Memorial Museum (James Freed), which opened in 1993.

Old Post Office

21C

A flurry of embassy construction in a mix of architectural styles ushered in the new millennium in DC. The new Italian chancery, juxtaposing elements of a Tuscan villa and a Florentine palazzo, provides Embassy Row with an eye-catching, if nonindigenous, example of historical eclecticism (2000, Piero Sartogo). The Nigerian embassy (2002, Shalom Baranes Associates), located in the International Center, north of the Washington Cathedral, is a modernist mix of glass and stone. Overlooking the Potomac in Georgetown, the Swedish embassy (2006, Wingårdh Arkitektkontor AB) inhabits a simple, yet striking five-story geometric construction of glass windows framed in layers of blond wood and stone. The largest chancery in Washington to date is the new 350,000sq ft Embassy of the People's Republic of China, currently rising in the International Center. Nearly a block long, the complex, designed by Pei Partnership Architects, is a series of multistoried buildings connected to a raised central courtyard. It is scheduled for completion in 2008.

Library of Congress

National Archives

Smithsonian Institution

Mall Museums

- Arthur M. Sackler Gallery
- Arts and Industries Building
- Freer Gallery of Art
- Hirshhorn Museum and Sculpture Garden
- National Air and Space Museum
- National Museum of African Art
- National Museum of American History
- National Museum of Natural History
- National Museum of the American Indian
- Smithsonian Institution Building: (The Castle)

Off the Mall

- Anacostia Museum
- National Portrait Gallery
- National Postal Museum
- National Zoological Park
- Renwick Gallery
- Smithsonian American Art Museum Steven F. Udvar-Hazy Center

New York City

- Cooper-Hewitt National Design Museum
  (🍃 See THE GREEN GUIDE New York City)

Robust modernism coupled with historic preservation was the formula for the renovation of the 800 block of F Street NW, which houses the International Spy Museum (2002, Shalom Baranes Associates). Sleek new high-rise office towers and condominiums are dotting the landscape with a modernist aesthetic: examples include BBGM's condominium building (2005) in brick and precast concrete at 12th and K streets NW; the bay-windowed, brick-paneled Rutherford condominiums (2005, Eric Colbert and Assocs.); and the glass and steel 1875 Pennsylvania Avenue office building (2006, Baranes Associates).

National Art Gallery

Gwen Cannon/MICHELIN

Cultural Scene

Traditionally considered a cultural backwater, Washington has emerged in recent decades as a vital center for the performing arts, thereby taking its place among the nation's leading cultural hubs.

MUSEUMS

Founded in 1846 through a bequest to the US from an English scientist named James Smithson, the **Smithsonian Institution** now constitutes the largest complex of museums in the world. Of its 17 museums and galleries in Washington, DC, ten are located on the Mall. (Although loosely affiliated with the Smithsonian, the National Gallery of Art is an independent institution.) The Smithsonian's National Zoological Park and five of its six other museums are also located in Washington.

The collections of the Smithsonian contain some 140 million objects, including cultural and scientific artifacts and artworks ranging from the prehistoric to the contemporary. Among them are revered relics that define the country's heritage: the Star Spangled Banner, the Wright Brothers' *1903 Flyer*, Dorothy's ruby slippers, Woody Guthrie's "This Land is Your Land" and the entire Folkways Records collection. The institution also maintains six special facilities sup-

Monumental Sculpture in the Capital

The following is a selection of noteworthy works of modern sculpture adorning the public spaces of Washington, DC (☞see also *Memorials* and *National Gallery of Art Sculpture Garden*):

Mountains and Clouds by Alexander Calder. Atrium of the Hart Senate Office Building, Constitution Ave. and 2nd St. NE.

Mobile (untitled) by Alexander Calder. Atrium of the National Gallery's East Building.

The Gwenfritz by Alexander Calder. Constitution Ave. and 14th St. NW on the grounds of the National Museum of American History.

The Spiral by Alexander Calder. Courtyard of the Old Patent Office Building.

Infinity by José de Rivera. Outside the Mall entrance of the National Museum of American History.

The Awakening by J. Seward Johnson. A striking aluminum sculpture depicting a giant emerging from the ground. Hains Point in East Potomac Park SW.

Mountains and Clouds by Alexander Calder

Architect of the Capitol

The plaza and the sculpture garden of the Hirshhorn Museum provide an open-air showcase for works by prominent modern artists such as Rodin, Matisse, Calder, Moore, Maillol and Smith, as well as pieces by contemporary sculptors.

porting work in the arts and sciences and sponsors public lectures, concerts, classes, festivals and tours.

In addition to the Smithsonian attractions, the capital boasts several fine privately owned museums created through the generosity of prominent Washington collectors. Foremost among these institutions are the Corcoran Gallery of Art, the Phillips Collection, Hillwood and Dumbarton Oaks. The area has preserved many historic house museums that offer visitors glimpses into the capital's illustrious past. The federal city also abounds in exemplary public buildings, many of which are open to the public. A visit to such sights as the Capitol, Supreme Court, FBI or the Bureau of Engraving and Printing can provide a unique learning experience in the workings of the US government. Throughout the year the area's cultural and educational institutions—both public and private—sponsor an impressive schedule of (usually free) exhibits, lectures and concerts catering to a wide range of tastes and interests.

PERFORMING ARTS

☞*For addresses, telephone numbers and other practical information, consult Your Stay in Washington, DC.* With the opening of the John F. Kennedy Center for the Performing Arts in 1971, Washington finally began to attract an increasing number of world-class performers. Housing four theaters and the resident National Symphony Orchestra, the center offers drama, concerts and dance performances, and a regular schedule of film festivals and events through its affiliation with the American Film Institute. The well-respected Arena Stage complex, entering its 53rd season, anchors the city's diverse and thriving theater community. Woolly Mammoth Theatre Company produces new and experimental works, while Shakespeare is the house playwright at the Folger Theatre. Touring Broadway musicals stop at the historic National Theatre, established on Pennsylvania Avenue in 1835 (and now a Kennedy Center affiliate).

The National Park Service maintains two theaters: historic Ford's Theatre located downtown and the acclaimed Wolf Trap Farm for the Performing Arts, an outdoor summer theater in the nearby Virginia suburbs, which features renowned dance troupes and musicians.

THE CITY TODAY

All three branches of US government are housed here, and in nearby Arlington, the command center for the entire American military establishment sprawls over 6.5 million square feet. The capital city is remarkably accessible, opening the doors of Congress, the White House and other federal institutions to hosts of visitors who come to witness democracy in progress.

The Federal Government

Under the system of checks and balances established by the US Constitution, the federal government is composed of three branches: the Legislative (both houses of Congress), the Executive (the president and the Executive Office) and the Judicial (the Supreme Court and all other federal courts). The White House, seat of the Executive branch, is situated within a mile of Capitol Hill, where the Capitol, home of Congress, and the Supreme Court building are located. Each of these branches fulfills specific functions and duties of its own, as well as overseeing and keeping in check the powers exercised by the other two branches.

THE LEGISLATIVE BRANCH

Conceived by the Founding Fathers as a bicameral system of government, the Congress comprises two bodies: the Senate and the House of Representatives. Jointly they are responsible for drafting and passing laws; for handling matters of national finance, such as setting and collecting taxes and coining money; for ensuring, in conjunction with the president, the defense of the nation; for regulating commerce; and for admitting new states to the Union. Within these broadly defined pow-

ers, each body has separate duties, as described below.

A specific Congress serves for two years (the 109th Congress convenes from 2004 to 2005), beginning new sessions each year in late January and generally recessing in August and again in the fall.

The **Senate** is composed of 100 senators, two from each of the 50 states in the Union. Senators are elected to six-year terms by popular vote, in accordance with the 17th Amendment, which was added to the Constitution in 1913 (originally, the Constitution specified that senators be elected by state legislatures).

Senate terms are staggered so that no more than one-third of the Senate seats are renewed each year. The vice president is the official presiding officer of the Senate, but in his absence, senators elect a president pro tempore from among their ranks. The Senate's specific duties include approving presidential appointments; ratifying foreign treaties by a two-thirds majority (a power now little used); and trying federal officials impeached by the House. (Only two US presidents have stood trial before the Senate: Andrew Johnson, Abraham Lincoln's successor, in 1868, and Bill Clinton in 1999. Both presidents were acquitted.)

The **House** is composed of 435 representatives (often referred to as congressmen and congresswomen), with the number of representatives per state based on population. California has the greatest number of representatives (53). The District of Columbia and the US territories of Guam, the Virgin Islands and American Samoa are represented by nonvoting delegates to the House, and the commonwealth of Puerto Rico sends a nonvoting resident commissioner.

Members of the House serve two-year terms, and their presiding officer is the Speaker of the House, elected anew with each Congress. Under the Constitution the House is responsible for originating all bills relating to taxes; impeaching (that is, charging federal officials with criminal actions); and determining the outcome of a presidential election if there is no clear electoral majority.

Historically Congress has been dominated by two opposing political parties, whose names and policies have changed over time. Today the major parties are Democratic and Republican, though nothing prevents "independents" or members of smaller parties from running for office.

In both houses, the dominant party elects a **majority leader** and a deputy, the **majority whip**. The minority party, likewise, elects its own leader and whip. If the majority party in one or both houses of Congress is different from the party of the president, legislation may bog down, as Congress votes against supported initiatives or the president vetoes congressional acts.

In both chambers, much of the work of formulating and drafting new laws is done within standing committees. There are 19 such committees in the House and 16 in the Senate. Normally a representative serves on two committees, a senator on three or four.

HOW A BILL BECOMES LAW

Any interested person or group, whether within or outside the political system, may draft a bill and seek the support of a US senator or representative to introduce it for congressional consideration. Of the many bills proposed annually, only a handful are enacted into laws. Throughout the legislative process described below, a corps of lobbyists is generally operating behind the scenes to persuade legislators to protect the interests of their clients.

Each bill begins its journey when it is introduced on the floor of either the House or the Senate chamber; in many cases a similar proposal is introduced simultaneously in both houses. The chamber's parliamentarian then assigns it to an appropriate **standing committee** for consideration, and if deemed worthwhile, the proposal is normally referred to a subcommittee for further study. The **subcommittee** holds hearings in which it elicits the opinions of experts and interested parties. Such hearings, especially in the House, are generally open to the public. The subcommittee must then "mark up" the bill, or rework the language and intent of various sections in light of the conclusions drawn from hearings. The marked-up bill then passes back to the full standing committee, which after further study either rejects the bill or "reports" it—that is, recommends its passage to the chamber. In the House, reported bills are then submitted to the Rules Committee before returning to the chamber. In the Senate, the leadership determines the course of action on each piece of legislation.

Having received committee approval, the bill is placed on the chamber's calendar, and at the scheduled time, it is debated, amended and put to a vote. At this point, a bill that has been introduced in only one chamber is sent to the other chamber, where the legislative process begins anew. If the bill has been introduced simultaneously in the Senate and the House and passed by both, the two versions are then referred to a **conference committee**, composed of members from both chambers who meet

House Chamber, November 17, 1947

to resolve differences in wording and intent. Their compromise version is then sent back to both the House and Senate, which separately vote on the identical version of the bill. After passage in both houses, the approved legislation next proceeds to the president, who may sign it into law or exercise his **veto** power by returning the bill to Congress unsigned, with a statement of his objections. Congress may override a presidential veto with a two-thirds majority vote in both chambers. The president has a third option: If he wishes to register his disapproval without actually vetoing, he may simply retain the unsigned bill, and after 10 days, it automatically becomes law, provided Congress is in session. If Congress is adjourned at that time, the president's failure to sign constitutes a "pocket veto," and the bill dies.

THE EXECUTIVE BRANCH

The president and vice president are the only elected officials of the branch's 4 million employees (including armed forces personnel). Presidential elections are held every four years, and a president may serve a maximum of two four-year terms in office, as stipulated by the 22nd Amendment (1951) to the Constitution.

The Constitution also requires that a presidential candidate be at least 35 years old, be born in the US and live in the US for 14 years prior to running for office. Presidential candidates choose their running mates at the commencement of campaigns. In the event of the president's resignation, impeachment, incapacitation or death, the vice president assumes the presidency.

The president serves as commander-in-chief of the Armed Forces, with ultimate control over the defense of the nation. However, as required by the Constitution and the War Powers Act of 1973, a protracted military action must be approved by Congress, which solely holds the power to declare war. In addition the president serves as the nation's chief executive. In this capacity he appoints all ambassadors, ministers, consuls and persons serving in cabinet-level positions and approves the appointments of many policy-making personnel within the Executive branch. Whenever a vacancy occurs on the Supreme Court or among other judges on the federal bench, the president makes a new appointment (which is subject to Senate approval). Through such appointments the president exerts an influence that may last far beyond his own tenure in office. The president is also empowered to grant pardons and reprieves to those convicted of committing crimes against the US government. Finally, the president, through his veto power, is instrumental in the lawmaking process.

The Executive branch comprises the **Executive Office of the President**— independent federal agencies, and all 14 **cabinet departments** (State, Treasury, Defense, Justice, Interior, Agriculture, Commerce, Labor, Health and Human Services, Education, Transportation, Housing and Urban Development, Energy, and Veteran Affairs). The "secretary," or head, of each cabinet department advises the president on setting national policy.

The Executive Office of the President includes the White House staff and a number of departments that assist and advise the president on policy, such as the Council of Economic Advisers and the Office of National Drug Control Policy (run by the nation's "Drug Czar"). A powerful component of the Executive Office is the **Office of Management and Budget,** which prepares the president's annual federal budget, works with Congress on legislative objectives and acts as an organizational overseer for the entire Executive branch.

Many crucial government responsibilities are executed by the dozens of federal agencies chartered by Congress and overseen by the president, such as the Central Intelligence Agency, the Post Office, the National Security Agency and the National Aeronautics and Space Administration and such important regulatory bodies as the Environmental Protection Agency, the Federal Trade Commission and the Securities and Exchange Commission.

THE JUDICIAL BRANCH

The smallest of the three branches, the Judiciary interprets the law of the land. It is composed of three levels: **US District Courts** (numbering 94), **US Courts of Appeals** (13) and the **US Supreme Court**. Judges at all three levels are appointed for life to the federal bench by the president and must be confirmed by the Senate.

Federal cases may be civil or criminal in nature. Criminal cases must concern a violation of federal law. For a civil case to be heard in federal court, it must involve one of the following criteria: a federal statute, a constitutional issue or litigants from different states in a case involving a sum in excess of $75,000.

Normally federal cases are first filed and tried at the district level, though they may begin in special federal courts, such as the US Claims Court or the Tax Court. Once a decision has been handed down in district court, a dissatisfied party who feels that the district wrongly applied the law may file an appeal with the US Court of Appeals serving his or her district.

The final court of review, the Supreme Court, is made up of eight associate justices and a chief justice. This body hears only about two percent of the

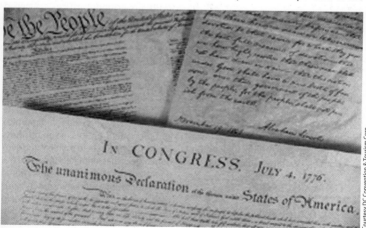

In CONGRESS. JULY 4, 1776.

The unanimous Declaration of the thirteen united States of America.

Historical Documents, National Archives

Courtesy DC Convention & Tourism Corp.

WELCOME TO WASHINGTON, DC

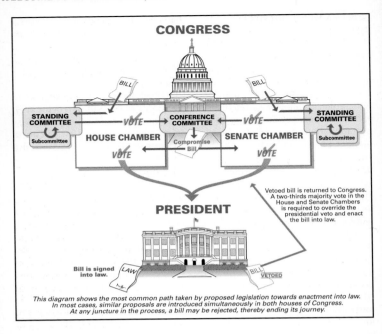

CONGRESS

STANDING COMMITTEE
Subcommittee

VOTE

HOUSE CHAMBER

BILL

CONFERENCE COMMITTEE

Compromise Bill

VOTE

SENATE CHAMBER

BILL

STANDING COMMITTEE
Subcommittee

VOTE

VOTE

PRESIDENT

Vetoed bill is returned to Congress. A two-thirds majority vote in the House and Senate Chambers is required to override the presidential veto and enact the bill into law.

Bill is signed into law. LAW

BILL VETOED

This diagram shows the most common path taken by proposed legislation towards enactment into law. In most cases, similar proposals are introduced simultaneously in both houses of Congress. At any juncture in the process, a bill may be rejected, thereby ending its journey.

petitions it receives annually, focusing attention on cases that call into question the constitutionality of existing laws or that challenge lower court interpretations of federal laws. Decisions handed down by the Supreme Court set the legal precedents for all other courts of the land.

How Washington Works

Washington's principal industry is government. The federal presence in the metropolis dominates the economy, directly through the civil service bureaucracy and indirectly through government-related businesses. Politics and government also influence the social climate of the capital city. With less than two percent of its work force involved in manufacturing, Washington functions like a white-collar town.

FEDERAL GOVERNMENT

Some 322,000 people living in the metropolitan area are on the federal payroll, from the president to park rangers, custodians to museum curators. Most permanent government positions are within the purview of the Office of Personnel and Management, an independent agency of the Executive branch. However, higher-level jobs are generally held by presidential appointment, and new appointees are customarily brought in with each change of administration. Daily, hordes of employees commute from the surrounding suburbs to work in the government offices scattered throughout the city. Some 23 percent of the city's land is federally owned. After hours, whole corridors of the city where government buildings are concentrated (particularly in Foggy Bottom) are virtually deserted.

Social life in the capital city tends to be conducted at private gatherings, where the nation's leaders, foreign diplomats and prominent figures in the business world informally share political and economic ideas that ultimately influence the direction of government. The national and international elite may meet in private homes, at embassy receptions, in reception rooms on Capitol Hill and in such private clubs as the Cosmos Club, Sulgrave Club and Metropolitan Club.

GOVERNMENT-RELATED SECTOR

In order to be near the federal nerve center, hundreds of national and international organizations have offices in Washington. The Pentagon, wellspring of the military industrial complex, supports innumerable defense contracting companies throughout the metropolitan area.

Since the 1970s a number of research and development complexes have been built around the Capital Beltway. Their fortunes are very much dependent on the political climate and the congressional appropriation of federal resources.

As many as 90,000 people engage in lobbying work in the capital. Washington-based **lobbyists** representing some 23,000 special interest groups, political action organizations (PACs), professional and trade associations, and foreign countries and businesses, work to persuade legislators to support laws helpful to their clients' interests. Many organizations employ their own staff lobbyists, but often such work is undertaken by well-connected attorneys at DC firms. The term "lobbyist" derives from the 19C, when such influence peddlers would haunt the lobbies of public buildings where politicians congregated. Today lobbyists conduct their business at fine restaurants and well-orchestrated social gatherings.

PRIVATE SECTOR

Exerting a powerful influence on the city's sociopolitical fabric is the **fourth estate**. Washington's formidable press corps is comprised of correspondents from national and regional newspapers, many of whom maintain Washington offices in the National Press Building (14th and F Sts. NW). The New Republic, National Geographic, US News and World Report, and USA Today (with its parent company, newspaper and media giant Gannett), are among the publications with their headquarters in or near the capital. Dominated by the Washington Post, one of the country's most influen-

tial newspapers, the press has become a major player in shaping public opinion. The Post's involvement in uncovering the Nixon-Watergate debacle in the mid-1970s broke new ground in investigative reporting.

The District also serves as headquarters for large corporations, such as Marriott; and for more than a thousand associations and interest groups, such as the AFL-CIO and AARP.

TOURISM

Attracted by the capital's renowned monuments and museums and by the numerous conventions held in the area, some 15.5 million visitors come to Washington each year. Tourism, the city's second-largest industry, brought in more than $5 billion in 2005 to hotels, restaurants and other service-related businesses that cater to visitors. Traditionally a place of pilgrimage for Americans, in recent years the capital has begun to draw more foreign tourists.

THE INTERNATIONAL ELEMENT

Once a rather provincial town with only a small contingent of foreigners, Washington has become, in recent decades, a cosmopolitan city. More than 150 foreign missions maintain embassies and consulates here, and such international organizations as the World Bank, International Monetary Fund and Organization of American States are based in the city.

The influx of Asian, Middle Eastern and African immigrants that began in the late 1970s has given the city a distinctly international flavor. Washington's shops, restaurants and festivals reflect this urban mix of cultures. Dining in the District has become a global experience, from Adams Morgan's Ethiopian and Mexican eateries and downtown's Spanish and Indian restaurants, to Chinatown's Asian cuisines and nearby Arlington's Vietnamese dining spots. French, Italian and American fare have long been staples of the city's dining scene.

Air Transportation Hall, National Air and Space Museum

Courtesy Air and Space Museum, Smithsonian Institution

CAPITOL HILL★★★

The city's high eastern ground, Capitol Hill is crowned by massive stone buildings serving the Legislative and Judicial branches of the federal government. Beyond them stretch the Hill's residential streets, neighborhoods of 19C row houses that reflect a true cross section of Washington's population.

- 🛈 **Information: Capitol Hill Business Improvement District** *(Union Station, bus level; ☎202-842-3333; www.capitolhillbid.org)*. Dressed in blue shirts bearing three gold stars, roving "concierges" on foot and bicycle answer visitors' questions and provide directions free-of-charge.
- 🅿 **Parking:** Union Station's multilevel garage *(open 24hrs/day; $6-$18)*.
- 🛇 **Don't Miss:** The Neptune Fountain, in front of the Library of Congress.
- 🄺 **Especially for Kids:** The postal museum.

A Bit of History

Seat of Government
In 1791 when L'Enfant chose this hilltop (then known as Jenkins Hill) as the site of the future home of Congress, he expected the city's residential core to develop on its east flank. In his design for the Capitol, William Thornton positioned the main facade on the building's east side. The establishment of the Navy Yard and the **Marine Barracks** (8th and Eye Sts. SE) in the early 19C encouraged the growth of neighborhoods stretching from the Capitol southeast to the river. After the War of 1812, the area grew steadily as a residential area, though never to the degree L'Enfant had expected. As the 19C drew to a close, the Hill became a middle-class enclave.

Federal Building Boom
At the turn of the 19C, the grandiose Beaux-Arts edifice housing the Library of Congress, now known as the Thomas Jefferson Building, was erected across from the Capitol. Later, Union Station and the City Post Office, both designed by Daniel H. Burnham, were built at the northern foot of Capitol Hill. In the 1930s the Folger Shakespeare Library, the John Adams Annex of the Library of Congress and the Supreme Court building were all built in the immediate vicinity of the Capitol. Meanwhile, the Senate erected three office buildings to the northeast of

the Capitol: the **Russell Building** (1909, Carrère and Hastings), the **Dirksen Building** (1958) and the **Hart Building** (1982). Similarly, the House raised three buildings on the south side: the **Cannon Building** (1908, Carrère and Hastings), the **Longworth Building** (1933) and the **Rayburn Building** (1965). In 1980 the Library of Congress added a third building, the James Madison Memorial Building, to its complex.

Revitalized Neighborhood
The social composition of Capitol Hill's residential streets fluctuated in the 20C. In mid-century its middle-class population gradually moved to the suburbs. Meanwhile, low-income families began to occupy the old, often run-down row houses. The streets between the Capitol and Lincoln Park underwent renovation as well-paid professionals bought up the 19C homes here. Since the 1970s the Hill's residents have gained a reputation as civic activists capable of effectively preventing development that would alter the residential character of this area. Today, **Eastern Market**, on the 200 block of 7th Street SE, is a nucleus for commerce. Independence Avenue, another commercial corridor, serves the Capitol's legislators. The latest landmark, the **Japanese American Memorial** is located in the triangular park at Louisiana and New Jersey avenues and D Street, NW.

THE CAPITOL★★★

The labyrinthine Capitol building, with its cast-iron dome topped by the statue of Freedom, is the city's most prominent landmark. This massive symbol of democracy in progress has housed the US Congress since 1800.

- **Information:** The office of The Architect of the Capitol; ☎202-224-3121; www.aoc.gov.
- ▶ **Orient Yourself:** Dividing the city into quadrants, the Capitol sits on downtown's high ground, at the eastern end of the Mall.
- Ⓟ **Parking:** Street parking is difficult to find; there are parking lots at Union Station and on North Capitol St.
- **Don't Miss:** The view of the Mall from the Capitol steps.
- Ⓞ **Organizing Your Time:** Phone ahead the day of your visit for ticket information (☎202-225-6827). In peak season arrive by 7:30am to get your choice of timed tickets.
- **Also See:** The US Botanic Garden and the Bartholdi Fountain.

A Bit of History

Early Construction

L'Enfant chose Jenkins Hill as the site for the Capitol in 1791. He himself was called upon to design the Capitol and other public buildings, but he was dismissed in 1792 before realizing a single project. President Washington and Secretary of State Jefferson elicited architectural plans for the Capitol by holding a public competition, but the entries proved so uninspiring that **Dr. William Thornton**, a respected amateur architect, was allowed to submit a drawing five months late. His entry called for a stone structure modeled after the Pantheon in Rome. The design met with immediate approval, winning Thornton $500 and a city lot.

On September 18, 1793, Washington presided over the laying of the cornerstone. A lack of skilled workers, tools and supplies in the then virtually nonexistent city hampered construction, as did a lack of funds. The revenue from the sale of city lots was expected to finance building costs, but few people were attracted by the high prices and rudimentary conditions. By 1800, however, Congress was able to leave the temporary capital of Philadelphia and move to the nascent federal city.

On November 22, 1800 President John Adams addressed the first joint session of Congress in the completed north wing (the original Senate wing) of the new Capitol.

Professional rivalry among the various architects working on the Capitol (including James Hoban, designer of the White House) led to Thornton's resignation. In 1803 British architect **Benjamin Henry Latrobe** was appointed surveyor of public buildings, and by 1807 he had completed the south wing (the original House wing). The two wings were linked by a wooden walkway crossing the present site of the rotunda. Latrobe began renovating and improving the north wing and submitted revised plans for the Capitol exterior that included a colonnaded central section.

Conflagration and Restoration

The War of 1812 saw the only enemy attack on the Capitol. In August 1814 the British set fire to it, gutting the interior. A providential downpour prevented total ruin, but when Congress returned in the fall, many members advocated abandoning the building and the city and finding a new home for the federal government. To discourage such a desertion, a group of private citizens had a temporary brick structure erected for

Thornton's Design for the Capitol

Congress on the site where the Supreme Court now stands.

From 1815 to 1817 Latrobe worked at restoring the Capitol's interior, adding low domes over the building's two original wings and redesigning the House chamber (now Statuary Hall) into its semicircular shape of today. Among the decorative elements are the tobacco fronds and ears of corn that top the columns lining the House chamber. Though the building's grace was admired, the cavernous space produced echoes. Red draperies were hung behind the gallery to help muffle sounds.

When Latrobe resigned because of a clash with the commissioner of public buildings, Boston architect **Charles Bulfinch** took over and Congress was able to again meet in the Capitol in December 1819. Bulfinch served as the official architect of the Capitol until 1829. During his tenure he completed the building more or less according to Thornton's original plans, substituting a copper-sheathed wooden dome for the stone vault designed by Thornton.

Civil War Years

In the early 19C the legislature, keeping pace with the nation it represented, grew rapidly. By 1850 it comprised 62 senators and 232 representatives. Spurred on by Sen. Jefferson Davis, who later became president of the Confederacy, Congress appropriated $100,000 for two new wings to house the cramped Senate and House. A contest was held, but no clear winner emerged. Rather, a composite design based on several entries was favored, and contestant **Thomas U. Walter** from Philadelphia was asked to draw up plans. Thomas Crawford designed the statue topping the new dome. His 19 1/2ft bronze **Freedom** is outfitted with flowing robes and an eagle's-head helmet.

With civil strife in the air, construction began. When war finally did come, Congress was not in session, and the War Department quartered troops in the Capitol for several months. Soldiers called it the "Big Tent," and Army bakers built enormous ovens in the basement committee rooms, producing enough bread to feed troops bivouacked around the city. A year later the Capitol served briefly as a hospital for the wounded Throughout the war, construction on the Capitol proceeded. Walter's enlarged dome, designed to replace the now disproportionately small dome built by Bulfinch, was made of cast iron and weighed almost nine million pounds. By 1863 the dome, considered a marvel of 19C engineering, was ready for Crawford's crowning statue. The two new wings were finally completed in 1867.

Expansion

The nation's foremost landscape architect, **Frederick Law Olmsted**, was appointed in 1874 to lay out the grounds. Olmsted's landscaping reflects his propensity for natural sweeps of lawn and trees. His addition of the broad plaza on the east and the marble stairway and terraces on the west facilitated the creation of much-needed office space in the building's lower levels.

For the next 75 years, interior changes such as electrification (1897), fireproofing and improved plumbing continued. Under Elliott Wood's term as architect of the Capitol (1902-23), a fourth floor was added, and the Latrobe domes were rebuilt in fireproof cast iron.

By the late 1950s Congress had again outgrown the Capitol. To provide more space the central section of the east facade was extended 32 1/2ft (*see drawing)*. The new marble front was designed as an exact copy of the original sandstone facade so as not to alter the essential appearance of this national landmark (the columns of the original facade are conserved at the National Arboretum).

Visit

Visit by guided 1hr tour only, year-round Mon–Sat 9am–4:30pm. Closed Thanksgiving Day & Dec 25. Visitors must obtain free timed tickets, on the day of their visit, from the Capitol Guide Service kiosk near the intersection of 1st St. SW & Independence Ave. ☎202-225-6827. www.aoc.gov. Tours start from the South Visitor Receiving Faciiity, but because of construction of an underground visitor center (projected completion fall 2007), it's best to phone ahead to find out where the tours will start. Recorded information includes a list of prohibited items. Be prepared to pass through metal detectors and/or have personal effects searched.

Main Floor

The Rotunda

On the east side of the rotunda, the eight-paneled, 10-ton bronze **Columbus doors** depict in high relief scenes from Christopher Columbus' life. Of the eight large paintings around the room, the four on the east side show early events in American history, such as the *Embarkation of the Pilgrims at Delft Haven, Holland* by Robert Weir, dated 1843 (**1**). The ornate Capitol **dome**★★— 180ft high and 98ft across—soars above rich artwork relating to the history of the country. The allegorical fresco in the eye of the dome, entitled the *Apotheosis of Washington*, was painted by Italian-born **Constantino Brumidi**, who had done restoration work in the Vatican. Brumidi worked on the Capitol from 1855 to 1880 and executed so many of its frescoes that he is often referred to as its "Michelangelo."

The grisaille frieze circling the base of the dome (total length of frieze: 300ft) records over 400 years of American history, from the landing of Columbus to the birth of aviation. Brumidi began the

CONSTRUCTION OF THE CAPITOL

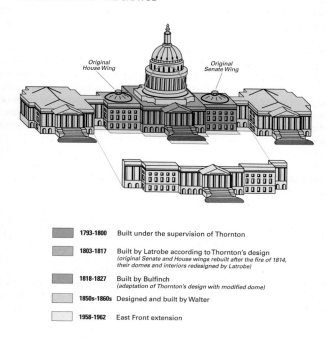

	1793-1800	Built under the supervision of Thornton
	1803-1817	Built by Latrobe according to Thornton's design *(original Senate and House wings rebuilt after the fire of 1814, their domes and interiors redesigned by Latrobe)*
	1818-1827	Built by Bulfinch *(adaptation of Thornton's design with modified dome)*
	1850s-1860s	Designed and built by Walter
	1958-1962	East Front extension

frescos when he was 72, but completed only six panels before he fell off the scaffolding, dangling for 15min before he was rescued. He died of poor health in February 1880. Filippo Costaggini carried on the work, but when he left in 1889, a 31ft gap remained in the frieze. Not until 1953 was the work completed by the American artist Allyn Cox.

The four paintings on the west side, all by John Trumbull, portray important moments of the Revolution, including the *Surrender of Cornwallis at Yorktown* (early 19C) (**2**). Statues of American leaders from Washington (**3**) and Jefferson (**4**) to Martin Luther King Jr. (**5**), encircle the room. During the Capitol's long history, such popular national figures as Abraham Lincoln and John F. Kennedy have lain in state here.

Statuary Hall

This elegant, semicircular, half-domed space was restored for the 1976 Bicentennial to its architectural appearance (unfurnished) of 1857, when it functioned as the House Chamber. A congressional act of 1864 allowed each state to place statues of two of its distinguished citizens in the Capitol. Until the 1930s these statues were all displayed in Statuary Hall. However, it was feared that their combined weight might cause the hall's floor to collapse, so some now stand in other Capitol corridors. Notable among the 38 still in the room are the statues of Robert E. Lee of Virginia (**6**), 19C social reformer Frances Willard of Illinois (**7**), 18C missionary pioneer Padre Junípero Serra of California (**8**) and King Kamehameha of Hawaii (**9**). The room's unusual acoustics considerably amplify words spoken within.

Old Senate Chamber

Also restored for the Bicentennial, this room maintains the general appearance and several of the furnishings it had during the period the Senate occupied it (1810-14, 1819-59). Note the gilt shield and eagle over the vice president's desk and the porthole portrait of George Washington (1823, Rembrandt Peale). From 1860 to 1935, the chamber housed the Supreme Court.

Visiting the Offices of Your Senators or Representative

Offices are located in six buildings accessible from the Capitol via the basement-level subway: Russell, Dirksen and Hart Bldgs. (Senate); Cannon, Longworth and Rayburn Bldgs. (House). For assistance in locating offices, call ☎202-224-3121 or inquire at the Senate and House Appointment Desks *(ground floor)*. For an appointment with your senator or representative, write in advance (🕮 *see Planning Your Trip).*

Viewing a Session of Congress
(3rd floor galleries)

Passes to view a House or Senate session must be obtained at the office of your senator or representative *(above)*. Certain committee sessions are also open to the public. Consult the *Washington Post* or ☎ 202-224-3121 for the recess schedule and the day's agenda. International visitors: Apply to the Senate and House Appointment Desks *(ground floor)*.

Ground Floor

Crypt

Forty Doric columns ring the low-ceilinged crypt directly below the rotunda. Original plans called for the body of George Washington to be enshrined in a vault below the crypt, but his relatives insisted that his remains be preserved at Mount Vernon. The crypt features displays on the history of the Capitol. The compelling sculpture of Lincoln's head (**10**) was done by Gutzon Borglum, who carved Mount Rushmore. He left off the statue's left ear as a symbol of Lincoln's unfinished life. A compass stone embedded in the floor (**11**) marks

New Visitor Center

Scheduled for completion in fall 2007, the new US Capitol Visitor Center will occupy 580,000sq ft beneath the East Grounds. It will include a 550-seat cafeteria, exhibit space, gift stores, orientation theatres and restrooms. The East Front Plaza will be relandscaped with trees and pavers. Tours of the Capitol will begin from the subterranean visitor center.

the zero point from which the city's four quadrants emanate.

▶ *Continue to the Senate wing.*

Old Supreme Court Chamber

An intimate chamber with red carpeting and green-topped desks, this room housed the Supreme Court from 1810 to 1860, except during the period of reconstruction after the War of 1812. Note the original 19C furnishings and the room's vaulting, designed by Latrobe. Here, the Marshall Court heard many of the cases that would profoundly influence the development of the young nation.

Brumidi Corridors

The arched ceilings and walls of these two intersecting corridors are embellished with Brumidi's classically inspired murals depicting nature, famous Americans and historical scenes. Interspersed among the murals are works of later painters, such as Allyn Cox's mural of the 1969 moon landing. Minton floor tiles further enhance the decorative scheme of the corridors.

▶ *Return to the crypt and continue to the House wing.*

A number of the state statues originally destined for Statuary Hall now stand among the tobacco-leafed pillars of the **Hall of Columns**. Paralleling this hall is the **Hall of Capitols**, which is decorated with murals by Allyn Cox depicting historic events as well as realistic scenes of everyday life.

Third Floor (Gallery Level)

House and Senate Chambers

See Viewing a Session of Congress. The east stairway in the House wing (not open to the pubic when the House is in session) leads to the third-floor visitors' gallery for the House Chamber. *The Scene of the Signing of the Constitution of the United States* (1940) by Howard Chandler Christy hangs on the second-floor landing. The **House Chamber**, a richly appointed room, is dominated by a broad podium faced by the seats of the 435 members of the House (Democrats

The US Capitol

© Brigitta L. House/MICHELIN

are placed to the right of the presiding Speaker of the House, Republicans to the left). Beside the podium hangs a full-length portrait of *George Washington* (1834) by John Vanderlyn, and to the right, a portrait of Washington's Revolutionary compatriot *General Lafayette* (1824) by Ary Scheffer. Medallions of historic figures hang on the gallery walls. A third-floor hallway extends along the east face of the Capitol to the Senate wing. Round windows and the stone of the building's original facade (prior to the late-1950s extension) are visible along the interior wall of this hall.

The **Senate Chamber** is more soberly appointed than the House Chamber. The only works of art on display are the busts of early vice presidents that occupy the niches on the gallery level. When the Senate is in session, the vice president (in his absence, the president pro tempore), flanked by the secretary of the Senate, the sergeant at arms and various clerks, presides from behind the veined marble podium. The 100 senators are seated at dark mahogany desks (Democrats on the right, Republicans on the left). Note on the second-floor landing of the east stairway in the Senate wing W.H. Powell's monumental painting *The Battle of Lake Erie* (1873).

Upon leaving the Capitol, stroll around the broad **west terrace**, where you can admire a sweeping **view**★★ across the Mall to the Washington Monument.

MAIN FLOOR

Committee on Appropriations

To Chamber Gallery

Congressiona[l]
Private Offices

8

HOUSE

Statuary Hall

3

CHAMBER

7

4

House Reception Room

6

9

To Chamber Gallery

Speaker's Office

Speaker's Formal Office

Ways and Means Committee

Not open to the public

0   100 ft
0   50 m

Th[e]

GROUND FLOOR

House Appointments Desk

Hall   of   Columns

Small House Rotunda

Hall   of   Capitols

Cap[itol]

THE CAPITOL

Senate
Private
Offices

2

Small Senate
Rotunda

TUNDA

1

Old
Senate
Chamber

umbus
ors

Senate Private Offices

President's
Room

SENATE

Marble
Room

CHAMBER

Senate
Conference
Room

To
Chamber
Gallery

V. President's
Office

MALL

—N→

Special
Services

Small Senate
Rotunda

ypt
1

**Old Supreme
Court Chamber**

Senate
Appointments Desk

Brumidi

Corridors

To Chamber
Gallery

Plaza

LIBRARY OF CONGRESS★★

1ST ST. AND INDEPENDENCE AVE. SE.
Ⓜ CAPITOL SOUTH OR UNION STATION.

A renowned Beaux-Arts landmark, the original Library of Congress is reputedly Washington's most richly ornamented building. The largest library in existence, it retains in its ever-growing collections more than 32 million books, as well as historical treasures. It functions as a reference library, open to anyone 18 years or older pursuing research. The general public is welcome to visit the complex.

- **Information:** Visitor information ☎202-707-8000; general information ☎202-707-5000. www.loc.gov. The visitor center is on the ground floor of the Jefferson Building.
- **Orient Yourself:** The Jefferson Building, the main building, lies just east of the Capitol and south of the Supreme Court.
- **Parking:** Parking lots lie within about a half mile at Union Station and N. Capitol St.; public transportation is handier.
- **Don't Miss:** The view of the Main Reading Room from the visitors' gallery.

A Bit of History

Congress' Library
In 1800, while still convening in Philadelphia, Congress appropriated $5,000 for the establishment of a library for its own use. Originally the library was housed in the Capitol for the convenience of the legislators. When the library's 3,000 volumes were destroyed in the Capitol fire of 1814, Thomas Jefferson offered his extensive personal library to Congress, which purchased the 6,487 volumes for $23,950. The collection was shipped in 10 horse-drawn wagons from Monticello, Jefferson's Virginia estate, to the Capitol. Unfortunately, another fire in 1851 destroyed two-thirds of the existing library collection. Congress immediately appropriated funds to replenish the holdings and to build a new, multi-tiered library along the west side of the Capitol. In honor of the library's Bicentennial in 2000, an effort was begun to reconstitute the lost volumes as a gift to the nation.

Great Hall, Jefferson Building, Library of Congress

A Library for the People

Though intended to serve only members of Congress and Supreme Court justices, the library was gradually opened to other governmental and diplomatic officials. In 1864 **Ainsworth Rand Spofford** was appointed librarian of Congress and began a process that changed the library into a public institution. To amass a more extensive collection, Spofford lobbied Congress to amend existing legislation so that the copyright for books, musical scores, maps and charts would be granted by the Library of Congress rather than the Department of Interior. This procedure ensured that newly published materials would find their way into the library's holdings, a practice that continues to this day.

In 1873 Congress approved a separate building for the library. In 1886 ground was broken, but the work progressed slowly, causing Congress to dismiss the building's principal architects, **John Smithmeyer** and **Paul Pelz**. They were replaced by Thomas Casey, the chief of Army engineers, and Bernard Green, a civilian engineer. Along with Casey's son Edward, Green planned the interior artwork and commissioned American artists to execute the decorative scheme, which blended mosaics, murals, marblework and sculptures. The library opened in 1897, under budget (total cost: $6.5 million) and ahead of schedule; it has functioned as the "national library of the United States" ever since.

In 1939 the library expanded to a second structure, the **John Adams Building** (2nd St. SE, behind the main building), noteworthy for its Art Deco ornamentation. At that time the original building was designated the Thomas Jefferson Building. A third facility, the austere marble **James Madison Memorial Building** (Independence Ave., between 1st and 2nd Sts. SE), was opened in 1980 and contains more than twice the floor space of either of the two older library structures. Its Memorial Hall (left side of the lobby) is dominated by a seated statue of James Madison, the fourth US president.

Main Reading Room, Library of Congress

Holdings

The Library of Congress retains more than 134 million items, which fill the equivalent of some 530 miles of shelves. These possessions include more than 59 million manuscripts; 5 million maps and atlases; 5 million musical items, such as scores, instruments and correspondence among musicians; 12 million photographs; and 32 million books. The library acquires new holdings at the rate of 10,000 items a day. Foremost among the valuable works of art owned by the Library of Congress are two mid-15C masterpieces: the manuscript Giant Bible of Mainz and a Gutenberg Bible. American artifacts include Jefferson's rough draft of the Declaration of Independence and President Lincoln's handwritten drafts of the Emancipation Proclamation and the Gettysburg Address. The library's renowned music division contains a noted collection of Stradivarius violins and original scores by Brahms, Liszt, Beethoven and other composers.

Visit

🕐 *Jefferson Building open year-round Mon–Sat 10am–5:30pm. Adams and Memorial Buildings 8:30am; closing hours vary.* 🕐 *Closed major holidays.* 🚶 *Guided tours (1hr) of the Jefferson Building are available Mon–Sat 10:30am, 11:30am & 1:30pm, 2:30pm, 3:30pm*

(Mon–Fri only). ☎202-707-8000. www. loc.gov. Tour tickets (free) may be required; inquire at the visitor center.

An orientation video (12min) is shown every 20min on the ground floor of the Jefferson Building in the visitor center. The Jefferson Building contains exhibits of items from the special collections. **Treasures of the Library of Congress** is an exhibit of continuously rotating rare library materials, such as George Washington's first inaugural address and Frank Lloyd Wright's architectural drawings. A copy of the Handbook of the New Library of Congress, which describes the library's history and architecture, may be purchased from the shop in the Jefferson Building or the Madison Building. A cafeteria is located in the Madison Building on the 6th floor (open to the public for lunch beginning at 12:30pm); a snack bar is located on the ground floor.

For current visitor information or assistance in using the research facilities, consult the touch-screen terminals located in the visitor center.

The library offers a regular series of concerts and features public lectures and poetry readings, as well as showings of old films in its Pickford Theater, located in the Madison Building. For schedules, consult the touch screens at the visitor center in the Jefferson Building. For concert information, call ☎ 202-707-5502.

The Thomas Jefferson Building

🕒 Open year-round Mon–Sat 10am–5:30pm. 🕒 Closed major holidays. 🐾 Guided tours (1hr) available. ♿☎202-707-8000. www.loc.gov.

Exterior

This Beaux-Arts showplace occupies a full block across from the Capitol on 1st Street SE. At street level the exuberant **Neptune Fountain** by Roland Hinton Perry depicts the sea god and his cavorting entourage.

The building's central section is vaulted by a massive green copper dome surmounted by a lantern that supports the symbolic "torch of learning" (step back from the facade across 1st St. to view). The intricate entrance stairway, replete with side flights, ornamented stone balus-

trades and candelabras, provides a ceremonial access to the edifice. The granite facade, which resembles the 19C Paris Opera House, features a second-story portico of paired Corinthian columns and massive quoins, or cornerstones. Busts depicting famous men of letters are framed in the oculi, or round openings, that punctuate the portico.

Interior★★

Murals, sculptures, detailed mosaics, marble columns and floors, and vaulted corridors make the two-story **Great Hall** one of the most impressive spaces in the city. The hall's vestibule is especially noteworthy for the gold leaf adorning its ceiling, while blue and amber stained-glass skylights punctuate the vaulting of the hall proper. At the rear of the hall stand glass cases containing a Gutenberg Bible and the Giant Bible of Mainz, which is one of the last hand-illuminated manuscript versions of the Bible. A grand staircase sculpted with elaborate bas-relief cherubs leads to the second-story colonnade, where a visitors' gallery overlooks the Main Reading Room. Occupying the vast rotunda under the library dome (height: 160ft from floor to lantern), the **Main Reading Room** is ringed by colossal Corinthian columns and arched windows, embellished with stained-glass state seals and eagles. In the lantern of the coffered dome is an allegorical mural entitled Human Understanding. The eight 11ft stone statues between the arches symbolize such subjects as commerce, law, poetry and science. Sixteen bronze statues along the balustrade of the galleries represent pivotal figures in the development of civilization. Rotating items from the library's permanent Americana and international collections are on view in the southwest and northwest galleries respectively.

Two rooms can be viewed by a special in-depth tour: the **Librarian's Room**, located at the east end of the Great Hall's north corridor; and the **Members of Congress Room**, a special reading room used today by members of the US Congress.

SUPREME COURT★★

1ST AND E. CAPITOL STS. NE.

🚇 CAPITOL SOUTH OR UNION STATION.

Positioned directly across the street from the Capitol, this white marble monument to the supremacy of law houses the highest court in the land. Within its walls the third branch of government exercises its mandate to protect and interpret the spirit of the US Constitution.

🛈 **Information:** ☎202-479-3211. www.supremecourtus.gov.

▶ **Orient Yourself:** Sessions are open to the public on a first-come, first-served basis. Consult the *Washington Post* for the daily schedule of Court hearings. When the Court is not in session, lectures on the Supreme Court are held in the courtroom on the half hour 9:30am–3:30pm. A film (24min) on the history and work of the Court is shown continuously in the theater at the end of the hall to the right of the Marshall statue.

A Bit of History

A Constitutional Basis

Article III of the US Constitution, ratified in 1788, called for a "supreme Court" of the land to act as a final arbiter of law and as a counterbalance to the other two branches of government (Executive and Legislative). The first US Supreme Court convened in 1790 at the Royal Exchange Building in the temporary capital of New York City. During the first three years, the Court, as a body, had little work. However, the individual justices were kept busy riding circuits, as they were required to do until 1891, hearing cases in their districts. Because of the difficulty of travel at the end of the 18C, many justices served only a few years.

One of the earliest judicial precedents was set in 1793 when President Washington asked the Court to advise him on questions of international law. Under its first chief justice, John Jay, it declined, explaining that in view of the Constitution's requirement of separation of powers, the Judicial branch had no place advising the Executive branch.

To jurists, the fourth chief justice, **John Marshall** (1755-1835), is the "Great Chief Justice." Appointed by President Adams in 1801, Marshall served until his death in 1835. During his long tenure he firmly established the fledgling Court as the supreme authority over the law of the land. Among the many important cases the Marshall Court ruled on, *Marbury v.*

Madison (1803) set a critical precedent. In this case the Supreme Court affirmed its power to declare an act of Congress unconstitutional. Other important decisions reached under Marshall, in such cases as *McCulloch v. Maryland, Cohens v. Virginia* and *Gibbons v. Ogden*, reaffirmed the power of the Union and its authority over state laws.

A Body of Controversy

"We are very quiet here, but it is the quiet of a storm center," explained Justice Oliver Wendell Holmes Jr., who served from 1902 to 1932. Throughout its history the Court has been involved in controversy, sometimes settling it, at other times kindling it. In 1857 the Court handed down perhaps its most infamous decision, when, under Chief Justice Taney, it heard the case of a slave named Dred Scott. The Court's ruling—that Congress had no authority to limit the expansion of slavery—helped bring on the Civil War and badly damaged public respect for the Court.

A Home of Its Own

In its early years the Court had no regular meeting place, convening in various public buildings in New York City, then Philadelphia. In 1800 it moved to the new federal city and occupied different rooms in the Capitol, including the room now known as the Old Supreme Court Chamber. After the British burned the Capitol in 1814, the Court was forced to

The Supreme Court

meet in a number of temporary locations, including a private home and a tavern. When the Capitol was sufficiently repaired, the Court returned to the Old Supreme Court Chamber, which it occupied from 1819 to 1860. It then moved upstairs to the Old Senate Chamber, which remained its home for the following 75 years.

William Howard Taft (1857-1930), the tenth chief justice (1921-30) and the only US president to serve on the Court, convinced Congress in 1928 to allocate funds for a building to house the Court. In October 1935 the present edifice was completed at a cost of $9,650,000 but to mixed reviews from the justices. Justice Harland Fiske Stone called the new structure "almost bombastically pretentious…."

Precedent-setting cases heard in the courtroom of the current building include *Brown v. Board of Education*, which established school integration nationwide; *Engel v. Vitale*, outlawing school prayer; cases involving the constitutionality of abortion; and the constitutionality of electoral procedures in the 2000 presidential election.

The Supreme Court Justices

The nominating president and the year in which the judicial oath was taken are shown in parentheses:

Chief Justice
John G. Roberts Jr. *(Chief Justice: Bush, 2005)*
Associate Justices
John Paul Stevens *(Ford, 1975)*
Antonin Scalia *(Reagan, 1986)*
Anthony M. Kennedy *(Reagan, 1988)*
David H. Souter *(Bush, 1990)*
Clarence Thomas *(Bush, 1991)*
Ruth Bader Ginsburg *(Clinton, 1993)*
Stephen G. Breyer *(Clinton, 1994)*
Samuel Alito Jr. *(Bush, 2006)*

The Court at Work

Woodrow Wilson called the Supreme Court "a kind of Constitutional Convention in continuous session." As the highest court in the country, it is the court of last appeal. The chief justice and associate justices are appointed by the president, with Senate approval, as vacancies occur. Only death, voluntary retirement or resignation, or congressional impeachment can remove a sitting justice. Sandra Day O'Connor is the most recent justice to retire; appointed in 1981, she served until 2006. Through his appointees to the Supreme Court, a US president might exercise influence long after his term has ended.

Congress, not the Constitution, sets the number of justices on the Court. In the Court's first century, that number changed six times. Now, based on the Judiciary Act of 1869, it is set at nine justices.

The Court's term begins on the first Monday in October. From October through April the Court hears oral arguments on cases it has consented to review. Of the 7,000-plus requests for review it receives annually, the Court hears about 100 cases per term. It typically sits two weeks a month, Monday to Wednesday (10am–3pm) with a lunch recess (noon–1pm). Most case arguments are limited to an hour, with 30 minutes allotted to each side. The rest of the week, the justices review arguments and consider requests for future reviews. From mid-May through June the Court convenes on Monday (10am) to deliver its opinions on the cases argued in that term.

Visit

🕐 *Open year-round Mon–Fri 9am–4:30pm.* 🕐 *Closed major holidays.* ✕ ♿ ☎ *202-479-3211. www.supreme courtus.gov.*
An oval plaza fronts the cross-shaped building of gleaming white marble, designed by Cass Gilbert. Flanking a broad staircase that leads up to a colonnade of 32 Corinthian columns are two massive allegorical figures. Sculpted by James Fraser, they represent the Contemplation of Justice *(left)* and the Authority of Law *(right)*. Carved under the bas-relief in the pediment are the words "Equal Justice Under Law."
A wide columned hall, adorned with a coffered 44ft-high ceiling and busts of chief justices, leads from the entrance to the **courtroom**. Here the justices sit on a raised bench positioned in front of 4 of the 24 massive veined columns that ring the 82ft-by-91ft chamber. The justices' places are ordered by their seniority, with the chief justice taking the center position.
Visitors may descend to the ground floor, which features changing exhibits on the history and function of the Court. Dominating the main hall on this level is a massive **statue of John Marshall**, depicting him in a relaxed seated pose that suggests his renowned affability and lack of pretense.

FOLGER SHAKESPEARE LIBRARY ★

201 E. CAPITOL ST. SE.
Ⓜ CAPITOL SOUTH OR UNION STATION.

The world's largest collection of Shakespeare's works is conserved behind this Art Deco exterior. Renowned as a research institution, the Folger also encourages a larger public appreciation of the traditions of Elizabethan England and the Renaissance through its program of exhibits, concerts, readings and theatrical performances.

A Bit of History

The Folger Bequest
The son of a Martha's Vineyard schoolmaster, Henry Clay Folger became a lifetime devotee of Shakespeare while attending Amherst College. There, in 1879, inspired by a lecture given by the aging Ralph Waldo Emerson, Folger bought a volume of Shakespeare's complete works.
Ten years later he made his first serious Shakespeare acquisition: a 1685 Fourth Folio edition purchased at an auction for $107.50. At the time, his finances were such that he was forced to request 30 days to raise the money. Through the years, however, his fortunes steadily increased, and he eventually became chairman of the board of the Standard Oil Co. of New York.
His wife and co-collector, Emily Jordan, was a schoolteacher and student of literature. She was particularly interested in acquiring different copies of the 1623 First Folio, the first collected edition of

Title Page of 1623 First Folio

Folger Shakespeare Library

Shakespeare's plays, for the sake of scholarly comparison.

In the 1920s the Folgers, who lived in New York state, began searching in both England and America for a site to establish a research library. They ultimately chose this nation's capital, and in 1930 the cornerstone was laid. Folger himself did not live to see the 1932 opening of the building that housed the 75,000 books, manuscripts, prints and engravings he and his wife had collected. Mrs. Folger continued to be active with the library until her death in 1936. The ashes of both are interred in the library, which today is administered by the trustees of Amherst College.

The Library's Holdings

Research facilities are not open to the general public.

The Folger now owns more than 300,000 books and manuscripts relating to the Renaissance period in England and other European countries. About a third of its holdings are considered rare, the most valuable being the only known copy of Shakespeare's early play *Titus Andronicus*. It was discovered in a cottage in Sweden and purchased for $10,000 by the Folgers in 1905.

The library holds 79 of the 240 first editions of the collected works of Shakespeare that are known to exist (Japan's Meisei University, the next-largest owner of first editions, owns only eight). The library also owns theatrical memorabilia—playbills, costumes, promptbooks, etc.—from 18C and 19C Shakespearean productions.

The Building

Paul Cret incorporated classical elements in this simple Art Deco marble facade, winning accolades from fellow architects for the "traditional modernism" of his design. Nine long rectangular windows covered in a geometrical grillwork are offset by bas-relief underpanels depicting scenes from Shakespeare's plays. Chiseled into the facade, above the windows, are quotes about the Bard, and above the two entrances appear the masks of Tragedy and Comedy. Along the 2nd Street side of the building is a freestanding marble statue of the character Puck from *A Midsummer Night's Dream*, inscribed with his famous quote "Lord, what fools these mortals be."

Visit

Open year-round Mon–Sat 10am–4pm. Closed major holidays. Guided tours (1hr) available Mon–Sat 11am (additional tour Sat 1pm). ☎202-544-7077. www.folger.edu.

The 190ft-long **Great Hall**, with oak paneling and a barrel-vaulted ceiling reminiscent of a Tudor gallery, features a changing series of exhibits based on the books, manuscripts and memorabilia in the library's collection.

The east end of the building houses a reproduction of an **Elizabethan theater**, its stage flanked by wooden columns. The Folger Consort, a resident chamber music ensemble, holds scheduled performances in the theater and in the Great Hall. The library also sponsors a rich program of poetry and fiction readings.

Outside, the small Elizabethan garden features a knot garden and plants well known in Shakespeare's day *(guided tours available Apr–Oct the third Sat of the month 10am and 11am).*

NATIONAL POSTAL MUSEUM ★

MASSACHUSETTS AVE. AND 1ST ST. NE.

Ⓜ UNION STATION.

Occupying part of the ground floor of the stately Beaux-Arts **City Post Office Building** next to Union Station, this Smithsonian Institution museum houses the world's largest philatelic collection and chronicles America's mail service from colonial times to the present.

A Bit of History

A gift of Confederate postage stamps in 1886 initiated the Smithsonian's philatelic collection. By 1908 the growing assemblage was housed on the Mall in the Arts and Industries Building; in 1964 it was transferred to the National Museum of American History. The landmark City Post Office Building (1914, Daniel H. Burnham) was chosen as the site for a new museum, which was established in 1990 by the joint efforts of the US Postal Service and the Smithsonian. It opened in 1993 after extensive renovation to the building, which also houses a large postal facility and other government offices. At present the museum comprises a research library, a theater and a discovery center, as well as six galleries, a stamp shop and a museum shop.

The 16-million-item collection includes historic postal artifacts, personal letters, photographs and transport vehicles, in addition to rare stamps and premier covers

Visit

Ⓚⁱᵈˢ Ⓞ*Open year-round daily 10am–5:30pm.* Ⓞ*Closed Dec 25.* ✎*Guided tours (30min) available; call for hours.* ♿☎*202-633-5534. www.si.edu/postal.* The lobby of the building, with its 40ft-high coffered ceiling, Ionic columns and marble floors, provides a grand passageway to the exhibit area *(located on the lower level)*, which is entered through a polished bronze and stainless steel **escalator arcade**. Three vintage mail planes, suspended from the ceiling, dominate the 90ft glass **atrium** gallery, where a walk-through railroad car with mail sorting bins, a Concord-style mail coach and a 1931 Model A Ford are also on view.

Eastern Market

7th St. between N. Carolina Ave. and C St. SE. Closed Mon. ☎*202-543-7293. www.easternmarket.net.* A nostalgically appealing market dating from the early 1870s, this brick building houses old-style butcher, produce and seafood stalls. On Saturdays it becomes the setting for a festive fair, when vendors selling everything from fresh flowers and potted herbs to ethnic artifacts and handicrafts set up outdoor stalls. By 10am the **Market Lunch** restaurant *(☎202-547-8444)* is typically edged with a long line of eager diners awaiting hearty pancake or waffle breakfasts. At noontime the queue is for local seafood lunches of crab cakes, fried fish and oysters.

Peter Wrenn/MICHELIN

Atrium Gallery , National Postal Museum

The **Stamps and Stories** gallery contains changing selections of philatelic rarities from the museum's collection, such as the first prepaid stamps (1840), called "penny blues." Other galleries showcase little-known pockets of postal history and stamp collecting, from the annual Duck Stamp contest that since 1934 has raised $500 million to acquire natural habitat for US waterfowl, to the more recent challenges posed by direct mail. Related activities like letter writing and envelope manufacturing may also be explored in exhibits complemented by novelties from the museum's far-ranging collection. A number of interactive videos, including an electronic souvenir postcard kiosk, invite visitor participation.

UNION STATION★

50 MASSACHUSETTS AVE. NE.
Ⓜ UNION STATION.

Located north of the Capitol, this monumental granite building has long served as the hub of the city's rail travel. It is a formidable embodiment of the oft-quoted premise of its architect Daniel H. Burnham: "Make no little plans." More than 70,000 people pass through the station per day.

A Bit of History

When the first trains pulled into the mammoth terminal in 1907, it was the largest train station in the world, measuring 760ft by 344ft (completed in 1908). Burnham designed the station with the colossal columns, arches and statues that characterize the Beaux-Arts style, of which he was a leading proponent. For half a century Union Station served as the city's main point of arrival, greeting soldiers, presidents, government representatives and royalty, as well as a steady flow of tourists.

With the demise of rail travel in the 1950s and 60s, the station steadily deteriorated. A renovation done in the 1970s met with much criticism, and an entirely new revamping was begun in 1986. The large-scale restoration project, which returned the station to its original

Union Station

splendor, was completed in 1988 at a cost of $160 million. In addition to being the main railway terminal for the metropolitan area, the station also houses scores of shops, eateries and a cinema complex.

Visit

🕐 *Public areas open daily year-round.* ✕ ♿ 🅿 ☎ *202-289-1908. www.union stationdc.com.*

A fountained plaza featuring a statue of Columbus and the Freedom Bell (a replica of the Liberty Bell) fronts the station, whose triple-arched, colonnaded entrance is modeled after Rome's Arch of Constantine. Another ancient Roman monument, the Baths of Diocletian, served as the inspiration for the station's cavernous main hall. A vaulted ceiling with gilded octagonal coffers soars 96ft, and 36 statues of Roman legionnaires look down from the second-story balcony rimming the hall.

SEWALL-BELMONT HOUSE

144 CONSTITUTION AVE. NE.

🚇 **UNION STATION OR CAPITOL SOUTH.**

Reputedly one of the oldest buildings on Capitol Hill, this gracious house was erected in 1799 by Robert Sewall. Today it serves as the headquarters for the National Woman's Party.

The residence remained in the Sewall family for 123 years and served as one of Washington's first social centers. Among its noted tenants was Albert Gallatin, secretary of the Treasury under presidents Jefferson and Madison. According to certain sources, Gallatin worked out the financial arrangements for the Louisiana Purchase on the premises. Over the years the house has undergone major exterior and interior alteration. In 1929 the building was purchased by the National Woman's Party, which has maintained its head offices there ever since.

Visit

🕐 *Open Tue–Fri 11am–3pm, Sat 10am–5pm (noon–4pm Labor Day–Memorial Day).* 🕐 *Closed major holidays.* ☜ *$5 contribution requested.* ☞ *Guided tours (30min) available on the hour.* ☎ *202-546-1210. www.sewallbelmont.org.*

Designated a National Historic Site, the building serves as the headquarters of the National Woman's Party (now solely an educational organization). It was the home of Alice Paul (1885-1977), the party's founder. Inside, exhibits commemorate the women's movement with portraits and busts of the suffragists—those who fought for passage of the 19th Amendment (1920) granting women the right to vote. Highlights include the museum's digital collection of vintage photographs, political cartoons, scrapbooks and other artifacts.

© Sewall-Belmont House

Sewall-Belmont House

THE MALL★★★

The Mall serves as the cultural heart of the capital and a political forum for the nation. Its imposing buildings and broad vistas underscore Washington's reputation as "the City Beautiful." The nation's revered memorials and a number of excellent national museums welcome the public free of charge.

- **Information:** The Castle, on the Mall; ☎202-633-1000; www.si.edu.
- ▶ **Orient Yourself:** The rectangular Mall stretches more than 2mi from the Capitol to the Lincoln Memorial between Constitution Ave. on the north and Independence Ave. on the south (♦ *see Visiting the Mall opposite*). The Smithsonian Information Center in the Castle is a great place to get an overview of the attractions on the Mall. Due to the proximity of the Mall museums to one another, touring the area on foot is recommended.
- **Parking:** Street parking is allowed, but spaces tend to be filled immediately after 10am, especially during the peak tourist season. There are lots several blocks away in the downtown area, but public transportation is easiest.
- **Don't Miss:** Sweeping views of the Mall, monuments and the Potomac River from the Lincoln Memorial.
- **Organizing Your Time:** Distances are long and museums are large; focus on one major museum in the morning and another in the afternoon.
- **Especially for Kids:** National Air and Space Museum, National Museum of Natural History and National Museum of American History are the big three.

A Bit of History

"A Vast Esplanade"
The city's designer, Pierre Charles L'Enfant, envisioned the Mall as a grand avenue extending from Jenkins Hill to the current site of the Washington Monument. In 1848 ground was broken for the Washington Monument and, a year later, for the Smithsonian Castle, paving the way for a growing institutional presence on the Mall.

After a severe flood in 1881, Congress appropriated funds for draining the Potomac flats south and west of the Mall. By the turn of the 19C, 621 acres had been reclaimed for the creation of Potomac Park. The Tidal Basin was formed to ensure a flow of fresh water through the Washington Channel.

Early-20C Development
The McMillan Commission, appointed in 1901 to assess the future development of the city, called for transforming the Mall into a broad, tree-lined promenade.

The commission succeeded in negotiating the transfer of the railroad facilities to the newly proposed Union Station (1903). In 1917, to accommodate wartime exigencies, barrackslike wooden structures known as "tempos" were constructed on the Mall. In 1923 the Smithsonian opened the Freer Gallery of Art on the south side of the Mall, and in 1941 the National Gallery of Art rose on the north side of the Mall, near the new National Archives. The southwestern portion of the general Mall area was extended in the late 1930s when the Jefferson Memorial was built on the shores of the Tidal Basin.

A Dream Realized
Following World War II, gardens, monuments and museums gradually replaced the unsightly tempos. Since the mid-1960s the Smithsonian has added six museums, and the National Gallery of Art has constructed its widely acclaimed East Building. The latest Smithsonian attraction in Washington, the **National**

Museum of the American Indian opened in 2004. In 2006, however, the Smithsonian Institute announced the site for its newest museum, the National Museum of African American History and Culture, which will be constructed just west of the National Museum of Natural History. The new museum will be the only national museum devoted solely to African-American art, history and culture.

Traditionally a rallying point for political demonstrations, the Mall also hosts major national events, such as the annual Independence Day celebration on the Fourth of July.

Visiting the Mall

Orientation

Known as the **East Mall**, the mile-long, tree-lined esplanade extending from the foot of Capitol Hill to 15th Street contains one of the world's densest concentrations of museums. The dominating presence here is the Smithsonian Institution, which operates nine museums on the Mall proper. The building on Jefferson Drive known as the Castle houses the Smithsonian Information Center. Comprising two structures, the independently administered National Gallery of Art dominates the northeast corner of the Mall. Just off the Mall are such governmental institutions as the National Archives, the Bureau of Engraving and Printing and the US Botanic Garden. The eastern end of the Mall is anchored by the Capitol Reflecting Pool, overlooked by an equestrian statue of President Grant that commemorates his leadership of Union troops in the Civil War. On the south side of the Reflecting Pool is a memorial to President Garfield, and on the north side there is an allegorical memorial to Peace.

Stretching from 15th Street to the Potomac River is the **West Mall**, an expansive greensward that contains the nation's best-known memorials. The monolithic Washington Monument is aligned on a north-south axis with the circular Jefferson Memorial, which overlooks the Tidal Basin. West of the Washington Monument stands Lincoln Memorial. South of it, the panhandle between the Potomac and the Tidal Basin serves as the setting for West Potomac Park.

Helpful Hints

Security continues to be a concern in the capital city. When entering national museums, be prepared to pass through metal detectors and/or have personal effects searched. All museums and attractions on the Mall are free of charge. Smithsonian sights are open daily (except Dec 25) 10am–5:30pm (The Castle opens at 8:30am). Several Metro stations serve the Mall, making a visit here free of time restraints. **Tourmobile** shuttle buses loop through the entire Mall area, including West Potomac Park, allowing visitors to get on and off at various sights (⊚ see Planning Your Trip). **Old Town Trolley** also serves sights on the Mall.

The information center in the Smithsonian Castle building should be the first stop, as it is designed to help visitors plan their time on the Mall and elsewhere in the city. You can also pick up a schedule of daily events at Smithsonian museums.

Cafes and cafeterias are located in many of the museums (indicated by the ✕ symbol in the sight descriptions that follow). Lines can be very long, so eating an early or late lunch is suggested. Street vendors along Independence Avenue sell hot dogs, soft drinks and snacks. On the Mall there are a number of pleasant spots to enjoy a picnic lunch.

In early July the Smithsonian holds its annual Festival of American Folklife. From Memorial Day to Labor Day, concerts are presented by military bands and other musical groups several times weekly in the Sylvan Theatre, an outdoor stage situated to the south of the Washington Monument (⊚ see Calendar of Events).

NATIONAL AIR AND SPACE MUSEUM★★★

INDEPENDENCE AVE. AT 6TH ST. SW.

Ⓜ L'ENFANT PLAZA.

FLOOR PLAN PP 92-93

This fascinating museum, commemorating man's aeronautical and astronautical achievements, welcomes more than nine million visitors annually, making it one of Washington's and the world's most popular museums.

▶ **Orient Yourself:** The museum encompasses an entire block on the south side of the Mall, opposite the National Gallery of Art.

🅿 **Parking:** With limited street parking, the most practical transportation is the Metro.

😊 **Don't Miss:** The Milestones of Flight gallery.

🕐 **Organizing Your Time:** Spend a full morning or afternoon here; if you're short on time, study the floor plan in this guide to pinpoint your interests. There is a cafe inside *(first floor, east end)*; vending carts are outside.

Kids **Especially for Kids:** Pretty much all the exhibits, but a Flight Simulator ride is among the most popular.

A Bit of History

In the Vanguard of Flight

In 1861 the Smithsonian's first secretary, Joseph Henry, encouraged Thaddeus Lowe's balloon experiments, resulting in President Lincoln's decision to use balloons in the Civil War. Fifteen years later kites brought from China for the Philadelphia Centennial Exposition were given to the Smithsonian and became

Courtesy National Air and Space Museum, Smithsonian Institution; photo: Eric Long

Space Hall, National Air and Space Museum

the cornerstone of the collection, which evolved into the museum.

The appointment in 1887 of **Samuel Pierpont Langley** (1834-1906) as the third secretary of the Smithsonian was a key factor in the development of flight in the US. Langley had gained renown as an astronomer, inventor, writer and researcher. In 1896 his Aerodrome No. 5 proved that sustained mechanical flight with a device heavier than air was feasible. He prepared the way for manned flight and what he forecast as "the great universal highway overhead."

In the 20C the idea for a museum dedicated to the history of flight evolved from the concern that the aircraft used by the US Air Force in World War II would be relegated to the scrap heap. With congressional support a conservation program was conceived, and in 1946 the National Air Museum was established by law. In 1966 the museum's scope was enlarged to include space flight. Companion facility to the Mall museum, the Steven F. Udvar-Hazy Center sits adjacent to Dulles International Airport in Virginia, 26mi west of Washington, DC.

The Mall Building

Designed by the St. Louis-based architect Gyo Obata, the building opened in

The Wright Brothers

A helicopter toy given as a present to young Wilbur (1867-1912) and Orville (1871-1948) Wright in 1878 sparked a passion for flight that remained with the brothers throughout their lives. As adults the self-taught engineers were among many in the US and abroad dedicated to making manned flight a reality. Drawing heavily from the experiences of Otto Lilienthal and other predecessors, they developed the 1903 *Wright Flyer*, an aircraft controlled by "wing warping," or changing the shapes of the wing tips to deflect the air. On December 17, 1903, in Kitty Hawk, North Carolina, their efforts succeeded. The longest of their four flights that day was 852ft in 59 seconds, after which a sudden gust of wind smashed the craft. There was little publicity about the brothers' breakthrough until 1905, but they patented their discovery and went on to build an airplane factory in Dayton, Ohio.

Orville and Wilbur Wright

Courtesy of National Air and Space Museum, Smithsonian Institution

1976 as a part of the nation's bicentennial celebration. The unadorned structure, measuring 635ft by 225ft and reaching nearly 83ft in height, comprises four massive rectangles connected by three glass "hyphens." Faced with Tennessee marble, the structure contains 23 galleries, a theater, a planetarium, museum stores and a research library *(open by appointment only)*. A glass annex housing a dining facility was added to the east end in the late 1980s.

The Collections

The museum possesses hundreds of aircraft and spacecraft, including manned vehicles, rockets, launching devices, space probes and satellites. As the museum has rights to all flown manned spacecraft from the US, its holdings constitute the most comprehensive collection of its kind in the world.

Authenticity is the keynote of the museum; nearly all the aircraft and most of the spacecraft in the galleries are genuine. As many spacecraft cannot be recovered once launched, the museum displays either the backup vehicle, a test vehicle, or a replica made from authentic hardware, as similar to the original as possible. Labels specifically note such distinctions.

Flight Time Line

Beginnings

early 16C — Leonardo da Vinci studies bird flight and draws plans for flying devices—precursors of the airplane, helicopter and parachute.

1783 — First manned balloon flight by the Montgolfier brothers in Paris.

1793 — George Washington witnesses first US balloon flight in Philadelphia.

1861-65 — Observation balloons are used in the Civil War.

1891-96 — Otto Lilienthal makes 2,000 glides in weight-controlled monoplanes.

1896 — The first successful engine-driven craft flight by Langley's Aerodrome No. 5 in Washington, DC.

20C Innovations

1903 — In Kitty Hawk, North Carolina, the Wright brothers successfully perform the first manned motorized flight in their 1903 Flyer.

1909 — Louis Bleriot crosses the English Channel in 36 minutes, flying a Type XI monoplane.

c.1910 — Glenn H. Curtiss develops the first seaplanes, which are used subsequently by the US Navy.

1911 — G.P. Rodgers makes the first coast-to-coast flight aboard the Wright EX Vin Fiz.

1918 — Scheduled airmail service begins with a route between New York City and Washington, DC via Philadelphia.

1920 — Beginning of regular passenger flights in Europe.

1923 — The first nonstop coast-to-coast flight in the Dutch-built Fokker T-2.

1924 — First round-the-world flight by two US Army Douglas World Cruisers.

1926 — The first liquid propellant rocket is developed.

1927 — Charles Lindbergh makes the first solo nonstop crossing of the Atlantic in the Spirit of St. Louis, covering 3,610 miles in 33 1/2hrs.

1932 — Amelia Earhart is the first woman to make a solo non-stop transatlantic flight.

1944 — The Germans begin launching the V-2, the world's first long-range ballistic missile.

1947 — Air Force pilot Charles E. "Chuck" Yeager flies the Bell X-1 Glamorous Glennis faster than the speed of sound

The Space Age

1957 — The Soviets launch Sputnik 1, the first artificial satellite.

1958 — The Boeing 707, the first US jet, begins commercial service. The National Aeronautics and Space Administration (NASA) is created.

1962 — In Friendship 7 John Glenn is the first American to orbit the earth.

1965 — Traveling aboard the Gemini 4 capsule, Edward White is the first American to walk in space.

1969 — Astronauts fly Apollo 11 to the moon and walk on its surface.

1970 — Beginning of regular commercial service of the supersonic Concorde.

1973-74 — The manned space missions of the Skylab orbital workshop conduct experiments and gather valuable data.

SECOND FLOOR

Flight and the Arts

Apollo to the Moon

Beyond the Limits: Flight Enters the Computer Age

0   100ft
0   50m

Explore The Universe

Looking at Earth

Lunar Exploration Vehicles

23

Space Hall
40

20

Rocketry and Space Flight

Space Race
21

FIRST FLOOR

NATIONAL AIR AND SPACE MUSEUM

(9) Suspended artifacts

Pioneer 10 is the first space-craft to reach Jupiter.

1977 — Voyager 1 and Voyager 2 are launched to photograph outer planets.

1979 — Voyager 1 and Voyager 2 reach Jupiter.

1981 — Voyager 2 reaches Saturn. Space shuttle Columbia is launched.

1986 — Voyager 2 reaches Uranus.

1989 — Galileo space probe is launched toward Jupiter.

1990 — Magellan space probe begins mapping the surface of Venus. Hubble Space Telescope is launched into orbit.

1991 — First close-up views of an asteroid obtained by Galileo probe.

1993 — The longest space-shuttle mission (14 days) to date is completed.

1996 — US space shuttle Atlantis and Russian Mir space station form largest structure ever assembled in space. Astro-naut Shannon Lucid remains in space for 188 days, longer than any American. The long-est flight in space-shuttle his-tory is achieved by Columbia (US)—a record 17 days, 15 hours, 54 minutes.

1997 — The Pathfinder mission lands on Mars. Sojourner, the first robotic rover, successfuly collects and transmits data concerning the red planet's geological and chemical composition.

1998 — John Glenn, the first American to orbit the earth, returns to space aboard the space shuttle Discovery, thirty-six years after his first mission aboard Friendship 7.

A new era in space flight begins with the initial construction stages of the International Space Station, the largest scientific cooperative endeavor in history.

2001 — Astronomers discover the first distant multiplanet system in which the planets have orbits similar to those in our own solar system.

2004 — In January twin Mars Exploration Rovers, Spirit and Opportunity, touch down on opposite sides of the red planet. Sent as robotic geologists to analyze rocks and soil on Mars, the rovers will relay photographs back to earth.

2006 — The first samples from a comet (Wild 2) are returned to earth by NASA's Stardust spacecraft.

2007 — In June the Space Shuttle Atlantis completes its mission to prepare the International Space Station for expansion.

Visit

Kids ⏰ *Open year-round daily 10am–5:30pm.* ⏰ *Closed Dec 25.* 🚶 *Guided tours (1hr 15min) available.* ✕ ☎202-633-1000. www.nasm.si.edu.
First go to the **Lockheed Martin IMAX® Theater** box office (**C**) to reserve a seat for one of the **films** (including the classic To Fly!) that are shown on a rotating basis daily (🎟$8.50; recorded information on films and screening times ☎202-633-4629). The theater's IMAX® projection system and five-story screen create the illusion of being airborne.
The **Albert Einstein Planetarium** presents shows in which the heavens are simulated on a 70ft overhead dome and discoveries of past centuries are

re-created (⏰ open year-round daily 10:30am–5pm; 🎟$8.50 and up; recorded information ☎202-633-4629).
🎟Circled numbers on the floor plan indicate artifacts that are suspended from the ceiling.

First Floor

On the west wall of the lobby, **Earth Flight Environment (A)**, a mural by Eric Sloane depicts an ever-changing sky. On the east wall, Robert McCall's **The Space Mural—A Cosmic View (B)** represents the artist's vision of the universe.

Milestones of Flight

In the large hall that occupies the central part of the building, several epoch-making airplanes and spacecraft are displayed. Among the highlights are Charles Lindbergh's Ryan NYP *Spirit of St. Louis* (**1**), Chuck Yeager's Bell X-1 *Glamorous Glennis* (**2**), John Glenn's *Friendship 7* (**3**) and *Apollo 11* (**4**). The exhibit also features the rocket-powered X-15 NASA (**5**) that set unofficial speed and altitude records of 4,520mph (Mach 6.7) and 354,200ft (over 67mi), as well as a replica of the Soviet satellite *Sputnik* (**6**), a surprisingly small (22.8in) polished sphere with four rod-shaped antennae. The Breitling Orbiter 3 (**7**) is the aircraft used in the first nonstop flight around the world. Visitors can touch a four-billion-year-old basalt moon rock (**8**) retrieved by the crew of Apollo 17 in 1972.

Air Transportation

Colorful aircraft fill this hall, illustrating the key stages of air transport. The sporty Pitcairn Mailwing (**9**) was designed to carry small loads for early mail routes in the eastern US. The all-metal Ford Tri-Motor (**10**) was a noisy but comfortable means of transport until the mid-1930s. Still used for passenger and cargo transport, the DC-3 (**11**), inaugurated in 1935, supplanted Ford's "Tin Goose" as the airlines' favorite workhorse. Boeing's 247-D (**12**) led the familiar series whose later models, the Stratoliners, could cruise above turbulence on long flights. In the At the Controls gallery, test your skills

The Physics of Flight

Flying is all about pressure and wing shape. To fly, an aircraft generates an upward force known as **lift**. To take off, lift must be greater than the aircraft's weight. An aircraft's **wings** are designed to be **curved** so that the air pressure at the top of the wing is different from the air pressure at the bottom of the wing. When the engines push the aircraft forward, air passes over the wings in such a way that a smaller pressure pushes down on the top of the wing and a higher pressure pushes up under the wing. This difference in pressure causes **lift**. The air coming off the wing is deflected downwards and the wing gets pushed upward. By varying this pressure difference, the pilot controls the altitude of the aircraft.

A pilot controls the amount of lift in two ways: by varying both the speed of the plane and the angle that the wing makes in relation to the plane's forward direction. In doing this, the pilot can make the aircraft climb, descend or fly level. Increasing speed increases lift. Increasing angle also increases lift. This is why the angle of the wing is so important. Varying the angle of the wing to the oncoming air changes the wing shape (and as such an airplane can fly upside down). Parts of the wing, such as flaps located in the back of the wing, can also be deflected to change the wing shape.

You might notice that at slower speeds, such as during climb or descent, the angle of the entire aircraft is high. The pilot is using angle to compensate for the lower speed. This allows the pilot to climb or descend at a controlled and desirable rate so as not to upset the passengers or to damage the aircraft.

© Brigitta L. House/MICHELIN

Wright Brothers' Flyer

in a MaxFlight® FS2000 Flight Simulator (☞$7).

The **Golden Age of Flight** celebrates the history of aviation between the two world wars. Highlights in this gallery include the Curtiss Robin (**13**) known as "Ole Miss," which achieved a world record of 27 days of sustained flight using air-to-air refueling, and a Hughes H-1 racer (**14**), designed and flown by Howard Hughes, who set a world-record flight speed of 352mph in 1935. In **Jet**

Aviation, the mural (**D**) spanning the length of the wall depicts 27 planes, from the Heinkel HE (1939) to the Concorde (1971) and the Airbus Industry A300B (1972). Opposite the mural are three jet fighters: a Messerschmitt Me262 (**15**), a Lockheed XP-80 (**16**) and a McDonnell FH-1 Phantom (**17**). **Early Flight** displays craft in a facsimile of a 1913 indoor aeronautical exhibition. Among other planes located in this gallery are a glider (1894) designed by Lilienthal, the Wright 1909

Military Flyer (**18**), which was the world's first military airplane, and a Bleriot Type XI monoplane (**19**).

How Things Fly includes exhibits on gravity and air, stability and control, and other principles of flight. Visitors can man the controls of a Cessna 150, activate a supersonic wind tunnel and interactive with other exhibits. The development of aerial photography and its applications is presented in **Looking at Earth**. A Lockheed U-2 is on display, along with touch screens that show a Landsat view of each of the 50 states.

Space Hall

Large rockets, guided missiles and manned spacecraft are featured in the exhibit entitled **Space Race**. On display is the infamous V-2 rocket (**40**) as well as a replica of the Hubble Space Telescope (**37**), a model of the *Columbia* space shuttle (**20**) and the *Apollo-Soyuz* spacecraft (**21**), which was used for a joint docking-in-space experiment with the Russians in 1975. Visitors can walk through the Skylab Orbital Workshop (**22**) *(accessible from the 2nd floor)*.

The **Rocketry and Space Flight** gallery displays historic rockets, engines for missiles and spacecraft, some rocket engines and a variety of space suits. The adjacent area is occupied by **Lunar Exploration Vehicles**, largely unmanned lunar probes that photographed the moon's surface. Although the *Apollo* lunar module (**23**) was never sent into space, it was nevertheless used for ground testing.

Explore the Universe examines the evolution of humanity's ability to search the heavens. Early **astrolabes** and Danish astronomer Tycho Brahe's portable **mural quadrant** represent the first steps taken in charting the skies while William Herschel's telescope tube, Edwin Hubble's camera, turn-of-the-19C spectrographs and the high-tech **Z machine** mark exceptional strides in the analysis of the ever-expanding frontier.

Second Floor

Pioneers of Flight

This open gallery houses planes that made historic flights. Among the arti-

facts displayed is Galbraith Perry Rodgers' Wright EX Vin Fiz (**24**), named after a grape drink his sponsor was making at the time. This plane was the first to succeed in a coast-to-coast flight. Rodgers crossed the continent from September 17 to November 5, 1911, covering 4,321 miles in 82 hours with an average speed of 52mph. The Fokker T-2 (**25**), built in the Netherlands and modified in the US, was the first to fly nonstop coast-to-coast. In 1923 this plane, manned by two pilots, flew almost 27 hours at an average speed of 92mph. The Douglas World Cruiser Chicago (**26**) was one of two biplanes to fly around the world, logging 27,553 miles in 175 days in 1924. **Amelia Earhart** (1898-1937), the legendary aviator who lost her life in the South Pacific while attempting an around-the-world flight, set two world records with her Lockheed Vega 5B (**27**) in 1932. In May of that year, Earhart became the first woman to fly alone nonstop across the Atlantic, covering a total of 2,026 miles in less than 15 hours.

A replica of the *Voyager 1* probe is the main attraction of **Exploring the Planets**, which presents an introduction to the solar system. **Great War in the Air** contrasts the realities of World War I with the war's romantic legacy, perpetuated in the films of Hollywood. Among aircraft on view is a 1918 German Fokker D VII (**38**). Some of the airplanes that determined the fate of nations can be viewed in **World War II Aviation**. Displays here include a Messerschmitt Bf 109 (**28**), a Mitsubishi Zero (**29**), a Supermarine Spitfire (**30**), a Macchi MC.202 (**31**) and a North American P-51D Mustang (**32**). The mural (**E**) was executed by Keith Ferris in 1976. **Sea-Air Operations** reproduces an aircraft-carrier hangar deck. Featured aircraft include the Boeing F4B-4 (**33**), the Douglas SBD-6 Dauntless dive-bomber (**34**), the Douglas A-4C Skyhawk (**35**) and the Grumman F4F Wildcat (**36**).

The Wright Brothers and the Invention of the Aerial Age delves into the lives and achievements of the famous duo. The centerpiece display is their *1903 Flyer* (**39**), resting on the floor.

Aviation Hanger, Steven F. Udvar-Hazy Center

Cynthia Ochterbeck/MICHELIN

The story of US manned spaceflight programs from Project Mercury to Apollo 17 is retold in **Apollo to the Moon**. Lunar samples are displayed along with space suits and lunar surface equipment such as a prototype of *Apollo 15's* Lunar Rover. **Beyond the Limits: Flight Enters the Computer Age** explores flight in the computer age. Here visitors find the Cray Serial 14 supercomputer used from 1978 to 1986 at the National Center for Atmospheric Research. Rotating works in **Flight and the Arts** feature interpretations of flight-related themes.

Steven F. Udvar-Hazy Center★★

Occupying 175 acres near Dulles International Airport in Virginia, this $311-million repository for aircraft and spacecraft (2003) consists of a 10-story-tall aviation hangar three football fields long, the James S. McDonnell Space Hangar, and the Donald D. Engen Observation Tower. The center's major benefactor (and a pilot), Steven Udvar-Hazy arrived in the US from Hungary at age 12. In 1973 he started a commercial-aircraft leasing business that became the world's top company of its kind. He donated $65 million to the Smithsonian Institution toward the construction of this facility.

Visit

14390 Air and Space Museum Pkwy., Chantilly, VA. From downtown, drive west on I-66 to Rte. 28 North (Exit 53B); continue 5mi north on Rte. 28 and exit at Air and Space Museum Parkway; follow the signs. ⏰*Open year-round daily 10am–5:30pm.* ⏰*Closed Dec 25.* ♿✕🅿 *($12)* ☎*202-633-1000. www.nasm.si.edu.*

At the Engen Observation Tower, watch planes take off and land at nearby Dulles Airport, and see exhibits on air-traffic control and airport equipment. Stop at the IMAX® Theater for a schedule of films (*$8.50*). In the Aviation Hangar, aircraft on display include the Lockheed SR-71 Blackbird, the world's fasted jet-propelled aircraft (speeds of over 2,100mph). The Boeing B-29 Superfortress, the Enola Gay, dropped the first atomic bomb, on Hiroshima, Japan, during World War II. Military and commercial aircraft include the supersonic Concorde. *Access the elevated walkway for a bird's-eye view of the artifacts.* In the Space Hangar, the Space Shuttle Enterprise served as an atmospheric test vehicle (the Enterprise never flew in space).

NATIONAL GALLERY OF ART★★★

MADISON DR. BETWEEN 3RD AND 7TH STS. NW.
Ⓜ ARCHIVES.
FLOOR PLAN PP 104-105

The National Gallery's world-class collection of masterpieces traces the development of Western art from the Middle Ages to the present. The West Building concentrates on European works from the 13C through the early 20C. Its contemporary counterpart, the East Building, highlights works of modern artists.

▶ **Orient Yourself:** Situated on the northeast corner of the Mall, the National Gallery is housed in the Beaux Arts-style West Building and the modernist East Building, the latter containing 20C works. Begin in the art information room of the West Building for an overview. Pick up the brochures on each building's collection highlights.

Ⓟ **Parking:** There are parking lots within a few blocks to the north.

☻ **Don't Miss:** West Building: Leonardo's "Ginevra de' Benci," Bernardino Luini's "Fresco Cycle," several Rembrandts. East Building: architecture, early Picassos.

🕐 **Organizing Your Time:** Allow 2hrs for a tour of the West Building's highlights, or an in-depth look at a few galleries; allow 1hr for the East Building. *⚫See Visiting the Museum opposite.*

A Bit of History

One Man's Dream

The financier, industrialist and statesman **Andrew Mellon** (1855-1937) was the impetus behind the National Gallery of Art. Mellon began collecting art in the 1870s, traveling to Europe with his friend Henry Clay Frick, benefactor of the famed Frick Collection *(⚫THE GREEN GUIDE New York City)*, for the purpose of acquiring 17C and 18C paintings. In the late 1920s, while serving as secretary of the Treasury, Mellon conceived of endowing a national gallery of art. From that time until his death in 1937, he became one of the world's foremost collectors of art. His intent was to amass masterpieces that would show the development of Western art from the 13C through the 19C. Among his acquisitions were 21 works from the Hermitage

The East Building

museum in Leningrad. They included paintings by such masters as van Eyck, Raphael, Titian and Rembrandt.

In 1937 Congress granted a charter to the new National Gallery of Art and pledged funds to support it. The stately building erected on the Mall was a gift from Mellon to the American people. Further, Mellon left the museum an endowment: 126 paintings and a collection of fine 15-16C Italian sculpture. The National Gallery's original building (the West Building) opened to the public in 1941.

Other Benefactors

Following Mellon's lead, other major American collectors have contributed to the gallery. Many of these collectors were able to assemble private collections rich in the works of Old Masters and Impressionists. Joseph Widener offered the renowned Widener family collection of painting, sculpture and decorative arts to the National Gallery in the 1930s. Samuel Kress, a self-made business magnate, already had plans drawn up for a museum in New York City to house his Italian paintings and sculptures when he was persuaded in 1939 to donate his collection to the uncompleted National Gallery.

Works by French Impressionists and post-Impressionists were donated by financier Chester Dale. Lessing J. Rosenwald left the gallery 22,000 prints and drawings, and Edgar William Garbisch and his wife, Bernice Chrysler Garbisch, gave a collection of 18C and 19C American naive paintings. More than 1,300 donors have contributed works of art to the National Gallery. Donations from Andrew Mellon's son, Paul, and his wife account for some 900 works of art, including those by Bonnard, Degas, Gauguin, Picasso and other masters.

A New Building

In only 30 years the expanding collections had outgrown the original building. **Paul Mellon** (1907-99), Ailsa Mellon Bruce and the Andrew Mellon Foundation funded the construction of a second building on the Mall just east of the original one. The $95 million East Building opened in 1978, establishing the National Gallery's reputation as a vital center for the presentation and appreciation of modern art.

The Collections

The gallery's collection of 106,000 paintings, sculpture, decorative arts, drawings, prints and photographs traces the development of Western art from the Middle Ages to the present. About 2,000 of these objects are on display at any given time. The Italian works constitute one of the finest collections of its kind in the world. The gallery's Ginevra de' Benci represents the only portrait by Leonardo da Vinci in the Western Hemisphere. Federal funds support museum operations and maintenance. However, all of its acquisitions are made through private means.

🐘 *Collection highlights appear in peach-colored boxes.*

Visiting the Museum

West Building

🕐*Open year-round Mon–Sat 10am–5pm, Sun 11am–6pm.* 🕐*Closed Jan 1 & Dec 25.* 🍴*Guided tours available.* ✕♿ ☎*202-737-4215, www.nga.gov.* 🐘*The West Building is undergoing long-term renovation. Some sections may be temporarily closed and some works of art mentioned below may not be on view. Check the Micro Gallery, accessible by the museum's website or at terminals in the art information room, to find out the status of specific works and collections.* The main entrance is located at the top of the steps on the Mall side between 4th and 7th streets. Wheelchair access is via the entrance at 6th Street. A checkroom is located to the right of the main entrance, beyond the Founders' Room. The art information room, with its state-of-the-art Micro Gallery, is to the left. The main floor of the West Building houses 13-19C European paintings and sculpture, and American art. Sculpture and decorative arts, prints and drawings, and temporary exhibits are presented on the ground floor. Artworks are displayed, for the most part, in chronological order by school.

We suggest you begin your visit at the art information room. Here you may obtain a list of current exhibitions, a schedule of docent-led tours and notices of temporary exhibits, lectures and special events. Spend 5–10min exploring the Micro Gallery, where 13 touch-screen monitors allow visitors to research artists and 1,700 works from the permanent collection. Along with historical commentary and analysis, this fascinating system provides the viewing status and location of specific works in the gallery. A random-access audio tour, The Director's Tour, offers curators' and conservators' perspectives on 130 works of art throughout the West Building and is available for rental (☜$5) from the desk in the rotunda. A new audio tour, *Adventures in Art* Kids (☜$3), introduces the Dutch and Flemish collection to younger visitors.

East Building

🕐*Open year-round Mon–Sat 10am–5pm, Sun 11am–6pm.* 🕐*Closed Jan 1 & Dec 25.* ☜*Introductory guided tours (50min) available.* ✕ ✆ *www.nga.gov.* ☎*202-737-4215.* The main entrance to the East Building is on 4th Street, across the plaza from the West Building. An underground concourse connects the two structures. Wheelchair access is to the left of the 4th Street entrance steps. All five levels of the East Building feature rotating exhibits drawn from the National Gallery's permanent collection of late-19C and 20C art. Works are not necessarily arranged in chronological order. The East Building's open interior space is easily adapted to changing exhibits; major traveling exhibits from all artistic periods are mounted here. Begin your visit to the East Building at the ground-level art information desk, where you may obtain notices of current exhibitions and events as well as the day's schedule of guided tours.

Sculpture Garden

🕐*Open year-round Mon–Sat 10am–5pm, Sun 11am–6pm (extended hours in summer).* 🕐*Closed Jan 1 & Dec 25.* ☎*202-737-4215. www.nga.gov.* On the National Mall between 7th and 9th streets *(across from the 7th Street entrance to the West*

Building), the Garden displays 17 major works of 20C sculpture in a pleasantly landscaped park.

West Building

The capital's leading proponent of Classical Revival architecture, John Russell Pope designed this formidable domed structure. The West Building's appeal derives from the seven shades of glowing pink Tennessee marble incorporated in the facade. Its sober exterior is adorned only by simple blind windows and pilasters. Ionic porticoes highlight the north and south sides. The 785ft-long edifice ranks as one of the world's largest marble structures.

Main Floor

🛈*A number of main-floor galleries may be temporarily closed; consult the Micro Gallery to verify the location of works mentioned below.*
Flanking the entrance hall on the Mall side are the art information room, with its **Micro Gallery** *(left)*, and the **Founders' Room** *(right)*, a lounge where portraits of major founding benefactors are prominently displayed. The hall leads to the **Rotunda**, where green-black Tuscan marble columns surround a fountain whose centerpiece is a statue of Mercury. The broad sculpture halls of the building's two wings extend from the rotunda past the galleries, culminating in garden courts. The **East Sculpture Hall** features classically inspired marble statuary from the 17-19C, while works in bronze, including a selection of Italian busts, are displayed in the **West Sculpture Hall.**

13-15C Italian Painting

Galleries 1-15. Representing the evolution of Western painting from 1200 to the early 1500s, this section begins with the stylized Byzantine iconography that developed in Constantinople, capital of the Eastern Roman Empire and cradle of the Orthodox faith. The **icons**, or devotional images, are painted in egg tempera on wooden panels and enhanced with gold leaf. The Byzantine tradition transplanted in Italy gave rise to a more natural style. The Sienese school, whose most influential master was Duccio di Buoninsegna (1255-1318), is particularly well represented in the collection. In the late 13C, Florentine artists, notably Giotto (c.1266-c.1337), developed a realistic rendering of space that ushered in the Italian Renaissance. Gradually, the strict iconography was replaced with secular portraiture and more sensual paintings that depicted biblical scenes. In the quattrocento (15C), Florentine artists like Fra Filippo Lippi and Botticelli looked to classical antiquity for its scientific notions of anatomy and perspective.

- *Madonna and Child* Giotto c. 1330
- *The Adoration of the Magi* Fra Angelico and Fra Filippo Lippi c.1445
- *Ginevra de' Benci* da Vinci c.1474
- *Giuliano de' Medici* Botticelli c.1478

East Garden Court, National Gallery of Art

- *The Small Cowper Madonna* Raphael c.1505
- *The Alba Madonna* Raphael c.1510
- *The Adoration of the Shepherds* Giorgione c.1510
- *The Feast of the Gods* Bellini and Titian c.1514/1529
- *The Conversion of Saint Paul* Tintoretto c.1545
- *Doge Andrea Gritti* Titian c.1548
- *Venus with a Mirror* Titian c.1555

Italian Sculpture and Furniture

Galleries 2, 5, 8, 11, 25-27 (The Cabinet Galleries) The marble, bronze, wood, porphyry, and painted terra-cotta sculpture (13-16C) displayed here closely follows the evolution in Italian painting: the earlier pieces depict religious themes, while in later works, portrait busts, particularly of prominent Florentines, begin to appear. The Italian Cabinet Galleries *(25-27)* were designed to evoke the interior of an Italian Renaissance palace or villa. They contain 40 items from the Gallery's permanent collection. A fresco cycle by Bernardino Luini (c.1480-1532) is showcased in Gallery 26. Small paintings provide a lustrous backdrop for bronze statuettes, glassware and porcelain.

- *Lorenzo de' Medici* Verrocchio and Benintendi c.1478/1521

16C Italian Painting

Galleries 16-28. The Renaissance that began in 15C Florence spread to northern Italy, in part through the works of Andrea Mantegna (1431-1506). His bold lines and sense of perspective influenced artists in Ferrara and Venice. Another very different innovation in Venetian art of the 15C came from Giorgione (c.1478-1510), whose delicate use of color gave this period its characteristic style. Giorgione's teacher, Giovanni Bellini (c.1427-1516), preferred the three-quarter portrait to the traditional Renaissance profile, thus allowing more expression of emotion and character. The High Renaissance of the early 16C, the cinquecento, attained an unparalleled level of delicacy and grace, enhanced by the manipulation of light and shadow as expressed in the art of such masters as Leonardo da Vinci (1452-1519) and Raphael (1483-1520). Titian (c.1490-1576), the prolific master whose outstanding talent was sought after by the leading European rulers of the day, dominated the 16C. Tintoretto (1518-94) carried innovations of his predecessors further with his own impressionistic, emotionally charged paintings. The allegorical representation of religious figures and classical gods and goddesses against a pastoral setting became the predominant subject of northern Italian art, with sensuality and color as its hallmarks.

17-18C Italian Painting

Galleries 29-34. Marked by the creative vision of Annibale Carracci (1560-1609), 17C Bologna was the birthplace of the exuberant art of the Baroque, which had its greatest flowering in papal Rome. In the next century Giovanni Battista Tiepolo (1696-1770) refined the Baroque's expansiveness into a lighter and more decorative style *(Gallery 32)*. Tiepolo's frescoes adorned ceilings throughout Europe, but his genius marked the end of Italian dominance in art. Thereafter, the main innovations in art came from new centers in northern Europe. Also popular in 18C Italy were detailed cityscapes and architectural representations, such as those of Canaletto and Panini, that reflected fashionable interests in the grand tour of Italian antiquities. Featured in gallery 36 are works by French artists Nicholas Poussin and Claude Lorrain, both of whom lived and painted in Rome.

- *River Landscape*
  Carracci c.1590
- *The Porta Portello, Padua*
  Canaletto c.1741
- *Wealth and Benefits of the Spanish Monarchy under Charles III*
  Tiepolo c.1762

Spanish Painting

Galleries 28, 29, 34 and 52. Restraint characterizes the work of most Spanish artists during the 16C, with the notable exception of El Greco (1541-1614). Born on the island of Crete and trained in Venice, El Greco is nonetheless considered a Spanish artist, whose elongated shapes and religious fervor distinguish his unique style.

The preeminent 17C Spanish artist Diego Velázquez (1599-1660) obtained in his later works "impressionistic" effects of color and light that foreshadow 19C stylistic trends. A court painter, Velázquez was renowned for his portraits of the Spanish royal family.

In the 18C Francisco de Goya (1746-1828) *(gallery 52)* was Madrid's most fashionable portraitist. His early works reflect the lighthearted Rococo spirit of the period, while his more probing later portraits anticipate the psychological Expressionism of the 20C.

Gallery 38 is devoted to European sculpture and painting from the 14C and 15C.

- *Laocoön*
  El Greco c.1614
- *The Needlewoman*
  Velázquez c.1650
- *Two Women at a Window*
  Murillo c.1660
- *Thérèse Louise de Sureda*
  Goya c.1804

German Painting

Galleries 35 and 35A. Albrecht Dürer (1471-1528), the preeminent German artist of the late 15C and early 16C, has been called the "Leonardo of the North." Renowned throughout Europe, Dürer was recognized as a master printmaker as well as an outstanding painter. Dürer's contemporary Matthias Grünewald (c.1475-1528) was a matchless interpreter of religious intensity, while Lucas Cranach the Elder (1472-1553) was known for both his religious works and his portraits. Hans Holbein the Younger (c.1498-1543) relocated to England and became a court painter to King Henry VIII. The artist was admired for his ability to convey a sense of nobility in the royalty he painted.

- *The Small Crucifixion*
  Grünewald c.1520
- *Portrait of a Clergyman*
  Dürer 1516
- *Edward VI as a Child*
  Holbein c.1538

Netherlandish Painting

Galleries 39-41A. Present-day Belgium, Holland, Luxembourg and even portions of France composed the Netherlands at the end of the Middle Ages. The wealthy regions of the Low Countries were a magnet for talented painters. During the 15C Flanders, in what is now part of Belgium, was a leading artistic center, thanks largely to Jan van Eyck (c.1390-1441). A technical virtuoso, van Eyck mastered the representation of interior space and, more importantly, is credited with having revolutionized painting by employing oil, as opposed to tempera, as the medium. This innovation, which allowed more subtlety in brushwork, attracted artists from throughout Europe to Flanders, among them Hans Memling (d.1494), whose delicate and serene paintings enjoyed great popularity. Rogier van der Weyden (c.1400-64), another Netherlandish master, achieved a virtuosity of brushstroke that influenced generations. François Clouet (c.1522-72) descended from a family of Flemish painters who lived in France. A celebrated court painter, Clouet is credited with popularizing bathing portraits.

- *The Annunciation*
  van Eyck c.1436
- *Portrait of a Lady*
  van der Weyden c.1460
- *A Lady in Her Bath*
  François Clouet c.1571

Dutch and Flemish Painting

Galleries 42-51. The Dutch and Flemish Cabinet galleries 50 A-C feature small paintings from the permanent collection as well as temporary exhibits. The robust vitality of Peter Paul Rubens (1577-1640) dominates the 17C Flemish Baroque. An artist of great versatility, Rubens enjoyed international renown for his allegories and portraits. His student Anthony Van Dyck (1599-1641) became one of Europe's most celebrated portrait painters *(Galleries 42 and 43).*

Among the numerous painters of the varied styles and genres developed in 17C Holland, Rembrandt van Rijn (1606-69) stands out as the abiding genius of this time *(gallery 48).* His mastery of chiaroscuro—the subtle play of light and shadow—influenced art for two centuries. *The Mill,* considered one of Rembrandt's finest landscapes, profoundly affected the work of 19C British artists such as J.M.W. Turner and Sir Joshua Reynolds. Rembrandt's deeply psychological approach to portraiture takes the inventiveness of a slightly earlier Dutch artist, Frans Hals (c.1583-1666), a step further. Employing lively brushwork, Hals had broken with the staid portraiture of the past to show his sitters with striking informality.

Johannes Vermeer (1632-75), another Dutch genius, used light and space in such a way that his scenes of the upper middle classes are infused with an ethereal quality. The numerous still lifes, landscapes and genre paintings that were produced by Dutch artists in the 17C often had allegorical meaning underlying their apparent realism.

- *Daniel in the Lions' Den*
  Rubens c.1615
- *Willem Coymans*
  Hals 1645
- *The Mill*
  Rembrandt c.1650
- *Self-Portrait*
  Rembrandt 1659
- *Woman Holding a Balance*
  Vermeer c.1664

17-18C French Painting

Galleries 36-37 and 53-56. During the reign of Louis XIV, the French Academy controlled all aspects of cultural life, and traditions of classicism prevailed in art. The most noted proponent of classicism, Nicolas Poussin (1594-1665) *(gallery 36),* worked much of his life in Italy yet strongly influenced French art. His works depict harmoniously composed subjects set against an Arcadian backdrop. Claude Lorrain (1600-82) *(gallery 36),* who also worked in Rome, shared Poussin's love of landscape but gave it a nostalgic interpretation. Louis Le Nain (1593-1648) and his two brothers *(gallery 37)* concentrated on realistic genre paintings. By the early 18C, Paris had

MAIN FLOOR

NATIONAL GALLERY OF ART

GROUND FLOOR

become the cultural hub of Europe, and the French Rococo style was the fashion. This florid style is best exemplified in the work of Antoine Watteau (1684-1721), who created whimsically poetic images that emphasize color and depict the sophisticated manners of 18C French society. Later, François Boucher (1703-70) introduced new sensuous pastoral reveries, while Boucher's student Jean-Honoré Fragonard (1732-1806) focused on French subjects, representing them in quick, colorful brushstrokes. Portraits by Elisabeth Vigée-Lebrun (1755-1842)

West Building

19C French

Special Exhibits

Rotunda

East Sculpture Hall

Spanish

Founder's Room

18C French

British

East Garden Court

American

MALL

| 0 | | 100 ft |
| 0 | | 50 m |

Avenue

(A) to Concourse East Building,

Café

(gallery 56), painter and confidante to Marie Antoinette, reflect her close ties to aristocratic French society. Traditional classicism persisted, however, in the works of Jacques-Louis David (1748-1825) and Jean-Auguste-Dominique Ingres (1780-1867).

- *Italian Comedians*
  Watteau c.1720
- *Madame Bergeret*
  Boucher 1746
- *A Young Girl Reading*
  Fragonard c.1776

Marcelle Lender Dancing the Bolero in "Chilpéric" (1895-1896) by Henri de Toulouse-Lautrec

19C French Painting

Galleries 80-93. In the early 19C the French Academy sanctioned the classicism of David and Ingres, but artists such as Eugène Delacroix (1798-1863) and Jean-Baptiste-Camille Corot (1796-1875) rebelled against such conventions, painting romantic landscapes in their own idiom. Gustave Courbet (1819-77), Honoré Daumier (1808-79) and Edouard Manet (1832-83) discarded romanticism in favor of an unsentimental realism that depicted everyday scenes. A group of young painters inspired by Manet's example broke from the state-sponsored Salon exhibitions in 1874 to show their works independently. Known as the **Impressionists** because of their unprecedented exploration of atmospheric light and color in natural landscapes and figure painting, the group was informally led by Claude Monet (1840-1926) and Pierre-Auguste Renoir (1841-1919). Edgar Degas (1834-1917) and Henri de Toulouse-Lautrec (1864-1901) depicted contemporary Parisian nightlife. Paul Gauguin (1848-1903), Paul Cézanne (1839-1906) and Dutch-born Vincent van Gogh (1853-90) each developed a highly personal style of modern art. American-born Mary Cassatt (1844-1926), known for her compositional structures and her evocative depictions of women and children, painted in Paris and exhibited with the Impressionists.

- *Agostina*
  Corot c.1866
- *The Artist's Father*
  Cézanne 1866
- *The Railway*
  Manet 1873
- *Woman with a Parasol – Madame Monet and Her Son*
  Monet 1875
- *A Girl with a Watering Can*
  Renoir 1876
- *La Mousmé*
  van Gogh 1888
- *Quadrille at the Moulin Rouge*
  Toulouse-Lautrec 1892
- *Fatata te Miti*
  Gauguin 1892
- *The Boating Party*
  Cassatt c.1894
- *Four Dancers*
  Degas c.1899

British Painting

Galleries 57-59, and 61. British painting first achieved a distinctive voice in the mid-18C with William Hogarth (1697-1764), whose works depicted the London middle classes. Later in the century Thomas Gainsborough (1727-88) created his romantic portraits of English nobility, while his rival Sir Joshua Reynolds (1723-92) adopted the formal grandeur of the Baroque in his portraiture.

In landscape painting the works of J.M.W. Turner (1775-1851), executed in swirls of colored light, are dramatically charged. The landscapes of his contemporary John Constable (1776-1837) are executed with scientific realism but convey a pastoral tranquillity. Both artists influenced the work of the French Impressionists.

- *A Scene from The Beggar's Opera*
  Hogarth 1729
- *Lady Caroline Howard*
  Reynolds 1778
- *Miss Juliana Willoughby*
  Romney 1783
- *Mrs. Richard Brinsley Sheridan*
  Gainsborough 1787
- *Wivenhoe Park, Essex*
  Constable 1816
- *Keelmen Heaving in Coals by Moonlight*
  Turner 1835

American Painting

Galleries 60-60B, 62-71. Like British painting of the 18C and early 19C, American art focuses on portraiture in the grand manner. Eminent artists of this period include Benjamin West (1738-1820), Thomas Sully (1783-1872), Charles Willson Peale (1741-1827), John Singleton Copley (1738-1815) *(Gallery 65)* and Gilbert Stuart (1755-1828), who was sometimes called the "court portraitist to the young Republic" because of his many paintings of early leaders.

By the mid-19C landscape painting emerged as the dominant force in American art, with painters such as Thomas Cole (1801-48) *(gallery 64)* and Frederic Edwin Church (1826-1900) depicting the awe-inspiring natural wonders of the New World. Highly personal expression, as evidenced in the works of Winslow Homer (1836-1910) and the mystical paintings of Albert Pinkham Ryder (1847-1917), followed later in the century. European influences are seen in the works of James McNeill Whistler (1834-1903), Thomas Eakins (1844-1916) and John Singer Sargent (1856-1925), all of whom either lived or studied abroad.

Gallery 68 showcases American naïve paintings culled from the Gallery's renowned collection of 18C and 19C folk art. These paintings by "naïve" artists, so-called for their lack of formal training, abound with talent and imagination. Bold colors, skewed perspective and discrepancies in scale characterize

Breezing Up (1873-1876) by Winslow Homer

these works, such as Edward Hick's *The Cornell Farm* (1848) and his *Peaceable Kingdom* (c.1834).

Galleries 72-79 are devoted to special exhibits.

- *Watson and the Shark*
  Copley 1778
- *The Skater*
  Stuart 1782
- *Benjamin and Eleanor Ridgely Laming* Peale 1788
- *Autumn–On the Hudson River*
  Cropsey 1860
- *The White Girl*
  Whistler 1862
- *Breezing Up*
  Homer 1876
- *Siegfried and the Rhine Maidens*
  Ryder 1891
- *Repose*
  Sargent 1911

Ground Floor

A number of ground-floor galleries may be temporarily closed; consult the Micro Gallery to verify the location of works mentioned below.

Sculpture and Decorative Arts

Small sculpture and medals in the collection date from the 15C to the early 18C. Marble busts and statuary, primarily French and Italian, date from the 17C and 18C. Works, mainly terra-cotta or marble, of 18C French sculptors such as Clodion and Houdon and 19C-20C sculpture by Degas, Rodin, Maillol, Bartholdi, Jo Davidson, Paul Manship and other masters round out the collection. Of special interest are Degas' *Dressed Ballet Dancer* (colored plaster, modeled 1881) and Rodin's *The Thinker* (bronze, 1880). Other noteworthy works include miniature bronze busts by Honoré Daumier.

Decorative arts in the collection include 15C and 16C Flemish and 18C French tapestries, as well as Italian Renaissance and 18C French Rococo furnishings. Small ecclesiastical artworks, such as enamels and stained glass, of the Middle Ages and Renaissance, include a 12C bejeweled chalice of sardonyx and silver gilt.

Prints, Drawings and Photographs

The National Gallery owns nearly 100,000 American and European works on paper and vellum, the vast majority of which were acquired in the postwar period. The **Armand Hammer collection** of drawings spans five centuries and includes the works of Leonardo da Vinci, Michelangelo, Dürer, Manet, Degas and Cézanne.

East Building

Generally considered Washington's most impressive example of modern architecture, the East Building (1978, I.M. Pei) houses the gallery's growing collection of Modern and Contemporary art, as well as a selection of small-format 19C French paintings.

The Architecture – The massive marble **building**★★ by **I. M. Pei** stresses line and angle over adornment. Pei's task was threefold: to design a structure that would showcase modern art, to harmonize with the West Building and to be monumental enough to anchor the northeast corner of the Mall. Given a trapezoidal lot formed by the intersections of Pennsylvania Avenue and the National Mall with 3rd and 4th streets, Pei chose a trapezoid formed of two distinct triangles. The northern isosceles triangle houses gallery space; the southern right triangle contains administrative and research facilities. Polygonal towers top the points of the isosceles triangle; each tower rises 108ft high, one foot less than the height of the West Building. The structure's marble facing came from the same Tennessee quarries as that of the West Building.

The 4th Street **plaza**, which fronts the East Building and links it visually to the West Building, is dominated by seven glass tetrahedrons, three-sided shapes that also serve as skylights for the underground concourse connecting the buildings. A fountain flows down a *chadar*, or water slide, that is visible from inside the concourse.

The Art – The gallery's stated goal is to "present the great European and American movements and masters of the century rather than to speculate on new trends." Works are displayed in large, fluid spaces on each of the building's five floors. Represented in the collection are the works of such 20C artists as Wassily Kandinsky, Henri Matisse, Constantin Brancusi, Pablo Picasso, Georgia O'Keeffe, Georges Braque, Joan Miró, Anselm Kiefer, Alberto Giacometti, Mark Rothko and Arshile Gorky.

Visit

Because works are shown on a rotating basis, not all artists mentioned will be represented at one time. Inquire at the ground-floor art information desk for current exhibits.

Henry Moore's monumental *Knife Edge Mirror Two Piece*, situated outside the main entrance, softens the building's exterior angles.

A skylit atrium opens from the low-ceilinged lobby of the ground level and is dominated by an immense red, blue and black mobile by Alexander Calder, specially commissioned for this space. Another commissioned work, a sculpture titled *National Gallery Ledge Piece*, by Anthony Caro, is displayed over the door to the administrative wing *(located near the escalator)*. On the opposite side of the building, outside the wall of windows, is a new installation, Andy Goldsworthy's *Roof* (2005). Created specifically for this site, nine domes of stacked slate crowd the outdoor courtyard. The view from the mezzanine reveals a hole in each dome, suggestive of a beehive.

Two intimate ground-floor galleries feature rotating exhibits of smaller works, including American art, as well as French paintings from the collections of Ailsa Mellon Bruce and Mr. and Mrs. Paul Mellon. Works by Degas, Bonnard, Renoir, Corot, Vuillard, Manet, Morisot and other masters line the walls of these smaller galleries.

Mezzanine galleries are generally devoted to large traveling exhibits from all time periods. Primarily reserved

East Building, Interior

Gwen Cannon/MICHELIN

for European paintings and sculpture, including monumental works, the upper-level galleries feature 20C artists such as Dubuffet, Derain, Mondrian, Picabia, Picasso, Miró, Gris, Brancusi, Modigliani, Giacometti, Magritte, Soutine and Gorky. The intimate tower gallery exhibits the museum's collection of **paper cutouts** by Matisse *(may be viewed Mon–Sat 10am-2pm, Sun 11am–3pm)*. The concourse galleries showcase predominantly American late-20C art, including works by Barnett Newman, Clyfford Still, Robert Motherwell, Andy Warhol, Agnes Martin, Louise Bourgeois, Roy Lichtenstein and Ellsworth Kelly.

Sculpture Garden

Opened in 1999, this spacious garden displays works from the National Gallery's collection of 20C sculpture amid trees, flowerbeds and twisting paths. Its central reflecting pool is used as an ice-skating rink in winter. The benches surrounding the fountain were carved out of the same pink Tennessee marble as the East and West buildings. Besides providing a relaxing outdoor escape from museum crowds, the six-acre space presents a who's who in contemporary sculpture: Louise Bourgeois, Claes Oldenburg, Coosje van Bruggen and Roy Lichtenstein are just a few of the artists whose works are on display.

ARTHUR M. SACKLER GALLERY ★★

THE SMITHSONIAN QUADRANGLE AT 1050 INDEPENDENCE AVE. SW.
Ⓜ SMITHSONIAN OR L'ENFANT PLAZA.

The Sackler Gallery is dedicated to the study and exhibition of the arts of Asia from the Neolithic period to the present. Major strengths of the collection are Chinese jades and bronzes, ancient Near Eastern gold and silverwork and 11-19C Islamic manuscripts. An underground gallery links the Sackler to the adjacent Freer Gallery, with which it is associated.

A Bit of History

The core of the museum's holdings was donated to the Smithsonian Institution in 1982 by **Dr. Arthur M. Sackler** (1913-87), a New York psychiatrist, medical researcher and publisher. Sackler began acquiring Asian art in the 1950s to supplement his collection of Western art. He was the principal benefactor of Harvard University's Arthur M. Sackler Museum, and he contributed generously to the Eastern art holdings of the Metropolitan Museum of Art (♨THE GREEN GUIDE New York City).

Visit

🕐Open year-round daily 10am–5:30pm. 🕐Closed Dec 25. 🗪Guided tours Thu–Tues 12:15pm. ♿ ☎202-633-4880. www.asia.si.edu.

Chinese Collections

Ancient Chinese culture placed particular importance on tradition: laws and customs were passed through the generations, and ancestor worship was a common practice, which explains in part the presence of ancestor figures in the decoration of ritual bronzes and jades. The economy was largely agricultural, and the attributes of nature became a powerful force in ancient Chinese religion. Clouds, rain, wind and stars appear frequently as symbolic ornamentation on vessels and objects, which the Chinese used presumably to deflect evil spirits and to invoke the protection of particular deities.

Jade Collection

The mountains of the Chinese provinces contained rich veins of nephrite jade, a gemstone so prized by the Chinese that they associate it with the five cardinal virtues of charity, modesty, courage, justice and wisdom. The Sackler's jade collection of some 450 decorated objects dates from about 3000 BC. Artifacts from the Neolithic period include ax blades (c.3000 BC) produced in most cases as ceremonial burial objects. The jades of the Shang dynasty (1700 BC) were used for ceremonial functions.

Chinese Bronzes

The gallery's bronzes date from the Shang through the Han dynasties (1700 BC-AD 220). Many of the objects are generously inscribed, providing a wealth of information about this period, which has long remained obscure to historians.

Ancient Near Eastern Gold and Silver

The civilizations that developed in ancient Iran, Anatolia (present-day Turkey) and the region around the Caucasus Mountains are credited with introducing metalwork as early as 7000 BC. Over the ensuing millennia, the craftspeople of these regions produced exquisite objects in copper, silver, gold and lead, employing a wide range of metallurgical techniques. Many of the gold and silver vessels and ornaments in the Sackler collection are gilded or inlaid with niello (an enamel-like alloy) and date from 3000 BC to 8C AD. These objects offer glimpses of often sumptuous court life in the nations that developed in the Tigris-Euphrates Valley.

FREER GALLERY OF ART★★

JEFFERSON DR. AT 12TH ST. SW.
Ⓜ SMITHSONIAN.

The Smithsonian's first museum on the Mall devoted exclusively to art, the Freer Gallery possesses an outstanding Asian collection and one of the world's largest collections of works by James McNeill Whistler (1834-1903).

A Bit of History

The Connoisseur

A successful railroad car manufacturer, Charles L. Freer (1854-1919) became, like Arthur Sackler, a keen collector of Asian art. From his first purchase in 1887 of a Japanese fan, he gradually amassed thousands of objects, many of which were acquired during his trips to Japan, India and China. In 1887 he also bought several Whistler prints, his initial acquisition of works by the artist who would become his good friend. Retiring at age 45, Freer became a full-time collector and world traveler, expanding both his Asian and American holdings. In 1904 he revealed plans to bequeath a significant portion of his collections to the Smithsonian Institution and to finance the construction of a building to house the art. At his death his bequest totaled some 9,000 works. Today the museum's Asian properties have grown to over 27,000 works (Freer stipulated that his American collection not be expanded).

The Building

After the announcement of his proposed gift, Freer embarked on a search for a suitable building design, visiting American and European museums to gather ideas as to gallery size, ventilation and lighting. In 1912 he hired New York architect Charles A. Platt, who employed Neoclassical symmetry in the marble and granite Renaissance-style structure that is built, as Freer had specified, around a central courtyard. The building's two entrances on Jefferson Drive and Independence Avenue are distinguished by triple arches. The arch motif is repeated in the bronze-framed Palladian windows and glass doors surrounding the 60sq-ft fountained courtyard, which is faced with white Tennessee marble. The stone balustrade of the exterior parapet appears again above the courtyard's arches. The museum was officially opened in 1923. After extensive renovation, begun in 1988, the museum reopened in 1993 with 19 galleries on the first level and study rooms, an auditorium, a conference room and a gallery shop on the lower levels. An underground exhibition gallery permits passage between the Freer and the Sackler Gallery.

Visit

🕐 *Open year-round daily 10am–5:30pm.* 🕐 *Closed Dec 25.* ⚑ *Guided tours Thu–Tue 12:15pm.* ♿ ☎ *202-633-4880. www. asia.si.edu. A floor plan can be obtained from the information desk.*

Asian Collection

Highlights of the Chinese holdings include ornamental implements of the emperors of the Ming (1368-1644) and Qing (1644-1911) dynasties; 15C blue-and-white porcelain bowls from the imperial workshop in Jingdezhen in southeast China; and bronzes, jades

Glazed Stoneware, Southern Song Dynasty, China 12C

Courtesy Freer Gallery of Art, Smithsonian Institution; photo: Neil Greentree

Harmony in Blue and Gold: The Peacock Room by James McNeill Whistler

and lacquerware from the Ancient Chinese collection, which dates from 3500 BC to the first century AD. Traditional Japanese painting and calligraphy can be seen on hanging scrolls (ink and color on silk or paper); 15-19C *byobu*, or folding screens; late-16-19C porcelain pieces and lacquered wooden boxes; and 13-17C stone and earthenware tea bowls. Korean ceramics from the 10C to the 14C, Indian 16-19C court paintings and Islamic manuscripts are showcased in separate galleries.

American Collection

Paintings by prominent American artists include Whistler's *Caprice in Purple and Gold: The Golden Screen* (1864) and John Singer Sargent's *Breakfast in the Loggia* (1910). Of special interest are Whistler's "Notes," miniature oils depicting Chelsea shops and English landscapes c.1882; and "Nocturnes," dramatic paintings of the Thames River at night, inspired by Japanese prints. Full of light and grace are his "Six Projects" of the late 1860s—varied compositions of figures against the backdrop of the sea *(all six paintings may not be on view)*. Oil portraits and landscapes by Abbott Henry Thayer, Thomas Dewing's paintings of

women in fields, and Dwight Tryon's large oil and pastel landscapes adorn other galleries devoted to the American collection.

Permanently installed in Gallery 12 is the **Peacock Room**★, Whistler's only extant interior design (1876-77). Freer purchased the room in 1904 from a London art dealer; prior to the museum's opening, it was transferred from his Detroit home to the premises. Asked by English shipping tycoon Frederick Leyland to redecorate portions of his 20ft-by-32ft London dining room, the artist began what evolved into a major (ostensibly unauthorized) overhaul. The result was a highly original, gilded setting for Leyland's blue-and-white Chinese porcelain collection. Intricate paintings of golden peacocks and peacock motifs embellish the walls, shutters and ceiling. Dominating the mantel is Whistler's painting *The Princess from the Land of Porcelain*, which Leyland had purchased. In the mural depicting two fighting peacocks *(south wall)*, the artist immortalized his dispute with Leyland over payment for his interior work. The porcelain pieces on view are similar to those in Leyland's collection and were acquired for the room's 1993 restoration.

HIRSHHORN MUSEUM AND SCULPTURE GARDEN★★

INDEPENDENCE AVE. AT 7TH ST. SW.
Ⓜ L'ENFANT PLAZA OR SMITHSONIAN.

An unmistakable architectural statement on the Mall, this cylindrical building houses one of the finest collections of modern art in the country. Its sculpture holdings, ranging from the realistic to the monumental and abstract, make up the world's most comprehensive collection of 20C works in that medium.

A Bit of History

The Benefactor

Born in Latvia on the eastern coast of the Baltic Sea, **Joseph Hirshhorn** (1899-1981) immigrated to Brooklyn with his widowed mother and 10 siblings when he was six years old. At age 13 he left school to help support his family, and at 18 he was a broker on Wall Street. He eventually became a wealthy financier and uranium magnate.

Hirshhorn traced his first interest in art to a series of paintings by Salon masters he saw reproduced in an insurance calendar. His early collecting followed in that vein, but by the late 1930s, his tastes had turned to the works of French Impressionists and post-Impressionists. That interest also passed, as he increasingly focused his collecting on contemporary American and European painting and on modern sculpture from around the world.

In 1962, with the first major public exhibition of his art treasures at the Solomon R. Guggenheim Museum in New York City, his collection drew international attention. Representatives from several foreign countries approached Hirshhorn, offering to establish museums for the collection in their respective countries. However, in the mid-1960s, President Lyndon Johnson and Smithsonian secretary S. Dillon Ripley convinced Hirshhorn to donate his collection to the Smithsonian. In 1966 Congress established the Hirshhorn Museum and Sculpture Garden, to which the benefactor contributed more than 6,000 works. He continued to be an avid collector until his death in 1981. At that time, he bequeathed another 6,000 works to the museum.

A "Doughnut" on the Mall

Almost every new addition to the Mall has met with a certain degree of controversy, but the so-called "doughnut" by architect **Gordon Bunshaft** incited harsh criticism, since it was the first unabashedly modern building erected on the prestigious national showplace. Dillon Ripley said of Bunshaft's design, "If it were not controversial in almost every way, it would hardly qualify as a place to house contemporary art." Elevated on four piers, the drum-shaped, unadorned concrete building wraps around a fountain plaza that extends beneath the raised building, serving almost as a first floor. Gallery windows along the interior circumference overlook the plaza.

The Collection

Some 5,000 paintings, 3,000 pieces of sculpture and mixed media and 4,000 works on paper compose the collection,

Lee Stalsworth/Courtesy Hirshhorn Museum and Sculpture Garden, Smithsonian Institution

The Burghers of Calais (1953-1959) by Auguste Rodin

roughly five percent of which is on view at any one time. The core collection is continually being refined and updated by an active acquisition program.

Visit

🕐 *Open year-round daily 10am–5:30pm.* 🕐 *Closed Dec 25.* 👣 *Guided tours (45min) available daily 1pm, 2pm & 3pm. Sculpture garden tours May–Oct Mon–Sat 12:15pm; rest of the year Mon–Sat 10:30am.* ✖ *(outdoors)* ♿ ☎ *202-633-1000. www.hirshhorn.si.edu.*

Paintings

The paintings in the collection are organized chronologically, beginning with early-20C American works on the third floor. Among the artists featured here are such renowned painters as George Bellows and John Sloan, adherents of the Ashcan school; and prominent 20C artists Edward Hopper, Marsden Hartley, Max Weber, Stuart Davis and Georgia O'Keeffe, among others. The third-floor galleries devoted to European and American modernism feature paintings and three-dimensional works by Constantin Brancusi, Alberto Giacometti, Jean Arp, Joan Miró, Isamu Noguchi, Jean Dubuffet, Francis Bacon, Willem de Kooning, Mark Rothko, and Richard Diebenkorn and others.

Also on this floor is a gallery titled **Directions**, devoted to rotating exhibits that highlight the work of emerging contemporary artists.

The second-floor galleries are reserved for major special exhibits and a variety of small, changing exhibits of art from the permanent collection.

Contemporary art is housed on the underground level. Featured are works by proponents of Pop Art (Jasper Johns, Robert Rauschenberg, Andy Warhol and others), and representative works of more recent tendencies by a rotating group of artists, including Bruce Nauman, Anselm Kiefer and Damien Hirst.

Also staged in this space, as part of the museum's **Black Box** series, are film and video works by emerging international artists such as Magnus Wallin, Takeshi Murata, Rivane Neuenschwander and Mircea Cantor.

Sculpture Ambulatories

On the second and third floors, continuous galleries following the interior circumference of the building feature small sculptural works. The display begins on the second floor with such 19C European artists as Maillol, Rodin, Degas and Renoir. The Hirshhorn's collection of sculptures by **Henri Matisse** is particularly rich. The third-floor ambulatory is devoted to 20C sculpture by such masters as Pablo Picasso, Alberto Giacometti and Alexander Archipenko. The Hirshhorn possesses one of the country's most extensive collections of works by **Henry Moore** (1898-1986), with some 60 sculptures and 20 works on paper that represent the entire career of the celebrated British sculptor.

Outdoor Sculpture

The **plaza** on which the building stands is a showplace for monumental contemporary sculpture, including works by Alexander Calder, Claes Oldenburg, Tony Cragg and Juan Muñoz.

Smaller figurative works are featured in the sunken and walled **Sculpture Garden** *(across Jefferson Dr.)*. Prominent among these are the works of Rodin, including his monumental *Burghers of Calais*, and Maillol. Also on display are sculptures by Gaston Lachaise and Henry Moore, as well as a series of rare relief plaques by Matisse *(Backs)*.

The Hirshhorn recently acquired a new work by **Yoko Ono** titled *Wish Tree for Washington D.C., 2007*. A gift to the museum by the artist, the white-flowering Japanese dogwood is the only wish tree of 10 created for the Cherry Blossom Festival that will remain in the capital as a permanent installation.

NATIONAL ARCHIVES★★

CONSTITUTION AVE. BETWEEN 7TH AND 9TH STS. NW.
Ⓜ ARCHIVES OR FEDERAL TRIANGLE.

This imposing Classical Revival "temple" just off the Mall holds the nation's documentary treasures, including the Declaration of Independence, the Constitution and the Bill of Rights.

A Bit of History

A Strongbox for the Nation

Completed in 1937, the National Archives filled a pressing need for a central repository of official and historical records. Before this institution's establishment, each department of the federal government stored its own archival material. Important documents were frequently lost or damaged due to haphazard treatment. In 1921 a fire destroyed all of the 1890 census records. That loss, coupled with the Public Building Act of 1926, finally precipitated plans to construct a fireproof federal archives building. Today the National Archives and Records Administration, as it is officially designated, safeguards 5 billion paper documents, 9 million aerial photographs, 6 million still photographs and 300,000 video, film and sound recordings. The collection includes such varied items as letters from private individuals to US presidents, Commodore Matthew Perry's journals from his historic 19C mission to Japan, Civil War photographs by Mathew Brady and the photo albums of Hitler's mistress, Eva Braun.

The Building

The massive rectangular limestone building, designed by John Russell Pope to engender a sense of awe, occupies an entire city block. Corinthian colonnades embellish its four facades, and elaborate bas-relief pediments top the entrance porticoes on the north and south sides of the building.

Inside, a sweeping staircase leads visitors up to the entrance of the National Archives' **rotunda**. Popularly known as "the Shrine," the cavernous, 75ft-high, half-domed space with its coffered ceiling inspires reverence. It is here that the nation's most revered documents are permanently enshrined. In late 2004 the Archives opened The Public Vaults, a permanent, interactive exhibit that allows visitors access to the Archives' stacks.

Gwen Cannon/MICHELIN

National Archives seen from National Gallery of Art Sculpture Garden

The Rotunda

Visit

The Rotunda

Enter from Constitution Ave. 🕐*Open daily 10am-5:30pm (extended hours mid-Mar–Labor Day.* 🕐*Closed Thanksgiving Day & Dec 25.* 🚶‍*Guided tours (1hr) available Mon–Fri; 6-week advance reservations required.* ✕♿║║║ ☎866-272-6272. www. archives.gov.

On view are the country's esteemed documents known as the **Charters of Freedom**★★★: the **Declaration of Independence**, all four pages of the **Constitution**, and the **Bill of Rights**. These six fragile pieces of parchment are sealed in specially designed argon-filled cases of titanium and aluminum.

Fourteen other cases display historical documents relating to the development of the Charters. Two 34ft-long murals, painted in the 1930s by Barry Faulkner, adorn the walls on either side of the dais. The left mural, *The Declaration of Independence,* is Faulkner's fictitious depiction of Thomas Jefferson presenting a draft of the Declaration to John Hancock, while the Continental Congress looks on. *The Constitution*, on the right, shows another imagined scene of James Madison offering the final document to George Washington at the Constitutional Convention.

Research Facilities

Enter from Pennsylvania Ave. 🕐*Open year-round Mon–Fri 9am–5pm (check online for monthly extended hours).* 🕐*Closed major holidays.* 🆔*Must be 14 years of age or older and present photo ID to enter facility.* ✕♿ ☎ 866-272-6272. The National Archives functions as a major source of historical material for researchers from the US and abroad. The ornately paneled **Central Research Room** *(2nd floor)* serves visitors engaged in scholarly research. Among the holdings are the papers of the Continental Congress, court and congressional records, historical correspondence and records of federal agencies deemed to be of "enduring value."

The **Microfilm Research Room** *(ground floor)* serves persons engaged in genealogical research. It contains such materials as census, military service and pension records and ship passenger arrival lists. Pamphlets and staff offer instruction on how to trace family histories.

As of 1978 certain presidential papers were declared federal property and came under archival jurisdiction. Most are housed in separate presidential libraries administered by the National Archives. The **Nixon Watergate tapes**, kept in an archives facility in College Park, Maryland, are accessible to the public (🕐*shuttle buses to the facility leave from the Archives Mon–Fri on the hour 8am–5pm).*

NATIONAL MUSEUM OF AFRICAN ART★★

THE SMITHSONIAN QUADRANGLE AT 950 INDEPENDENCE AVE. SW.
Ⓜ SMITHSONIAN OR L'ENFANT PLAZA.

Originally located in a row of Capitol Hill town houses, the National Museum of African Art today occupies more spacious quarters in the underground Smithsonian Quadrangle complex. Devoted to the research, acquisition and display of traditional African arts, especially those of the sub-Saharan regions, the museum possesses a permanent collection of over 7,000 items.

Visit

🕐Open year-round daily 10am–5:30pm. 🕐Closed Dec 25. ♿ ☎202-633-4600. www.nmafa.si.edu. Obtain a floor plan from the information desk. ☺Only a small selection of the collection is exhibited at any particular time.

Collection Highlights

Pieces in bronze, copper, wood, ivory and fiber are exhibited on a rotating basis. The sculptures, utilitarian objects, architectural elements, decorative arts and textiles on display are organized by regions, thereby emphasizing how geography determines the selection of materials, as well as form and style. The museum's collection of **Royal Benin Art** from the historic West African kingdom of Benin (present-day Nigeria) includes several cast-copper alloy sculptures on permanent display. The ceremonial figures, heads, pendants and plaques were created between the 15C and 19C and reveal the elaborate rituals and ornate regalia of the Benin oba (king) and his entourage. Note especially the figure of an *oba* (19C); his regalia symbolizes his role as a divine ruler. A 16-17C carved ivory spoon, produced specifically for export, illustrates foreign influences on the style of Benin art.
Objects on display evidence the tremendous variety of shapes, proportions and designs present in African sculpture. Among the fine pieces that may be on display are initiation masks, woman-and-child figures created as icons of human perfection and fertility, and reliquary guardian figures. The permanent collection also includes a number of **ritual objects** that are believed to be conduits of communication with spirits. Medicinal figurines, arranged in a Chokwe fiber divination basket, play a significant role in the healing process. Finely sculpted Sherbo Bullom stone figures, like those owned by the museum, are still used by the Mende people of the Guinea coast to assure a good harvest. An Igala shrine figure was part of an altar created as an intermediary space between the spiritual and physical worlds.

Recent Acquisition

The museum's most significant acquisition in recent times is the 525-object **Walt Disney-Tishman African Art Collection**, a gift in 2005 by the Walt Disney World Co. Predominately masks and figures from west and central Africa, the collection was amassed by Paul and Ruth Tishman, beginning in 1959. They sold their holdings to the Walt Disney

Mask (Pwo), Chokwe Peoples, Zaire

Franko Khouri/National Museum of African Art, Smithsonian Institution

Company in 1984 in anticipation of its permanent display at Epcot; however, the collection was reserved for exhibit loans instead. Pieces on view at the museum include an exquisitely carved, late-15C ivory hunting horn from Sierra Leone; a carved 16C ivory armlet, rich in detail; a late 19C to early 20C wooden door of the Tsogo peoples, Gabon; and an early 20C crown fashioned of cloth, glass beads, iron and plant fiber from the Yoruba peoples in Nigeria.

NATIONAL MUSEUM OF AMERICAN HISTORY★★

CONSTITUTION AVE. BETWEEN 12TH AND 14TH STS. NW.
Ⓜ FEDERAL TRIANGLE OR SMITHSONIAN.
FLOOR PLAN OPPOSITE

The repository for such popular national icons as the Star-Spangled Banner, the boxing robe of "Rocky Balboa" and the First Ladies' gowns, this unique museum captures the essence of America by presenting the objects and ideas that have figured prominently in the nation's material and social development. The museum is closed until mid-2008 while undergoing a major architectural renovation and updating of infrastructure.

▶ **Orient Yourself:** The museum stands just east of the Washington Monument on the north side of the Mall. Use the floor plan below for inside the museum.
🅿 **Parking:** Downtown lots are blocks away; public transportation is preferable.
⊙ **Don't Miss:** The Star-Spangled Banner, the First Ladies and the American Presidency exhibits.
🕐 **Organizing Your Time:** Plan to spend at least 2hrs.
Ⓚⁱᵈˢ **Especially for Kids:** The hands-on science center and Icons of American Culture are particularly popular with children.

A Bit of History

Totaling more than 3 million objects, the museum's collections trace their origins to 1858, when the models from the US Patent Office were transferred to the Smithsonian Institution. Beginning in 1881, selections from this collection were exhibited in the Arts and Industries Building. To provide adequate space for the rapidly expanding collection of diverse artifacts illustrating America's scientific, cultural, political and technological achievements, the current marble structure was opened in 1964 as the National Museum of History and Technology. Renamed the National Museum of American History in 1980, this institution has in recent years committed itself to presenting issue-oriented exhibits that explore key events and social phenomena in American culture.

In September 2006, the museum closed for extensive architectural renovation and overhaul of infrastructure. A state-of-the-art gallery for the Star-Spangled Banner is being constructed. The museum's projected reopening is mid-2008.

Visit

☞*The museum is closed for renovation until summer 2008. During the renovation, some 150 objects from the historical collections are on view at the National Air and Space Museum.*
Ⓚⁱᵈˢ*Enter the museum from Constitution Ave. The following refer to customary opening hours.* 🕐*Open daily 10am–5:30pm (extended summer hrs).* 🕐*Closed Dec 25.* ☞*Guided tours (1hr) available.* ✗♿☎*202-633-1000. http://americanhistory.si.edu.*

NATIONAL MUSEUM OF AMERICAN HISTORY

THIRD FLOOR

SECOND FLOOR

FIRST FLOOR

Facts about the Flag

(the Star-Spangled Banner will be showcased in a new state-of-the art gallery)

Size: 30ft by 34ft (originally 30ft by 42ft).

Design: Fifteen hand-sewn white cotton five-pointed stars (approximately 24in wide) on blue field of English wool bunting. 15 handsewn stripes (8 red, 7 white, approximately 24in wide) of wool bunting.

Weight: 40-50 pounds.

Crafted by: Mrs. Mary Pickersgill of Baltimore.

Date: July–August 1813.

Features: The red V is of unknown origin and date. The irregular "fly edge" has resulted from the flag's snapping in the wind and from the cutting of pieces during the 1800s.

Jeff Tinsley/National Museum of American History

Star-Spangled Banner

Pre-Renovation Layout

First Floor

The **post office-general store** situated to the left of the entrance was constructed in Headsville, West Virginia and transferred to the museum in 1971.

A small exhibit, **A Material World: Testing Materials**, occupying a corner in the central gallery, displays the raw matter used to produce pencils and a machine that tests the strength of materials.

East Wing

The galleries in this wing illustrate the extent to which agriculture, transportation and power machinery made the "good life" possible in America.

The **John Bull** (1831) is the nation's oldest operable steam locomotive. This type of locomotive replaced the likes of the buckboard, the Concord coach, and the riverboat, all of which were too slow and too labor-intensive to satisfy the demands put upon them. Farm implements on display reflect the importance of **Agriculture** throughout the nation's development. Around the turn of the 19C, the wooden plow, the cradle scythe and the Holt combine gave way to internal combustion tractors. The advent of **"Old Red"** (1), the International Harvester mechanical cot-

ton picker, marked the end of the labor-intensive cotton industry and paved the way for modern large-scale farming.

American Maritime Enterprise retraces the evolution of sailing ships and offers a look at new forms of motive power—such as steam- and, later, gasoline-operated vessels.

America on the Move illustrates the history of US transportation, especially rail and automotive, and its impact. The 280-ton Pacific-type locomotive 1401 on view here was used by the Southern Railway between 1926 and 1951, when the age of steam came to its close. Automobiles such as the 1903 Winston touring car sent the horse-drawn wagon into retirement. **Lighting a Revolution** gives prominent coverage to Thomas Edison's inventions and presents the new motors and engines that sparked the industrialization process. **Engines of Change: The American Industrial Revolution 1790-l860** gives an overview of not only the machines but also the work habits and ideas that provided the impetus for the evolution from manual to industrial labor.

West Wing

Near the escalators in the West Wing stand three unassuming glass cases that nonetheless contain some of the most popular artifacts in the museum: **TV objects** such as Mr. Rogers' zippered red cardigan, Archie Bunker's threadbare armchair and the Fonz's leather jacket. **Science in American Life** highlights the country's scientific history from 1876 to the present. On display are over 1,000 instruments and appliances. Completing the exhibit are interactive videos, a hands-on science center and a biotechnology unit where a DNA game introduces children to the origin of life.

The **Information Age** explores the history of information transfer and its effects on American economy and society. Telegraphs dating from the 1840s, and Alexander Graham Bell's induction telephone (1876) are on view.

Second Floor

East Wing
The **Ceremonial Court** at the center of the East Wing replicates White House interiors as they appeared in the early 20C. **First Ladies: Political Role and Public Image** profiles the lives of White House wives and displays some of the inaugural gowns worn by them.

West Wing
Commissioned by Congress in 1832, Horatio Greenough's majestic **sculpture** (2) of George Washington looms at the end of the hall. **Field to Factory** is a dramatic chronicle of the African-American migration from the rural South to the industrialized North between 1915 and 1940. The popular **Star-Spangled Banner**★ exhibit allows visitors to observe the enormous flag (originally 30ft by 42ft) that was "still there" on the morning of September 14, 1814, after an intensive British bombardment of Fort McHenry in Baltimore during the War of 1812. In British custody during the attack, Francis Scott Key saw this flag still waving at dawn and penned the poem that was later set to music and, in 1931, proclaimed the national anthem of the United States of America. The adjacent

exhibit **Whatever Happened to Polio** celebrates the 50th anniversary of Jonas Salk's vaccine. The **Communities in a Changing Nation** exhibit explores the evolution of three American communities during the 19C. **Within These Walls** showcases a 240-year-old house from Ipswich, Massachusetts. Five families who once lived in the Georgian-style structure are profiled in the exhibit.

Third Floor

In **The American Presidency**★, 900 objects illustrate the winners' personalites: John Quincy Adams' chess set, Abe Lincoln's top hat, Warren Harding's silk pajamas, Teddy Roosevelt's chaps, and Bill Clinton's saxophone are some of the quirkier objects. Yet the star of this exhibit is the office itself, deemed by various holders "A Hell of a Job."

East Wing
This wing is devoted to **The Price of Freedom: Americans at War**. An overview of the country's military history and the armed services' role in society, the interactive exhibit includes such artifacts as George Washington's military commission from Congress and Andrew Jackson's War of 1812 uniform.

West Wing
In the hallway between the East and West wings is a selection the museum's 50,000-piece collection of quilts, looms and other sewing paraphernalia. Adjacent are several gigantic dollhouses. **Popular Culture**★ preserves in glass cases objects that have been immortalized by musicians and film stars, such as the red-sequined shoes worn by Judy Garland in the 1939 classic The *Wizard of Oz*. In **Printing and Graphic Arts**, a replica of an early-19C print shop holds the 1720 press (4) on which journeyman Benjamin Franklin may have worked. Jazz legends Duke Ellington and **Ella Fitzgerald** are honored in a tribute that includes sheet music and concert posters. A small collection of **musical instruments** is also on display.

NATIONAL MUSEUM OF NATURAL HISTORY★★

CONSTITUTION AVE. AT 10TH ST. NW.
Ⓜ SMITHSONIAN.
FLOOR PLAN P 124

This museum, part of the Smithsonian Institution, ranks as one of the most visited museums in the world. Two floors of exhibits and two large-format cinemas explore life on earth through clues nature has left behind—among them dinosaur skeletons, prehistoric fossils and gemstones, as well as artifacts of human cultures.

▸ **Orient Yourself:** The museum is located in the north center of the Mall. Use the floor plan to get your bearings within the museum.
🅿 **Parking:** Downtown lots are several blocks away; public transportation is preferable.
🅐 **Don't Miss:** The Gem and Mineral collection.
🕓 **Organizing Your Time:** Go first to the box office if you plan to see an IMAX show *(about 40min)*. Allow 2-3hrs to visit the museum. Take a break in the Atrium Cafe *(ground floor)* or Fossil Cafe *(first floor)*.
Kids Especially for Kids: Insect Zoo, Giant Squid exhibit,

A Bit Of History

Soon after the completion of the Arts and Industries Building (1881), more space was needed to accommodate the rapidly expanding Smithsonian collections. In 1903 Congress authorized the construction of the Smithsonian's third building, today known as the National Museum of Natural History. Designed by Hornblower and Marshall in the Classical Revival style, the original four-story granite structure faced with a seven-column entrance portico was completed in 1910. Its octagonal rotunda is 80ft in diameter and rises to a height of 124.15ft. The addition of the six-story east and west wings in 1963 and 1965 brought the building's footprint up to 16 acres. Today the museum encompasses 300,000sq ft of exhibit space and two large-format theaters, conserves 126 million specimens and provides laboratory facilities for 500 geologists, zoologists, botanists, anthropologists and paleontologists.

A new **Secret Life of Soils** exhibit will debut in 2008, and the new **Ocean Hall** is anticipated to be completed by late 2008.

Visit

Kids Enter from the Mall (Madison Dr.). Open year-round daily 10am–5:30pm (extended hours Mar–Aug). Closed Dec 25. Guided tours (75min) available Tue–Fri 10:30am & 1:30pm. ✕⚕ ☎202-633-1000. www.mnh.si.edu.

Theater

At the rear of the hall is the box office for the Samuel C. Johnson IMAX® theater. Shows last about 40min. *Tickets (☞$8.50) may be purchased up to two weeks in advance online or by phone: www.mnh.si.edu; ☎202-633-4629 or 877-932-4629.*

Some exhibits listed below may be temporarily relocated or not on view.

First Floor

The rotunda is dominated by a 13ft-tall **African bush elephant**, which weighed nearly 12 tons at its death in 1955 at the age of 50. Surrounding exhibits describe the sights and sounds of the savanna, home to creatures ranging from tiny dung beetles to giant elephants like this one.

Dinosaurs

"Hatcher," a **triceratops** skeleton, was created by 3-D computer modeling technology, which allowed scientists to show the 65- to 70-million-year-old dinosaur in a natural pose. The skeleton was discovered in Wyoming by bone collector John Bell Hatcher in 1891. Shown doing battle with **Tyrannosaurus rex**, Hatcher is also kept company by a 90ft **Diplodocus skeleton**, a life-size model of a **pterosaur**, a **Stegosaurus stenops** and four new casts of **pachycephalosaurs**, or bone-headed dinosaurs.

Fossil Galleries

Encircling galleries describe the parade of life from the big bang 4.6 billion years ago through the Cenozoic era, which began 65 million years ago and extends through the present. Evidence for many of the theories presented here lies in the fossil record. Stone imprints of microorganisms and stubby shoreline plants chart the first four billion years on earth, after which emerged a wild panoply of animals. In the Fossil Mammals gallery, a re-created 5ft **eryops** skeleton from the Permian era, a 50-million-year-old rhinocerous-like **uintatheres** skeleton and a large array of Oligocene mammals, including a mesohippus (tiny horse), are on view. The giant sea turtle and the massive mosasaur are highlights in the **Life in the Ancient Seas** gallery.

Ice Age Mammals

A brief presentation of glacial history precedes this display of fossilized mammal skeletons from the Pleistocene epoch, also known as the Ice Age. The woolly mammoth and the mastodon are both "cousins" of the elephant. The saber-toothed cat was recovered from Los Angeles' La Brea tar pits, where it met its sticky end along with more than one million other animals.

Mammals

In the Kenneth E. Behring Family Hall of Mammals, tall glass panels and cases offers the visitor an overview of the mammal class in all its diversity. Along with more familiar animals, the exhibit includes specimens of such exotic creatures as the jaguar, kinkajou, tapir, dingo, African civet, okapi and Chinese pangolin. Lifelike settings illustrate habitats and survival mechanisms (such as food gathering, migration and defense strategies) that either led these mammals to their present stage of development or caused them to perish. Mock thunder and lightning add a sense of realism.

African Voices

This large-scale exhibit uses film clips, recorded narratives, poetry excerpts and music, along with 400 artifacts from the museum's permanent collection, to explore African history. Starting from the west entrance, a path leads through the millennia, as human life takes form, the Nile cultures rise and

National Museum of Natural History, Smithsonian Institution

African Bush Elephant in the Rotunda

NATIONAL MUSEUM OF NATURAL HISTORY

SECOND FLOOR

FIRST FLOOR

Constitution Avenue Entrance

(Ground Floor)

THE MALL

fall, and tribal cultures spread across the continent, producing a wealth of traditions and arts. An *aqals*, or Somalian portable house, is on display, as is a stunning 8ft-tall antelope mask made of corn husks by the Chewa people of Malawi. Exhibits on more recent history tell African stories of survival and protest: the slave revolts of the 1800s; the 1960s independence movements in Congo, Nigeria, Senegal and Kenya; the successful fight against apartheid in South Africa; and the ongoing struggle against the AIDS epidemic.

Discovery Room

Open year-round Tue–Fri noon– 2:30pm, weekends 10:30am–3:30pm. This hands-on educational exhibit offers visitors the opportunity to touch and examine various objects and artifacts (fossils, minerals, and animals both living and preserved) that are representative of those found in the museum.

Ocean Hall

Projected opening late 2008. A large section at the rear of the first floor was closed in 2004 in preparation of the new 23,000ft Ocean Hall, with 52ft high ceilings. Featured exhibits will include the world's largest collection of marine specimens; a giant squid exhibit; a 1,500-gallon aquarium with a live coral reef; and 50ft model of a North Atlantic right whale hanging from the ceiling.

Second Floor

Geology Hall

The **gem and mineral collection**★★★ is housed in the Janet Annenberg Hooker Hall of Geology, Gems and Minerals. The largest blue diamond in the world at 45.5 carats, the legendary **Hope Diamond**, greets visitors. The 330-carat **Star of Asia** Sapphire from Sri Lanka and the 138.7-carat **Rosser Reeves Ruby** are among the finest in the collection. Set in a brooch containing 138 diamonds is the 75-carat **Hooker Emerald.** A flawless 127.88in Burma **quartz ball** and a headlight-size **golden topaz** from Brazil, the largest cut gemstone in the world at 22,892.5 carats, highlight the array. **Diamonds** on view show a remarkable range of sizes and colors, from the 253.7-carat **Oppenheimer Diamond**, which is uncut and unpolished, to the 2.9-carat pink beauty from Tanzania.

Large mineral samples as well as smaller interesting specimens are on view. Smithsonite, or zinc carbonate, was first identified by James Smithson, founder of the Smithsonian. Minerals are largely grouped in families of increasing chemical complexity or arranged by their places of origin.

Actual crystal pockets and ore veins are re-created in the **mine gallery**, and how earthquakes, mountain chains and volcanoes result from the movement of the earth's plates is illustrated in **plate tectonics.**

The **Moon, meteorites and the solar system** exhibit shows how moon rocks have contributed to our understanding of the solar system. Samples in the collection were brought to earth by astronauts on four different *Apollo* flights *(Apollo 14-17)*. Also on view are pieces of more than 150 meteorites, including a fragment of the 4.6 billion-year-old Allende meteorite.

Insect Zoo

The Insect Zoo is closed until fall 2007. Until then, visitors can hold insects in Bug Corner, across from the Discovery Room.

The arthropod group comprises 90 percent of animal life on earth. Many insects in the O. Orkin Insect Zoo exemplify the adaptations that have enabled arthropods to survive for 475 million years. Most are contained in low cases, enabling children to see physical details. Video monitors on a re-created 18ft African termite mound show the tiny builders at work. An ant farm forms a complete, small-scale society, and a beehive is equipped with an exit tube to the outdoors, allowing inhabitants to forage for food. *Tarantula feedings Tue–Fri 10:30am, 11:30am & 1:30pm; weekends 11:30am, 12:30pm & 1:30pm.*

Butterfly Exhibit

Opens November 2007. An enclosed pavilion holds a new permanent exhibit entitled **Butterflies and Plants: Partners in Evolution**, wherein living specimens and plants are spotlighted.

Korea Gallery

Korea's long history and remarkable culture are portrayed in this new permanent exhibit through themed sections. Topics cover such diverse interests as the family, the writing system, natural and constructed landscapes, and visual arts. Paintings, sculpture, ceramics, textiles and other works on display span the 6C BC to the present.

Western Cultures

The remainder of the exhibit space is devoted to dioramas illustrating aspects of Western civilization and prehistoric North America, as well as to bones of mammals and reptiles.

Butterfly Garden

Outside, on the 9th Street side, between the museum and the National Gallery of Art's Sculpture Garden, is the Smithsonian Butterfly Garden. Four separate habitats have been created—wetlands, woods, meadow and urban—to demonstrate butterflies' natural partners. Host plants for different species are labeled, and informative panels illustrate how visitors can make their gardens bee- and butterfly-friendly.

NATIONAL MUSEUM OF THE AMERICAN INDIAN★★

4TH ST. AND INDEPENDENCE AVE. SW.
Ⓜ FEDERAL CENTER.

Opened in September 2004, the National Museum of the American Indian (NMAI) is the first national museum dedicated to Native Americans and the first new museum on the Mall since 1987. Fifteen years in creation, the museum holds 800,000 objects that represent more than 1,000 indigenous cultures spanning some 10,000 years of North, South, and Central American history.

▶ **Orient Yourself:** Obtain a floor plan from the information desk as you enter.
🍽 **Don't Miss:** An opportunity to try indigenous food in the Mitsitam Cafe.
🕐 **Organizing Your Time:** Allow at least 90min for a visit if you eat in the cafe.

A Bit of History

The museum's holdings grew from the comprehensive collection of wealthy New York banker George Gustav Heye (1874–1957), which he amassed over a 45-year period. Heye was a member of the American Anthropological Association and the American Museum of Natural History; he was also a life fellow of the American Geographical Society, a fellow of the American Association for the Advancement of Science, and an honorary fellow of the Royal Anthropological Institute. His collection first opened to the public in 1922 in New York's Museum of the American Indian. Among NMAI's treasures are Northwestern wood carvings and masks, Plains Indians clothes and feather bonnets, Southwestern pottery and basketry, Costa Rican ceramics, Mayan jade objects, and Andean gold. Some 8,000 objects are on display at any given time.

Visit

🕐 *Open year-round daily 10am–5:30pm.* 🕐 *Closed Dec 25.* 🚶 *Guided tours (1hr) Mon–Fri 1:30pm & 3pm, weekends 11am, 1:30pm & 3pm.* ☎ *202-633-1000. www. americanindian.si.edu.*

Exterior

A curving golden-hued limestone exterior, suggesting a Native American cliff dwelling, stands in contrast to surrounding Classical-style buildings. The

National Museum of the American Indian

4.25-acre site includes wetlands and 40 boulders, enhancing the museum's emphasis on man as part of the natural world.

Interior

Inside, a prism window reflects sunlight into a 120-foot-high atrium, and a wall of video screens welcomes visitors in 150 native languages, indicating the vitality and diversity of Indian ways.

Major exhibits focus on such topics as native cosmologies, history from Indian points of view, and the lifestyles of 21C Indians. The **Our Universes** exhibit concentrates on philosophies related to the nature of the universe and to the relationship between humans and the natural world. In **Our Peoples**, the past 500 years of history is presented through the perspectives of the Seminoles of Florida, the Brazilian Tapirape, the Kiowa Tribe of Oklahoma, the Tohono O'odham Nation of Mexican Nahua, and the Wixaritari of Mexico. These various histories relate tribal struggles for survival in the face of European invasion. The **Our Lives** exhibit explores contemporary life in eight native communities ranging from the Igloolik of Canada to the Pamunkey of Virginia. Stories show

Native Lunch

The museum's **Mitsitam Cafe** continues the aboriginal theme with native cuisines from various regions. Indigenous, and often organic, ingredients are used where possible. Diners can try cedar-planked, fire-roasted salmon; chicken tamales wrapped in corn husks; pinto bean and corn enchiladas; or buffalo burgers and chile fries. For a drink, try the hibiscus flower aqua fresca and for dessert the cinnamon fry bread. "Mitsitam" is Piscataway for "let's eat."

how native languages, traditional arts, and cultural integrity have been kept alive in modern times.

Native dress, baskets and artifacts, displayed in glass cases *(3rd and 4th levels)*, can be researched on interactive touch screens in front of the cases.

A demonstration area in the atrium offers an opportunity to see native arts in action; the construction of an Inuit kayak or a Pueblo necklace, for example, gives context to the museum's exhibits.

US BOTANIC GARDEN★★

1ST ST. SW.
Ⓜ FEDERAL CENTER.

Situated at the foot of Capitol Hill, this conservatory serves as the nation's living plant museum and provides a pleasant respite from the activity of the Mall.

A Bit of History

This federally owned institution was chartered by Congress in 1818. The first greenhouse was established in 1842 to conserve the collection of exotic specimens brought from the South Seas by a team of US explorers. Originally located on the premises of the Patent Office Building, the collection was transferred to the Mall in 1850. The present conservatory, built in 1931, completed a four-year renovation in 2001. The garden features a skillful blend of two building

types traditionally used for storing and displaying plants: the 19C iron and glass

US Botanic Garden

greenhouse and the stone orangerie of French palace gardens, with its full-length arched windows.

Visit

Mall entrance on Maryland Ave. ⏱*Open year-round daily 10am–5pm.* ⚑*Guided tours available.* ♿ ☎*202-225-8333. www.usbg.gov.*
The garden court, the setting for seasonal floral exhibits, leads into a large glass pavilion with towering subtropical plants. The two smaller pavilions flanking this central space house flowering orchids, medicinal plants, desert flora, and a collection of cycad trees similar to those existing on earth 200 million years ago.

The park situated across Independence Avenue blooms with myriad seasonal flowering plants that provide a colorful setting for the cast-iron **Bartholdi Fountain**, executed by Frédéric-Auguste Bartholdi (1834-1904), sculptor of the Statue of Liberty.

US HOLOCAUST MEMORIAL MUSEUM★★

SOUTH OF INDEPENDENCE AVE. BETWEEN 14TH ST. AND RAOUL WALLENBERG PL. SW.
Ⓜ SMITHSONIAN.

A deeply moving, wholly absorbing history lesson awaits visitors to this large museum-research complex, conceived "to commemorate the dead and to educate the living." Occupying nearly 2 acres of land just off the Mall, the striking edifice houses a compelling permanent exhibit that focuses on the Nazi extermination of millions of Jews and others during World War II.

▶ **Orient Yourself:** The permanent exhibit covers three floors. Visitors take an elevator to the 4th floor and walk down through the exhibits to the 2nd floor.

🅿 **Parking:** There's a parking garage at 12th and C St., SW, east of the museum *($4/hr)*; hourly metered parking along Independence Ave. is 3 to 5 blocks away.

🕐 **Organizing Your Time:** Allow 2.5hrs to visit the museum.

🧒 **Especially for Kids:** "Daniel's Story: Remember the Children" is available for young visitors instead of the permanent exhibit.

A Bit of History

The Museum Takes Shape

In 1980 Congress chartered the United States Holocaust Memorial Council—the museum's governing body—and the federal government donated a museum site just south of the Washington Monument. Soon thereafter, the council began extensive fund-raising and international artifacts-collecting efforts. In 1986 the New York firm of I.M. Pei & Partners was chosen, with James Freed as principal architect, to design an appropriate structure. Construction commenced on the $90-million building in 1989, and the museum formally opened in 1993.

An Unconventional Building

Given the museum's highly charged subject matter, the challenge to design a suitable structure, able to match its powerful message with dignity and sensitivity, was immense. The main five-story brick and limestone building is a post-Modern "penitentiary," with its series of "watchtowers" lining the north and south walls. The exposed metal beams, railings and metal-framed glass doors of the building's 7,500sq ft glass-roofed central atrium, the **Hall of Witness**, amplify the feeling of imprisonment. The contrasting hexagonal, 6,000sq ft beige limestone annex *(located on the west side)* houses, on the second floor, the 60ft-high **Hall of Remembrance**, an unadorned, natural-light-filled space provided for quiet contemplation and commemorative ceremonies. Four nonrepresentational works by prominent artists were commissioned for the museum: wall art by Ellsworth Kelly and Sol LeWitt graces transition rooms between the floors of the permanent exhibit; Richard Serra's steel monolith anchors the atrium's lower staircase; and Joel Shapiro's monumental sculpture fronts the west entrance. The 250,000sq ft complex also contains an auditorium, a theater, museum shop, education center and learning center as well as temporary exhibit space.

Gwen Cannon/MICHELIN

US Holocaust Memorial Museum

Visit

🕐*Open early Apr–mid-Jun Tue & Thu 10am–7:50pm, Fri–Mon & Wed 10am–5:30pm. Rest of the year daily 10am–5:30pm.* 🕐*Closed Yom Kippur & Dec 25. Free timed passes, available at the box office on the day of visit, are required for the permanent exhibit; advance passes obtainable from Tickets.com (☎800-400-9373) carry a service charge.* ✖️♿ ☎202-488-0400. www.ushmm.org.
🔲*Daniel's Story: Remember the Children exhibit is for young visitors, in lieu of the permanent exhibit.*

Before entering the elevator, visitors are given a keepsake photo identification card containing the background and fate of a Holocaust victim.

In the darkened surroundings of the fourth floor are photographs, archival films and artifacts in the exhibit entitled Nazi Assault 1933-1939. Informative panels begin the tragic story of the calculated deprivation of the property, human rights, dignity and eventually the lives of nearly six million European Jews, and some five million others, including three million Soviet POWs, as well as Slavs (Czechs, Poles and Russians), Gypsies, communists, homosexuals, Jehovah's Witnesses and people with disabilities. The exhibit is augmented by documentaries, newspaper headlines, vintage newsreels, documents, letters and architectural casts. Two small theaters offer continuous showings of films on anti-Semitism *(14min)* and on the Nazi regime's rise to power *(13min)*.

Ghetto and concentration camp life is evoked on the third floor in Final Solution: 1940-1944. Personal articles, food and work implements are interspersed with an actual railcar, which visitors can walk through, and a scale model of a gas chamber. Especially sensitive topics are presented discreetly, for optional viewing, by way of sunken video monitors surrounded by chest-high walls. In Voices of Auschwitz visitors can listen in a glass-paneled sitting area to survivors' stories.

In Aftermath 1945 to the Present on the final floor of the permanent exhibit, the valor and success of various rescue and resistance efforts are hailed. Here, resistance fighters' weapons and hundreds of photos of rescuers, prison martyrs and survivors are on view, as are photos of "death" marches. Shown continuously is film footage recording the liberating armies' arrival at the camps, and the Nuremburg trials. A display is devoted to Raoul Wallenberg, the Swedish diplomat stationed in Budapest who led the War Refuge Board's mission to save Hungarian Jews. Near the exit a small, open theater presents filmed interviews with Holocaust survivors.

BUREAU OF ENGRAVING AND PRINTING ★

14TH AND C STS. SW.

Ⓜ SMITHSONIAN.

This nondescript 20C building at the foot of the 14th Street Bridge calls itself, justifiably, "the nation's money factory." Here, paper currency and many of the official documents issued by the US government are produced.

A Bit of History

Early Exchange

The most widely circulated currency during the colonial period was the Spanish *peso de 8 reales*, or "piece of eight." During the Revolution the hoarding of *reales* and other coins led to a shortage and consequently to the Continental Congress' issue of its own currency. Under the Articles of Confederation enacted after the war, the dollar was adopted as the unit of currency, but paper money was not issued until 1861 when noninterest bearing "demand notes" were first issued by the US government as an emergency measure to help pay the costs of the Civil War.

Growth of the Bureau

Functioning as a division within the Treasury Department, the Bureau initially consisted of four women and two men who, working in the basement of the Treasury Building, sealed and separated notes printed by private companies. By 1878 it was responsible for all currency printing. The green ink, chosen for one side of these bills because of its resistance to physical and chemical change, earned the notes the name "greenbacks." In 1880 the bureau moved into its own building, now part of the Department of Agriculture. In 1914 the Bureau moved to its current building, and in 1938 the annex building was constructed across 14th Street. Engraving facilities are now housed in the annex (⊶ *not open to the public*). The total floor space of bureau operations encompasses 30 acres. In addition to bills, these facilities also produce Executive and Treasury seals, official engravings of presidents and governmental buildings, presidential invitations and military certificates.

Visit

🐚 *Visit by guided tour (50min) only, May–Aug Mon–Fri 9am–10:45am, 12:30pm–3:45pm & 5pm–7pm. Rest of the year Mon–Fri 9am–10:45am, 12:30pm–2pm.* 🕐 *Closed Dec 25–Jan 1 & major holidays. Same-day free tickets from the kiosk (open 8am) on the bureau's west side (R. Wallenberg Pl.) are required Mar–Aug.* 👁 *It is advisable to pick up tickets before 11:30am. Congressional visits available (* 🕐 *Planning Your Trip).* 👤 ▥ ☎ *202-874-2330. www.moneyfactory.com.*

The entrance hall contains displays and a film *(7min)* on the history of currency and US paper-money production. The remainder of the tour leads past four processing rooms. In the first room, $20, $50 and $100 bills undergo the coloring process. In the second room, bills are printed by a process called intaglio printing, whereby impressions are made by pressing inked engravers' plates into the currency fabric, a blend of 75 percent cotton and 25 percent linen. Each fabric sheet holds 32 bills.

In the third area, sheets are trimmed and examined for imperfections. Any defective sheets, called "muts" (an abbreviation of mutilated) are shredded. However, 99.9 percent of the printed bills are without defect. The fourth processing room is devoted to printing Treasury seals and serial numbers on the bills. After this final printing the bills are cut, stacked and banded in preparation for their dispersal to the 12 Federal Reserve banks throughout the country. The tour ends in an exhibit hall displaying bills and historical materials.

SMITHSONIAN QUADRANGLE★

INDEPENDENCE AVE. BETWEEN 9TH AND 12TH STS. SW.
Ⓜ SMITHSONIAN OR L'ENFANT PLAZA.
DRAWING PP 132-133

Topped by a street-level garden, this underground complex occupies a prime site in the shadow of the Castle building. Opened in 1987, the quadrangle comprises two Smithsonian museums—the National Museum of African Art and the Arthur M. Sackler Gallery—and an education center, the S. Dillon Ripley Center.

A Bit of History

The Smithsonian Quadrangle is the brainchild of S. Dillon Ripley, secretary of the Smithsonian from 1964 to 1984. During his tenure Arthur Sackler pledged a portion of his Asian artifacts to the Smithsonian, but the institution lacked space for their display. Ripley also had to find a larger facility for the Museum of African Art (👆see entry heading). He spearheaded a project for an "international center of advanced study."

In 1982 Congress appropriated $36.5 million (about half the total cost) for the project. In 1983, construction began on the quadrangular site bordered by the Castle, the Freer Gallery and the Arts and Industries Building.

Visit

Enid A. Haupt Garden

🕐Open year-round daily 6:30am–dusk. 🕐 Closed Dec 25. 🐛 Guided tours May–Sept. Wed 1pm. ♿ ☎202-633-1000. www.si.edu.

This 4-acre garden, named after its New York benefactor, is a haven of antique benches, urn planters and 19C-style lampposts. The centerpiece is the ornamental parterre, adorned in 19C fashion with seasonal plantings. The iron and red-sandstone gate opening onto Independence Avenue is based on designs by James Renwick, architect of the Castle.

On either side of the gate stand entrance pavilions to the two underground museums. Behind the Sackler Gallery (👆see entry heading) pavilion is an intimate garden with a circle-in-square fountain, based on the Temple of Heaven in Beijing, and two 9ft pink granite "moon gates." Adjacent to the Museum of African Art pavilion are fountains and canals terminating in a *chadar*, or water wall, inspired by the Alhambra gardens in Granada, Spain.

Concourse

3rd underground level; accessible through the street-level kiosk situated between the Freer Gallery and the Castle. 🕐Open year-round daily 10am–5:30pm. 🕐Closed Dec 25. ☎202-633-1000. www.si.edu.

Visitors enter the glass-enclosed kiosk and descend one floor down a circular staircase, flooded with light from above. An escalator ride completes the descent to the third-level Ripley Center, where a passageway leads to an open concourse complete with trees and a fountain. A trompe-l'œil mural by Richard Haas dominates the eastern wall. Classrooms and offices line both sides of this airy concourse.

Kiosk
(access to concourse level)

★★ Freer Gallery of Art

1st level

← Freer Gallery
2nd level

3rd level

Arthur M. Sackler
Gallery ★★

Concourse

ARTS AND INDUSTRIES BUILDING

JEFFERSON DR. AT 9TH ST. SW.

Ⓜ SMITHSONIAN OR L'ENFANT PLAZA.

This 19C brick and Ohio sandstone building has long served the Smithsonian Institution as a storehouse for various collections and as a showcase for art, history, science and culture. ⚬━*The building is closed for renovation.* ♿ ☏*202-357-2700. www.si.edu.*

A Bit of History

In 1876 the US celebrated its centennial by hosting the nation's first world's fair, known as the International Exhibition, in Philadelphia. When it ended, 60 freight cars full of centennial exhibits were shipped to the Smithsonian. Congress authorized the construction of a national museum, now called the Arts and Indus-tries Building, on the Mall. Adolph Cluss designed the elaborate structure with four turreted wings radiating from a skylit fountained rotunda. Completed in 1881, the museum was the setting for President Garfield's inaugural ball.

A restoration undertaken for the 1976 Bicentennial celebration returned the building to its former glory.

The Castle

Arts and Industries Building

nid A.

ot Garden

National Museum of

African Art ★★

© 1989 Washington Post

THE CASTLE

SMITHSONIAN INSTITUTION BUILDING
JEFFERSON DR. AT 10TH ST. SW.
Ⓜ SMITHSONIAN.

The turreted red sandstone "castle" on the Mall has become the symbol of the
Smithsonian Institution. The building functions as a visitor information center
providing orientation to the Smithsonian's many museums and to other Washington sights.

A Bit of History

The Gift of an Englishman

The Smithsonian Institution is the brainchild of an Englishman who never visited
America: **James Smithson** (1765-1829),
an enlightened thinker and prominent
Oxford scientist. As the illegitimate son
of Elizabeth Macie and Hugh Smithson,
the first duke of Northumberland, James
Smithson spent the first 34 years of his
life as James Macie. Eventually the Brit-

ish Crown granted his petition to bear
the Smithson name.
Smithson wished to acknowledge blood
ties before all else, and he consequently
left his wealth to his only surviving
relative, a nephew. When the nephew
died in 1835 without descendants, the
remaining money went, as Smithson's
will had stipulated, to the US, "to found
at Washington, under the name of the
Smithsonian Institution, an Establish-

The Castle

ment for the increase and diffusion of knowledge."

A National Institution
Thanks primarily to the efforts of John Quincy Adams, Congress finally passed a bill establishing the Smithsonian Institution in 1846, thereby ending years of heated debate. The bill called for the formation of a board of regents that would include the chief justice of the Supreme Court, the vice president, members of both houses of Congress and private citizens. Smithson's assets were worth roughly $515,000 at the time.

In 1846 Congress appointed the respected American physicist Joseph Henry as the Smithsonian's first secretary. During his controversial 32-year tenure, Henry resolutely insisted on focusing the institution's role on scientific research rather than on museum development.

It was Henry's assistant secretary and successor, the biologist Spencer Fullerton Baird, who developed the Smithsonian as a federal institution of public exhibitions. Over the decades, the institution has grown through the generosity of major benefactors as well as the general public. Today it is the largest museum complex in the world. Exhibits range from Charles Lindbergh's plane, the *Spirit of St. Louis*, to Picasso's paintings to the Hope Diamond. In addition the institution administers the National Zoological Park.

Renwick's "Castle"
The Smithsonian's first building, an example of Romanesque Revival architecture, was designed by **James Renwick** in the late 1840s and completed in 1855 (renovated in 1989). Inspired by 12C Norman architecture, the asymmetrical building is topped with nine towers that soar above a battlemented cornice..

Visit

Open year-round daily 8:30am–5:30pm. Closed Dec 25. Guided tours (1hr) Mon & Fri 9:30am, Sat 9:30am & 10:30am, Sun 10:30am. 202-633-1000. www.si.edu.

The Castle's state-of-the-art **information center** features interactive touch screens and wall maps, as well as three-dimensional maps and an orientation film *(20min)* that summarizes each Smithsonian museum.

A crypt containing the body of James Smithson, which was moved here in 1904, lies in the north foyer. Located at the south entrance, the **Children's Room**, commissioned in 1899 by Smithsonian secretary Samuel Pierpont Langley, contains the original ceiling mural depicting a vine-covered arbor. The Castle also houses administrative offices.

For the best little places, follow the leader.

Looking for the latest news on today's best hotels and restaurants? Pick up the Michelin Guide and look for the Bib Gourmand and Bib Hotel symbols. With 45,000 addresses in Europe, in every category and price range, the perfect place to dine or stay is never far away.

THE MEMORIALS★★★

Offset by the graceful Tidal Basin and the Potomac River, the landscaping in the West Mall lends both grandeur and contemplative beauty to the memorials to presidents Washington, Jefferson and Lincoln. Skillfully positioned at major focal points of the city's monumental axes, these three memorials command striking vistas that further enhance their tremendous emotional impact. By contrast, the design of recent memorials often seeks to blend in with the existing landscape, making more subtle yet equally powerful statements.

- **Information:** National Park Service; 202-426-6841; www.nps.gov.
- ▶ **Orient Yourself:** The memorials lie in the western part of the Mall (west of 15th Street) and around the Tidal Basin. In this chapter, they are described in alphabetical order. Use the Map of Principal Sights to orient yourself.
- **Parking:** There is street parking along Ohio Dr. along the Potomac.
- **Don't Miss:** The memorials at night, aglow with lighting.
- **Organizing Your Time:** The memorials must be seen on foot: group them into two or three at one visit; then take a meal break or save some for another day. The park is open 24 hours a day. Park rangers are on duty to answer questions 9:30am to 11:30pm every day.

A Bit of History

The National Park Service administers what it has designated the National Mall and Memorial Parks: the sweep of national parkland that stretches from the Capitol building to the Potomac River, including the memorials. The centerpiece of **West Potomac Park** is the impressive **Reflecting Pool**, which stretches 350ft beyond the east facade of the Lincoln Memorial. Created in the 1970s, **Constitution Gardens**, with its 45 acres of landscaped grounds surrounding a pleasant pond, borders the pool to the north. The small island in the pond provides a placid setting for the semicircular memorial to the signers of the Declaration of Independence, which was dedicated in 1984. Discreetly positioned in the northwest corner of Constitution Gardens is "the Wall," a simple but revered black granite monument to America's soldiers who were killed or captured or remain missing in Vietnam. A classically inspired memorial (1924) to DC veterans graces the green expanse on the south side of the Reflecting Pool. The Korean War Veterans Memorial, also located south of the Reflecting Pool, was

dedicated in 1995, and the Franklin D. Roosevelt Memorial was completed in 1997. Two additional memorials, honoring Virginia statesman George Mason and World War II veterans, are the most recently completed memorials. Groundbreaking for a monument to Martin Luther King Jr. took place in November 2006. The memorial to Dr. King is scheduled to be completed in 2008 on a four-acre site in the northeast corner of the Tidal Basin near the Jefferson and Roosevelt memorials.

Encircling the Tidal Basin are the city's famous **Japanese cherry trees**★★ (generally in bloom late March or early April), which originated as a gift from the mayor of Tokyo to Washington, DC in 1912. In 1958 the Japanese presented the city with two additional gifts: a 17C granite lantern to commemorate Commodore Perry's voyage to Japan (1853-54) and a stone pagoda. Both objects now stand among the cherry trees on the west bank of the Tidal Basin.

East Potomac Park, the peninsula projecting southeast from the Tidal Basin, is also bordered by cherry trees. The park is devoted to general recreational uses.

Franklin Delano Roosevelt Memorial★★★

Tidal Basin, west of the Jefferson Memorial.

Situated on 7.5 acres bordering the Tidal Basin, this memorial to the nation's 32nd president combines sculpture, water and natural landscape to forge a dramatic setting for recounting the lifetime events and terms of office of Franklin D. Roosevelt (1882-1945).

In 1955 Congress authorized a commission to oversee the construction of a memorial to Roosevelt. The present site in West Potomac Park was set aside in 1959. After years of rejecting design submissions, the Commission of Fine Arts approved a design by Lawrence Halprin in 1978. In the 1980s Congress authorized construction and partial funding. The groundbreaking ceremony was held in September 1991, followed by a fund-raising drive to raise an additional $10 million from private sources for construction, which began in the fall of 1994. The memorial opened to the public in May 1997.

Visit

🕐*Open year-round 24 hours daily.* 🕐*Closed Dec 25.* 🚶*Guided tours (20min) available on request.* ♿ ☎*202-426-6841. www.nps.gov/fdrm.*
Ornamental plantings, trees, waterfalls and quiet pools lend a sense of tranquility and seclusion to this expansive memorial. Four outdoor galleries constructed of red South Dakota granite contain sculptured figures and cascading water walls designed to symbolize each of FDR's terms as president (1933-45). The First-Term Room (1933-37) symbolizes the dedication of the president and his determination to overcome the nation's economic problems with optimism and courage. A country in the depths of the Great Depression is represented in the Second-Term Room (1937-41). World War II's devastation

is symbolized by strategically placed, rough-hewn granite blocks in the Third-Term Room (1941-45). In the Fourth-Term Room (1945), a bronze bas-relief, *Funeral Cortege*, depicts the president's death, while a statue of Eleanor Roosevelt honors and commemorates her role as First Lady, champion for human rights, and first delegate to the United Nations.
President Bill Clinton dedicated an addition to the memorial in January 2001. A bronze statue, sculpted by Robert Graham and sited at the memorial's entrance, depicts FDR sitting in the wheelchair he designed and used daily after his crippling bout with polio in 1921. While the depiction of FDR in his wheelchair was met with great controversy, it was decided that the statue's demeanor emphasizes his indomitable spirit.

Jefferson Memorial★★★

South bank of Tidal Basin.

In a peaceful shaded spot on the south shore of the Tidal Basin, the nation's third president is commemorated with a 20C adaptation of the ancient Roman Pantheon. Inscribed on its marble walls are Jefferson's own writings concerning the role of government in safeguarding human liberties.

The Man

Statesman, architect, musician, inventor, horticulturalist, philosopher and president, **Thomas Jefferson** (1743-1826) was one of the country's greatest geniuses. He brought his talents to bear on many of the issues facing the new nation, helping to formulate its system of government, assisting in the planning of its capital city and developing such fundamental principles as public education and religious freedom. In 1962 President Kennedy paid Jefferson a lasting homage when he greeted a group of Nobel Prize winners by saying that they were "the most extraordinary collection of talent, of human knowledge, that has ever gathered together at the White House—with the possible

Jefferson Memorial

exception of when Thomas Jefferson dined alone."

Early Years

Born into a well-respected Virginia family, Jefferson spent his boyhood on the edge of what was then the Western frontier, in Albemarle County. His father, Peter, was a civil engineer and prominent local figure, serving as a justice of the peace, a colonel of the local militia and a member of the House of Burgesses. While a student at the College of William and Mary in Williamsburg, Virginia, young Tom turned his prodigious intellect to the study of the natural sciences, the arts and especially law, which he believed shaped the social and political conditions of man.

After studying law for five years with the famous Virginia jurist George Wythe, Jefferson practiced on his own for another seven years. In 1769 he was elected to the House of Burgesses and, while serving, participated in the colonists' protests against British taxation. In 1774 he was elected to the first Continental Congress in Philadelphia. At the second Continental Congress a year later, he was appointed to a five-man committee charged with drafting a statement to the British Crown that justified the colonists' stand on independence. Noted for his eloquent writings, Jefferson was encouraged by his fellow committee members to draft the document himself. On July 4, 1776, his Declaration of Independence was signed by the Continental Congress.

Serving the New Nation

In 1790 President Washington appointed Jefferson as the first secretary of State. Along with Washington, he was a major force behind implementing plans for the new federal city. It was also at this time that he became embroiled in his historic conflict with secretary of Treasury Alexander Hamilton. Their strident opposition to one another's views on the power of state versus federal governments under the Constitution led to the formation of a two-party political system. From 1797 to 1801 Jefferson served as vice president under John Adams before becoming the third US president, as well as the first to be inaugurated in Washington. During his two terms in office (1801-09), the US negotiated the Louisiana Purchase, effectively doubling the size of the country and strengthening its position in the international arena. The accession of this vast territory, which included lands west of the Mississippi purchased from France for $27,267,622, led to the country's westward expansion. Jefferson's administration also sponsored the Lewis and Clark expedition, which explored and charted this new land.

The Final Years

In 1809 Jefferson retired to his beloved Monticello, the domed plantation house he had designed in his elegant brand of Neoclassicism, outside Charlottesville, Virginia. Here, he pursued his long-cherished dream of founding an institution of public education. Jefferson personally conceived both the architecture and the educational approach for the University of Virginia in Charlottesville, which opened in 1825. On July 4, 1826—the 50th anniversary of the signing of the Declaration of Independence—Thomas Jefferson died at Monticello.

A Controversial Monument

In 1934 Congress enacted a resolution authorizing this memorial, which became the last in the city's triumvirate of presidential monuments along with those honoring Lincoln and Washington. From the beginning, the project was beset by controversy. John Russell Pope, the designer of numerous federal buildings in the capital city, planned the structure as an adaptation of the Pantheon in Rome, in deference to Jefferson's love of classical architecture. Critics demanded that a more contemporary architectural plan be used or that a utilitarian building, such as a national auditorium or stadium, be built instead of a monument. Ultimately Pope's design, though scaled down to half its initial size, triumphed.

The site lies on an axis with the White House, thus creating a monumental north-south perspective consistent with the spirit of L'Enfant's original plan for the city.

Visit

🕐 *Visitor facilities open year-round daily 8am–11:45pm;* 🕐 *closed Dec 25.* 🌿 *Guided tours (20min) available on request.* ♿ 🅿 ☎ *202-426-6841. www. nps.gov/thje.*

The wide, paved plaza in front of the monument along the Tidal Basin offers a sweeping **view** of the capital's famous cherry trees, which bloom around late March and early April. Stairs lead from the plaza to the monument's entrance portico, which supports a sculpted marble pediment depicting Jefferson surrounded by the four other members of the committee chosen to draft the Declaration of Independence (from left to right: Benjamin Franklin, John Adams, Jefferson, Roger Sherman and Robert Livingston).

Encircled by an Ionic colonnade, the open-air interior of the monument is dominated by a 19ft bronze **statue** of Jefferson by Rudulph Evans. Standing on a 6ft pedestal, the likeness of a middle-aged Jefferson, in knee breeches and a fur-collared coat, clutches a rolled parchment on which the Declaration of Independence is written. The four wall panels surrounding the statue are inscribed with Jefferson's writings, including portions of the Declaration of Independence, admonitions against slavery, and statements promoting religious freedom in government.

Situated near the Tidal Basin's inlet bridge, southwest of the Jefferson Memorial, the **George Mason Memorial Garden** commemorates the author of the first document in America to call for freedom of the press, religious tolerance, and other rights that citizens take for granted today. George Mason (1725-92) wrote the Virginia Declaration of Rights in 1776, and refused to put his name to the Constitution because it did not contain a Bill of Rights—a document added, largely due to his steadfast urging, in 1791. The memorial garden features a bronze statue of Mason seated beneath an arbor and flanked by stone walls inscribed with his words. A project of the regents of Gunston Hall Plantation, the garden was completed in 2002.

Korean War Veterans Memorial★★★

Independence Ave. at French Dr. SW.

Located southeast of the Lincoln Memorial, this compelling ensemble of statues, freestanding wall and circular pool honors the members of the US armed forces who served in the Korean War (1950-53). The $18 million memorial was funded by private contributions and dedicated in 1995 by President Bill Clinton and Kim Young Sam, president of the Republic of Korea at the time.

"The Forgotten War"

American veterans of the Cold War attached this sobriquet to a war they felt was overshadowed by the magnitude of World War II and the controversy of Vietnam. As memories of Korea faded from the national consciousness, veterans began pursuing a means to formally commemorate the war. In 1986 Congress authorized the American Battle Monuments Commission to oversee the design of a memorial, and in 1988 the current 2-acre site on the Mall was approved. A team of architects from Pennsylvania State University won the design competition in 1989 but withdrew from the project when reviewing agencies requested alterations. Washington, DC firm Cooper-Lecky Architects completed the project. The human figures were sculpted by Frank Gaylord and the granite "mural" was crafted by Louis Nelson. At the groundbreaking ceremony in 1992, President George Bush stated that the memorial's realization would assure that "no American will ever forget the test of freedom" faced by US troops. Of the 1.5 million Americans serving in the Korean War, more than 54,000 died, over 110,000 were captured or wounded and some 8,000 were declared missing.

Visit

🕐 *Open year-round daily.* 🕐 *Closed Dec 25.* 📞 *Guided tours (20min) available on request 8am–11:45pm.* ♿ ☎202-426-6841. www.nps.gov/kowa.

Nineteen larger-than-life stainless-steel statues (each about 7ft tall) of men wearing combat raingear stand in patrol formation within a triangular plot of junipers. One side of this "field" is lined with a 164ft-long wall of polished black granite, etched with the faces of more than 2,500 servicemen and women. The wall recalls the neighboring Vietnam Memorial, but it provides no written identification of those who lost their lives in the war. Mounted in the granite apex, an American flag stands guard over the dedicatory inscription: "Our nation honors her sons and daughters who answered the call to defend a country they never knew and a people they never met." A circular pool behind

the flagpole is interrupted by a lower, separate wall bearing the words "Freedom is not free." Etched on the rim of the pool, the statistics of the war's toll bear witness to this poignant summary.

Lincoln Memorial★★★

The Mall at 23rd St. NW.

From this stately memorial the famous marble likeness of a seated, brooding Lincoln stares across the Reflecting Pool to the Washington Monument and to the Capitol beyond. On the southwest side of the monument, Arlington Memorial Bridge serves as a symbolic link between Lincoln and the South's great hero, Robert E. Lee, whose home, Arlington House, overlooks the monument from the Virginia bluffs.

Preserver of the Union

Born in Kentucky in 1809 to a poor farming family, **Abraham Lincoln** (1809-65) was a self-educated, self-made man who became this country's 16th president and perhaps its most admired political hero. He is remembered by an affectionate public as "Honest Abe," the down-home, commonsensical statesman; as the Great Emancipator who ultimately freed the country of slavery; and as the president who fought a protracted civil war in order to keep the nation intact. Catapulted from state politics to the presidency, Lincoln was faced with a nation in turmoil even before he took the oath of office in March 1861. South Carolina, knowing Lincoln to be an opponent of slavery, seceded from the Union shortly after he was elected. Other southern states quickly followed suit. The month after Lincoln's inauguration, Confederate and Union troops exchanged fire at Fort Sumter, South Carolina. For the next four years, Lincoln waged a war to bring the Southern states back into the Union.

In 1863 he issued his renowned **Emancipation Proclamation**, decreeing that slaves in the Confederate states would thereafter be free. Though this was more a symbolic gesture than a real

Allison Simpson/MICHELIN

Lincoln Memorial

reversal of slavery nationwide, it helped set the stage for the eventual passage in 1865 of the 13th Amendment to the Constitution, which did in fact abolish slavery.

In April of 1865, at the start of Lincoln's second term, Robert E. Lee surrendered to Ulysses S. Grant at Appomattox, Virginia. With the long war over, the president turned his thoughts to the reconstruction of the South, but his plans of reconciliation were never realized. On April 14, 1865—five days after Lee's surrender—he was shot at Ford's Theatre by the actor John Wilkes Booth. The following day, at age 56, President Abraham Lincoln died of his wound.

An Anchor for the Mall

A congressional commission was established two years after Lincoln's death to plan a monument in his memory. It was not until 1901 that the McMillan Commission, with the backing of the Commission of Fine Arts, endorsed a memorial at the western end of the recently extended Mall.

Inspired by Greek architecture, the monument's designer, Henry Bacon, produced his version of a Doric temple, reminiscent of the Parthenon in Athens. However, Bacon positioned the main entrance on the long side of the structure, overlooking the Mall. Work began on the memorial in 1914; it was dedicated in 1922 in a ceremony attended by Robert Todd Lincoln, the president's only surviving son.

A National Forum

Over the years this monument epitomizing Lincoln's ideals has served as the forum for public protests and demonstrations. The acclaimed black opera singer Marian Anderson gave a historic outdoor concert here in 1939, after being refused permission to perform at the DAR's Constitution Hall. It was here in 1963 that Martin Luther King Jr. inspired a crowd of 200,000 with his famous "I Have a Dream" oratory. During the Vietnam War, President Richard Nixon paid an unofficial late-night visit to the protesters gathered here.

Visit

🕐*Visitor facilities open year-round daily 8am–11:45pm.* 🕐*Closed Dec 25.* 🔊*Guided tours (20min) available on request.* ♿ ☎202-426-6895. *www.nps. gov/linc.*

Reproduced on copper pennies and $5 bills, the facade of this building is easily identifiable. Thirty-six Doric columns form a continuous colonnade ringing the edifice and symbolize the states in the Union at the time of Lincoln's death. The names of the 36 states are inscribed in the entablature above the columns. The parapet crowning the structure is adorned with a frieze sculpted with bas-relief swags and bearing the names of

DISCOVERING WASHINGTON, DC

the 48 states that existed at the time the monument was completed.

Lincoln's craggy aspect comes into view as you ascend the long flight of marble stairs of the memorial. **Daniel Chester French** collaborated with Bacon to create a statue of Lincoln that would harmonize with the architecture. French's powerful marble **statue**★★★, 19ft high, depicts a contemplative Lincoln and captures the force of the man himself. The right wall is inscribed with Lincoln's second inaugural address and a mural by Jules Guerin, allegorically portraying the freeing of slaves. The Gettysburg Address (1863), the celebrated oratory that begins with the oft-quoted words "Four score and seven years ago," is chiseled into the left wall and topped by a similar Guerin mural showing the unity of the North and South.

The monument steps afford a **view**★★ of the Mall from the Reflecting Pool to the Washington Monument.

National World War II Memorial★★★

The Mall at 17th St. NW. Ⓜ *Smithsonian.*

The **National World War II Memorial** was dedicated on Memorial Day 2004. Encompassing 7.4 acres, it pays homage to the more than 400,000 Americans who lost their lives in what has been called the most devastating war in history. It also stands as a testament to all those who served in the American Armed Forces as well as those who contributed to the wartime effort at home.

In 1993 President Bill Clinton signed an act authorizing the establishment of the memorial; $195 million was received in private donations and $16 million from government sources. A symbolic groundbreaking took place on Veterans Day, November 11, 2000, and construction began in September 2001. Though its location has been hotly contested by those who believe it mars the open spaces and vistas of the Mall, the memorial itself is not under debate. Architect Friedrich St. Florian's design maintains 70 percent of the area as a parklike setting of water, grass and trees, with the remaining 30 percent as hard surface.

A War of World Proportions

The Second World War (1939-45) was fought on all but one of the seven continents and involved most of the world's powerful nations. Some 50 million people were killed, millions wounded and millions left homeless. In this global conflict, the Axis powers of Germany, Italy and Japan confronted the Allied Forces of Great Britain, France, the Soviet Union, China and a number of smaller nations, joined in 1941 by the United

World War II Memorial

States. By September 1945, the last surrender was signed; the Allies were finally victorious.

Visit

🕐*Visitor facilities open year-round 24 hours daily;* 🕐*closed Dec 25.* ♿ ☎ *202-426-6841. www.nps.gov/nwwm.*

At the 17th Street entrance to the memorial, a low-lying granite block, aligned with the Lincoln Memorial, is inscribed with a dedicatory message to "those 20C Americans" who struggled and sacrificed to preserve liberty. Bas-relief sculptures depicting wartime activities line the sidewalks leading down to an oval-shaped plaza. Larger than a football field, the plaza features a central pool graced with fountains. Flanking the plaza on the north and south, identical arched pavilions symbolize the Atlantic and Pacific theaters of the war. Each bearing a bronze wreath, 56 pillars representing US states and territories line the ends of the plaza. Backdropped by the Reflecting Pool, a Freedom Wall bears 4,000 gold stars, each star symbolic of 100 American war-related deaths.

Vietnam Veterans Memorial★★★

Constitution Gardens at Constitution Ave. and 22nd St. NW.

Though it was conceived in controversy, this long, solemn black wall has become one of the nation's most cherished and moving memorials. Tucked away in the sylvan setting of Constitution Gardens, it bears the names of all those killed or missing in the Vietnam War.

"Serenity, Without Conflict"

The impetus for this monument came from a small group of Vietnam veterans living in the capital. Troubled by the public's indifference toward those Americans who served in the Southeast Asian conflict, they formed the Vietnam Veterans Memorial Fund in 1979, soliciting congressional support and contri-

Vietnam Veterans Memorial

Gwen Cannon/MICHELIN

butions from individuals and corporate donors. In July 1980, President Jimmy Carter signed a joint congressional resolution authorizing the placement of the monument on a 2-acre plot in Constitution Gardens just northeast of the Lincoln Memorial.

The fund then held a national design competition for the memorial and appointed an eight-member jury of internationally-known artists and designers to judge the entries. Among the criteria was that it make no political statement about the Vietnam War. The competition attracted 1,421 entries. The winning design was submitted by **Maya Ying Lin**, a 21-year-old architectural student at Yale University. Lin's wall was conceived as a symbol of healing.

The Wall

Begun in March 1982, the monument, known as "the Wall," was completed and dedicated by November of the same year. Its abstract simplicity aroused controversy, and in an attempt to quell the dissatisfaction, a realistic sculpture by Frederick Hart was added nearby in 1984. The life-size work, portraying three young soldiers of different ethnic origins, is intended to commemorate all US military men who served in the conflict. However, the Wall quickly became accepted as the moving shrine it was intended to be, a place of healing where family and friends could touch the names of loved ones lost in battle.

Visit

🕐*Open year-round daily.* 🕐*Closed Dec 25.* 👥*Guided tours (20min) available on request 8am–11:45pm.* ♿ ☎*202-426-6841. www.nps.gov/vive. Directories specifying the memorial panels on which names appear are located at the approaches to the Wall.*

Inset in a low hill, the memorial is actually two triangular walls that join at a 125° angle, with their ends pointing toward the Washington Monument and the Lincoln Memorial. Composed of granite from Bangalore, India, they are intended to reflect the surroundings in their polished surface. The memorial extends 493.5ft in length and rises to a height of 10ft at its apex. The names of the more than 58,000 men and women incised in the Wall are arranged chronologically, beginning with the first casualty in 1959 and ending with the last in 1975 (more than 200 names were added in 1996). Those who died in the war are indicated by a diamond; those missing or imprisoned are denoted by a cross.

A grove of trees just south of the Wall is the site of the **Vietnam Women's Memorial.** Dedicated in 1993, it features a bronze statue (1992, Glenna Goodacre) nearly 7ft high depicting three military women tending a wounded male soldier. It stands as a memorial to the more than 265,000 women who served in the US armed forces in Vietnam.

Washington Monument Statistics

Height:	555ft 5 1/8in
Weight:	90,854 tons
Thickness at base:	15ft
Thickness at top:	18in
Width at base:	55ft 1 1/2in
Width at top:	34ft 5 1/2in
Depth of foundation:	36ft 10in
Cost:	$1,187,710

Washington Monument★★★

The Mall at 15th St. NW. Ⓜ *Smithsonian.*

The capital's most conspicuous landmark, and the world's tallest free-standing stone structure, this austere white marble obelisk rises from the middle of the Mall. Though it took nearly four decades to complete, the monument, stands as a commanding memorial to the man who was "first in the hearts of his countrymen," and as an indelible symbol of the city that bears his name.

Military Commander

Soldier, statesman and leader, **George Washington** (1732-99) began his long service to this country while in his early 20s, distinguishing himself as a commander during the French and Indian War in the 1750s. Following the war Washington served as a loyal British member of the Virginia House of Burgesses in Williamsburg, Virginia. However, as tension over British taxation grew among the colonists, Washington became increasingly disenchanted with the mother country. In 1774 he served as one of seven Virginia delegates to the Continental Congress in Philadelphia. A year later, at the second Continental Congress, he was unanimously elected head of the Continental Army. For eight years Washington spearheaded the fight against Britain, frequently keeping the war effort alive through the strength of his own convictions. In addition to battling the superior forces of the British, Washington had to contend with poorly trained troops, as well as a Congress reluctant to provide necessary funds or moral support. After countless setbacks and lost battles, the Continentals, thanks to Washington's military brilliance and the help of French allies, won a decisive victory against Lord Cornwallis' troops on October 19, 1781, at Yorktown, Virginia.

Father of the Nation

For six years, from 1783 to 1789, Washington enjoyed a respite from public life at his plantation, Mount Vernon, near Alexandria, Virginia. But in 1787, when growing anarchy and lack of centralized government threatened the new confederation of states, he presided over the Constitutional Congress in Philadelphia. Judicious and nonpartisan, Washington served as a stabilizing force that allowed the contentious delegates to arrive at a mutually acceptable Constitution for the young Republic. Two years later, in 1789, the new electoral college unanimously voted Washington the first president of the nation. On April 30, 1789, he took the oath of office on the steps of Federal Hall in New York City. Faced with defining the presidency, Washington proceeded cautiously. He managed to keep the young country out of European wars, and to establish federal authority over individual states and presidential authority over issues of foreign policy. He argued (unsuccessfully) against the adoption of a partisan political system, and he set a standard of ceremonial decorum for his office. He also approved and began construction of the new federal city that would bear his name. After eight years and two terms as president, he refused a third and in 1797 retired for a final time to Mount Vernon.

A Monument to the Man

In 1783 the Continental Congress passed a resolution to erect an equestrian statue honoring the hero of the Revolution. Lack of funds delayed the project for decades. Finally, in 1833, a group of prominent citizens formed the Washington National Monument Society. Having raised $28,000 by 1836, the group held a contest to choose a design for the monument. The well-respected architect **Robert Mills** won. The cornerstone was laid July 4, 1848.

Progress was slow due to insufficient funding. Work ceased when the funds finally ran dry in 1853, leaving the monument a truncated 152ft shaft that languished in neglect for nearly 25 years, until President Ulysses S. Grant approved

Washington Monument seen from Constitution Gardens

Gwen Cannon/MICHELIN

an act authorizing the federal government to complete the project. Dedicated on February 21, 1885, the monument opened to the public in 1888.

Visit

🕐*Open year-round daily 9am–4:45pm.* 🕐*Closed Dec 25. Timed tickets (free) are required year-round and can be obtained from the 15th St. kiosk. Advance tickets obtainable from the National Park Reservation Service (☎ 877-444-6777) carry a service charge.* 🚶*Guided tours (1hr) available weekends 10am & 2pm (phone the day of your tour).* ♿ 🅿 ⚟ ☎202-426-6841. www.nps.gov/wamo.*

A state-of-the-art elevator makes a 70-second ascent from the ground to the observation room at the summit of the monument. Eight small windows afford the best **panorama**★★★ of the city. The south-facing windows overlook the Tidal Basin and the Jefferson Memorial; the western view highlights the Reflecting Pool and the Lincoln Memorial; the north faces the Ellipse and the White House; and the east overlooks the long stretch of Mall ending at the Capitol. Photographs above the windows reproduce the views and identify major landmarks.

WHITE HOUSE AREA★★★

Inspired by the stately presence of the Executive Mansion, this area maintains a decorous gentility, with manicured parks, elegant row houses and grandly conceived public structures.

▶ **Orient Yourself:** Area attractions form a horseshoe around the White House and Ellipse, with Lafayette park at the top. Make your first stop the White House Visitor Center.

▣ **Parking:** Garages on New York and Pennsylvania Aves. and 17th and 18th Sts.

☺ **Don't Miss:** The view of the White House from Lafayette Park, pew 54 in St. John's Church, and the Corcoran and the Renwick galleries.

🕐 **Organizing Your Time:** Allow 3hrs. The White House tour takes less than 1hr.

A Bit of History

Lafayette Square

In the early 19C, Jefferson ordered Pennsylvania Avenue extended in front of the still incomplete White House. The 7-acre plot to the north of it became a public park known as President's Square. In 1824 the park was renamed Lafayette Square to honor America's French ally in the Revolution, the Marquis de Lafayette. That same year **Blair House** (no. 1651) was built on Pennsylvania Avenue. Today it serves as an official guest house for foreign dignitaries (⚠ not open to the public). An equestrian statue of Andrew Jackson stands in the center of the park; other statues are of foreign heroes of the American Revolution: Lafayette (1891, southeast corner); Jean-Baptiste Rochambeau (1902, southwest corner); Friedrich von Steuben (1910, northwest corner); and Thaddeus Kosciuszko (1910, northeast corner). Following the Civil War, the first major landscaping of the park was carried out in keeping with an 1850s design prepared by Andrew Jackson Downing.

Lafayette Square and the Ellipse (below) have been integrated into a **President's Park**, which includes plazas, paved walkways, plantings and outdoor seating.

Grandiose Buildings

Though work began on the White House in 1792, the building evolved gradually. On its east side is the stately Treasury Building, completed in 1869. To the west is the colossal Old Executive Office Building, completed in 1881.

In the late 19C and early 20C, the 17th Street corridor south of the White House witnessed the construction of several dignified buildings, including the Corcoran Gallery of Art, the headquarters for the American Red Cross, the Daughters of the American Revolution complex and the Organization of American States.

From "White Lot" to Ellipse

South of the White House, the open expanse of ground called the **Ellipse** was once marshy lowland. During the Civil War, military livestock was enclosed here behind a whitewashed fence that gave rise to the designation "white lot." In the late 19C the area was reclaimed. At the corner of Constitution Avenue and 17th Street, a stone **lock keeper's house** still stands as a reminder of the Washington Canal. Across the avenue, on either side of the Ellipse, are a pair of gatehouses, designed by Charles Bulfinch, that once stood on the Capitol grounds.

In the mid-20C, the Ellipse became a ceremonial grounds for the White House. On its north side is the **Zero Milestone**, from which all distances in the federal city are computed. Also here is the **National Christmas Tree**, a blue spruce planted during Jimmy Carter's presidency.

WHITE HOUSE★★★

1600 PENNSYLVANIA AVE. NW.

Ⓜ MCPHERSON SQUARE, METRO CENTER, OR FEDERAL TRIANGLE.

For almost two centuries the White House has been the home of America's first families. More than just an official residence, the stately structure has become a universally recognized symbol of the US presidency. Today its public rooms house an exemplary collection of Americana, both furnishings and historic memorabilia, reflecting the tastes of the nation's leaders.

🛈 **Information:** White House Visitor Center; ☎202-456-7041; www.whitehouse.gov.

▶ **Orient Yourself:** Stop first at the White House Visitor Center, just east of the Ellipse, on E Street at 15th in the Commerce Building (🖢 *see below*).

🅿 **Parking:** No street parking is available near the White House.

A Bit of History

The President's Palace

L'Enfant had envisioned the "President's house" as a grand palatial structure, five times its current size, but after the Frenchman's dismissal in 1792, a design competition for the official residence was held. The $500 prize went to **James Hoban**, a young Irish builder. His plan called for a three-story stone structure reminiscent of a Georgian manor, with a hipped roof surrounded by a balustrade. The main facade featured a columned portico with an eagle carved in the pediment.

The cornerstone was laid on October 13, 1792, but due to a lack of skilled labor and public funds, the work proceeded slowly. Faced with financial challenges, the city commissioners approached President Washington with a plan to reduce the mansion's dimensions. In October 1793 Washington compromised by agreeing to omit the third floor, and Hoban redrew plans for a two-story building. (It was not until 1927 that a third floor was actually added to create additional living quarters.)

First Occupants

The structure was not completed during Washington's presidency. In November 1800 the second president, **John Adams** (1797-1801), became the first president to occupy the mansion. Though conditions in the still incomplete house were drafty and unpleasant, Adams none-

The White House

© Brigitta L. House/MICHELIN

theless left a lasting benediction on it. After his first night there, he wrote, "May none but honest and wise men ever rule under this roof!"

Thomas Jefferson, the mansion's first long-term resident (1801-09), turned his architectural attentions to the design of the White House, as the whitewashed sandstone building had come to be known. Collaborating with his surveyor of public buildings, **Benjamin H. Latrobe**, Jefferson designed colonnaded wings on the east and west sides to house domestic and office spaces. Latrobe also replaced the mansion's heavy slate and mortar roof with a lighter one of steel.

Fire and Reconstruction

James Madison's stay in the Executive Mansion (1809-17) was marked by disaster. In August 1814, during the War of 1812, the British entered the city and set fire to several public buildings, among them the White House. Thanks to the forethought of Mrs. Dolley Madison, many important documents, as well as a Gilbert Stuart portrait of George Washington that now hangs in the East Room, were saved from destruction. Had a summer rain not put out the fire, the mansion might have burned to the ground. The city commissioners called on James Hoban to salvage the mansion; he demolished weakened stone walls and began rebuilding. In 1818 President James Monroe was able to occupy the house. During his administration (1817-25) the south portico was added, and the French Empire pieces that remain at the core of the White House's historic furniture collection were acquired.

Throughout the 19C, architectural changes and redecorating occurred as funds were available. In order to customize the house to his own taste, a new president frequently resorted to raising funds by selling old furnishings at public auction. Congressional appropriations for the upkeep and refurbishing of the chief executive's home were generally dependent on the political and economic climate. During the popular administration of Andrew Jackson (1829-37), for example, bountiful funds allowed for the purchase of new china and glassware,

the installation of indoor plumbing and the completion of the north portico. In other administrations, however, furnishings became seriously dilapidated. During James Polk's tenure (1845-49), gas lights were added and long-term interior transformations were initiated. Chester A. Arthur (1881-85) undertook a major refurnishing of the mansion in 1882. According to contemporary reports, he had 24 wagonloads of old furniture carted away for public auction. He then called on the celebrated New York designer Louis C. Tiffany to redecorate the interior. Electricity was installed in the White House in 1891.

20C

In 1902 vast changes were again wrought on the mansion by Theodore Roosevelt (1901-09), who entrusted the prominent architectural firm McKim, Mead and White with large-scale renovation. The extensive greenhouses that had flanked the west and south sides of the house for decades were demolished. The west wing was added and an expansive carriage porch built on the east. The interior, whose old plumbing, wiring, heating and flooring were in dangerous disrepair, was revamped and modernized. The Roosevelt renovation began the process of restoring the White House to its original appearance—a process that has been continued by succeeding presidents. In 1942, while Franklin D. Roosevelt was in residence (1933-45), the current east wing was built. Under Roosevelt's successor, Harry S. Truman (1945-53), another major structural renovation was undertaken to shore up and replace the weakened flooring, walls and foundations. The second-story balcony was added to the south portico during the Truman presidency.

During her stay in the White House (1961-63), Jacqueline Kennedy began a campaign to acquire items of historic and artistic interest. Following her precedent, in 1964 President Lyndon Johnson (1963-69) established the Committee for the Preservation of the White House, which provided for a permanent curator. The curatorial staff today continues to expand and document the White House collection.

Visiting the White House

White House Visitor Center

15th and E Sts. NW. ◷*Open year-round daily 7:30am–4pm.* ◷ *Closed Jan 1, Thanksgiving Day & Dec 25.* &.☎202-456-7041. www.whitehouse.gov.

Housed in the spacious, ground-floor Baldrige Hall in the Commerce Building, the center features an information booth staffed by National Park Service rangers, displays and a souvenir sales area. Obtain a map of the White House area to familiarize yourself with the grounds and entrance gates. If you have time, see the 30min film titled *Where History Lives.*

White House Tours

☜Visit by group (10 people minimum) tour only. Submit your request up to six months in advance through members of Congress, or if a foreign national, the American Embassy in one's country two months in advance (&see Congressional Visits). ⊜As the White House may close without advance notice for official functions, phone the 24hr information line the morning of your visit for current tour information ☎202-456-7041.

Tour

◷*Visit by advance reservation only (&see above), Tue–Sat 7:30am–12:30pm.* &.☎202-208-1631. www.whitehouse.gov.
The White House is set off by 18 acres of flower gardens, lawns and trees *(grounds not included on tour).* A balustraded roofline, Ionic pilasters and windows with alternating rounded and triangular pediments adorn the rectangular facade of the main structure. The columned and balconied south portico extends out in an expansive bay overlooking the sweep of the south lawn and the Ellipse beyond. The colonnade of the north portico facing Pennsylvania Avenue and Lafayette Park supports an unadorned pediment. Elaborate carvings grace the area above the fanlight of the double entrance doors. Pavilions connect the one-story east and west wings to the main mansion. The west wing (○━ *not open to the public)* houses the Cabinet Room, several staff and reception rooms, and the president's Oval Office, which opens onto the Rose Garden.

In the mansion, the ground-floor and first-floor rooms function as formal state reception areas, while the first family's private living quarters are located on the second and third floors.

Ground Floor

Visitors first enter a security building on East Executive Ave.

In the paneled entrance hall of the east wing, as elsewhere in the mansion, portraits of first ladies and presidents adorn the walls. A glassed colonnade overlooking the intimate **Jacqueline Kennedy Garden** displays exhibit panels explaining the history of the White House. Portraits of recent first ladies hang in an elegant vaulted marble corridor, and a large Sheraton breakfront holds an assortment of presidential porcelains. The **library**, which opens off the right side of the hall, is decorated in late Federal style and contains some 2,700 volumes. The **Vermeil Room**, situated directly across the hall, is so named for its collection of French and English gilded silver, or vermeil, dating from the 17C to the early 20C.

First Floor

The vast and ornate **East Room**, the setting for White House concerts, dances and official ceremonies, contains elaborate plaster ceiling decorations and entablatures, fluted pilasters, Bohemian cut-glass chandeliers and four marble mantels. Because it is used for a variety of purposes, the gold and white room is sparsely furnished. The legendary 1797 **portrait of George Washington** that Dolley Madison saved hangs in this room. The small drawing room off the East Room is known as the **Green Room**, owing to the color scheme it has retained since the days of President John Quincy Adams (1825-29). An intricately patterned Turkish Hereke carpet complements the room's green watered-silk wall coverings and the tones of the upholstered Sheraton-style chairs and settees, many from the early-19C work-

State Dining Room

North Entrance Ha

Red Room

Blue Room

South Portico

Diploma
Recepti
Room

White House Receptions Rooms

Second and Third Floors
(reserved for the Presidential family)

ss Hall

en Room

East Room

ina Room

Library

Vermeil
Room

Entrance

Jacqueline Kennedy
Garden

(drawing) by R.W. Nicholson / c White House Historical Assoc.

Presidents of the United States of America

President	Years	President	Years
George Washington	1789-1797	Grover Cleveland	1885-1889
John Adams	1797-1801		1893-1897
Thomas Jefferson	1801-1809	Benjamin Harrison	1889-1893
James Madison	1809-1817	William McKinley	1897-1901
James Monroe	1817-1825	Theodore Roosevelt	1901-1909
John Quincy Adams	1825-1829	William H. Taft	1909 1913
Andrew Jackson	1829-1837	Woodrow Wilson	1913-1921
Martin Van Buren	1837-1841	Warren G. Harding	1921-1923
William Henry Harrison	1841	Calvin Coolidge	1923-1929
John Tyler	1841-1845	Herbert Hoover	1929-1933
James K. Polk	1845-1849	Franklin D. Roosevelt	1933-1945
Zachary Taylor	1849-1850	Harry S. Truman	1945-1953
Millard Fillmore	1850-1853	Dwight D. Eisenhower	1953-1961
Franklin Pierce	1853-1857	John F. Kennedy	1961-1963
James Buchanan	1857-1861	Lyndon B. Johnson	1963-1969
Abraham Lincoln	1861-1865	Richard M. Nixon	1969-1974
Andrew Johnson	1865-1869	Gerald R. Ford	1974-1977
Ulysses S. Grant	1869-1877	James Carter	1977-1981
Rutherford B. Hayes	1877-1881	Ronald Reagan	1981-1989
James A. Garfield	1881	George H. Bush	1989-1993
Chester A. Arthur	1881-1885	William J. Clinton	1993-2000
		George W. Bush	2001-

shop of Duncan Phyfe. On the dropleaf sofa table is the silver-plated coffee urn that John Adams considered one of his "most prized possessions."

The French Empire furnishings in the elliptical **Blue Room** include seven of the original Bellange gilded armchairs ordered from Paris by James Monroe. The gilded wood chandelier and Carrara marble mantel contain classical motifs mirrored in the wallpaper frieze that forms a border around the wainscoting and entablature. Portraits of the first presidents to live in the house are among the paintings hanging in this reception room. The three long casement windows afford a striking **view** of the Washington Monument and the Jefferson Memorial beyond. From this standpoint the visitor can easily discern the extent to which the Washington Monument is positioned off the axis that links the White House with the Jefferson Memorial. The small parlor known as the **Red Room** also contains French Empire-style furnishings prevalent from 1810 to 1830, including gilded chairs upholstered in red and gold damask. Displayed on the wall between the windows is a bust by

Hiram Powers of President Martin Van Buren (1837-41). Above the fireplace hangs a painting depicting Van Buren's daughter-in-law and official hostess, Angelica. Note that the bust is featured in the painting.

In the gold and white **State Dining Room**, the Neoclassical pilaster, wall paneling and ceiling molding are modeled on decor found in late-18C English estates. Gold upholstered Queen Anne-style chairs surround the long mahogany dining table, which holds the gilded plateau from a service ordered by James Monroe.

Over the mantel is the Lincoln portrait executed by George P.A. Healy in 1869. Marble-topped side tables with gilded eagle pedestals rim the room. When prepared for a state dinner, this room can seat 140 people.

Marble columns separate the long **Cross Hall** from the North Entrance Hall. Both halls are hung with portraits of recent presidents. The carpeted marble staircase, connecting the state rooms to the first family's private quarters, is frequently used by the president and first lady to make ceremonial entrances.

CORCORAN GALLERY OF ART★★

17TH ST. AND NEW YORK AVE. NW.
Ⓜ FARRAGUT WEST OR FARRAGUT NORTH.

In a city now dominated by federal museums, the Corcoran Gallery of Art can claim to be the capital's oldest institution and its most venerable private gallery. Although it houses a fine collection of European art, the Corcoran is primarily known as a showcase for American art.

🄸 **Information:** ☎202-639-1700. www.corcoran.org.

A Bit of History

A self-made man, self-educated connoisseur and philanthropist, **William Wilson Corcoran** (1798-1888) halted construction of a museum to house his private collection in 1861, when he left wartime Washington. His Southern sympathies had made him unwelcome. Upon his return in 1865, the building, now the Renwick Gallery, was completed and opened as one of the first major galleries of art in 1874.

In 1897 a larger building (Ernest Flagg) opened several blocks south to hold the expanded 700-work collection. Frank Lloyd Wright considered it "the best designed building in Washington."

Highlights

🕑 *Open year-round Sun, Mon & Wed 10am–6pm, Thu 10am–9pm, Fri–Sat 10am–5pm.* 🕑 *Closed Jan 1, Thanksgiving Day & Dec 25.* 🎫$14. 🍴♿ ☎202-639-1700. www.corcoran.org. 🄳*Exhibits change frequently, as do the specific locations of pieces of art within the museum.*

First Floor.

One of the Corcoran's best-known works, Hiram Powers' nude sculpture **The Greek Slave** (1846) *(second floor),* scandalized Victorian audiences when it was first shown in the Renwick Gallery. In a gallery off the far end of the south atrium, Rembrandt Peale's *Washington Before Yorktown* (1825) dominates an entire wall. The **Salon Doré** was bequeathed to the Corcoran by Senator William Clark of Montana. Appointed with gilded woodwork, the salon is considered one of the country's finest French-Rococo interiors.

Second Floor

Highlights include *The Old House of Representatives* (1822) by Samuel F.B. Morse, inventor of the Morse code, and Frederic Edwin Church's **Niagara** (1857). In the third gallery are Thomas Eakins' genre painting **The Pathetic Song** and John Singer Sargent's painting of **Madame Edouard Pailleron** (1879).

The works of John Sloan, Robert Henri and George Bellows reflect the **Ashcan school** of early-20C realism. *Into Bondage* by Aaron Douglas is part of the Tibbs collection of African-American art.

Niagara (1857) by Frederic Edwin Church

Courtesy Corcoran Gallery of Art

DAUGHTERS OF THE AMERICAN REVOLUTION★

17TH AND D STS. NW.

🚇 FARRAGUT WEST.

This stately complex occupies an entire city block and is reputedly the world's largest group of structures owned and maintained exclusively by women. The national headquarters of the Daughters of the American Revolution (DAR), it houses an extensive collection of genealogical materials and artifacts relating to the colonial and early Republic periods through the mid-19C.

A Bit of History

The DAR was established in 1890 by a group of women who were descended from Revolutionary War patriots. The organization has achieved a national reputation for perpetuating "the memory and spirit of the men and women who achieved American independence." Today it is supported by 168,000 members belonging to chapters throughout the US.

The Beaux-Arts edifice known as **Memorial Continental Hall** was designed at the turn of the 19C by Edward Pearce Casey, who also collaborated on the construction of the Library of Congress. Facing the Ellipse, the original entrance is dominated by a porte-cochère, or carriage entry, covered by a pedimented roof. The semicircular portico that rises from the balustraded terrace on the C Street side features 13 columns, representing the 13 colonies. In the 1920s, having outgrown its original building, the DAR commissioned John Russell Pope to design **Constitution Hall**, a colossal structure whose columned, pedimented entrance faces 18th Street. The building contains a U-shaped, 3,800-seat auditorium, where the Daughters meet for their annual convention. In addition, the hall functions as a public auditorium where a variety of concerts and lectures are held.

Visit

🕐 *Museum open year-round Mon–Fri 9:30am–4pm, Sat 9am–5pm. Period rooms open year-round Mon–Fri 10am–2:30pm, Sat 9am–4:30pm.* 🕐 *Closed major holidays and 2 weeks in late Jun.* 🔊 *Guided tours available.* ♿ ☎202-628-1776. www.dar.org.

Memorial Continental Hall houses 33 **period rooms** depicting scenes of early American life, including a colonial home, tavern, church and other historical interiors dating from the late 17C to the mid-19C. Of note are the Georgia Room, portraying the late-18C Peter Tondee Tavern in Savannah; the brick-floored Oklahoma kitchen; and the Virginia room, reproducing an 18C dining room.

The original meeting hall, an enormous room overhung by a vaulted skylight and elaborate Neoclassical trim, is now the DAR library, a renowned repository of genealogical material. The **DAR Museum** regularly displays ceramics, silver, glass and textiles.

Additional pieces from the permanent collection of more than 30,000 objects are placed on view in changing exhibits. Unless it is reserved for DAR or other functions, Constitution Hall is visited on the tour.

DECATUR HOUSE★

1610 H STREET NW.
Ⓜ **FARRAGUT WEST OR FARRAGUT NORTH.**

For almost a century and a half, this sedate brick town house on the northwest edge of Lafayette Square figured prominently in the social and political life of Washington. The first home built on the square and the last to remain in private ownership, it served as the residence of military heroes and renowned statesmen.

A Bit of History

The Decatur Years

Stephen Decatur, a 19C naval hero, had the house built in 1818. Substantial prize money from his military successes against the Barbary pirates off the coast of North Africa and against the British in the War of 1812 enabled him to commission the eminent architect **Benjamin H. Latrobe** to design a home in elegant style. The three-story structure, 51ft wide and 45ft deep, cost Decatur $11,000. He and his wife, Susan, entertained lavishly here, but only for a brief 14 months. At the age of 41, the young commodore was killed in a duel with a discredited naval captain who believed Decatur responsible for his disgrace. Bereft, Mrs. Decatur moved to a Georgetown town house and rented the Lafayette Square house to a succession of dignitaries. In the 1820s Secretary of State Henry Clay, the "Great Compromiser," lived in Decatur House. After Clay, Martin Van Buren, then secretary of State and soon to be president, occupied the house. In 1836 the hotelier John Gadsby purchased it from Mrs. Decatur. During the Civil War Decatur House was appropriated by the government as a commissary facility.

The Beale Era

Edward Fitzgerald Beale, a renowned Western adventurer, became owner of the house after the Civil War. In 1847 Beale, accompanied by his cohort Kit Carson, brought back word of California's accession to the Union. A year later Beale again crossed the country, in a record-breaking 47 days, to officially report the discovery of gold in California.

When Beale and his wife, Mary, took possession of Decatur House in 1872, it was in disrepair from wartime use. Following the fashion of his day, Beale added such Victorian embellishments as sandstone trim around the entrance and windows. He also had the Latrobe fanlight and side lights around the front door removed and the first-floor windows lengthened. For two decades the Beales were prominent members of the capital's social circles. President Grant frequently crossed Lafayette Square to visit Beale, who was one of his closest friends.

In 1902 the house passed to the Beales' son, Truxtun. He and his second wife, Marie, made Decatur House a focal point of Washington society. One of the capital's most important annual events, a dinner following the White House Diplomatic Reception, was given here for three decades. Mrs. Beale, considered the city's premier hostess, continued to entertain diplomats, royalty and statesmen after her husband's death in 1936. In the early 1940s, recognizing the historic significance of her home, Mrs. Beale engaged the noted restoration architect Thomas Tileston Waterman to recover the Latrobe character of the house. In 1956 she bequeathed it to the National Trust for Historic Preservation, which operates it today.

Visit

🕐*Open year-round Tue–Sat 10am–5pm, Sun noon–4pm.* ⬦*Guided tours available.* 🕐*Closed Jan 1, Thanksgiving Day & Dec 25.* 💰*$5 contribution requested.* ♿ ☎*202-842-0920. www.decatur house. org.*

Latrobe's vestibule combines domes, arches and recesses to achieve an effect of understated elegance. Off the vestibule to the left lies the parlor, which, like

Decatur House (1882) by E. Vaile

the dining room adjacent to it, is deco-rated with furnishings appropriate to the Decatur period. Among the parlor furnishings is a *secrétaire à guillotine*, so called for its sliding front panel. The room off the right side of the vestibule was later discovered to be the former kitchen of the house, which has been restored to its original use. Curving double doors, fit to the contours of the vestibule's rear wall, lead to a separate hallway and the main staircase. The second floor has been restored to reflect its original appearance.

DWIGHT D. EISENHOWER EXECUTIVE OFFICE BUILDING ★

17TH AND G STS. NW.
Ⓜ FARRAGUT WEST OR FARRAGUT NORTH.

The massive granite pile that rises like a tiered wedding cake to the west of the White House is one of Washington's foremost architectural treasures. Having survived years of derision and neglect, it has been restored to its former gran-deur and houses several key government offices of the Executive branch. The building is no longer open to the public for tours.

A Bit of History

Second Empire Landmark

Erected as headquarters for the depart-ments of State, War, and Navy, this grand building (1888) symbolized the renewed vitality of the post-Civil War government. Its chief architect was Alfred Mullett, who designed the north wing of the Treasury Building. Mullett opted for the French Second Empire style, following the example of the Corcoran Gallery (now the Renwick Gallery). Known in the US as the General Grant style because of the popularity it enjoyed during the Grant administration (1869-77), this style is characterized by mansard roofing and prominent corner and central pavilions. With 900 exterior columns, 1,572 win-dows, more than 550 rooms, nearly 2 miles of corridors and 4 1/2ft-thick gran-ite walls, this construction was Wash-ington's largest and most lavish office building and is generally considered to be the finest surviving example of the Second Empire style in the country.

A Threatened Monument

By the time the edifice was completed in 1888, the Second Empire style had already passed out of fashion. Over time, the building was allowed to deteriorate, and demolition seemed inevitable. Gradually the original occupants moved to more modern quarters around the city. After the State Department's move in 1947, the Executive Office of the President appropriated the building as an annex to the adjacent White House (hence the structure's name).

The Kennedy administration was instrumental in promoting the building's rehabilitation. In addition to the president's office, among the most influential divisions of the Executive branch housed in the building today are the Office of Management and Budget, the National Security Council, and the Office of the Vice President.

☞ *The Executive Office Building is not open to the public for tours. For an online tour, www.whitehouse.gov/history/eeobtour.*

Interior Highlights

The sumptuous halls, stairways and offices, designed primarily by Mullett's successor, Richard von Ezdorf, provided a splendid workplace. Theodore Roosevelt, Franklin D. Roosevelt, Taft, Hoover, Eisenhower, Johnson, Ford and George H. Bush all had offices here before moving into the executive mansion next door. The **cast-iron detailing**, employed throughout the building for fire protection, is an outstanding feature.

Executive Office of the President Libraries

Four stories of alcoves enclose the library's central reading area, crowned by a vault pierced by a skylight. The upper three stories are adorned with white cast-iron balconies, resembling pieces of lacework.

The three-story law library features dark cast-iron balconies. The floors of both libraries are laid with Milton tiles arranged in geometric patterns.

Indian Treaty Room

Originally the Navy's library and reception room, this hall contains a lacy cast-iron balcony featuring eagles, anchors, shells and other nautical motifs.

Office of the Secretary of the Navy

The original fireplace, mirrors and stenciled walls of this spacious suite have been restored to their former splendor. Note the four **corner domes** and **two central rotundas**, especially the skylight of the **west rotunda**, covered in gold leaf and tinted in soft yellow, peach and pale green colors.

Dwight D. Eisenhower Executive Office Building

Gwen Cannon/MICHELIN

RENWICK GALLERY ★

PENNSYLVANIA AVE. AND 17TH ST. NW.

Ⓜ FARRAGUT WEST OR FARRAGUT NORTH.

The earliest major example of the Second Empire style in America, and embodying Victorian tastes, this ornate brick building is home to the Smithsonian American Art Museum's contemporary craft program. Inside, its galleries highlight the best works of contemporary and traditional American craftsmanship.

A Bit of History

The City's First Art Museum

In 1858 the wealthy financier William Wilson Corcoran commissioned one of the period's most influential architects, **James Renwick**, to design a building to house his private art collection. Impressed by the innovative contemporary architecture he had seen on a recent visit to Paris, Corcoran requested that Renwick adopt the fashionable Second Empire style.

In 1874 the Corcoran Gallery of Art, as the building was then called, opened as Washington's first art museum. By 1897 the collection had outgrown the original building and the museum moved down 17th Street to the building it occupies today.

Renewal and Rebirth

Sold to the government, the old building was used by the US Court of Claims until 1964, the year in which demolition was proposed. The successful campaign to preserve the threatened landmark was championed by the Kennedy and Johnson administrations. Renamed the Renwick Gallery in honor of the building's architect, it became part of the Smithsonian Institution in 1965. To return the structure to its original appearance, restoration architects used old drawings and the photographs of Mathew Brady. The refurbished Renwick opened as a department of the Smithsonian American Art Museum in 1972.

Visit

🕐 *Open year-round daily 10am–5:30pm.*
🕐 *Closed Dec 25.* ♿ ☎ *202-633-1000.*
www.americanart.si.edu.

Exterior

The brick facade is embellished with sandstone pilasters, vermiculated quoins, garlands and window trim. Filigreed ironwork caps the ridges of the building's mansard roof. On the long western facade, niches hold statues of Rubens and Murillo, replicas of two of the original eleven statues of artists that once adorned the facades. The capitals of the two pilasters flanking the entrance feature sculpted tobacco fronds and ears of corn. Above the entrance bay is a medallion profile of Corcoran, inscribed with his motto: "Dedicated to Art."

Interior

A red-carpeted staircase leads from the entryway to the second-floor **Grand Salon**. Decorated in the style of a Victorian picture gallery, the 90ft-long room is furnished with red velvet "poufs"—circular settees—and brocade sofas and chairs. Paintings, hung in tiers, cover its raspberry walls from the wainscoting to the ceiling molding. Among the paintings and sculptures on display from the Smithsonian American Art Museum are a suite of three stunning views of Yellowstone and the Grand Canyon by Thomas Moran. Other artists represented include George Catlin, George Inness, Edmonia Lewis, Rembrandt Peale, Hiram Powers and John Twachtman.

The **Octagon Room** *(directly opposite the Grand Salon)* showcases works by Winslow Homer, Albert Pinkham Ryder and Thomas Wilmer Dewing, also from the Smithsonian American Art Museum's permanent collection.

The galleries on both sides of the Octagon Room feature selected pieces from the Renwick's permanent, comprehensive collection of outstanding **American crafts**. Highlights include the elaborate metalwork of Albert Paley's *Portal Gates,* Larry Fuente's playful *Game Fish,* Wendell Castle's trompe-l'oeil *Ghost Clock,* Kim Schmahmann's elegant *Bureau of Bureaucracy* and Beth Lipman's tour-de-force glass sculpture, *Bancketje,* a recent museum acquisition.

Portal Gates by Albert Paley

Courtesy Smithsonian American Art Museum

ORGANIZATION OF AMERICAN STATES

17TH ST. AND CONSTITUTION AVE. NW.
Ⓜ FARRAGUT WEST.

Conceived as a symbolic amalgam of North and South American architecture, this white marble building with a terra-cotta roof has the gracious ambience of a Spanish Colonial villa. As the headquarters for the Organization of American States (OAS), the building serves as a forum for discussions and conferences affecting the political and economic climate of the Western Hemisphere.

A Bit of History

Established in 1890 as the International Union of American Republics, this organization is the oldest such alliance of nations in the world. Created to engender peaceful relations and economic cooperation among the independent countries of the Americas, it has grown from 24 member nations to 35. The US was a charter member.

In the early 20C Washington was chosen as the site for this headquarters building because it was the only city in which all member nations maintained permanent legations. Congress donated the tract of land, which then became international territory. In addition to housing the offices of the permanent staff, the building serves as headquarters of the General Secretariat, the 700-member body responsible for OAS administration and policy implementation.

Visit

🕐 *Open year-round Mon–Fri 9am–5:30pm.* 🕐 *Closed major holidays.* ♿ ☎ 202-458-3000. www.oas.org.

Headquarters Building

For their innovative blending of classical elements and traditional Latin motifs, Paul Cret and Albert Kelsey won the architectural competition to design the structure. A plaza fronts the triple-entry arches, which are flanked by allegorical statues.

The lobby is dominated by the **tropical patio**, designed after a Spanish Colonial courtyard. A fountain occupies the

159

Headquarters Building

center of the patio, whose lush vegetation includes the enormous "peace tree," a grafted fig and rubber tree planted at the building's dedication in 1910. The coats of arms of the member nations embellish the entablature around the roofed overhang. A gallery behind the patio features changing exhibits, generally from the collection of the OAS museum *(below)*.

On the second floor the columned **Hall of the Americas** contains three Tiffany rock-crystal chandeliers and Tiffany stained-glass windows. The adjacent Old Council Room features bronze bas-relief friezes depicting scenes in the histories of the Americas.

Museum and Grounds

Behind the main building, the Aztec Gardens display contemporary and traditional sculpture. The stuccoed loggia fronting the garden pool is the rear of a building designed by Cret and Kelsey to serve as the residence of the OAS secretary-general. In 1976 it was converted to the **Art Museum of the Americas** (*open year-round Tue–Sun 10am–5pm; closed major holidays; guided tours available Tue–Fri, reservations required; 202-458-6016; www. museum.oas.org*). The museum rotates works of the modern Caribbean and Latin American artists represented in its permanent collection of some 700 pieces.

Hall of the Americas

ST. JOHN'S CHURCH

LAFAYETTE SQUARE AT 16TH AND H STS. NW.
Ⓜ MCPHERSON SQUARE.

Occupying a prominent corner of Lafayette Square since 1815, this elegant structure is one of the most historic and prestigious churches in Washington. Since its inception, every chief executive has worshiped in this "church of Presidents" while in office.

A Bit of History

In the early 19C parishioners of the capital's only Episcopal church, Christ Church on Capitol Hill, began to consider creating a new parish in the area that was then developing around the White House. In 1815 **Benjamin H. Latrobe** was engaged to draft plans for the building. Latrobe's church took the shape of a Greek cross.

Throughout the church's history, its vestry has attempted to maintain the integrity of Labrobe's design even as the building has been expanded and altered. A pillared porch was added to the west side in 1822; thereafter this side replaced Latrobe's south entrance as the main entrance. The bell tower was also added at this time, and the west transept extended, changing the church's shape to a Latin cross.

In 1883 James Renwick, oversaw further renovation to the church, including the addition of a Palladian window behind the altar and stained-glass windows designed by Madame Veuve Lorin, curator at Chartres Cathedral in France.

Visit

🕐 Open year-round Mon–Sat 9am–3pm, Sun 8am–3pm. 🕐 Closed major holidays. ♿☎202-347-8766. www.stjohns-dc.org.

Latrobe's graceful, saucered dome and lantern draw the eye to the midpoint of the low-ceilinged church. A brass plate on **pew 54** indicates the president's pew, where attending chief executives are seated. The kneeling stools in this and nearby pews are covered in needlepoint patterns bearing the presidential seals and the names of presidents. Adjoining the church on H Street is Ashburton House, a Federal-style structure (1836) that now functions as the parish house.

TREASURY BUILDING

15TH ST. AND PENNSYLVANIA AVE. NW.
Ⓜ METRO CENTER.

Pictured on the back of the $10 bill, the stately Treasury Building, which flanks the executive mansion on the east, is the seat of government finances and a prominent architectural landmark in its own right.

A Bit of History

Department of the Treasury

The Treasury was established in 1789 as a department of the Executive branch. The Postal Service, General Land Office (now the Department of the Interior), departments of Commerce and Labor, and the Coast Guard all initially began as arms of the Treasury.

Today the Treasury Building houses executive and support offices for the secretary of the Treasury. A number of bureaus administered by the department are housed elsewhere in the city. Among these are the Bureau of Engraving and

Printing, where currency is printed; and the Internal Revenue Service.

The Building

One of the few official buildings completed when Congress moved to Washington in 1800, the first Treasury Building, designed by George Hadfield, was burned down during the British invasion of 1814. Its replacement, designed by James Hoban, was destroyed in a fire set by arsonists in 1833.

The current building was begun in 1836, with the construction of the T-shaped east wing, designed by **Robert Mills**. Mills employed brick vaulting to fireproof the interior and, in compliance with the wishes of Congress, used Aquia Creek sandstone, an ill-suited material that was also used in the construction of the White House and the Capitol.

In 1851, due to political wrangling, Mills was dismissed and eventually replaced by Thomas U. Walter, who modified Mills' E-shaped structure by adding a west wing that would enclose the E in a square and create two interior courtyards. The south, west and north additions took 14 years to complete and were supervised by a number of architects who added their own embellishments. The granite building (the Aquia Creek sandstone exterior and east colonnade were replaced in 1909) covers two blocks and reflects the Greek Revival style prevalent in the 1830s and 40s. The building's most distinctive feature is the Ionic colonnade of 30 monolithic columns, each 36ft high, that adorns the east facade. The south, north and west entrances are approached by wide plazas. The south plaza contains a statue of Alexander Hamilton, first secretary of the Treasury (1789-95), and the north plaza, one of Hamilton's successor, Albert Gallatin (1801-14). Both statues were designed by James Earle Fraser.

Visit

🔊 Visit by guided tour (1hr) only, by advance reservation through your senator or representative (🕯 see Congressional Visits). 🔊 Use the south building entrance at 15th St. and Hamilton Pl. NW (Washington Monument side); enter through the gate in the iron fence by pressing the call button for admittance. ♿ ☎202-622-2000. www.ustreas.gov/curator.

The hallways in the original T-shaped east wing were conceived by Mills with Doric columns and groin- and barrel-vaulted ceilings. The more elaborately ornamented hallways of the south, north and west wings exemplify the Greek Revival style. Cast-iron pilasters lining the hall feature eagles and a hand holding the Treasury key. Cast-iron balustrades adorn the circular staircases.

The third-floor corridors serve as a portrait gallery hung with paintings of the secretaries of the Treasury, arranged in chronological order. The **Secretary's Conference and Reception Rooms** have been created to reflect the decor popular in the late 1860s through the 1880s. The conference room features a painting of George Washington attributed to portraitist Gilbert Stuart and one of Salmon Chase (Treasury secretary under Lincoln from 1861 to 1864) attributed to Thomas Sully.

The **Andrew Johnson Suite** has been restored to its appearance in 1865, when the suite served as the Executive Office for President Andrew Johnson following Lincoln's assassination. Johnson had his office in the Treasury building until Mrs. Lincoln vacated the White House. The walls and ceilings of the **Secretary Salmon Chase Suite** are decorated with stenciling, allegorical figures and gilt detailing.

The second floor holds the Treasurer's Office, where a cast-iron **vault wall**, designed by Isaiah Rogers in 1864, is visible. Incised with seals and medallions, the wall was obscured behind other vault extensions and forgotten about for 80 years. Its interior lining of steel balls, intended to prevent burglary, can now be viewed through a wall cutaway.

The north lobby, fronting Pennsylvania Avenue, opens onto the **Cash Room**★, designed by Alfred Mullett. The site of Ulysses S. Grant's inaugural reception in 1869, the impressive 72ft-by-32ft chamber features immense bronze chandeliers, a coffered ceiling, and walls and floors faced in seven different kinds of marble. A mezzanine with ornate pilasters and an elaborate bronze railing rims the room. Intended to inspire public trust in paper money, which the government first issued in 1862, the Cash Room functioned to redeem government-issued certificates and to supply commercial banks with coins and currency. It ceased operations in 1976 and is now used for official functions.

Treasury Building

© Brigitta L. House/MICHELIN

DOWNTOWN★★

Traditionally the commercial heart of Washington, Downtown reflects the flavor of the city's past and present. Large office buildings and retail complexes tower above 19C shopfronts, and the process of revitalization continues as new condominiums, restaurants, shops and attractions make the area their home.

- **Information:** Downtown D.C. Business Improvement District; ☎202-638-3232; www.downtowndc.org. The district's roving "concierges," attired in red jackets, are on hand to answer questions and give directions at no charge. Information kiosks are located Downtown as well.
- ▶ **Orient Yourself:** Sights covered here lie east of the White House and north of the Mall, an area compact enough to be walkable.
- **Parking:** Several lots are scattered throughout; many offer early-bird specials. The former Convention Center *(9th St. NW between New York Ave. & H St.)* has been converted to a 1000-space garage *($20 maximum weekdays; $10 weekends)*.
- **Don't Miss:** One of the best views of Washington's skyline from the Old Post Office Tower, as well as Ford's Theatre ranger presentations.
- **Organizing Your Time:** Allow 2 days to see the sights and get a feel for this vibrant section of Washington.
- **Especially for Kids:** The International Spy Museum, particularly the gift shop.

A Bit of History

19C

Conceived by planner L'Enfant to link the White House and the Capitol, **Pennsylvania Avenue** was the capital's first major thoroughfare, and as such it gave rise to the city's commercial district. In 1801 President Jefferson authorized the building of a central market on the avenue between 7th and 9th streets, and in 1807 construction began on the ill-fated Tiber Creek canal, which was eventually covered over in the 1870s. For much of the 19C, Pennsylvania Avenue was lined with hotels, boardinghouses and theaters, in keeping with L'Enfant's intent that this be a thoroughfare "attractive to the learned and affording diversion to the idle." Among the diversions were the **National Theatre**, an institution still in operation between 13th and 14th streets, and the **Willard Hotel** (& *see Where to Stay*), for decades Washington's premier hostelry. Established in the 1850s, the Willard has occupied several buildings on the same site. The present building (1901) was designed by H.J.

Hardenberg, architect of Manhattan's celebrated Plaza Hotel.

As the city grew, F Street became the site of major government buildings and fashionable residences. North-south growth occurred along 7th Street, where two- and three-story brick buildings housed shops and residences. In the 1830s 7th Street was chosen as the site for the Patent Office and became an enclave for German immigrants working in the dry-goods trade. By the turn of the 19C, their businesses had made this street the commercial hub of Downtown.

Decline and Rebirth

During the first half of the 20C, Downtown continued to thrive, with major new development occurring in the land bordered by Pennsylvania and Constitution Avenues. Known as **Federal Triangle**, this cluster of Classical Revival government buildings was designed by a group of eminent architects working in collaboration.

After World War II Downtown declined as it lost business to suburban malls. When John F. Kennedy's inaugural parade moved down Pennsylvania

Avenue, the thoroughfare was described by one cabinet member as "a vast, unformed, cluttered expanse." A cabinet committee established by Kennedy in 1960 began a redevelopment process gradually revitalized the avenue. At the core of this rebirth was the renovation of the Old Post Office while other landmark construction includes the 53,879sq ft **Navy Memorial** dedicated in 1987. An international trade center, the 3 million sq ft **Ronald Reagan Building** (1997, Pei Cobb Freed & Partners, and Ellerbe Becket), houses federal offices and conference rooms, restaurants, exhibit space and the Washington, DC Visitor Information Center.

Mixed-use complexes such as Hartman-Cox's Market Square (1984), near the site of the old city market, have risen on Pennsylvania Avenue. The Landsburgh complex (7th, 8th and E Sts.), home of the **Shakespeare Theatre** (1992), was the result of the overhaul of several buildings. Both Market Square and the Landsburgh are part of **Pennsylvania Quarter**, the designation for the avenue's north side between 6th, 9th and E streets.

21C Growth

Today a refurbished Willard Hotel overlooks Pershing Park, a pleasant square with an outdoor cafe. Nearby **Freedom Plaza**, designed by the prestigious architectural group, Venturi, Rauch and Scott Brown, has a large-scale copy of **L'Enfant's city plan** incised in its pavement. Anchoring the northern portion of Downtown rises the new **Washington Convention Center** (2003). On G and 9th streets stands the **Martin Luther King Memorial Library** (1972), an austere building designed by Mies van der Rohe, one of the 20C's most influential architects. **Chinatown**, a small stretch of restaurants and shops on H Street between 6th and 7th streets, is recognizable by its ornate Friendship Archway. Chinatown neighbors the **Verizon**

Center (formerly the MCI Center, 1997), a 20,000-seat sports arena for the city's basketball and hockey teams. The old Atlas and Le Droit buildings on F Street, between 8th and 9th streets, were revitalized to house the **International Spy Museum** (2002). At Pennsylvania Ave. and 6th Street, the **Newseum**, relocated from Arlington, is slated to open in the fall of 2007 in a new six-level, 215,000sq ft building. The interactive museum of news will feature a large "window on the world" overlooking Pennsylvania Avenue and the Mall, a state-of-the-art broadcast studio, a 535-seat theater, and six levels of exhibits showcasing the news media past and present.

Also in the fall, **Madame Tussauds** is expected to open a $16 million, 27,000 sq ft wax museum in the former Woodward & Lothrop building *(10th and F Sts. NW)*. Featured likenesses will include politicos George W. Bush, Al Gore and Bill and Hillary Clinton as well as pop icons like Beyoncé and Angelina Jolie, and traditional historical figures.

Fall 2007 will also see the Downtown debut of Shakespeare Theatre Company's **Harman Center for the Arts**. The facility in Penn Quarter will comprise two theatres, a newly constructed 776-seat Sidney Harman Hall *(6th and F Sts. NW)* and the existing 451-seat Lansburgh Theatre. The additional space will allow the company to offer eight plays, rather than five, per season.

In the same block as the Lansburgh Theatre will be a new, second site for the **Textile Museum**, now situated in Embassy Row. The 23,400sq ft venue, to be located at 421 7th Street NW, is expected to open in early 2008.

From April through mid-November, Penn Quarter is the site of a **farmers' market** every Thursday from 3:00pm–7:00pm *(north end of 8th St., between D and E Sts.; ☎202-362-8889; www.freshfarmmarkets.org)*. Throughout the year, countless festivals and celebrations are held in Downtown.

INTERNATIONAL SPY MUSEUM★★

9TH AND F STS. NW.
Ⓜ GALLERY PLACE.

The late-19C exteriors of the renovated Atlas and Le Droit buildings disguise the sleek interior that now holds this intriguing, interactive museum. Opened in 2002, the museum gives visitors access to the largest and most fascinating collection of spying paraphernalia ever to be displayed in public.

▶ **Orient Yourself:** Self-guided tours move from the third floor to the first-floor.
🐾 **Don't Miss:** Spy gadgets like the lipstick pistols.
🕐 **Organizing Your Time:** Allow 90min for the museum, 30min for gift shop.
Kids **Especially for Kids:** The interactive code-breaking room.

Visit

Kids 🕐 *Open late May–mid-Aug daily 9am–8pm. Late Aug–Oct & Jan–mid-May daily 10am–closing hrs vary. Nov–Dec daily, hrs vary; check online.* 🕐 *Closed Jan 1, Thanksgiving Day & Dec 25.* ⬚$16. *Advance tickets recommended.* ✕♿ ☏202-393-7798. www.spymuseum.org. Visitors enter a high-tech security portal and take elevators to the third floor. There, visitors choose a "cover" identity from those on display, and in the Briefing Theater, view a film (5min) on the real world of spying. Then begins a self-guided tour of third- and first-floor exhibits. **School for Spies** features, among other gadgets, buttonhole cameras, lipstick pistols and equipment for listening in on bugged conversations. A fully equipped Aston Martin, boasting machine guns and rotating license plates, highlights the exhibit. **The Secret History of History** traces spying from George Washington's era to the beginnings of the Secret Service. Intelligence-gathering during World War II is depicted in **Spies Among Us**, highlighted by an interactive code-breaking room. In **War of the Spies** (*1st floor*), visitors enter a replicated section of Berlin, complete with a cafe and a tunnel for eavesdropping on the Soviets. The exhibit showcases spy technology spawned during the Cold War, from shoe phones to satellites. Challenges confronting today's intelligence community are revealed in the final exhibit, **The 21st Century.**

NATIONAL PORTRAIT GALLERY★★

OLD PATENT OFFICE BUILDING
8TH AND F STS. NW.
Ⓜ GALLERY PLACE.
PLAN P168

Sharing the interior of the Old Patent Office Building with the Smithsonian American Art Museum since 1968, this museum serves as the nation's family album. Modeled after its namesake in London, the National Portrait Gallery conserves some 19,400 paintings, sculptures, photographs, engravings and drawings of "men and women who have made significant contributions to the history, development and culture of the people of the United States." Portraits hung here must be original works of art, preferably taken from life.

▶ **Orient Yourself:** Use the floor plan to get your bearings. The portrait gallery and the art museum are connected by hallway galleries.
☺ **Don't Miss:** The presidential portraits *(2nd floor)* and the Great Hall *(3rd floor).*
🕐 **Organizing Your Time:** Allow 2hrs, minimum.

A Bit of History

Home for the Arts
In the mid-1830s Congress authorized a "temple of the useful arts"—a patent office—to be constructed on this site. In 1836 construction began on the Greek Revival edifice designed by William Parker Elliott. The monumental stone **Old Patent Office Building**★★ features a pedimented Doric portico on each of its four sides and encloses a central courtyard. Robert Mills oversaw construction of the south wing (1840), whose golden sandstone contrasts with the granite of the rest of the building.

The War Years
During the Civil War, the building served as a hospital for Union soldiers. Clara Barton, a Patent Office copyist and founder of the Red Cross, ministered to the wounded, as did poet Walt Whitman, who read to them from his works. In 1865 Lincoln's second inaugural reception was held here. A benefit to raise funds for the families of Union soldiers, the gala took place in the 264ft-long, marble-pillared hall on the third floor of the east wing.

Structure Preserved
When completed in 1867, the building also housed, at various times, the Department of the Interior and the Civil Service Commission. In 1958 Congress saved the building from demolition and gave it to the Smithsonian Institution. In July 2006 the building reopened after a six-year overhaul, financed in part by a $45 million gift from the Donald W. Reynolds Foundation of Las Vegas. The museums are known collectively as the Donald W. Reynolds Center for American Art and Portraiture. Their individual names, however, remain the same. As a result of the renovation, which included structural repairs and replacement of aging infrastructure, three floors are now exclusively devoted to exhibits (former staff offices have been moved to another building). A new conservation center allows visitors to view the conservation process. New visible storage has expanded the display space, and a 346-seat auditorium has been added. A renovated courtyard is scheduled to open in fall 2007.

Visit

🕐*Open year-round daily 11:30am–7pm.*
🕐*Closed Dec 25.* ✕&☎202-633-8300. *www.npg.si.edu.*

First Floor
To the right after entering from F Street. In an ongoing special exhibit "Americans Now," figures of contemporary fame such as Gore Vidal, Tom Wolfe, Edward Albee and Toni Morrison are portrayed in paintings, photographs and sculpture. The long corridor along 7th Street presents a chronological overview of prominent people and events from 1600-1900 in **American Origins**. Included are protraits of Pocahontas, Ben Franklin, John Singleton Copley (*Self-Portrait*, 1784), Seminola chief Osceola, Thomas Edison, Walt Whitman and Frederick Douglass. The end of the corridor is devoted to the **Civil War** period, where likenesses of Abraham Lincoln, Julia Ward Howe, abolitionist John Brown, generals Ulysses S. Grant and William Tecumseh Sherman, and other renowned figures are on view. Mounted in the hallway leading to the G Street lobby is a selection of the museum's recent acquisitions.

Second Floor
The museum's series of **presidential portraits**, featuring representations in various media of the Americans who have held the nation's highest office, occupy much of the second floor (*to*

SECOND FLOOR

WPA

to third floor

to third floor
(Great Hall)

Special Exhibits

233

Hall of
Presidents

American Colonies

Graphic Arts

251

252

**NATIONAL PORTRAIT GALLERY/
AMERICAN ART MUSEUM**

FIRST FLOOR

G Street

M
GALLERY
PLACE

M
GALLERY
PLACE

Recent Aquisitions

9th Street

7th Street

Special Exhibits

American Origins

Archives

Folk Art

American Experience

Special Exhibits

0   50 ft
0   25 m

F Street

| | American Art Museum | | National Portrait Gallery |
| | Shops | | Archives of American Art |

the right of the landing); the highlight is Gilbert Stuart's celebrated **Lansdowne portrait**★ of George Washington. Flanking this full-length portrait are Stuart's **Athenaeum Portraits** of George and Martha Washington. The Athenaeum portrait is the most widely known representation of the first president, since it served as the model for the portrait that appears on the $1 bill. Stuart's **Thomas Jefferson portrait** is also noteworthy.

George P.A.Healy's oil painting depicts a pensive, seated Abraham Lincoln, and particularly moving is the famous **"cracked plate" photograph of Abraham Lincoln** taken on February 5, 1865, just two months before his assassination.

The remaining galleries are reserved for special exhibitions. An entire gallery *(opposite the G Street elevators)* is devoted to works by the noted sculptor

Jo Davidson (1883-1952), who immortalized in bronze, stone or terra-cotta many prominent figures of his period including Clare Boothe Luce, Robinson Jeffers and Fiorello La Guardia.

Third Floor

The entire south wing of the museum on this floor is occupied by the **Great Hall**, whose decor of multicolored Milton tiles, carved ceiling medallions, and a yellow and blue central skylight reflects late-19C tastes. The frieze of six relief panels illustrating sources of technology is a reminder that the hall was originally designed to display miniature patent models.

The exhibit **20th-Century Americans** dominates both sides of the hall and features portraits of historical and contemporary Americans such as Rachael Carson, Jackson Pollock, James Baldwin, James Dewey Watson and Jonas Salk. In the section devoted to American Justice are likenesses of such human-rights advocates as Thurgood Marshall, César Chávez, Malcolm X, Shirley Chisholm and Christover Reeves.

On its long sides the hall is flanked by mezzanines. **BRAVO!** showcases portraits of popular figures in the Performing Arts, including great names in American theater, film and music, such as Marian Anderson, Benny Goodman, Will Rogers, Elvis Presley, Joan Baez and Jerry Seinfeld. Lined with paintings and photographs, as well as hanging banners, **Champions** features well-known sports figures Arthur Ashe, Lance Armstrong, Muhammad Ali and many others.

FEDERAL BUREAU OF INVESTIGATION★

E ST. BETWEEN 9TH AND 10TH STS. NW.
Ⓜ FEDERAL TRIANGLE.

Officially known as the J. Edgar Hoover FBI Building, this immense, fortresslike structure bordering Pennsylvania Avenue houses the national headquarters of the Federal Bureau of Investigation (FBI).

A Bit of History

An arm of the Justice Department, the FBI traces its beginnings to 1908, when a permanent investigative force of special agents was placed under the control of the attorney general. In 1935 this force was designated the Federal Bureau of Investigation and its powers broadened in an effort to combat rampant gangsterism. Under the 48-year leadership (1924-72) of director **J. Edgar Hoover,** the bureau became the supreme federal authority in matters of domestic crime. Begun in 1963, the headquarters building was completed 12 years later in 1975, at a cost of over $126 million. Stanley Gladych's design exemplifies the New Brutalism school of architecture, which features exposed concrete and little embellishment. Covering a city block, the building wraps around an interior courtyard. An exterior arcade along the perimeter is lined with rows of massive pillars. The building houses nearly 8,000 workers. In addition, the FBI maintains 56 field offices and over 400 resident agencies, employing more than 12,000 agents.

Visit

⚊ *FBI tours have been suspended until further notice.* ♿ ☎*202-324-3447. www.fbi.gov.*

A small exhibit hall contains displays on the history of the bureau and its procedures. The remainder of the tour is devoted to various research facilities housed here, such as the labs where bullet, firearm and fiber analyses are conducted. A live firearms demonstration often concludes the tour.

FORD'S THEATRE
AND PETERSEN HOUSE★

10TH ST. BETWEEN E AND F STS. NW.

Ⓜ METRO CENTER.

In the heart of Downtown, amid a stretch of 19C structures, stands old Ford's Theatre, where Abraham Lincoln was shot by an assassin, and Petersen House, where he died of his wound.

A Bit of History

A Tragic Gala

On the evening of April 14, 1865, President and Mrs. Lincoln attended a performance at Ford's Theatre. The capital was in a festive mood as, only five days before, Confederate Gen. Robert E. Lee had surrendered to Union Gen. Ulysses S. Grant at Appomattox, Virginia. Grant and his wife had, in fact, been in Washington on April 14 and were to have attended the theater with the Lincolns, but they made the decision to leave town earlier in the day. In their stead, Clara Harris, daughter of Sen. Ira Harris, and her fiancé, Maj. Henry Rathbone, attended. That night the theater was full of Washingtonians hoping for a glimpse of Grant, who had rarely visited the city. In preparation for the president's arrival, boxes no. 7 and no. 8 had been draped with flags and the partition between them removed to allow the presidential party more space. The Lincoln party was engrossed in the third act of the play when **John Wilkes Booth** silently entered the box and shot the president at close range. The bullet from the small, single-shot derringer entered behind Lincoln's left ear and lodged behind his right eye. Major Rathbone immediately tried to subdue the attacker, but Booth defended himself with a large knife, stabbing the major in the left arm. Booth leaped over the balustrade of the box, but as he did so, his feet got tangled in the draped flags. He landed off balance on the stage 12ft below, breaking a small bone in his leg. Most accounts claim that Booth then stood and flourished his knife, declaring "Sic semper tyrannis!" ("Thus always with tyrants"). The audience, believing that Booth's appearance was part of the play, was slow to respond. In the theater alley Booth mounted a horse he had sequestered and escaped.

Lincoln's Final Hours

Three army surgeons in the audience immediately attended the stricken Lincoln. Recognizing the seriousness of the wound, they ordered him moved to the nearest bed; the president was carried across the street to a boarding house owned by a tailor named Petersen. He was laid in a first-floor back room then being rented by a young man in the Union Army. Due to Lincoln's height, he had to be placed diagonally across the bed. As the night passed, Cabinet ministers, physicians and other prominent people gathered in the back parlor, while Mrs. Lincoln was consoled by friends in the front parlor. Lincoln never regained consciousness. At 7:22am the following morning, he died.

After official ceremonies in Washington, Lincoln's body was taken by train to Springfield, Illinois, for burial. Along the route he lay in state in several large cities. Abraham Lincoln was buried at Springfield's Oak Ridge Cemetery on May 4.

The Assassination Plot

A successful actor who appeared several times on the stage of Ford's Theatre, John Wilkes Booth apparently sought to achieve lasting fame for himself by what he considered his "heroic" act on behalf of the Confederacy. He was the ringleader of a band of conspirators who had initially plotted the kidnapping of Lincoln. When logistics prevented this approach, Booth hatched a plot in which he would kill Lincoln and his accomplices would assassinate other high government officials. Only Booth was successful.

Once he had inflicted the mortal wound, Booth made for the home of Dr. Samuel Mudd in the southern Maryland countryside. Mudd set his leg, and Booth continued his flight, accompanied by a fellow conspirator, David Herold. The two men crossed into Virginia and were apprehended the night of April 26 by a cavalry detachment in Port Royal, Virginia. Herold surrendered, but Booth refused, forcing his pursuers to set on fire the barn in which he was hiding. As the building burst into flames, the assassin was fatally shot through the neck by one of the soldiers.

Ford's Theatre

Library of Congress

Abraham Lincoln

🕘*Open year-round daily 9am–5pm.* 🕘*Closed Dec 25 and during rehearsals & performances. Narrative talks available.* ☏*202-426-6924. www.nps.gov/foth.*

When John Ford opened the doors of this brick structure in 1863, it was one of the grandest theaters in the country, with an advertised seating capacity of 2,500. Though its facade was adorned only with arched door bays, window trim, pilasters and an undecorated pediment, its interior was lavishly appointed. A cantilevered "dress circle," or balcony, flanked by private boxes, sloped toward the stage.

After Lincoln's assassination, the theater was ordered closed by the federal government. John Ford's announced intention to continue dramatic productions in the theater met with threats, so the War Department leased the building from Ford and began converting it into office space, ultimately purchasing it a year later for $100,000.

In 1893 another tragedy occurred here when collapsing floors killed 22 office workers. Thereafter the building was used only for storage until 1932, when the government opened it as a Lincoln museum, displaying memorabilia relating to the life of the 16th president. In the mid-1960s Congress authorized a restoration of the building to its 1865 appearance. Ford's Theatre reopened in 1968 as both a memorial and an active playhouse.

The **box** where Lincoln sat is decorated as it was on the night of April 14, 1865, with upholstered Victorian period pieces, including the settee that had been specially placed there for the president and his guests. On the balcony level is an imposing **bronze head of Lincoln** by Carl Tolpo, which was presented to Ford's Theatre in 1965.

In the basement, the refurbished Lincoln Museum (🕘*same hours as the theater*) displays such artifacts from the assassination as Booth's derringer and the clothes Lincoln was wearing.

Petersen House

Across the street from the theater at 516 Tenth St. 🕘*Open year-round daily 9am–5pm.* 🕘*Closed Dec 25.* ☏ *202-426-6924.*

The simple three-story brick row house where Lincoln died on April 15, 1865 was built in 1850 by William Petersen, a tailor. Its three first-floor rooms, a front and back parlor and bedroom, decorated in Victorian period furnishings, are open to the public.

NATIONAL MUSEUM OF WOMEN IN THE ARTS ★

1250 NEW YORK AVE. AND 13TH ST. NW.
Ⓜ METRO CENTER.

Behind this Beaux-Arts exterior is the world's only major museum devoted exclusively to the works of women artists. The 3,000-piece permanent collection includes works from the 16C to the present, covering every medium from native American pottery to abstract sculpture.

A Bit of History

Local philanthropists Wilhelmina and Wallace Holladay founded the museum in 1981 as a private institution "to encourage greater awareness of women in the arts." The Holladays donated their own collection to form the core of the museum's holdings, which today comprise works from more than 800 women artists.

A limestone and granite trapezoid, the edifice housing the museum was once a Masonic temple (Waddy B. Wood, 1908). It was designated a National Historic Landmark in the early 1980s.

In 1983 the newly founded museum purchased the building from the fraternal order of Masons and formally opened at this new location in 1987. An $8 million renovation transformed the interior into three levels of exhibit space,

a library and research center and a 200-seat auditorium, where public lectures, workshops, films and concerts are held. The Kasser Wing, which houses additional exhibit space, a conference room and an expanded museum shop, was completed in 1997.

Visit

🕐Open year-round Mon–Sat 10am–5pm, Sun noon–5pm. 🕐Closed Jan 1, Thanksgiving Day & Dec 25. ⊛$10. ✕👤 ☎202-783-5000. www.nmwa.org.

The main floor is dominated by the **Great Hall**, a two-story expanse of rose, white and gray Turkish marble (and *faux marbre*) overhung by three crystal and gold-leaf chandeliers. The mezzanine level is rimmed with a heavy marble balustrade that extends along the twin staircases on opposite sides of the hall. The gilded lions' heads topping the columns on this level and the ornate ceiling are the only features from the building's original interior. Light is admitted through the mezzanine's large arched windows.

Selected works from the permanent collection are hung in the Great Hall and on the mezzanine on a rotating basis; the second floor is reserved for temporary exhibits.

The third-floor galleries, arranged chronologically, are devoted to works from the **permanent collection** (⊛ take elevator to 3rd floor). The earliest works (displayed in the 16-18C gallery) are primarily still lifes and portraits, characteristic of the subject matter of early women artists. The oldest work in the collection is the *Portrait of a Noble-*

Lady with a Bowl of Violets (c.1910) by Lilla Cabot Perry

Courtesy The National Museum of Women in the Arts, Gift of Wallace and Wilhelmina Holladay woman (c.1580) by Lavinia Fontana, a 16C Italian painter from Bologna who is considered the first professional woman artist. *Still Life of Fish and Cat* by Clara Peeters, a 17C Flemish artist, highlights her contributions to the development of that genre. Two still lifes of flowers are representative of the work of Rachel Ruysch, a 17C Dutch artist. This gallery also contains a portrait by the court painter of Marie Antoinette, Elisabeth Vigée-Lebrun (1755-1842).

The 19C gallery displays works by the well-known animal portraitist Rosa Bonheur and *The Cage*, a still life by the famous French Impressionist Berthe Morisot, as well as the sculpture *Young Girl With a Sheaf* by Camille Claudel. Among the 19C American works are an early portrait by Cecilia Beaux, and *The Bath*, from a renowned series of graphics by Impressionist Mary Cassatt. Lilla Cabot Perry, who introduced the work of Monet to Americans, is represented by her *Lady with a Bowl of Violets* and *Lady in Evening Dress*.

The museum's notable collection of **19C sculpture** includes the works of Malvina Hoffman, Anna Vaughn Hyatt Huntington, Bessie Potter Vonnoh and Evelyn Beatrice Longman.

The 20C galleries feature paintings by Helen Frankenthaler, Elaine de Kooning, Lee Krasner and others. Mexican artist Frida Kahlo's *Self-Portrait*, painted in homage to Trotsky, reflects her revolutionary zeal and introspection.

SMITHSONIAN AMERICAN ART MUSEUM ★

OLD PATENT OFFICE BUILDING, 8TH AND G STS. NW.

Ⓜ GALLERY PLACE.

PLAN P168

Housed in the landmark Old Patent Office Building, this museum contains the country's oldest federal collections of art. Its holdings run the gamut of American art from early-18C portraiture and 19C landscapes to the free-form sculpture and large, abstract canvases of contemporary artists.

▶ **Orient Yourself:** ♿ See the National Portrait Gallery above.

◉ **Don't Miss:** George Catlin Gallery and the Folk Art collection.

A Bit of History

The museum traces its beginnings to the efforts of a Washingtonian named John Varden. In 1841 his collection of art, artifacts and natural history specimens was joined with that of the congressionally mandated National Institute. The combined collections were exhibited in the Patent Office Building.

In 1862 the collection was donated to the Smithsonian Institution, which exhibited selected pieces in several buildings in the city. In 1906 the collection was officially designated the National Gallery of Art, but it still had no permanent home. Even its title was short-lived, since the new museum being built on the Mall to house the Mellon Collection was officially named the National Gallery of Art in 1937.

The National Collection of Fine Arts, as it was then called, remained in the Museum of Natural History until 1968, when it was permanently installed in its original quarters—the Old Patent Office Building. Since then, the collection has increased fivefold and now includes more than 41,000 objects. It received its previous name, the National Museum of American Art (NMAA), in 1980, to reflect its mandate to display exclusively the works of US artists. In 2000 President Bill Clinton signed into law a bill renaming the museum the Smithsonian American Art Museum. In July 2006 the building was reopened after a six-year renovation. *For details, see the National Portrait Gallery.*

Visit

Open year-round daily 11:30am–7pm. Closed Dec 25. ✕ ♿ ☎202-633-7970. www.americanart.si.edu.

First Floor

The **American Experience** *(to the left of the F Street lobby)* showcases 19C landscape paintings as well as works by renowned 20C artists such as Hans Hoffman, Milton Avery, Joseph Stella, Richard Diebenkorn, Georgia O'Keeffe, Edward Hopper and the sculpture of Isamu Noguchi, among others.

Not to be missed in the **Folk Art** section is James Hampton's **Throne of the Third Heaven of the Nations' Millennium General Assembly**. This three-dimensional work depicts the throne of God surrounded by altarlike pulpits and offertories. While employed as a Washington janitor from 1946 to 1960, Hampton created this work from discarded furniture, bottles and other items that he wrapped in aluminum and gold foil. Paintings, toys, quilts and sculpture from the museum's collection of 19C and 20C American folk art are also on view. The remainder of the corridor is reserved for special exhibits.

Second Floor

American art from colonial times through 1940 is exhibited on this floor *(to the left of the landing)*. The first three rooms on the right are reserved for changing displays of graphic arts. Opposite, the **American Colonies** includes works by artists Ralph Earl, Thomas Sully and John Trumbull. John Singleton Copley's portrait of *Mrs. George Watson* (1765) is especially noteworthy.

The two opposite rooms *(galleries 251 and 252)* at the end of the 7th-Street Corridor showcase late 18C and early 19C furniture, such as a 1790 mahogany dining table. The **Early Republic** spotlights Albert Bierstadt's *Among the Sierra Nevada* (1868). **Western Art** includes sculpture such as *The Dying Tecumseh* by Ferdinand Pettrich (1856) and a gallery devoted to the early-19C paintings of American Indians by artist-anthropologist **George Catlin** (1796-1872). In the central hall, a standout is Eastman Johnson's *The Girl I Left Behind Me* (1875). Gallery 233 features black and white photos from the **Civil War**. Next door, floral still life and a portrait of *Elizabeth Winthrop Chanler* (1893) by John Singer Sargent are highlights. American **Impressionism** includes works by Childe Hassam, John Henry Twachtman (*Round Hill Road,* c.1900) and Mary Cassatt (*The Caress,* 1902).

Galleries at the end of the corridor display works by artists of the **Gilded Age**, such as John La Farge, Abbott Thayer, and Augustus Saint-Gaudens, whose bronze Adams Memorial sculpture dominates the hallway.

The spacious gallery devoted to Modernism highlights major schools and trends in mid-to-late-20C art.

In the center of the G Street corridor, art from the **WPA** (Works Progress Administration) includes works by Thomas Hart Benson and Morris Kantor's delightful *Baseball at Night* (1934).

Third Floor

Art Since 1945 and Contemporary Art feature works by Jesus Moroles, Chaim Gross and Paul Feeley. Don't miss the humorous *Any Questions* sculpture (1985) by William King.

Luce Foundation Center

Extending over three floors *(3rd, 3rd-floor mezzanine and 4th)*, this open storage displays some 3,500 works of American Art enclosed within glass partitions. In-depth information on individual objects is available from computer kiosks.

MARIAN KOSHLAND SCIENCE MUSEUM

6TH AND E STS. NW.
Ⓜ JUDICIARY SQUARE.

This museum (2004) operates under the auspices of the National Academy of Sciences in Washington, DC, and seeks to "explore current scientific issues at the core of many of the nation's public policy decisions." Established with a gift from molecular biologist Daniel Koshland, the facility is named for his wife, Marian Koshland (1921-1997), also a molecular biologist, known for her work in the field of immunology.

Visit

Kids ⏱ *Open year-round Wed–Mon 10am–5pm.* Closed Thanksgiving Day, Dec 25. $5. ☎202-334-1201. www.koshland-science-museum.org. Exhibits are designed to appeal to visitors 13 years of age and older.

The museum's permanent exhibit, **Wonders of Science**, opens with a film about the behavior and composition of the universe. Interactive stations allow visitors to manipulate satellite images of earth's nighttime illuminations, for example, and view a real-time representation of DNA.

Temporary exhibits on global warming and DNA investigate, among other topics, the role of cows in climatic changes and the use of DNA fingerprinting in the conviction of criminals.

NATIONAL AQUARIUM

14TH ST. AND CONSTITUTION AVE. NW.
Ⓜ FEDERAL TRIANGLE.

This small aquarium is the nation's oldest. Established in 1873 under the auspices of the Federal Fish Commission, it has occupied various locations, including ponds on the grounds of the Washington Monument. In 1932 the aquarium was moved to its present location in the basement of the Department of Commerce Building. Since 1982 the aquarium has functioned independently of the government as a private, nonprofit organization.

Visit

Kids ⏱*Open year-round daily 9am–5pm (last admission 4:30pm).* Closed Thanksgiving Day & Dec 25. $5. Shark feeding Mon, Wed & Sat 2pm. Piranha feeding Tue, Thu & Sun 2pm. Alligator feeding Fri 2pm. ☎202-482-2825. www.nationalaquarium.com. Exhibit renovations may be underway, but the aquarium remains open.

The aquarium's tanks house some 1,500 specimens of aquatic life, including sea turtles, lemon sharks, piranhas, moray eels and lungfish. A touch tank allows visitors to handle such marine life as sea urchins and hermit crabs, and a theater features presentations on the underwater world.

NATIONAL BUILDING MUSEUM

401 F ST. NW (NORTH SIDE OF JUDICIARY SQUARE).
Ⓜ JUDICIARY SQUARE.

Formerly known as the Pension Building, the colossal brick edifice was long considered one of the capital's most monumental eyesores. Painstakingly refurbished, this example of 19C eclecticism now houses a museum devoted to America's achievements in the building arts.

A Bit of History

"Meigs' Old Red Barn"

In the 1880s US Army engineer Gen. **Montgomery Meigs** (1816-92) was commissioned to design a permanent workplace for the 1,500 employees of the Pension Bureau, the federal agency responsible for distributing government pensions. Nicknamed "Meigs' Old Red Barn," the **Pension Building**★ occupies an entire city block. The massive rectangular edifice stands almost 160ft tall. The exterior design, with its prominent overhanging cornice and three stories of pedimented and linteled windows, is a double-scale version of the Palazzo Farnese in Rome. The 3ft-high terra-cotta **frieze** around the entire structure was created by 19C sculptor Casper Buberl as a memorial to the Civil War Union dead. The oversized "palazzo" is crowned by a roof of intersecting gable-ended clerestories, designed to provide light within and to conserve heat in winter. Meigs incorporated a ventilation system that afforded a crosscurrent between the roof, windows and the openings below each window. The structure was made fireproof by the use of brick and metal. The Pension Bureau transferred to more spacious accommodations in the 1920s. In the 1950s demolition was considered, but the building's survival was ensured, thanks to its designation as a National Historic Landmark. The Pension Building is now the home of the National Building Museum (NBM), created in 1980 by congressional mandate to commemorate American architecture. Since 1885 the Great Hall has been the setting of **inaugural balls** for 13 presidents.

Visit

🕐Open year-round Mon–Sat 10am–5pm, Sun 11am–5pm. 🕐Closed Jan 1, Thanksgiving Day & Dec 25. 👓Guided tours (45min) available Mon–Wed 12:30pm, Thu–Sun 11:30am, 12:30pm & 1:30pm. ✕⛦ ☏202-272-2448. www.nbm.org.

National Building Museum

Upon entering the vast interior court known as the **Great Hall**, the visitor is impressed by its staggering proportions. Measuring 116ft by 316ft, this monumental space is punctuated by eight 75ft Corinthian columns made of brick and painted to resemble Siena marble. These colossal pieces of solid masonry support the central roof structure, which admits abundant light. The court is flanked by two stories of galleries lined with 72 Doric and 72 Ionic columns. The third-floor parapet is ornamented by plaster replicas of the terra-cotta urns originally designed for the building. In the cornice of the hall's central section high above the colossal columns, 244 niches (best seen from the upper floors) contain life-size busts symbolic of American builders and craftsmen. Deep-set brick stairways are covered by pure-lined barrel and groin vaulting.

The exhibit Washington: Symbol and City *(1st floor)*, featuring models of prominent monuments, offers an overview of the development of architecture in the nation's capital.

OLD POST OFFICE

PENNSYLVANIA AVE. AND 12TH ST. NW.
Ⓜ FEDERAL TRIANGLE.

Saved from the wrecker's ball at the eleventh hour, this rejuvenated Pennsylvania Avenue landmark has been converted into a "festival market" that attracts residents and tourists throughout the year.

A Bit of History

Designed in the then-outmoded Richardsonian Romanesque style, the massive granite structure met with public disfavor after its completion in 1899. Built as the headquarters of the US Postal Service, the building greatly deteriorated in the decades following the postmaster general's move to new quarters in 1934.

In 1971 demolition was officially approved, but preservation groups ultimately saved the structure. A $30 million, federally funded restoration project (1978-83) transformed the Old Post Office into a multifunctional complex with commercial space.

Visit

🕐 *Tower open Memorial Day–Labor Day Mon–Sat 8am–7:45pm, Sun 10am–5:45pm; rest of the year Mon–Sat 10am–7:45pm, Sun noon–5:45pm* 🕐 *Closed Jan 1, Thanksgiving Day & Dec 25.* ✕ ♿ ☎ *202-289-4224. www.oldpostofficedc. com.*

Interior

The central glass-roofed **courtyard** (160ft high) is surrounded by seven floors of offices for federal agencies. The first three levels accommodate restaurants, cafes, fast-food stands, souvenir shops and a stage for live entertainment. Called the Pavilion, this spot has been the setting for annual festivities, including a New Year's celebration.

Tower

Ascending the 315ft clock tower by means of the glass elevator *(in the northwest corner of the courtyard)* allows visitors to appreciate the vastness of the courtyard. Near the summit are the **Congress bells** donated to the US government by the Ditchley Foundation of Great Britain in 1983 to commemorate the end of the American Revolution. Cast in London in 1976, the 10 bells are played for state occasions and to mark the opening and closing of sessions of Congress. The observation deck, the area's second-highest public vantage point (surpassed only by the Washington Monument), offers a **view** of the surroundings.

FOGGY BOTTOM★★

Once industrialized riverfront, this bottomland lying west of the White House was transformed after World War II into an administrative quarter. Today it houses private institutions, government departments, a celebrated performing arts complex and the city-styled campus of **George Washington University**.

- 📄 **Information:** ☎202-661-7581; www.culturaltourismdc.org.
- ▶ **Orient Yourself:** This neighborhood lies west of the White House and south of Washington Circle, extending eastward from the Potomac River.
- 🅿 **Parking:** Garage parking at the Kennedy Center for patrons; limited metered spaces in the immediate area of the State Department.
- 🎭 **Don't Miss:** A free performance *(daily 6pm)* at the Kennedy Center's Millennium Stage.
- 🕐 **Organizing Your Time:** Reserve your State Rooms visit 90 days in advance. Group the sights geographically, given the distances between them; and see Kennedy Center by attending a performance.

A Bit of History

Breweries and Gasworks
In the early 19C a glassworks and brewery attracted Germans here, but the area called Foggy Bottom—presumably because of the mists that hovered over its marshy ground—developed slowly. An early home in the area was The Octagon. In 1856 the Washington Gas Light Storage Facility was built in Foggy Bottom and became a major employer, particularly for the Irish immigrants who lived in Connaught Row, south of Virginia Avenue.

The growing black population in the area commissioned James Renwick to design **St. Mary's Episcopal Church**. Established in 1886, the Gothic Revival church still stands at 728 23rd Street. Two breweries, the Heurich Brewery and the Abner Drury Brewery, employed many of the neighborhood's German residents. Waterfront warehouses added to the industrial character of this malarial bottomland, and rows of brick tenements provided residences.

Transformation
In 1912 George Washington University moved to the northern end of Foggy Bottom. Yet the lowlands near the Potomac remained an industrial area of substandard housing. Then in 1947 the State Department moved into a large, new headquarters building at 23rd and D streets. The century-old gas plant ceased operations, and Foggy Bottom took on a new respectability.

In the 1950s the neighborhood shifted to middle-class professional. Office-residential buildings were constructed, and in the 1960s the Potomac shoreline became the site of the John F. Kennedy Center for the Performing Arts. Beside it, the exclusive **Watergate complex** of condominiums and shops further enhanced the riverfront. In the 1970s the complex gained notoriety as the site of the Democratic National Committee break-in that ultimately led to President Richard Nixon's resignation. Pleasant 19C row houses can still be found in the vicinity of the university *(18th-25th Sts. and E-K Sts.)*. In Foggy Bottom's southern quarter are the administrative headquarters of the **World Bank** *(1818 H St.)* and the **Pan-American Health** and **World Health organizations** *(both at 523 23rd St.)*, as well as government departments. The north side of Constitution Avenue is lined with the **Department of the Interior** (1937), the **Federal Reserve** buildings (1937), the **American Pharmaceutical Assn.** (1934) and the **National Academy of Sciences** (1924), whose grounds hold a monument to physicist Albert Einstein.

DIPLOMATIC RECEPTION ROOMS ★★
DEPARTMENT OF STATE
23RD ST. BETWEEN C AND D STS. NW.
Ⓜ FOGGY BOTTOM.

Housed in an undistinguished 1960s government office building, these reception rooms have been transformed into architectural masterpieces of 18C interior design. They are furnished with one of the most impressive collections of American decorative arts in the country.

A Bit of History

When the State Department headquarters building opened in 1961, its eighth-floor rooms, used for official functions in honor of visiting dignitaries, were furnished in a stark, streamlined decor in keeping with the building's concrete and glass modernism. Before long, an effort called the **Americana Project**, under the direction of the Fine Arts Committee of the State Department, was begun to upgrade these reception areas.

Spearheaded by Clement E. Conger, then the department's deputy chief of protocol and curator of the White House, the project solicited private donors for contributions of funds and furnishings. Over the past three decades, it has amassed a collection of **American decorative arts** ★★ from the period between 1725 and 1825 valued at approximately $90 million.

Edward Vason Jones, a Georgia architect, dedicated the last 15 years of his life to redesigning the rooms in the style of great 18C American manor houses. The ornately plastered ceilings, pilasters, paneling, entablatures and pediments complement the fine furnishings.

Visit

🚶Visit by guided tour (45min) only, by 90-day advance reservation, year-round Mon–Fri 9:30am, 10:30am & 2:45pm. 🕐Closed major holidays. 🚸Tour is not recommended for children under 12. ♿☎202-647-3241. www.state.gov.

From the austere modernism of the building lobby, elevators ascend to the Edward Vason Jones Memorial Hall. Originally a nondescript elevator hall, it now serves as an elegant **foyer** appointed with marbelized pilasters and entablatures and rare King of Prussia gray marble floors.

The **Entrance Hall** contains the Chippendale furnishings, oriental rugs and English cut-glass chandeliers characteristic of the 18C American decor seen throughout most of the reception rooms. The mahogany bombé secretary-bookcase in this hall is the oldest dated and signed piece of bombé furniture in

W. Brown/Diplomatic Reception Rooms, US Department of State

Bombé Desk and Bookcase (1753)

North America. It was made by Benjamin Frothingham of Boston in 1753.

A short passageway opens onto the **Gallery**, a long, narrow room that was lightened and enlarged by adding Palladian windows at either end. Among the **Chippendale and Queen Anne furniture** is a bombé chest of drawers made in Boston about 1765 and considered one of the finest examples of its kind in the world. Also made in Boston about the same time, the mahogany secretary belonged to an 18C colonial shipping magnate of Massachusetts. Two portraits by John Singleton Copley hang here. The five-part breakfront holds Chinese export porcelain in the Fitzhugh pattern. Ordered from England about 1800, the 65-piece set arrived in Philadelphia with an incorrect family monogram. It remained in its original shipping boxes until put on display here.

In the large 18C-style **John Quincy Adams State Drawing Room**, guests are greeted by officials and other dignitaries in receiving lines. Wall paneling, door and window cornices, an elaborate mantelpiece and oriental rugs ornament this formal room. Portraits of Mr. and Mrs. John Quincy Adams hang on the walls. The original **portrait of John Jay** (1784) by Gilbert Stuart is considered the finest painting in the collection. The English Sheraton tambour, or desk, where Jay signed the Treaty of Paris, Britain's formal acceptance of American Independence, is among the room's furnishings, as is the simple architectural desk on which Thomas Jefferson may have drafted the Declaration of Independence.

The Neoclassical proportions and Doric entablature of the **Thomas Jefferson State Reception Room** reflect Jefferson's own architectural tastes. A copy of the David Anger statue of Jefferson that stands in the US Capitol occupies a pedimented niche at the end of the room. Several Jefferson portraits, including Thomas Sully's 1822 work, are on display. A fine pastel portrait of Benjamin Franklin by Jean-Baptiste Greuze also hangs here. The Savonnerie carpet is a reproduction of one originally made for the palace at Versailles.

The cavernous **Benjamin Franklin State Dining Room** was redesigned by John Blatteau and completed in 1985. Red-veined scagliola columns are set off by gilded capitals and entablatures. An 8,000-pound **Savonnerie** rug in rose and gold covers the floor, and eight cut-glass chandeliers flank a gilded Great Seal of the US in the ceiling. Above the mantel hangs Benjamin Franklin's favorite portrait of himself, painted by David Martin.

JOHN F. KENNEDY CENTER FOR THE PERFORMING ARTS★★

NEW HAMPSHIRE AVE. AT ROCK CREEK PARKWAY.

Ⓜ FOGGY BOTTOM.

Its gleaming horizontal mass dominating Foggy Bottom's riverfront, the Kennedy Center today ranks as one of the country's leading cultural institutions. Designation as the capital's official memorial to the 35th president of the US has greatly contributed to the center's popularity as a tourist attraction.

▶ **Orient Yourself:** Take the guided tour; it's free and lasts about 1hr.

🅿 **Parking:** The center's underground garage ($15 if attending a performance).

☺ **Don't Miss:** A performance here.

Kids **Especially for Kids:** A performance in the Family Theater.

A Bit of History

"A Living Memorial"

Although the idea of establishing a national cultural center in Washington dates back to the early days of the capital, it was only in 1958 that such an undertaking received congressional approval. In that year President Eisenhower signed the National Cultural Center Act authorizing the creation of a national showplace for the arts.

A prime Foggy Bottom site comprising just under 10 acres of government property was chosen for the facility's location, and architect Edward Durell Stone was commissioned to design the complex. Due to a lack of sufficient private funds, the project lagged until early 1964, when Congress unanimously voted to designate the center as the capital's only monument to assassinated President John F. Kennedy. Unlike the other presidential memorials erected in Washington, the John F. Kennedy Center for the Performing Arts, as the complex was renamed, was to be "a living memorial." To hasten construction of the privately funded project, Congress appropriated $23 million in federal matching funds. The groundbreaking ceremony took place in December 1964. Over 40 foreign governments offered gifts—primarily works of art—to adorn the presidential memorial.

To mark the center's official opening on September 8, 1971, the world premiere of Leonard Bernstein's *Mass* was performed in the Opera House. In 2004 plans for a 10-year expansion were approved, which would make the Kennedy Center less isolated and integrate it with the Mall; a new 8-acre plaza as well as two buildings, were to be designed by noted architect Rafael Viñoly, for administrative, educational and rehearsal purposes. In 2005, however, the project was placed on indefinite hold after being unfunded by Congress.

Operation of the Center

Headed by a board of trustees appointed by the US president, the Kennedy Center operates as a nonprofit institution supported by private gifts and ticket sales.

As a presidential memorial, the building and its property (excluding theater and administrative facilities) are maintained by the National Park Service.

The complex houses six theaters with a total seating capacity of over 7,000, as well as an educational resource center. Home of the National Symphony Orchestra, the Kennedy Center schedules a wide spectrum of world-class entertainment in music, dance and theater, including hit Broadway shows.

Visit

🕐 *Open year-round daily 10am–9pm.* 👟*Guided tours (1hr) available Mon–Fri 10am–5pm, weekends 10am–1pm.* ☎ *202-416-8340. Tickets must be purchased for most performances.* ✕ ♿ 🅿 ☎*202-467-4600. www.kennedy-center.org.* 🚌*Free shuttle to/from Foggy Bottom Metro station and Kennedy Center Mon–Fri 9:45am–midnight, Sat 10am–midnight, Sun noon–midnight every 15min.*

Exterior

The low rectangular structure (630ft by 300ft) is surrounded on all sides by a colonnade of metal piers supporting a roof terrace, above which rises the building's central section. Clad in white Carrara marble (a gift from Italy), the stark structure seems to echo the overall design of

Grand Foyer

J. F. Kennedy Center

the Lincoln Memorial, situated just a half mile downstream.

Interior

The two principal entrances, situated on the east facade, lead to a pair of lofty galleries clearly designed to inspire awe. The dizzying effect experienced upon entering is created by the relative narrowness of these spaces. The **Hall of States** *(north side)* displays flags of the 50 states, while the **Hall of Nations** *(south side)* is decked with flags of all foreign countries diplomatically accredited by the US. These parallel halls traverse the building's width, separating the three main auditoriums and ultimately connecting with the **Grand Foyer**, reputedly one of the largest rooms in the world (630ft long, 40ft wide, 60ft high). Occupying the entire length of the river facade, this awesome space is lined with 60ft-high mirrors (a gift from Belgium) that reflect the river terrace outside the foyer's floor-to-ceiling windows. Eighteen Orrefors crystal chandeliers (donated by Sweden) illuminate the gigantic expanse. In the central section of the foyer, note the expressive bronze bust of President Kennedy by Robert Berks.

The foyer serves as a vestibule to the three main auditoriums: the **Opera House** (2,300 seats), flanked by the **Concert Hall** (2,442 seats) and the **Eisenhower Theater** (1,100 seats). Renowned for their excellent acoustics, these theaters contain gifts, in the form of stage curtains, chandeliers and artwork, from foreign countries that contributed to the project.

Occupying the former site of the American Film Institute Film Theater, the **Family Theater** (324 seats) made its debut in December 2005. Incorporating state-of-the-art technology, the theater stages performances geared to the young. (AFI moved to new facilities in Maryland.)

The roof level *(accessible by elevators in the Hall of States and Hall of Nations)* houses two additional theaters, the educational resource center, restaurants and exhibit spaces. A gift from Japan, the **Terrace Theater** *(off the north gallery)* was designed by noted architects Philip Johnson and John Burgee. This 513-seat performing space hosts concerts of chamber music as well as recitals and small-scale dance and theatrical performances. The **Theater Lab** (350 seats) is designed for experimentation in sound research.

THE OCTAGON★

1799 NEW YORK AVE. NW.
Ⓜ FARRAGUT WEST.

One of Washington's earliest and finest residences, this many-sided architectural gem played a decided role in the history of the young Republic. Still retaining its Federal appearance, the Octagon houses period rooms and a gallery of exhibits organized under the auspices of the American Architectural Foundation, which administers the property.

A Bit of History

Historical Role

In the 1790s wealthy Virginia planter, Col. John Tayloe commissioned Dr. William Thornton to build a town house for him. Tayloe's lot was triangular. To harmonize the house with its setting, Thornton conceived a multisided structure. The Tayloes used it as their winter residence after its completion in 1801, entertaining the capital's most influential figures here. During the 1814 burning of Washington by the British, the French Minister was in residence at the house, and at his request, the British spared the Octagon.

The White House, however, was gutted by fire, and while it was being repaired, President Madison lived in the Octagon. During the Madisons' stay, peace was negotiated, ending the War of 1812. The Treaty of Ghent, signed by the British in Ghent, Belgium, on December 24, 1814, was brought to Washington and signed by James Madison at the Octagon, on February 17, 1815.

Decline and Revival

By the time of Mrs. Tayloe's death in 1855, the house had deteriorated. By the late 19C it had become an ill-kept tenement, but its architectural integrity attracted the **American Institute of Architects** (AIA). In 1902 the institute purchased the building, moved its headquarters here and began a meticulous restoration. In 1972 the AIA built the modern structure that wraps around the rear of the Octagon to house its offices, library facilities and bookstore. The courtyard that separates the buildings features a sculpture by James Rosati titled *Triple Arc 1* (1984).

Visit

🔊*Visit by group tour only (10 people minimum), by advance appointment.* ⊜*$5.* ☎*202-638-3221. www.arch foundation.org.*

Though its name suggests eight sides, this brick structure is actually six-sided, with a rounded front pavilion that serves as an entrance foyer. The main hall is dominated by an oval staircase. Opening off the main hall are two large public rooms, furnished in Federal style. The drawing and dining rooms are notable for their rare mantels of Coade stone, an artificial material produced in England until the mid-19C. In the symmetrical, Adam-style dining room hang portraits of Col. and Mrs. Tayloe by Gilbert Stuart. The circular study on the second floor is known as the Treaty of Ghent Room. President Madison signed the historic document at the round mahogany table in the center of the room. The two flanking rooms are devoted to changing exhibits on architecture.

The brick-floored basement houses a kitchen, servants' quarters and a wine cellar.

B'NAI B'RITH KLUTZNICK NATIONAL JEWISH MUSEUM

2020 K ST. NW.

Ⓜ FARRAGUT NORTH OR FARRAGUT WEST.

Sponsored by B'nai B'rith International, the world's oldest Jewish service organization, this museum (seventh floor) houses an extensive collection of Judaic ceremonial, folk and fine art.

Visit

🕐*Visit by advance reservation only, year-round Mon–Thu noon–3pm.* 🕐*Closed Jewish holidays and major holidays.* ♿ ☎*202-857-6603. http://bnaibrith.org.*

Changing exhibits from the permanent collection feature antique and contemporary ritual objects, such as Torah implements, spice boxes, Esther scrolls, Hanukkah menorahs and kiddush cups. Photographic and other temporary exhibits are also presented.

DEPARTMENT OF THE INTERIOR MUSEUM
DEPARTMENT OF THE INTERIOR BUILDING

C ST.

BETWEEN 18TH AND 19TH STS. NW.

Ⓜ FARRAGUT WEST.

This small museum, located in the Interior Department building (first floor), has retained the flavor of the late 1930s, when it first opened to the public.

A Bit of History

In 1849 Congress created the Department of the Interior to conserve and manage the country's natural resources, including public lands, mineral resources, forests and wildlife. The department was also given the responsibility for American Indian reservations and the US island territories. Today the department's principal bureaus are Reclamation, Indian Affairs, Land Management, Minerals Management, Surface Mining, US Geological Survey, US Fish and Wildlife, and National Park Service. In 1935 Secretary of the Interior Harold Ickes suggested that space for a museum be included in the Interior building, which was completed in 1936. Opened in 1938, the museum contained a gallery for every bureau to display its equipment, documents, maps, models, natural history specimens and other artifacts. The museum became such a popular attraction that opening hours had to be extended into the evening and maintained even during World War II.

Visit

🕐*Open year-round Mon–Fri 8:30am–4:30pm & 3rd Sat of the month (call for hours).* 🕐*Closed major holidays.* ♿ ☎*202-208-4743. www.doi.gov/interiormuseum.* Seven bureaus have gallery space in the museum. The Bureau of Mines closed in 1996, but its exhibit continues to be on display. Throughout the museum **dioramas** depict historic or characteristic scenes from the nation's past, such

as the meeting of generals Washington and Lafayette at Morristown in 1780 and a 19C Indian trading post in 1835. The dioramas, and the **metal cutouts** of the first two sections, were executed by artists in the 1930s.

The **Native American section**—featuring a canoe, pottery and baskets—presents only a small fraction of the department's rich collection. In the passageway leading to the other exhibits hang four paintings by artist William H. Jackson depicting some of the earliest survey teams on assignment in the West during the second half of the 19C. Working from authentic period photographs, Jackson executed these paintings in 1938 when he was in his 90s.

Surveying equipment such as zenith and meridian telescopes used at the turn of the 19C, as well as facsimiles of early documents granting land to homesteaders and to military personnel, are on display in the section devoted to the Bureau of Land Management.

Artifacts from various Pacific islands, such as Micronesia, the Marshall Islands and American Samoa include watercraft and a wooden Palauan storyboard. Storyboards are carved and painted rafters, taken from traditional clubhouses, that depict a legend or commemorate a historic event.

Upon leaving the museum, stop in at the shop across the hall, where American Indian arts and crafts are on sale (🕐*open year-round Mon–Fri 8:30am–4:30pm; 3rd Sat of the month 10am–4pm;* 🕐*closed major holidays;* ♿ ☎*202-208-4056; www.indiancraftshop.com).*

GEORGETOWN ★★

Washington's choicest neighborhood, Georgetown today is an amalgam of popular nightspots, restaurants and shops surrounded by quiet residential streets. Predating Washington itself, this historic quarter functions as a well-preserved village, bounded on the south by the Potomac and on the east by Rock Creek. Congressional representatives, foreign dignitaries and the capital's intelligentsia live in many of its fine late-18C and 19C homes.

🛈 **Information:** Georgetown Visitor Center; 1057 Thomas Jefferson St. NW; ☎202-653-5190; www.nps.gov/choh.

▶ **Orient Yourself:** Wisconsin Ave. and M Street are Georgetown's chief commercial thoroughfares.

🅿 **Parking:** Garages and street parking are scarce. There is no Metrorail service, so you may want to take the bus line (nos. 32, 34, 36, and 38) that runs from Washington along Pennsylvania Ave., M St. and Wisconsin Ave.

☺ **Don't Miss:** A boat ride on the C&O Canal.

🕐 **Organizing Your Time:** Allow a full day for Georgetown sights.

A Bit of History

A Rock and a Knave

In 1703 Ninian Beall, a Scottish immigrant, patented a 795-acre tract on which most of present-day Georgetown now stands. Thirty years later George Gordon acquired an adjacent tract of land and established a tobacco inspection house on it. A small settlement of Scottish immigrants began to grow up here, and in 1751 the inhabitants petitioned the Maryland Provisional Assembly to establish a town. The assembly agreed, appointing commissioners to negotiate the sale of lots on the lands of George Gordon and those of George Beall, who had inherited the holdings of his father, Ninian. To this day no clear consensus on the town's namesake—the former owners George Gordon and George Beall or King George II—has been reached by historians.

The Golden Age

Positioned at the head of the Potomac's navigable waters, Georgetown thrived in the late 18C as a port of entry for foreign goods and as an exporter of products from the fertile Ohio Valley in the West. Even during the Revolution the town prospered, as a base of supplies and munitions.

After the war, the town thrived during the building of the capital. Well established and respected, Georgetown was considered the "court end" of the still rough federal city.

During this golden age, such grand manors as Evermay (1623 28th St.) and Tudor Place dotted the hills of upper Georgetown, and elegant Federal-style town houses lined its lower residential streets. In 1789 the first Catholic institution of higher learning in the country, Georgetown College—now **Georgetown University**—was founded.

Decline and Rebirth

By the late 1820s Georgetown found itself being eclipsed by Washington. In 1828 construction on the Chesapeake and Ohio Canal, with its eastern terminus in Georgetown, was begun in an attempt to stimulate commerce and westward migration. As the canal was being built, so too was the Baltimore and Ohio Railroad. The efficiency of train travel gradually brought an end to barge transport. At the same time, the advent of steam navigation, which required deeper ports than the town could provide, spelled doom to Georgetown's shipping business.

By midcentury, as the town continued its decline, residents began a movement to consolidate Georgetown and Washington, but those plans were waylaid by the Civil War. Georgetown counted both Union and Confederate sympathizers among its residents. Many of its churches and public buildings were used as hospitals for the Union wounded, and as elsewhere in Washington, the area was consumed with the war effort.

In 1871, with the war over, Georgetown was consolidated with the District of Columbia. To incorporate it into Washington's gridiron street plan, its original street names were changed to the letters and numbers used in Washington. From the late 19C through the first half of the 20C, Georgetown fell into decline. Though its great houses remained in the hands of the wealthy, many of its old row houses were divided into apartments and rooming houses and adorned with Victorian flourishes. Only in the last 40 years has the neighborhood regained its prestige. Under the Old Georgetown Act of 1950, the area was declared a National Historic District. Demolition, new construction and renovation are subject to review by the Commission of Fine Arts.

Today Georgetown's residential streets, with their carefully restored Federal-style and mid-19C houses, exude refinement. At the exclusive private parties held in these homes, much of the business of government, politics and private enterprise is conducted. Georgetown's commercial district is concentrated almost exclusively on Wisconsin Avenue and M Street, which are lined with numerous restaurants and small trendy boutiques. **Georgetown Park**, a large-scale urban mall, is situated at the intersection of these two streets. Anchoring the intersection of these two main thoroughfares is the golden dome of the former Riggs National Bank (now PNC), a prominent Georgetown landmark. Along the canal and the waterfront, redevelopment has generally taken the form of large brick office complexes. An exception is the riverfront showcase **Washington Harbour** (1986), a glittery complex of condominiums, offices, shops and restaurants. Its elaborately terraced and fountained courtyard affords a fine **view** down the Potomac.

The old towpath along the canal, saved through the efforts of conservationists, remains a quiet walker's thoroughfare reminiscent of the town's historic past.

GEORGETOWN

C&O CANAL AND VICINITY★★

LOCAL MAP

Georgetown is the terminus for the old **Chesapeake and Ohio Canal**, which runs 185 miles through 75 lift locks to Cumberland, Maryland. In 1971 the entire canal was designated a National Historic Park. At lift lock no. 3, a **bust (1)** of Supreme Court Justice William O. Douglas commemorates his work in spearheading the movement to preserve the canal as a recreation area.

▮ **Information:** 1057 Thomas Jefferson St. NW; ☎202-653-5190; www.nps.gov/choh.

▶ **Orient Yourself:** See the local map in this chapter.

Ⓟ **Parking:** Nearby street parking is difficult to find.

🕓 **Organizing Your Time:** Follow up the walking tour (allow 90min) with a 1hr ride on a mule-drawn boat on the canal *(departs from 1057 Thomas Jefferson St.* 🕓*open Apr–Oct Wed–Sun 11am, 1:30pm & 3pm (call ahead to confirm departure times);* 👜*$7;* ☎ *202-653-5190; www.nps.gov/choh).*

Walking Tour

▶ *1.5 miles. Begin at the corner of the towpath and 30th St. NW.*

At the intersection with Thomas Jefferson Street, the brick Federal structure (c.1810) at **no. 1058** originally housed the Potomac Masonic Lodge, whose early members were present at the ceremonies for the laying of the Capitol cornerstone. The quaint **row houses** just past it along the towpath were built after the Civil War as residences for artisans and laborers.

▶ *Turn right on 31st St. and then right on M St., one of Georgetown's main thoroughfares.*

Old Stone House

3051 M St. 🕓*Open year-round Mon–Sun noon–5pm.* 🕓*Closed major holidays.* 💬*Guided tours (30min) available by reservation only.* ☎*202-426-6851. www. nps.gov/rocr.*

The front of this two-story house, one of the oldest structures in Washington, was built by Christopher Layman around 1765. Since 1960 the National Park Service has maintained it as a visitor center and museum house characterizing colonial life. Note the paneling in the dining

Canal boat on the C&O Canal

C&O Canal/National Park Service

room. A large garden in the rear offers a respite from the bustle of M Street.

▶ *Continue east on M St.*

The twin buildings at nos. 3037 and 3039 (known as the Nathan Loughborough houses) date from the turn of the 19C. The Junior League of Washington, a women's civic organization, restored them in 1963 and now uses them as its DC headquarters. The late-18C buildings at **nos. 3001 and 3003** were the home of Thomas Sim Lee, governor of Maryland and friend of George Washington. In 1951 the buildings were saved from demolition under the strictures of the Old Georgetown Act.

▶ *Turn left on 29th St., then right on N St.*

N Street★

This handsome street contains some of the finest Federal-style architecture in the city. The elegant brick residence at **no. 2812** was built in the early 19C. Susan Decatur is said to have lived here after her departure from Decatur House.

▶ *Return to the corner of N and 29th Sts. and continue to 30th St.*

A bastion of Southern support during the Civil War, the **3000 block of N Street** boasts many of Georgetown's most distinguished town houses.
At the corner of N and 30th streets stands the **Laird-Dunlop House** (no. 3014), a brick building constructed in 1799 by John Laird, a wealthy tobacco merchant. Laird's daughter Barbara married James Dunlop, a law partner of Francis Scott Key, who penned "The Star-Spangled Banner." In 1915 Abraham Lincoln's son Robert Todd, who had been a secretary of War and minister to Britain, bought the house from Dunlop heirs. He added the attached dwelling at no. 3018.
The large house across the street at **no. 3017** was built in the 1790s by Thomas Beall, descendant of original Georgetown landowner Ninian Beall. **Jacqueline Kennedy** briefly lived here in 1963, after President Kennedy's death. The

dwelling at no. 3038, with its elegant doorway and shingled dormers, is a fine example of the smaller town houses built during the early 19C.

▶ *Turn right on 31st St. and left on Dumbarton Ave.*

Surrounded by a lush garden and a white picket fence, the imposing residence at **3123 Dumbarton Avenue** was built by Henry Foxall, a prominent Georgetown businessman, for his daughter Mary Ann McKenney. Dating back to the early 19C, the house is considered one of the most architecturally pristine structures in the area. According to local legend it also houses a famous Georgetown ghost—a maiden lady who came to luncheon at the McKenneys' and never left.
The yellow-brick **Dumbarton United Methodist Church** (no. 3133) was constructed in 1849 in the Romanesque Revival style. During the Civil War the church was used as a hospital, and poet Walt Whitman, serving as a nurse, ministered to the Union wounded here. The current facade was added in an 1894 renovation.

▶ *Continue across Wisconsin Ave. and turn left on O St.*

Note the remnants of the old trolley track embedded in this brick-paved street.

St. John's Church

3240 O St. 🕐*Open year-round Mon–Thu 9am–4pm, Fri 9am–3pm, Sun 9am–noon.* 🕐*Closed major holidays except Thanksgiving Day & Dec 25.* ♿☎202-338-1796. *www.stjohnsgeorgetown.org.*
Built between 1796 and 1804, the interior walls of this Federal-style stucco structure make it the oldest Episcopal church in Georgetown. Thomas Jefferson donated money for its building, and Francis Scott Key served as one of its vestrymen. In 1831 the church was abandoned due to lack of funds. Financier and art patron William Wilson Corcoran purchased it as a philanthropic gesture in 1837 and gave it back to the church two years later.
The 3300 block of O Street has a typical Georgetown mix of Federal and late-19C structures.

Bodisco House

3322 O St. Built about 1815, the handsome, porticoed Federal dwelling was home to Robert E. Lee's mother after she left Alexandria. The residence is most renowned, however, for the romantic tale surrounding another of its former occupants—Baron Alexander de Bodisco, the Russian minister to the US in the mid-19C. At that time the structure housed the Russian legation. After the 62-year-old baron married a 16-year-old Georgetown belle, Harriott Beall Williams, he and his new bride used the house as the setting for lavish parties that became legendary. For years it was a focal point of Georgetown society.

▶ *Turn left on 34th St. and left again on N St.*

Cox Row★

This handsome group of five Federal houses (nos. 3339-3327), adorned with swags and high dormers, was built in 1805 by Col. John Cox. Georgetown's first mayor elected by popular vote, Cox held that office for 22 years (1823-45). No. 3339 was Cox's residence for a time. In 1824 he entertained the Marquis de Lafayette in no. 3337.

Sen. **John F. Kennedy** purchased **no. 3307** in 1957 as a present for his wife, Jacqueline. The Kennedys lived here until moving into the White House in 1961. This house and its twin at no. 3311 were built in 1811.

Like a number of Georgetown homes dating from the Federal period, the facade of no. 3311 has been embellished with 19C Italianate detailing (elaborate cornice and door frame, and hooded window crowns with brackets).

Smith Row★

An unbroken, manicured block of Federal row houses extends from no. 3267 to no. 3255. Their exteriors have been little altered since they were built by Clement and Walter Smith in 1815.

DUMBARTON OAKS★★

1703 32ND ST. NW.

Renowned for its outstanding collection of Byzantine and pre-Columbian art, this museum and research institution is situated on a 16-acre estate set on a ridge above Rock Creek Park. The harmonious ensemble of buildings is surrounded by beautiful gardens.

▶ **Orient Yourself:** To get to Dumbarton Oaks, take any even-numbered 30s bus, or D2, D4, or M 12 bus to Wisconsin Ave. and R St. and walk one block east on R St.

🅿 **Parking:** Two-hour street parking near the museum on weekdays; unlimited street parking on Sun.

☺ **Don't Miss:** The gardens.

A Bit of History

The Oaks

In 1800 and 1801 Sen. William Dorsey of Maryland purchased 22 acres on the northern edge of Georgetown, and constructed the brick Federal-style home still standing at Dumbarton. He and his family lived here for only a year before personal and financial problems forced Dorsey to sell. The property passed through a succession of prominent owners, among them Edward Linthicum, a self-made businessman who, in the 1860s, added substantial wings to the original structure and renamed it "The Oaks," because of the stand of white oaks surrounding it.

A Marriage of Taste and Wealth

In 1920 Robert and Mildred Bliss purchased the estate. From adolescence the

Blisses had known each other, because their separate, widowed parents had wed, making them stepbrother and stepsister. Cultured, widely traveled and independently wealthy, the Blisses transformed Dumbarton Oaks, as they renamed it, into an elegant "country house in the city." With the help of the architectural firm McKim, Mead and White, the interior was restructured and the exterior restored to its original Federal style. In 1929 a large music room was added. Beatrix Jones Farrand, a noted landscape architect, designed the extensive gardens.

Robert Bliss' career in the foreign service prevented the couple from living here until 1933. During their years abroad, they acquired Byzantine artifacts, and once settled at Dumbarton they continued collecting, amassing an extensive research library. A west wing was added with two pavilions and an enclosed courtyard to function as a museum open to the public.

In 1940 the Blisses gave the house, grounds, their Byzantine collection, a library of some 14,000 volumes and an endowment to **Harvard University**, which maintains the estate. They also donated an adjacent 27-acre tract known as Dumbarton Oaks Park (○open year-round daily dawn–dusk) to the National Park Service. In 1944 the famous **Dumbarton Oaks Conferences**, involving representatives from the US, the United Kingdom, China and the Soviet Union, were held at the Blisses' former home. The accords reached among the participants ultimately resulted in the creation of the United Nations.

Museum

○━Museum closed for renovation until 2008. ○Gardens open (○see opposite below). ♿ ☏202-339-6401. www.doaks. org.

Byzantine Collection★★

The collection comprises some 1,500 artifacts—all examples of the artistic production of the Byzantine empire, which held sway over the eastern Mediterranean region from the 4C to 15C. The collection of 12,000 Byzantine coins is one of the most extensive in the world. The columned interior courtyard is devoted to artifacts predating, or created on the periphery of, the Byzantine empire. Displays include late Roman and early Byzantine bas-reliefs, Roman glass and bronze (1-5C), textiles from Egypt and the eastern Mediterranean (6-12C) and a 6C Syrian floor mosaic. The adjacent gallery displays 6C ecclesiastical silver from the Sion Treasury, found in present-day Turkey, and Byzantine icons, lamps, liturgical vessels, crosses and enameled adornments.

Pre-Columbian Collection★

In 1962 Robert Bliss donated his pre-Columbian collection to Dumbarton Oaks, and commissioned architect **Philip Johnson** to design an addition to house it. Johnson's concept consists of eight circular, glass-walled pavilions built around a central fountain.

Arranged by cultures, the pavilions house Olmec figurines and masks (gallery II); Mayan architectural reliefs and ceramics (III-IV); stone yokes and axes from Veracruz (V); gold jewelry from Central America (VI); pottery, gold and tapestries from ancient Peruvian and Bolivian cultures (VII); and Aztecan carvings, frescoes, masks and vessels (VIII).

Music Room★

This hall is dominated by a stone chimney piece from the Château de Thébon (16–17C) in France's Bordeaux region. The wooden ceiling beams are modeled on those in the 17C Château de Cheverny in the Loire Valley. Flemish and German tapestries hang on the walls, as does El Greco's Visitation (c.1610) (left

Gold Medallion of Constantine I (c.326)

Courtesy Dumbarton Oaks/Byzantine Collection

Pebble Garden at Dumbarton Oaks

Joseph Mills/Courtesy Dumbarton Oaks Research Library and Collection

wall). The frescoes adorning the arched stair alcove *(far wall)* were painted by Allyn Cox, who executed many of the murals in the Capitol. During the Blisses' residency, a number of famous musicians performed here, including Ignace Paderewski, Nadia Boulanger and Igor Stravinsky, whose *Concerto in E-flat*, also known as the *Dumbarton Oaks Concerto*, was commissioned by the Blisses for their 30th anniversary.

A rotating selection of rare books from the permanent collection of the garden library is displayed in the hall to the right of the entrance pavilion.

Gardens★★

Entrance at 31st and R Sts. ⏰*Open mid-Mar–Oct Tue–Sun 2pm–6pm. Rest of the year Tue–Sun 2pm–5pm.* ⏰*Closed major holidays and in inclement weather.* 💲*$8 (free Nov–early Mar).* ☎ *202-339-6401. www.doaks.org.* 🖐*In the flowering season, a map is available at the garden gate.*

Beatrix Jones Farrand planned broad terraces leading from the house to the lower garden, planted with flowering trees, shrubs and bulbs. Several "garden rooms" function as extensions of the house itself. The grounds include 10 acres of formal terraces devoted to such plantings as rose and herb gardens. Paths lead to secluded fountains, pools, terraces and arbors, offset by flowering trees and shrubs. The centerpiece of the lovely **Pebble Garden**, added in the 1960s, is a shallow pool framed by Rococo borders of moss and paved with a mosaic of Mexican stones arranged to represent a wheat sheaf.

TUDOR PLACE★
1644 31ST ST. NW.

The landmark mansion and stately grounds of Tudor Place were home to the prominent Peter family for six generations. The estate now functions as a house museum and a monument to old Washington traditions.

▶ **Orient Yourself:** To reach Tudor Place, take any no. 30s bus to Wisconsin Ave. and Q St. Walk east on Q St. and then turn left on 31st St.

🅿 **Parking:** Street parking is usually available.

A Bit of History

Tudor Place was built as the home of Thomas Peter and his wife, Martha Custis Peter, the granddaughter of Martha Washington. In 1805, with the $8,000 inheritance Martha Peter received from her stepgrandfather, George Washington, the Peters purchased an 8-acre city block in Georgetown Heights. Dr. William Thornton, the first architect of the Capitol, was commissioned to design the house. Thornton's project called for a two-story central structure to be joined to the preexisting east and west wings by means of one-story hyphens. The stuccoed brick mansion was finally completed in 1816.

At her death in 1854, Martha Peter left the estate to the youngest of the three Peter daughters, Britannia Wellington Peter Kennon, who had been widowed after only a year of marriage. During the Civil War years, Britannia, a staunch Southern sympathizer and relative of Robert E. Lee, allowed Union officers to use Tudor Place as a boardinghouse. Illustrious 19C visitors to this respected Washington residence include the Marquis de Lafayette, Andrew Jackson, Daniel Webster and John C. Calhoun.

The estate remained in the family until 1983. It then passed to the Tudor Place Foundation, which opened the property to the public in 1988.

Visit

Mansion visit by guided tour (1hr) only, year-round Tue–Fri 10am, 11:30am, 1pm & 2:30pm, Sat 10am–3pm hourly, Sun noon–3pm hourly. Grounds open year-round Mon–Sat 10am–4pm. Closed Jul 4. $6. 202-965-0400. www.tudorplace.org.

The simple Federal-style north facade fronts a boxwood-edged carriage drive. The centerpiece of Thornton's distinctive design is the circular south portico. The recessed semicircular wall of the portico projects into the interior, creating a convex glass wall in the central salon. A number of furnishings come from Mount Vernon. The first-floor rooms as well as the bedrooms on the upper story contain memorabilia from various eras in the family's history.

The 5 1/2 acres of **grounds** surrounding the house are devoted on the north side to more formal plantings, including a flower "knot," a circular garden and a bowling green. The south lawn slopes in a broad green expanse. Against the south facade of the house is a border of old roses, a few dating from Martha Custis Peter's occupancy.

Tudor Place, South Facade

DUMBARTON HOUSE
2715 Q ST. NW.

This brick Federal-style house serves as a house museum and the headquarters of a national women's organization.

A Bit of History

Built in the last years of the 18C, the house quickly passed through several owners until 1804, when it was purchased by Joseph Nourse, registrar of the US Treasury. In the early 20C, Georgian Revival quoins, balustrades and other embellishments were added, and in 1915 the house was moved 100 yards north to accommodate the eastward extension of Q Street. After the move, the present east and west wings were added to the house. In 1928 the **National Society of the Colonial Dames of America**, a women's organization dedicated to historic preservation, bought the property and renamed it Dumbarton House, after the original Rock of Dunbarton tract that once included much of present-day Georgetown. With the consultation of the architectural preserver Fiske Kimball, the Dames had the house restored to its Federal appearance.

Visit

Visit by guided tour (45min) only, year-round Tue–Sat 10:15am, 11:15am, 12:15pm & 1:15pm. Closed major holidays. $5. 202-337-2288. www.dumbartonhouse.org.

The exterior features a columned portico with a fanlight over the doorway and stone lintels above the windows. A sweeping staircase dominates the wide interior entrance hall, flanked by a formal library, a dining room, a music room and a parlor. The rooms, furnished in the Federal period, display china, crystal, quilts and clothing that belonged to Martha Washington and her granddaughter Eliza Custis Law. Also notable is a 1789 painting by Charles Willson Peale. It portrays the children of Benjamin Stoddert, first secretary of the Navy, with a view of old Georgetown and the Potomac River in the background. The second floor contains four bedrooms, also furnished predominantly in the Federal style.

Dumbarton House, Front Facade

© Dumbarton House

Benjamin Stoddert's Children by Charles Willson Peale

OAK HILL CEMETERY
3001 R ST. NW.

One of the city's oldest cemeteries, Oak Hill occupies a wooded 25-acre tract of land along the west bank of Rock Creek.

▶ **Orient Yourself:** To reach Oak Hill Cemetery, take any no. 30s bus to Wisconsin Ave. and R St. Walk east on R St. to 30th street.

A Bit of History

William Wilson Corcoran, financier and founder of the Corcoran Gallery of Art, donated the original 15 acres of ground to the cemetery company, incorporated by Congress in 1849.

Visit

Entrance at R and 30th Sts. ⏱Open year-round Mon–Fri 10am–4pm. ⏱Closed during funeral services and inclement weather. ☎202-337-2835.

James Renwick, the architect of the Castle and the first Corcoran Gallery (now the Renwick Gallery), designed the **Gothic Revival chapel** (1850) and the cast-iron gate that encloses the cemetery along R Street. Most graves date to the 19C. Corcoran's own grave is marked by a replica of a Doric temple, designed by 19C Capitol architect Thomas U. Walter. Among the many other prominent citizens buried here are John Howard Payne, composer of "Home, Sweet Home"; Dean Acheson, secretary of State under Truman; and relatives of George Washington.

ARLINGTON ACROSS THE RIVER ★

Arlington is a mixture of high rises, middle-class neighborhoods and ethnic enclaves. Along its Potomac shoreline, a network of pleasant parkways, dotted with memorials and statues, connects Arlington to the capital

🛈 **Information:** Arlington Visitors Orientation Center, Pentagon Row shopping center, 1301 South Joyce St.; ☎703-416-0784; www.stayarlington.com.

▶ **Orient Yourself:** Arlington lies across the Potomac, west of The Mall.

🅿 **Parking:** Street parking and parking garages are available.

🕐 **Organizing Your Time:** Allow 5hrs for Arlington sights if a tour of the Pentagon (*1hr; two-week advance reservation required*) is included in your itinerary.

A Bit of History

The Beginnings
By the mid-17C, much of the present county had been claimed by absentee landholders. Chief among them were members of the Alexander family, after whom the town of Alexandria, established in 1748, is named.

Throughout the colonial period and into the 19C, the Arlington region was bound, both administratively and economically, to Alexandria, which served as the urban focus for the area's small farms.

Part of the Capital City
By a 1789 act of the Virginia General Assembly, land along the Potomac was ceded for the new federal city. These former Virginia lands officially became the County of Alexandria of the District of Columbia. For the first half of the 19C, the current jurisdiction of Arlington was part of the capital. In 1846, disillusioned with their association with the nation's capital, the county's residents voted by public referendum to retrocede to Virginia.

War and Devastation
During the Civil War, Arlington's lands were occupied by Union forces guarding the southern flanks of the capital city against Confederate incursions. Robert E. Lee's own home, Arlington House, became the headquarters for various Union commanders.

After the war, Virginia's adoption of a new constitution added to the community's troubles. Under the 1870 law, cities with populations of 5,000 or more became independent units, separate from any county jurisdiction. Alexandria thus became an entity divorced from the County of Alexandria, leaving Arlington to fare on its own. It took 30 years to recover from the war, but business slowly returned. Between 1910 and 1920, Arlington's population grew by 60 percent, in large part due to an influx of workers in the World War I years. In 1920 the Virginia General Assembly recognized the county's growing prominence by changing its name from the County of Alexandria to Arlington County, named in honor of General Lee's Arlington home.

Arlington Today
In the last six decades, Arlington has continued its phenomenal growth, largely as a bedroom community for government workers. World War II saw federally funded housing for this white-collar work force sprout up in the southern part of the county, as did military buildings, including the Pentagon. Some 200,000 people now live in Arlington's 25.7sq mi. While its affluent northern neighborhoods retain their suburban character, south Arlington is home to many Hispanics and South Asians, some of whom operate small specialty food stores or restaurants in the area.

ARLINGTON NATIONAL CEMETERY★★

ON THE ARLINGTON SIDE OF MEMORIAL BRIDGE.

MAP P198

A sylvan retreat situated just minutes from the hubbub of the Mall, Arlington National Cemetery is the country's most revered burial ground and one of the capital's most poignant sights. This vast military cemetery, lined with endless rows of gleaming white headstones, contains the graves of a host of distinguished Americans.

▶ **Orient Yourself:** The cemetery is located on the Arlington side of Memorial Bridge, about 3/4mi from the Lincoln Memorial. By Metro: Ⓜ Arlington Cemetery. By foot: a short walk across Memorial Bridge. By car: see Parking *(below)*. By Tourmobile: access to the cemetery is included on the standard Washington tour. A **Tourmobile shuttle** operates within the cemetery: tickets for the cemetery tour *(⌖$7)* can be purchased at the cemetery visitor center, in front of which shuttles depart continually from opening time to a half hour prior to closing.

🅿 **Parking:** Cross Memorial Bridge to the parking lot *(hourly charge)* situated adjacent to the visitor center.

☺ **Don't Miss:** Tomb of the Unknowns, Changing of the Guard, Arlington House.

🕐 **Organizing Your Time:** The cemetery grounds can be explored on foot *(allow half a day and wear comfortable walking shoes)*. If you are pressed for time, ride the special Tourmobile shuttle *(⌖see Orient Yourself above)*, making stops at the most popular sights within the cemetery.

A Bit of History

A Vengeful Act

At the outbreak of the Civil War, Arlington House was established as the headquarters for the defense of Washington, and military installations were erected around the 1,100-acre estate. As much of the early fighting took place around the

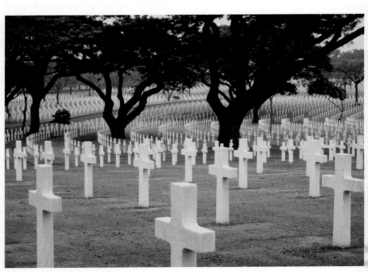

Arlington National Cemetery

capital, the need for burial space soon became evident.

In 1864 Quartermaster-General of the Army Montgomery Meigs (architect of the Pension Building), who was responsible for overseeing the appropriation of government land for military purposes, recommended that the grounds of Arlington House be used to inter war casualties. With the approval of secretary of War Edwin Stanton, 200 acres of the estate were designated as a burial ground, and on May 13, 1864, the first soldier was laid to rest there. Showing considerable vindictiveness toward Lee, whom he viewed as a traitor, Meigs ensured that the first graves were situated in the immediate vicinity of the mansion as a deterrent to the return of the Lee family.

In 1883, following a Supreme Court decision that the Arlington estate should be returned to the Lees, the family accepted $150,000 as compensation rather than demanding the restitution of the estate, which by that time contained the remains of some 16,000 war casualties. In that same year, Arlington became the official national cemetery of the US.

A National Shrine

The cemetery now comprises 612 acres and contains the graves of more than 300,000 military personnel, their dependents and others buried here. Among those laid to rest in the cemetery are veterans of every armed conflict in which the US has participated since the Revolutionary War.

Tour

The cemetery is situated on a tract of hilly terrain crisscrossed with meandering paved routes. Car traffic is permitted only for disabled visitors and for relatives of persons interred in the cemetery.

Cemetery Grounds

🕐Open Apr–Sept daily 8am–7pm. Rest of the year daily 8am–5pm. ♿🅿 ☎703-607-8000. www.arlingtoncemetery.org.

Situated at the entrance to the cemetery, the **Women in Military Service for America Memorial** is a testament to all US women who have served in the armed forces from the Revolutionary War to the present. Two US presidents are buried in Arlington Cemetery: President **William H. Taft** (1857-1930); and President **John F. Kennedy** (1917-63), whose simple grave is marked by an eternal flame. The grave of **Robert F. Kennedy** (1925-68), marked by a white cross, lies close to that of his older brother.

Designed by Carrère and Hastings, the 5,000-seat **Memorial Amphitheater** (1920) is used for special ceremonies such as Memorial Day and Veterans Day services. As the country's most prestigious burial ground, Arlington Cemetery has been chosen to house numerous **memorials** dedicated to special groups or particular events in the nation's history. Scattered throughout the cemetery, these memorials include group headstones, statues, plaques and even trees. Especially moving is the **Tomb of the Unknowns** (located behind the Memorial Amphitheater) containing the remains of soldiers from each of the two world wars and the Korean War. The remains of these soldiers represent symbolically all the men and women who lost their lives in those conflicts as well as the Vietnam War. Not to be missed at the tomb is the **Changing of the Guard**, whereby visitors can witness the precision and skill of the military sentries (🕐Apr–Sept daily on the half-hour; rest of the year daily on the hour). The cemetery's most prominent memorial, Arlington House, occupies a hilltop site overlooking the cemetery.

Arlington House/ The Robert E. Lee Memorial★

Surrounded by the white headstones of Arlington Cemetery, the dignified mansion that has been designated the official Robert E. Lee Memorial tops a high bluff overlooking Washington. Lee, hero of the Confederacy, called this his home for 30 years.

ARLINGTON NATIONAL CEMETERY

⊙ Tourmobile stop

1 Seabees Memorial
2 United Spanish War Veterans Memorial
3 Admiral Richard E. Byrd Memorial
4 101st Army Airborne Division Memorial
5 Women in Military Service for America Memorial
6 Memorial to service personnel killed in Beirut, 1983
7 USS Serpens Memorial
8 Mary Roberts Rinehart: mystery writer, war correspondent
9 William Jennings Bryan: Secretary of State
10 US Coast Guard Memorial
11 John P. Pershing: General of the Armies
12 Argonne Cross (dedicated to Americans killed in France during WWI)
13 Virgil Grissom and Roger Chaffee: Apollo I astronauts
14 Walter Reed: instrumental in combating yellow fever
15 Nurses Memorial
16 John Foster Dulles: Secretary of State
17 Rough Riders Memorial
18 Confederate Monument
19 USS Maine Memorial
20 Shuttle Challenger Astronauts Memorial
21 Memorial to service personnel killed in the attempt to rescue US hostages in Iran, 1980
22 Frank Reynolds: broadcast journalist
23 Joe Louis: heavyweight boxing champion
24 George C. Marshall: General, Secretary of State
25 James Parks: Arlington House slave
26 Claire L. Chennault: Commander of the WWII Flying Tigers
27 Montgomery Meigs: Quartermaster-General, engineer, architect
28 Johnny Clem: youngest soldier in the US Army
29 Lockerbie, Scotland, Pan Am 103 Memorial
30 Anita Newcomb McGee: first female Army surgeon
31 Tomb of the Unknown Dead of the War of 1812
32 Tomb of the Unknown Civil War Dead
33 Pierre Charles L'Enfant: planner of Washington DC
34 Oliver Wendell Holmes Jr.: Supreme Court Justice
35 Richard E. Byrd (grave): polar explorer
36 George Westinghouse: inventor
37 Dashiell Hammett: detective novelist
38 Medgar Evers: civil rights leader

A Bit of History

The Custises

Arlington House, as the mansion is commonly known, was built by George Washington Parke Custis, whose father, John, was the son of Martha Washington by her first husband. When John Custis died during the Revolution, George and Eleanor (Nelly), the youngest of his four small children, were brought to Mount Vernon and raised by the Washingtons. George Custis spent his childhood among the Washingtons' illustrious circle of acquaintances.

Washington died in 1799 and Martha in 1802. Mount Vernon passed to Bushrod Washington, a nephew of George Washington, and the 21-year-old Custis moved to a 1,100-acre tract of land his father had left him across from the newly established federal city.

Custis began planning a mansion worthy of housing the Mount Vernon memorabilia he had acquired through inheritance or purchase. Architect George Hadfield's building, incorporating the lines of a Doric temple, was the area's first example of the Greek Revival style. By 1804 the south wing was completed. In the same year Custis married Mary Lee Fitzhugh. About this time he also renamed his estate Arlington, after a Custis family property in Northhampton County, Virginia. The mansion was completed in 1818.

Sophisticated and talented, Custis was a poet, playwright and painter. Much of his skill and enthusiasm went to perpetuating the memory of his guardian and idol, George Washington.

The Lees

Robert E. Lee, a distant relative of the Custises, grew up in nearby Alexandria and visited their home often as a boy. In 1831 he and Mary Anna Randolph Custis, the Custises' only surviving child, were married at Arlington House. For the next 30 years, the Lees were posted to various locations as Robert pursued his military career. During this time they considered Arlington House their true home and spent many winters here. Arlington House was the birthplace of six of the seven Lee children. At the Custises' death, title to the house passed to the Lees. In January 1861, fearing the consequences of mounting hostilities between the North and South, Lee wrote to a friend, saying "There is no sacrifice I am not ready to make for the preservation of the Union, save that of honour." Three months later, on April 18, he was called to Blair House and offered the command of the Union troops. He refused, and on April 20 at Arlington House, he wrote his letter of resignation from the US Army. On April 22 he left Arlington House for Richmond, Virginia, where he accepted command of the Virginia forces. He would never return to his beloved home again.

Confiscation

In May 1861 Union troops crossed the river to Virginia and quickly made the strategically located Arlington House into the headquarters for the Army of the Potomac. Throughout the war the estate grounds were turned into fortifications, and ultimately into a national cemetery for the Civil War dead (Arlington National Cemetery).

In 1864 Arlington House was claimed by the federal government due to a dubious tax law that required Mrs. Lee to pay a $92 property tax in person. Mrs. Lee, in poor health, chose not to travel to Washington, sending a cousin instead. The government refused payment from the cousin, seized the property, and offered it up for public auction. As no

Courtesy National Park Service

Robert E. Lee

bidders were forthcoming, the government bought it for $26,800. After a legal battle that was decided by the Supreme Court, the Lees' eldest son, George Washington Custis Lee, won a suit for the return of the property. In 1883 Lee accepted the congressional appropriation of $150,000, based on the estate's market value, rather than reclaiming the land, which by then had the character of a cemetery. Congress designated the house a national memorial to Robert E. Lee in 1925, and the National Park Service began administering it in 1933.

Visit

🕐 *Open year-round daily 9:30am–4:30pm.* 🕐 *Closed Jan 1 & Dec 25.* 🅿 ☎ *703-235-1530. www.nps.gov/arho.* ♿ *Arlington House remains open during a major restoration. Furnishings have been removed until the project's completion in 2010. Call ahead the day of your visit to confirm operating hours.*

The mansion commands a fine **view**★★ of Washington, with Memorial Bridge stretching to the Lincoln Memorial in the near distance and the city beyond it. The main facade, with eight large Doric columns supporting an unadorned pediment, provides a gracious entrance to the off-white stucco structure.

Interior

Off the entrance hall to the right is the family parlor, where the Lees were married. Over the simple mantel is a portrait of a young Mary Custis painted by Auguste Hervieu just prior to her marriage. The room, and most of the rest of the house, is furnished with period pieces from the first half of the 19C.

Beyond the parlor is the well-lit room that served as an artist's studio for George W.P. Custis and for Mary Lee, who, like her father, was a painter. On an easel rests Custis' *Battle of Monmouth, New Jersey*, which hung in the US Capitol for several years.

On the lawn in front of Arlington House is the **tomb of Pierre L'Enfant**, whose remains were moved here in 1909. A marble plaque incised with his original city plan for Washington commemorates his unique contribution. A small museum *(behind the house and to the north)* has exhibits highlighting Lee's career.

This table is selective, showing only those figures mentioned in the guide.

MARINE CORPS WAR MEMORIAL★

IWO JIMA MEMORIAL

OFF N. MEADE ST. - MAP P198

This striking sculpture, honoring all US Marines who have lost their lives in military duty, ranks as one of the nation's most famous war memorials. Its prominent location across the Potomac in near-perfect alignment with the Mall's principal axis visually links the memorial to the heart of Washington.

Information: ☎202-433-6060.

▶ **Orient Yourself:** By Metro: Ⓜ Arlington Cemetery or Rosslyn. By car: Leave Washington via Memorial Bridge heading toward Rte. 50 West and follow signs to the memorial and Fort Meyer. To reach the memorial from the grounds of Arlington Cemetery, exit by the Ord and Weitzel Gate.

Visit

🕐*Open daily year-round. The US Marine Corps Sunset Parade is held here Jun–Jul Tue 7pm–8:30pm; Aug 6:30pm–7:30pm.* The sculpture depicts six Americans raising the Stars and Stripes on Mount Suribachi in 1945 during the assault of the Japanese-controlled island of Iwo Jima (hence the memorial's popular name). The capture of this strategically located island is considered one of the Marines' greatest victories and marked a turning point in the American campaign in the Pacific. Based on the Pulitzer Prize-winning war photograph by **Joseph Rosenthal**, the memorial was designed by Horace W. Peaslee and sculpted by Felix de Weldon. The work's poignancy is further intensified by the incessant waving of the US flag that rises from the bronze statue group.

The nearby tower, known as the **Netherlands Carillon**, is a gift from the Dutch people in appreciation of American assistance during and after World War II. Reminiscent of the pure geometrical style of the 20C Dutch masters Rietveld and Mondrian, this lofty metal structure contains 50 bells of various dimensions. **Carillon concerts** are given here from May to September. *For concert information, ☎703-289-2552; www.nps.gov/gwmp/carillon.*

The grounds of the US Marine Corps Memorial and the Netherlands Carillon afford excellent **vistas**★★ of the Mall area. The eye is drawn across the Potomac past the Lincoln Memorial and the Washington Monument to the dome of the Capitol in the distance.

Marine Corps War Memorial

W. Clark/Courtesy National Park Service

PENTAGON

I-395 AT WASHINGTON BLVD.
Ⓜ PENTAGON.

The heart of the American military establishment, this enormous pentagonal building houses the offices of the highest authorities of the armed services—the secretary of Defense and the joint chiefs of staff (Army, Navy, Air Force and Marines)—all of whom answer to the commander in chief, the president of the US.

▸ **Orient Yourself:** The Metro stop Ⓜ Pentagon City is closer than parking (♿*see below*) and walking to the Pentagon from the parking garage.

🅿 **Parking:** Park in the Fashion Center at Pentagon City mall parking garage; then it's a 10min-walk to the Pentagon.

A Bit of History

Conceived during World War II, the Pentagon combined for the first time all of the branches of the Department of War, as it was then called, under one roof. Army engineers were given one weekend in July 1941 to design the building, which was to be situated on the Arlington shore of the Potomac. Since the lot was five-sided, they devised a pentagonal shape for the building. Though the new structure was not ultimately constructed on the original lot, the five-sided shape was retained. Built of reinforced concrete faced with limestone, the five-story Pentagon was constructed in a relatively short 16 months and was completed on January 15, 1943.

On September 11, 2001 the west wall of the Pentagon was struck by a hijacked commercial airliner resulting in the loss of 184 lives. This event, coupled with the attack, on the same day, on New York City's World Trade Center, was the worst terrorist attack on US soil in the nation's history.

Visit

🐌*Visit by guided group tour (1hr) only, by reservation Mon–Fri 9am–3pm. Tours (minimum 5 people) must be requested two weeks in advance through your state representative's office.* 🕐*Closed major holidays.* 🪪*Visitors must show a photo ID.* ♿ ☎*703-697-1776. http://pentagon.afis.osd.mil.*

An introductory film *(12min)* explains the history of the construction of the Pentagon. The remainder of the tour walks visitors through office corridors displaying military art (battle scenes, portraits of high-ranking officers) and the **Hall of Heroes**, where the names of those who have received the Congressional Medal of Honor are listed.

Pentagon Profile

The Pentagon contains six and a half million sq ft, making it one of the world's largest single-structure office buildings. Its interior comprises five concentric circles that enclose a five-acre central courtyard. Each of its five sides is larger than the Capitol, and together they contain 17 1/2 miles of corridors. Some 23,000 personnel, about half of whom are military, work here in round-the-clock shifts.

DUPONT CIRCLE ★

At the beginning of the 20C, this neighborhood was the preferred address of Washington's moneyed elite. Back in vogue, the Dupont Circle area today boasts many of the city's finest boutiques, galleries, restaurants and cafes.

- **Information:** ☎202-661-7581; www.culturaltourismdc.org.
- ▶ **Orient Yourself:** Use the map and take the walking tour described herein.
- 🅿 **Parking:** Street parking may be available on the less busy side streets.
- 🐾 **Don't Miss:** The Phillips Collection.
- 🕐 **Organizing Your Time:** Allow 4hrs for the walk and the museum visits.
- Kids **Especially for Kids:** National Geographic Museum at Explorers Hall.

A Bit of History

Early Development

It was during the public works projects overseen by Alexander "Boss" Shepherd in the early 1870s that the Dupont Circle area developed. The improvements attracted a group of real estate investors that included Sen. William Stewart of Nevada. In 1873 he began constructing an elaborate home between Massachusetts and Connecticut avenues. Stewart's Castle was an extravagant Second Empire estate, complete with a stable of thoroughbreds. The mansion was razed in 1901; a branch of Riggs Bank stood on the site from 1924 until 2005, when PNC acquired it.

In 1874 the British legation constructed an impressive Second Empire structure at N Street and Connecticut Avenue. The side streets in the area developed as a modest working-class neighborhood. Not until the 1890s did the area become a "millionaires' colony," peopled mostly by Americans who had made fortunes elsewhere and chose to settle in the nation's capital. Typical of these millionaires was Levi Leiter, a Chicago department store magnate who in 1891 built a 55-room mansion on the circle.

In the early 20C, Massachusetts Avenue became a corridor of elegant Beaux-Arts palaces. The Virginia architect Waddy B. Wood designed more than 30 mansions in this area and in **Kalorama**, another prestigious neighborhood just northwest of Dupont Circle.

As the mansions rose along the avenue, the working-class houses on the side streets gave way to stylish brick row houses. A number of foreign missions were built in the area.

20C Vicissitudes

In the 1920s the character of Dupont Circle gradually shifted toward the commercial; a number of the fine homes were torn down to build offices and stores. With the Great Depression, the flamboyant lifestyle of the old Massachusetts Avenue residents ended, and the area gradually lost its cachet as a neighborhood of the fabulously rich. By the 1950s many of the mansions were occupied by private clubs and businesses, and the row houses had been converted into boardinghouses. During the 1960s these dwellings became the homes of student activists and "hippies," as Dupont Circle became a haven of the counterculture.

The Tax Reform Act of 1969 encouraged the demolition of old buildings and led to the loss of many of the area's surviving grand structures. To counter the razing, citizen groups petitioned the city to provide legal protection for the Dupont Circle environs. In 1978 the streets around the circle and north to T Street were designated a historic district. Now the neighborhood's renovated 19C row houses are once again home to professionals, and great efforts have been made to preserve the elegant old mansions that still grace Massachusetts Avenue.

DUPONT CIRCLE AND VICINITY ★

Ⓜ DUPONT CIRCLE-19TH ST. EXIT.

MAP BELOW

Situated at the junction of five thoroughfares—Massachusetts, Connecticut and New Hampshire avenues, and 19th and P streets—this bustling intersection has become a focal point of the city's Northwest quadrant. It is here that planner Pierre Charles L'Enfant's proposed arrangement of streets and avenues converging on a central green with a monument at its center can best be appreciated.

A Bit of History

Originally known as Pacific Circle, it was renamed in 1884 to honor Rear Adm. Samuel F. Du Pont (1803-65), the Civil War hero who directed Union naval operations along the south Atlantic coast. A bronze statue of Du Pont stood in the center of the circle until 1921, when the hero's family transferred the memorial to Wilmington, Delaware. Shortly thereafter, the Du Ponts replaced the statue with the marble **fountain** that now occupies the center of the circle. Designed in 1921 by Daniel Chester French, sculptor of the statue of Abraham Lincoln in the Lincoln Memorial, the fountain consists of a wide basin resting atop a central pillar adorned with figures symbolizing the sea, wind and stars—references to Du Pont's naval career.

During the 1960s and 70s, Dupont Circle gained prominence as a major gathering place for the counterculture and political activists. Today this busy urban park is frequented by a representative cross section of Washington's diverse residential population, making it one of the capital's best outdoor spots for people watching.

Walking Tour

▶ *1-1/3miles. Begin at the Circle. Then cross over to Massachusetts Ave. south of P St. on the east side of the Circle.*

Sulgrave Club (Wadsworth House)
1801 Massachusetts Ave. NW.
⊶Not open to the public.

Dupont Circle

This buff brick mansion was the residence of Herbert and Martha Wadsworth, from upstate New York. Constructed around 1900 (architect unknown), this two-story structure is crowned by a roof balustrade and features a Palladian window above the principal entrance *(on Massachusetts Ave)*. In 1918 Wadsworth donated his residence to the Red Cross, which occupied the mansion until 1932. It was then sold to a group of Washington women who established the Sulgrave Club, one of the city's private social clubs.

▶ *Continue on Massachusetts Ave. to the corner of 18th St.*

The 1700 block of Massachusetts Avenue contains four buildings by **Jules Henri de Sibour** (1872-1938), a French-born architect who trained at Yale and at the École des Beaux-Arts in Paris.

National Trust for Historic Preservation (McCormick Apartments)

785 Massachusetts Ave. NW. ⏰*The lobby is open to the public year-round Mon–Fri 9am–5pm.* ⏰*Closed major holidays.* ♿ ☎ *202-588-6000. www.nationaltrust.org.* Completed in 1917, the five-story edifice takes its name from the original owner, Stanley McCormick, son of Cyrus McCormick, inventor of the reaper and founder of the International Harvester Co. The two principal facades are accented by a rusticated first story, bas-relief panels and a balcony with cast-iron railings. The steep mansard roof is lined with chimneys and pedimented dormers adorned with characteristic Beaux-Arts ornamentation. The original interior reflected the fabulous lifestyle of the early-20C millionaires. Each floor held a single apartment (except the ground floor, which was divided into two) containing six bedrooms and measuring 11,000sq ft, with ceilings more than 14ft high.

Today the landmark building is the headquarters of the National Trust for Historic Preservation.

▶ *Continue east on Massachusetts Ave.*

Across the street stands **no. 1780**, built by de Sibour in 1922 for the Ingalls, another wealthy Washington family. The building has been remodeled to accommodate the Yater Clinic, which has occupied the site since the 1950s.

The five-story limestone and brick mansion at **no. 1746** was commissioned in 1906 by Clarence Moore, a West Virginia tycoon who perished on the ill-fated Titanic (1912). The building housed the Canadian diplomatic mission from 1927 until 1988.

The brick and sandstone building (1889), now the **Chilean chancery** (no. 1732), was constructed as a private residence by local architect Glenn Brown. It served as the headquarters of the Washington chapter of the Daughters of the American Revolution (DAR) from 1940 to 1973.

The dignified mansion at the corner of Massachusetts Avenue and 17th Street, now the **Peruvian embassy** *(no. 1700)*, was designed by de Sibour in 1910 for the widow of Beriah Wilkins, a congressman from Ohio and publisher of the *Washington Post*. Its imposing facade is reminiscent of a Renaissance palazzo.

▶ *Walk back up Massachusetts Ave. toward Dupont Circle, turn right on 18th St. and left on P St.*

On the corner of P and 18th streets, note the **embassy of Iraq** (1801 P St.), a tan brick structure with Richardsonian detailing. Completed in 1893, the building was designed by the architectural firm Hornblower and Marshall.

▶ *Continue on P St. to Dupont Circle.*

Washington Club (Patterson House)

15 Dupont Circle NW. ⊶*Not open to the public.* This ornate white marble and terra-cotta mansion, which resembles a Mannerist palazzo, was built in the early 20C by Stanford White of the New York firm McKim, Mead and White. Commissioned by the Chicago socialite Mrs. Robert Patterson, this opulent residence was yet another setting for lavish entertaining in the capital. The Pattersons' daughter, Cissy (1884-1948), publisher of the *Washington Times-Herald*, assumed the role of the capital's premier hostess in the 1930s and early 40s.
During the renovation of the White House in the summer of 1927, Patterson House served as the temporary residence of President and Mrs. Coolidge. In the course of their stay, the Coolidges hosted the nation's hero, Charles Lindbergh, just back from his historic transatlantic flight.
The family's Washington residence was donated to the Red Cross after Cissy's death in 1948. Three years later the mansion was sold to the Washington Club, the elite women's organization that now occupies the building.

▶ *Walk clockwise along the circle.*

Note the **Euram Building** at 21 Dupont Circle. Designed in 1971 by the Washington architectural firm Hartman-Cox, this glass, brick and concrete office building enclosing a handsome courtyard is one of the capital's most innovative works of contemporary architecture.

▶ *Turn left on New Hampshire Ave. and continue one block to the intersection of New Hampshire Ave., 20th St. and Sunderland Pl.*

The Brewmaster's Castle (Heurich Mansion)

1307 New Hampshire Ave. NW. 🔍*Mansion visit by guided tour (1hr) only, year-round Wed–Fri 11:30am & 1pm, Sat 11:30am, 1pm & 2:30pm.* ⊛*$5. Garden open Memorial Day–Labor Day Mon–Fri 10am–4pm, Sat 11am–4pm.* ☎*202-429-1894. www.heurichhouse.org.*
This landmark Richardsonian Romanesque building is one of the city's best-preserved house museums.
The imposing mansion (1894) was commissioned by Christian Heurich, the German-born founder of a brewery that stood on the present site of the Kennedy Center. The house remained in the Heurich family until 1956, when Heurich descendants donated the building to the Columbia Historical Society (later renamed the Historical Society of Washington, DC), founded in 1894. The society maintained the property as its headquarters and a museum until 2003, when the society moved to Mount Vernon Square. Two of Christian Heurich's grandchildren established a foundation for the purchase of

Washington Club

R. Corbel/MICHELIN

the mansion, and in fall 2003, Heurich House reopened to the public as a house museum.

▶ *Upon leaving the building, cross over to 20th St. and continue north to the corner of Massachusetts Ave.*

Blaine Mansion

2000 Massachusetts Ave. NW. ⚊ Not open to the public.
This severe brick edifice (1881) is Dupont Circle's oldest surviving mansion. It was built for **James G. Blaine** (1830-93), cofounder of the Republican Party. Displeased with the high maintenance costs, the Blaines leased it to Chicago real-estate baron Levi Leiter from 1883 until the early 1890s. Inventor George Westinghouse purchased the Blaine mansion in 1901 and lived there until his death in 1914.

▶ *Continue west on Massachusetts Ave.*

Indonesian Embassy (Walsh Mansion)

2020 Massachusetts Ave. NW. ⚐ Visit by guided tour (45min) only, year-round Mon–Fri 9am–5pm. ⊘ Closed Indonesian and major holidays. Phone before visiting. ♿ ☎ 202-775-5200. www.embassyof indonesia.org.
This turn-of-the-19C mansion was designed by Danish-born architect Henry Andersen for Thomas Walsh, an Irish immigrant who struck it rich in the Colorado goldfields.
The Walshes were prominent social figures, using their palatial home for lavish parties. At Mrs. Walsh's death in 1932, the house passed to her daughter Evalyn. Married to Edward Beale McLean, whose family owned the *Cincinnati Enquirer* and the *Washington Post*, Evalyn Walsh McLean was a Washington socialite and the last private owner of the celebrated Hope Diamond (⚐ see *National Museum of Natural History*). In 1951 she sold the home to the Indonesian government.

▶ *Continue west on Massachusetts Ave.*

Society of the Cincinnati Museum (Anderson House)★

2118 Massachusetts Ave. NW. ⊘ Open year-round Tue–Sat 1pm–4pm. ⊘ Closed major holidays. ⚐ Guided tours (30min) available. ♿ ☎ 202-785-2040. www. thesocietyofthecincinnati.addr.com.
This edifice serves as the headquarters of the Society of the Cincinnati and a house museum displaying its collection of Revolutionary artifacts.

The Society – George Washington was the first president-general of this patriotic organization, founded in 1783 by former officers of the Revolution. Named for a 5C Roman military hero and farmer, the society extols the ideal of the soldier returning to civilian life and spearheaded military pensions in America. Membership passes, by tradition and charter, through the line of eldest sons.

The Andersons – Larz Anderson, who had the 50-room house (1905, Little and Brown) built, was a member of the society. At her husband's death in 1937, Mrs. Anderson donated the house to the Society of the Cincinnati.

Visit

Arched carriage gates lead into a walled courtyard dominated by a rounded portico. Inside the front hall is a bust of Washington by Thomas Crawford, who designed the statue that tops the Capitol. The small room to the right is lined with late Renaissance choir stalls. On the wall above is a frieze by Henry Siddons Mowbray that depicts awards. In the billiard room hang military portraits by Gilbert Stuart, John Trumbull and George Catlin. The great stair hall contains cases with battle dioramas, French miniatures of soldiers and other memorabilia. *The Triumph of the Dogaressa Anna Maria Foscari* in the Year 1424, by Jose Villegas y Cordero, dominates the staircase landing. On the second floor, the reception room is notable for its Siena and white marble floor bearing the pattern of the Greek key. The allegorical wall and ceiling friezes were painted by Mowbray. A Louis XV-style parlor displays jade trees from the Andersons' Ching dynasty collection.

Among the furnishings in the adjoining English parlor are Hepplewhite pieces, English portraiture and Chinese porcelains from the 16C to the 19C. The long corridor contains Asian antiques and Italian paintings, while the formal dining room is decorated with early-17C Belgian tapestries. This room opens onto a musicians' gallery, overlooking the grand **ballroom**. Over the ballroom mantel is a portrait of Gen. Henry Knox, considered the society's founder. A solarium overlooks a walled sculpture garden. The reflecting pool is faced by an 18C statue of a Japanese Buddha.

▶ *Cross Massachusetts Ave.*

Cosmos Club (Townsend House)
2121 Massachusetts Ave. NW. ⚬🚇 *Not open to the public.*
Set behind a landscaped entrance driveway, this limestone mansion is the headquarters of one of the country's most exclusive social clubs. In 1899 Richard Townsend, the president of the Erie and Pittsburgh Railroad, and his wife, Mary, heiress to the Pennsylvania Railroad fortune, commissioned Carrère and Hastings to design a palatial residence. The architects received strict instructions to integrate the site's preexisting brick house into their plan because Mrs. Townsend had been warned by a fortune-teller that calamity would strike if she were to settle into a brand-new

house. Despite the precautions taken, Mr. Townsend died from a riding accident in 1902, the year following the house's completion. In accordance with the Townsends' request for a house in the style of the 18C Petit Trianon at Versailles, the architects designed a central facade composed of three bays separated by colossal pilasters and crowned by a roof balustrade. A mansard roof punctuated by dormer windows constitutes the fourth floor. The two-story wings that flank the central section lend balance to the design.

Mrs. Townsend gained fame among the capital's affluent circles for her extravagant entertaining. In the 1930s the mansion was home to the Townsends' daughter, Mathilde, and her second husband, Sumner B. Welles, undersecretary of State during most of the Roosevelt administration. The Welleses hosted President and Mrs. Roosevelt for several weeks in January 1933 before the first family moved to the White House. In 1950 the residence was purchased by the Cosmos Club, a social club founded in 1878 for men of distinction in the fields of science, literature and the fine arts. Inscribed in its prestigious register are the names of three US presidents and more than 80 Nobel and Pulitzer Prize recipients.

▶ *Continue one block east on Q St. to the corner of 21st St.*

THE PHILLIPS COLLECTION★★

The Phillips Collection, the nation's first museum of modern art, exhibits outstanding works by prominent American and European artists in an intimate setting and hosts a year-round schedule of music, gallery talks and films.

A Bit of History

The Collector
The grandson of one of the cofounders of the Jones and Laughlin Steel Co., **Duncan Phillips** (1886-1966) developed an interest in art during his studies at Yale and in travels abroad. In 1908 Duncan and his brother, James, began expanding the small private collection

that hung in the family's unpretentious brick and brownstone home built by the firm of Hornblower and Marshall in 1896. Following James' death in 1918—only 13 months after the death of his father—Duncan devoted himself to transforming the family's private collection into a public memorial to his beloved father and brother. In the fall of 1921, eight years before the founding of the Museum of

Modern Art in New York City, the Phillips Memorial Art Gallery, occupying two rooms of the family home, opened to an appreciative public.

That same year Phillips married Marjorie Acker, a talented painter in her own right. During the 1920s they acquired many of the collection's most famous paintings, including Renoir's *Luncheon of the Boating Party*, which was purchased for the record sum of $125,000 in 1923. By 1930 the collection had assumed its basic form, containing paintings by all the major French Impressionists, post-Impressionists and Cubists as well as outstanding works by several 17C and 18C masters, including Goya and El Greco. In 1931 Phillips and his family moved out of their home to provide space for the expanding collection. A new wing was added in 1960 (Goh Annex), and in 1961 the museum was renamed the Phillips Collection. The annex was expanded in 1989. Most recently, an expansion was completed in 2006 that included additional gallery space for large-scale works and a re-sited Rothko Room (Sant Building), an auditorium, and an expanded cafe and museum shop.

The Collection

Throughout his life Duncan Phillips eschewed the cold formality of the art establishment. He and his wife relied on their judgment and taste, rather than the advice of curators or art dealers. Phillips did not adhere to any one specific doctrine or school of art and largely avoided the avant-garde and cult movements of the day. While concentrating primarily on modern art, he frequently juxtaposed 19C and 20C works with Old Masters paintings to suggest sources from which modern artists might have sought inspiration. Phillips conceived his collection as "a museum of modern art and its sources."

Most of the museum's nearly 2,500 works, primarily from the 19C and 20C, were selected by Phillips and his wife. Artists represented in the collection include Daumier, Degas, Cézanne, Monet, Bonnard, van Gogh, Matisse, Klee and Picasso, along with noted American painters such as Ryder, Marin, Dove, O'Keeffe and Tack.

Visit

1600 21st St. NW. Ⓜ*Dupont Circle.* ⏰*Open year-round Tue–Sat 10am–5pm (Thu til 8:30pm), Sun 11am–6pm.* ⏰*Closed major holidays.* 💲*$10 weekends (weekdays by contribution).* ✕🚻☎*202-387-2151. www. phillipscollection.org. "Artful Evenings" of*

Luncheon of the Boating Party (1880-81) by Pierre Auguste Renoir

Courtesy The Phillips Collection

gallery talks on art are held year-round Thu 5pm–8:30pm (admission charged). To the right of the street-level entrance hovers the bas-relief of a bird in flight, based on a work by Georges Braque, one of Phillips' favorite painters.

Paintings are hung in simply furnished rooms to create an informal domestic setting that Phillips considered conducive to the appreciation of art. The works, which are rotated frequently, are not arranged chronologically, but large-scale contemporary pieces are generally found in the ground-floor galleries. The house's largest room, the oak-paneled **Music Room** *(1st floor)*, which features a ceiling decorated with raised plaster medallions, and the foyer, with its dark oak staircase and molding, showcase works from the permanent collection. Added to the house in 1907 as a library, this room is the setting for Sunday concerts *(Oct–May 4pm)*.

The second floor of the house contains additional gallery space for the permanent collection.

The Goh Annex *(floors G2 and G3)* is linked to the original building by two glass-enclosed walkways. Among the works displayed on a rotating basis in the annex are paintings from the **Bonnard Collection**, reputed to be the country's largest collection of the French artist's paintings. One room holds works by renowned Swiss painter **Paul Klee** (1879-1940). Also on exhibit in the annex *(floor G2)* is the museum's most renowned treasure: **Luncheon of the Boating Party** (1881) by Renoir.

Off the annex, in the newly added Sant Building, a small gallery is exclusively devoted to four works by Abstract Expressionist **Mark Rothko** (1903-70), known for his hauntingly simple canvases of large expanses of color.

The third-floor galleries are reserved for temporary exhibits.

Outside, off the cafe, the newly completed Hunter Courtyard (2006) is graced with sculptures by Ellsworth Kelly and Barbara Hepworth.

NATIONAL GEOGRAPHIC MUSEUM AT EXPLORERS HALL

17TH AND M STS. NW.
Ⓜ FARRAGUT WEST OR FARRAGUT NORTH.

The National Geographic Society's century-long support of explorers, archaeologists, oceanographers and other scientists is showcased in this museum. Housed in the society's three-building headquarters complex, the hall was opened in 1964. It occupies the ground floor of a 10-story marble and glass structure designed by Edward Durell Stone, architect of the Kennedy Center.

Visit

Kids ⏱*Open year-round Mon–Sat 9am–5pm, Sun 10am–5pm.* ⏱*Closed Dec 25.* ♿ ☎*202-857-7588. www.national geographic.com/museum.*

The museum at Explorers Hall showcases 3-D models, from its permanent collection, of Mount Everest, the Grand Canyon and other regions. Interactive displays involve visitors in such topics as underwater exploration, dinosaurs and other aspects of natural history. Changing exhibits on cultural, geographic or scientific topics, generally feature photographs and discoveries made by photographers and researchers who work for the National Geographic Society.

Explorers Hall

EMBASSY ROW

Embassy Row is the popular name of the two-mile portion of Massachusetts Avenue between Scott Circle and Observatory Circle where some 50 diplomatic missions are concentrated. The buildings housing the chanceries (the embassies proper) and the ambassadors' residences (which may be separate from the chanceries) are recognizable by the colorful flags or plaques that generally adorn their facades.

- **Information:** ☎202-661-7581; www.culturaltourismdc.org.
- **Orient Yourself:** From 22nd Street to Observatory Circle is considered the most distinctive and elegant segment of Embassy Row. Use the map on page 212.
- **Parking:** Street parking should be available on the less busy side streets.
- **Don't Miss:** The Spanish Steps.
- **Organizing Your Time:** Allow 2hrs for the walking tour and 2hrs for the museums. Embassies are usually open for official business or social functions only. Contact the individual embassy about possible tours open to the public.

A Bit of History

Massachusetts Avenue beyond 22nd Street developed as an extension of the Dupont Circle residential enclave. Overlooking Rock Creek Park, this area offered spacious, relatively inexpensive lots suited to the construction of the palatial residences fashionable before the advent of income tax. By 1915 the Sheridan Circle area was home to some of the capital's wealthiest residents.

After the 1929 stock-market crash and Great Depression, formerly affluent residents were forced to set up households in more modest quarters. In 1931 the governments of Great Britain and Japan constructed new embassy compounds in the area. The two-mile stretch between Scott Circle and Observatory Circle soon supplanted the Meridian Hill district as the capital's premier diplomatic quarter.

In the construction boom that followed World War II, some of Embassy Row's buildings were sacrificed to make way for modern structures, but the avenue's upper portion (north of Florida Avenue) has conserved its elegant character.

In **Kalorama**, the residential neighborhood north of Florida Avenue between Massachusetts and Connecticut avenues, additional diplomatic missions have been established in reconverted upper-middle-class dwellings.

Beaux-Arts Architecture

The upper portion of Embassy Row preserves a concentration of private residences designed in the Beaux-Arts style. Derived from the preeminent art academy in Paris, the École des Beaux-Arts, this term, as applied to American architecture, generally refers to the classically inspired styles advocated by the École in the second half of the 19C. Among the Americans who trained in Paris during this period were the Washington-based architects George Oakley Totten Jr. (1866-1939), Waddy B. Wood (1869-1944) and Nathan C. Wyeth (1870-1963). The returning expatriates imported such European styles as the Chateauesque and Georgian and Renaissance Revivals, but the most popular Beaux-Arts style was derived from tall apartment buildings that rose in Paris' elegant residential quarters at the turn of the 19C. The American edifices were characterized by symmetrical design, exuberant decorative details (swags, garlands, carved panels, ornamented keystones and brackets), a rusticated first floor generally with an entry canopy, and a mansard roof rising above a stone balustrade.

211

EMBASSY ROW AND VICINITY

Ⓜ DUPONT CIRCLE.

MAP BELOW

It's best to visit this area on foot, particularly the most noteworthy portion of Embassy Row—Massachusetts Avenue between 22nd Street and Observatory Circle. Part of Massachusetts Avenue below 22nd Street is included on the Dupont Circle walking tour (see Dupont Circle chapter). Unless otherwise specified, all sights described or mentioned on the tour are located on Massachusetts Avenue NW.

Walking Tour

▶ *1mi (not including visits). Begin the tour at the corner of Massachusetts Ave. and 22nd St.*

2200 Block

This gently sloped portion of Massachusetts Avenue, flanked by attached town houses, provides entry to Sheridan Circle, situated on a rise to the northwest. The limestone mansion at no. 2200, which today houses the **embassy of Luxembourg**, was designed by Jules Henri de Sibour for Alexander Stewart (1829-1912), a lumber magnate and congressman from Wisconsin. Completed in 1909, the building incorporates characteristic Beaux-Arts features: symmetrical design, a rusticated first floor, arched windows, and a mansard roof rising above a stone balustrade. The embassies of Togo and the Sudan are located at nos. 2208 and 2210 respectively. At **no. 2230** stands the smallest of the four Embassy Row residences built by George Oakley Totten Jr. Completed in 1907, this brick-faced row house was designed in the so-called Chateauesque manner—an eclectic style briefly in vogue around the turn of the 19C. Derived from large-scale 16C European estates, Chateauesque buildings are characterized by gabled dormers, steeply pitched hipped roofs and balconies carved with reliefs or tracery. With elegant facades on both

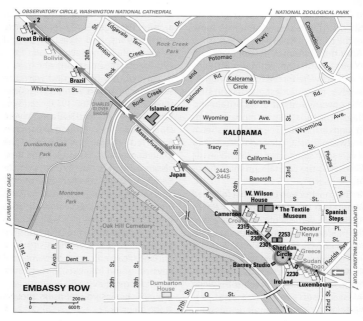

Massachusetts Avenue and Sheridan Circle, **no. 2234** was erected in 1909 as a private residence by William Cresson (1873-1932), an architect turned rancher, diplomat and law professor. Cresson's training at the École des Beaux-Arts is reflected in the building's overall design and ornamental details. Since 1949 the building has housed the embassy of Ireland. The freestanding structure across the avenue is the embassy of Greece.

Sheridan Circle
Originally called Decatur Circle in honor of the early-19C naval hero Stephen Decatur, the park was renamed in 1890 after Gen. Philip H. Sheridan (1831-88), leader of the Union cavalry. Dedicated in 1908, the bronze equestrian **statue** of Sheridan was designed by Gutzon Borglum, renowned for the colossal presidential heads at Mount Rushmore.
This circle, with its well-tended park rimmed with age-old ginkgo and linden trees, provides a graceful setting for the surrounding palatial mansions and town houses. At **no. 2301** the four-story mansion with a convex facade and Palladian arch is the residence of the Egyptian ambassador.
Other embassy buildings facing the circle are the residence of the ambassador of the Philippines at **2253 R St.** and the embassy of Kenya (2249 R St.).

▶ *Continue to the corner of 23rd St. and Sheridan Circle.*

Embassy of Turkey (Everett House)
1606 23rd St. Designed by George Oakley Totten Jr., this grandiose structure (1915) was the home of Edward H. Everett, multimillionaire industrialist and inventor of the fluted soft-drink bottle cap.
The glass-covered carriage porch, the semicircular columned portico and the balustrade crowning the roof lend an air of opulence to the structure. Totten incorporated a colonnaded porch above the south wing.
The interior, richly appointed with carved wood paneling and inlaid floors, featured an indoor swimming pool and a ballroom with walls hung with gold-thread damask. Mrs. Everett, an opera singer, hosted a concert series featuring world-renowned divas and attended by Washington's cultural elite. Now located at no. 2525, the Turkish chancery occupied the mansion from 1936 to 1999. Today Everett House serves as the Turkish ambassador's residence.

▶ *Continue clockwise along the circle.*

Barney Studio House
2306 Massachusetts Ave. ⊶*Not open to the public.*
Rather modest by Embassy Row standards, this town house on the southwestern rim of Sheridan Circle played a pivotal role in the cultural life of Washington in the early 20C.
Built about 1902 by Waddy B. Wood, the five-story structure, inspired by Spanish Colonial architecture (stucco facade, quatrefoil windows, curved parapet and red tile roof), was the home of Alice Pike Barney (1857-1931). Painter, playwright and trendsetter, Barney established her studio-home to serve as one of the capital's earliest private artistic centers. During her lifetime it provided the setting for much-needed cultural events. In 1960 the building was donated to the Smithsonian Institution by Barney's two daughters.

▶ *Continue north on Massachusetts Ave. (right side).*

2300 Block
Occupying adjacent lots just steps from Sheridan Circle, the Beaux-Arts mansions at **nos. 2305 and 2311** were designed between 1909 and 1910 by architect Nathan Wyeth (who also drew up the plans for the Key Bridge linking Georgetown with Arlington). Sold to the Chilean government in 1923, no. 2305, with its gracefully curved central section and roof balustrades, is the ambassador's residence. No. 2311, faced with colossal Corinthian pilasters and surmounted by a steeply pitched mansard roof, was owned by the Nationalist government of China (Taiwan) from the 1940s to the 1970s; it was subsequently purchased by the government of Haiti.
Located on a prominent triangular lot on the corner of Massachusetts Avenue and

R. Corbel/MICHELIN

No. 2315 Massachusetts Avenue

Decatur Place, the mansion at **no. 2315** boldly completes this distinguished block. The stucco Beaux-Arts pile, built in 1909 for the Moran family by George Oakley Totten Jr., is dominated by an imposing round tower adorned with limestone and terra-cotta detailing— oval cartouches, swags and bas-relief decorative panels. It was formerly occupied by the embassy of Pakistan, which relocated to a new chancery in 2003.

▶ *Cross Decatur Pl. past the Croatian embassy (no. 2343) to the intersection of Massachusetts Ave. and 24th St.*

Embassy of Cameroon (Hauge Mansion)

No. 2349. This prominently situated lime-stone "chateau" was the first of the four Embassy Row residences designed by George Oakley Totten Jr.

Christian Hauge, Norway's first minister to the US, commissioned the building to serve as both his private residence and his government's legation offices. However, in 1908, less than a year after the mansion's completion, Hauge died accidentally in Norway. For 19 years thereafter it was the home of Hauge's American wife, Louise, a prominent East Coast socialite. Like the sumptuous Sheridan Circle mansion of the Everetts, Mrs. Hauge's residence was, according to a local newspaper, "the scene of much of Washington's most brilliant entertaining." After almost 40 years as the Czechoslovakian foreign mission, the mansion was sold to the Cameroon government in 1972.

The Hauge mansion is the city's finest example of the Chateauesque manner.

Much bolder in scale and design than the row house at 2230 Massachusetts Avenue that Totten designed at about the same time, this freestanding struc-ture is based on the 16C French chateau Azay-le-Rideau, in the Loire Valley. The mansion's outstanding architectural feature is the imposing rounded tower with its candlesnuffer roof.

▶ *Turn right on 24th St. and right again on S St.*

Woodrow Wilson House

2340 S St. ⟲*Visit by guided tour (1hr) only, year-round Tue–Sun 10am–4pm.* ⟲*Closed major holidays.* ⟲*$5.* ♿ ☎*202-387-4062. www.woodrowwilsonhouse.org.* The 28th president of the US chose this residence as his place of retirement upon completing his second term in the White House in 1921. The brick Geor-gian Revival town house was designed in 1915 by Waddy B. Wood.

The house has been converted into a **museum**, which preserves the lifestyle of an upper-middle-class family in the 1920s and serves as a window on the family life of the president who led the US through World War I and into a posi-tion of world leadership.

▶ *Continue on S St.*

The Textile Museum★

2320 S St. ⟲*Open year-round Mon–Sat 10am–5pm, Sun 1pm–5pm.* ⟲*Closed major holidays & Dec 24.* ⟲*$5 contri-bution suggested.* ⟲*Guided tours (1hr) available.* ☎*202-667-0441. www. textilemuseum.org.*

Founded in 1925 by George Hewitt Myers, this small private museum occupies a pair of town houses built by two renowned Washington architects. The building serving as entrance to the museum was designed in 1913 by the prolific John Russell Pope as a private home for Myers. The adjoining house was designed in 1908 by Waddy B. Wood, who later constructed the adja-cent Woodrow Wilson House.

The museum focuses on the collection, study and preservation of handmade textiles and carpets. Its holdings com-prise more than 14,000 textiles and

Franko Khoury/Textile Museum

Peruvian Nasca Tunic Fragment (c.700 AD)

1,400 rugs, primarily from the Near and Far East and South America, including an outstanding **pre-Columbian collection** from Peru. Changing exhibits present textiles from the US and abroad.

In early 2008 the museum expects to open a second location, in Pennsylvania Quarter, at 421 7th Street NW.

Less than a block east, the **Spanish Steps**, which connect S Street with Decatur Place, offer a quiet spot to sit and enjoy the lion-head fountain and seasonal plantings.

▶ *Return to Massachusetts Ave.*

Note the low complex of white buildings (nos. 2443-2445) on well-maintained grounds, formerly housing the embassy of Venezuela, which relocated to Georgetown.

▶ *Cross the avenue.*

Embassy of Japan

2520 Massachusetts Ave. This Georgian Revival structure dominating a tree-lined cobblestone courtyard was built in 1931 for the Japanese government. The design, conceived by the architectural team Delano and Aldrich and reputedly approved by Emperor Hirohito, contains a hint of Oriental aesthetics in the delicately curved roofline. Note the depiction of a chrysanthemum, the imperial symbol of the Japanese emperor, that emerges from the balcony recess over the front entrance. The starkly modern chancery building to the right was added in 1986.

▶ *Continue on the opposite side of the avenue.*

At no. 2525 the Embassy of Turkey's chancery (1999, Shalom Baranes Assoc.) embodies traditional Turkish architecture with a contemporary look.

Islamic Center

2551 Massachusetts Ave. 🕐*Open year-round daily 10am-5pm. Proper attire is required while visiting the mosque: arms, legs and women's heads must be covered and shoes removed.* ☎*202-332-8343.*

This long white edifice, surmounted by a slender minaret, serves as a place of worship and instruction for the metropolitan area's sizable Islamic population. Completed in 1957 with funds and materials donated primarily by the governments of Islamic countries, the center houses one of the first mosques in the US.

Operation of the Center

A board of governors, composed of the heads of Islamic diplomatic missions in Washington, sets policies for the center's activities. In accordance with Muslim practice, prayer services are held five times daily. The call to prayer, traditionally chanted from a raised place by the muezzin, can be heard *(10am–5pm only)* from the loudspeaker installed on the minaret. Every Friday, the Muslims' holy day, the faithful meet for congregational prayers. Marriages and funerals are also performed in the mosque.

Visit

The limestone construction incorporates characteristic features of Islamic architecture, including horseshoe arches, roof cresting and a minaret, which reaches a height of 160ft. The two-story buildings facing Massachusetts Avenue house the library and the administrative offices. The double row of arches linking the two buildings leads to a small courtyard enclosing a pink marble fountain. From this point the visitor should note the oblique alignment of the mosque's facade, explained by the fact that, like all mosques, this building is oriented in the direction of Mecca. The **mosque** proper is an open, square space flanked by colonnades richly ornamented in a profusion of calligraphy and geometric and floral patterns (the Koran forbids the representation of human or animal forms). The lower parts of the walls are faced with 7,000 blue tiles donated by the Turkish government. The gifts from Egypt include the 2-ton copper chandelier in the center of the mosque and the carved wood pulpit, or *minbar*. To the left is the *mihrab*, the niche that indicates the direction of the holy city of Mecca to which the faithful pray.

Cross the Charles Glover Bridge, a 420ft-long single-span construction (1940) that rises 75ft above a heavily wooded section of Rock Creek Park.

▶ *Go to the corner of Whitehaven St.*

Embassy of Brazil

3000 Massachusetts Ave. This edifice was built in 1909 for an American diplomat by John Russell Pope. Inspired by Italian Renaissance palaces, the architect designed four proportioned stories topped with a prominent cornice. The sober facade is punctuated by a recessed entry with two pairs of columns. The building, which was purchased by the Brazilian government in 1934, today serves as the ambassador's official residence.

The dark-glass rectangular structure resting on concrete legs at **no. 3006** houses the chancery. Erected in 1971 by the Brazilian architect Olavo Redig de Campos, it is one of the few buildings of contemporary design constructed on Embassy Row.

Continue beyond the embassy of Bolivia *(nos. 3012-3014)* to the **Winston Churchill statue (1)** on the left. One of the greatest public figures of the 20C, Prime Minister Churchill was given honorary American citizenship in 1963 by President John F. Kennedy. Three years later, this statue by William McVey was unveiled.

British Embassy

3100 Massachusetts Ave. This embassy complex (1931), designed by British architect **Sir Edwin Lutyens** (1869-1944), resembles an early-18C English country estate. The building facing the avenue is the main chancery—a U-shaped brick structure trimmed in white stone with steep roofs accented by tall chimneys. The ambassador's residence is linked to the rear of the chancery (the two chimneys rising above the chancery's roof are the only parts of the residence visible from the avenue).

The nondescript office building rising to the west of Lutyens' building is the chancery annex. In 1957 the cornerstone for this addition was laid by Queen Elizabeth. The circular glass capsule near the entrance gate is a multifunctional space used primarily for conferences.

Opposite, the **Kahlil Gibran Memorial (2)** commemorates the Lebanese-born (1883-1931) author of *The Prophet*.

THE ANACOSTIA RIVERFRONT

Somewhat off the beaten track, the banks of the Anacostia River host historic military installations and the southeast neighborhood known as Anacostia, an area rich in black history. Targeted by the Anacostia Waterfront Commission for extensive development, the area will soon host a new baseball stadium that is expected to initiate an infusion of new businesses and recreational venues.

▶ **Orient Yourself:** Refer to the map on page 25 (BZ), in the Planning Your Trip: Getting There section of the guide.

🕐 **Organizing Your Time:** Make advance reservations for the Navy Museum. Given the distances among attractions, allow one full day for a visit to this area.

A Bit of History

The Beginnings

The Nacotchtank Indians inhabited the area when Capt. John Smith explored it in 1608. Later explorers misheard Nacotchtank as "Anacostia," the name now applied to the eastern branch of the Potomac and its southeast shore. By mid-17C tobacco plantations, worked by black slaves, dotted the riverfront. Thomas Jefferson had recommended that the land south and east of the river be included in the new federal district, as it offered a position from which to defend the city. The lower Southeast became the site of military installations, the first being the Navy Yard in 1799. With the demise of the tobacco economy, slaves were increasingly given or allowed to buy their freedom; by the early 19C the area had a large population of freed blacks. In addition, the liberal attitude of the federal circuit court toward black landownership and the rights of blacks encouraged many freemen to settle here.

The First Suburb

In the 1850s the area took on a suburban tenor with the establishment of Union-town, whose row houses still stand along U, V, and W streets east of Martin Luther King Jr. Avenue. In 1862 Congress enacted a bill emancipating slaves in the District. After the Civil War a Freedman's Bureau was established under Gen. O.O. Howard, for whom Washington's **Howard University** is named. The

bureau quietly purchased 375 acres in 1867 and resold plots to black families eager to own land. Within a year 500 families lived here. In 1877 **Frederick Douglass**, the nation's most prominent black spokesman, moved to Anacostia.

20C

Throughout the first half of the 20C, Anacostia's demographics reflected a mix of black and white working-class residents, who lived in single-family homes. Low-income housing projects were built here in the 1950s and 60s. By 1970 the population of the area was predominantly black (86 percent). The area suffered the serious social and economic problems afflicting many city neighborhoods. But in 1986 the district government designated Anacostia one of three development zones, and a line of the Metro was extended into the area.

Future Growth

A new stadium (*S. Capitol, First and N Sts. and Potomac Ave.*) for the Washington Nationals baseball team, to be completed by April 2008, is expected to jumpstart new mixed-use waterfront development. Construction of an entertainment, residential, office and retail district is anticipated. In early 2007 one entrance of the Navy Yard Metro station was closed while it is overhauled to accommodate ballpark crowds. The west side of the new Anacostia Riverwalk between the Navy Yard and the ballpark is scheduled for completion in late 2007.

FREDERICK DOUGLASS NATIONAL HISTORIC SITE ★

1411 W ST. SE.

Known as Cedar Hill, this Victorian house was the last residence of black states-man, orator and abolitionist Frederick Douglass. The estate tops a grassy, shaded knoll overlooking the Anacostia River and the Mall area beyond, and serves as a perpetual monument to Douglass' ideals and spirit.

▶ **Orient Yourself:** The site lies southeast of the Mall and south of the Anacostia River. By car: From downtown, cross the 11th St. Bridge to Martin Luther King Jr. Ave. and turn left on W St. By Tourmobile: in summer.

▣ **Parking:** Park *(free)* in the visitor center parking lot.

☺ **Don't Miss:** The film *(17min)* about Douglass shown in the visitor center.

🕐 **Organizing Your Time:** Allow 1hr for a visit.

A Bit of History

Father of the Civil Rights Movement

Born into slavery in Talbot County, Maryland about 1818, **Frederick Douglass**, christened Frederick Augustus Washington Bailey, was the son of a black mother and an unidentified white father. As a boy he worked as a house servant in Baltimore, where he was taught reading and writing by the household's white mistress. However, as a young man he was sent to work in the fields and suffered physical deprivation and abuse at the hands of a notorious slave overseer. Later his owner allowed him to leave the fields and learn the trade of ship's caulker.

In 1838 Douglass escaped bondage and fled north, settling with his wife Anna Murray in New Bedford, Massachusetts. In 1841 he became involved with the Massachusetts Anti-Slavery Society and was soon a respected and well-known abolitionist and publicist. After the publication of his first autobiographical work, *Narrative of the Life of Frederick Douglass, An American Slave*, in 1845, Douglass departed for Europe. While abroad Douglass became a free man thanks to English sympathizers and friends who purchased his freedom in 1846. During the Civil War Douglass exerted his efforts in recruiting black troops and in persuading Lincoln to legally end slavery. After the war he was involved with Reconstruction and moved to Washington, first settling in a row house on Capitol Hill, then in 1877, on his Cedar Hill estate. During his years in Anacostia, Douglass received several presidential appointments to serve in district government. In 1882 his wife died, and in 1884 his remarriage to Helen Pitts, a white woman, caused controversy but did not ultimately detract from Douglass' influence as a powerful spokesman for civil rights. In 1895, after attending a women's rights meeting, Douglass died suddenly of a heart attack at his home.

National Archives 200(s)FL-22

Frederick Douglass

Cedar Hill

The neat white house with its broad columned front porch was originally built as a speculative property in the late 1850s by John Van Hook, one of the developers of the area's first planned residential community, Uniontown. When Douglass purchased the 9-acre estate from Van Hook, the house had never been lived in. Douglass expanded the property to 15 acres and added seven rooms to the rear of the house In 1900 Douglass' widow, Helen, founded the Frederick Douglass Memorial Assn., which, in conjunction with the National Assn. of Colored Women, opened the house for tours. The house was donated to the National Park Service in 1962; the Park Service restored the estate and opened the historic site to the public. Early 2007 saw the completion of a $2.7million preservation effort that, among other improvements, restored the house to its 1893-95 appearance.

Visit

🕐 *Visitor center open year-round daily 9am–4pm.* 🕐 *Closed Jan 1, Thanksgiving Day & Dec 25.* 🚶 *House visit by guided tour (30min) only, year-round daily 9am, 12:15pm, 3pm, 3:30pm & 4pm (reservations encouraged ☎877-444-6777; www.recreation.gov; 💲$1.50 service fee).* ♿ 🅿 ☎202-426-5961. www.nps.gov/frdo.

The house is decorated with Victorian furnishings and memorabilia, most of which belonged to the Douglass family. The ground floor consists of a formal parlor and a family parlor, a dining room, kitchen, Douglass' study and a pantry and washroom. Note the rare Douglass portrait by Sarah James Eddy in the formal parlor. Douglass sat for the artist during a visit to Massachusetts. The five bedrooms on the second floor include those of Douglass and his two successive wives, and two guest rooms. Behind the house, a small reconstructed stone building served as a second study, which Douglass called "the Growlery."

ANACOSTIA COMMUNITY MUSEUM

1901 FORT PLACE SE.

Located on the high ground of old Fort Stanton, a Civil War fortress now converted into a public park, this museum was conceived by the Smithsonian Institution as a neighborhood museum. Since its inception in 1967, it has focused on African-American communities, including Anacostia.

▶ **Orient Yourself:** By car: From downtown, cross the 11th St. Bridge to Martin Luther King Jr. Ave. and turn left on Morris Rd., which becomes Erie St. before ending at Fort Pl.

🅿 **Parking:** On-site parking is free.

Visit

🕐 *Open year-round daily 10am–5pm.* 🕐 *Closed Dec 25.* ♿ 🅿 ☎202-633-4820. www.anacostia.si.edu.

The museum holds a permanent collection of more than 6,000 objects dating from 1800 to the present, including photographs, furniture, works of art, musical instruments and textiles. Changing exhibits on black history, culture and achievements are mounted year-round.

CONGRESSIONAL CEMETERY

1801 E ST. SE.

Ⓜ POTOMAC AVE.

Established in 1807 by private investors, this grassy site above the Anacostia River was intended to serve as the burial grounds for the new federal city. In 1812 the cemetery was deeded to nearby Christ Church, whose vestry in turn allocated 100 plots for the burial of members of Congress, adding a further 300 in 1823. Congress bought more sites; provided funds for walls, a gatekeeper's house, vaults and other improvements; and in the process named it the Congressional Cemetery.

Visit

🕐 *Open year-round daily dawn–dusk.* 🕐 *Closed Jan 1 & Dec 25.* 🅿 ☎*202-543-0539. www.congressionalcemetery.org.* Many prominent individuals involved with the history of the nation are buried on the 32-acre grounds. Notable among these are Civil War photographer Mathew Brady; "March King" composer John Philip Sousa (who was born in nearby Anacostia); and Push-ma-ta-ha, a Choctaw chief who served with Andrew Jackson in the War of 1812.

In addition, more than 70 former members of the House and 20 former senators lie here.

FORT LESLEY J. MCNAIR

4TH AND P STS. SW.

Ⓜ WATERFRONT.

Strategically positioned at the confluence of the Anacostia River and the Washington Channel, this complex, dating back to 1794, is one of the nation's oldest military installations in continuous operation. Known by various names over the years—Turkey Buzzards Point, Fort Humphreys, and the US Arsenal—the post was renamed Fort Lesley J. McNair in 1948 in honor of the commander of the army ground forces who was killed in Normandy in 1944.

A Bit of History

It was on this site in 1865 that four of John Wilkes Booth's fellow conspirators in the Lincoln assassination plot were imprisoned and hanged. One of them, Mary Surratt, was the first American woman executed by federal order. At the turn of the 19C, Maj. Walter Reed, who was instrumental in identifying the carrier of yellow fever, conducted research in the fort's military hospital.

Occupying a 98-acre site, Fort McNair today is the headquarters of the US Army Military District of Washington and the home of the prestigious National Defense University.

Visit

🕐 *The visitors gate is open daily year-round. Visitors are allowed to drive or stroll only around the grounds.* 🆔 *A photo ID must be presented for entry.* ♿🅿 *Because the fort is an active military base,* 🔑 *buildings are open only to military personnel.*

The post is laid out in a long quadrangle with a central esplanade bordered by rows of neat brick houses that serve as residences for officers and enlisted personnel. At the southern tip of the grounds rises the **National War College** (1907), designed by McKim, Mead and White.

Among the other noteworthy institutions on the post are the Industrial College of the Armed Forces and the **Inter-American Defense College** (1962). The Defense College trains senior officers from 19 countries in the Western Hemisphere.

WASHINGTON NAVY YARD

9TH AND M STS. SE.
Ⓜ NAVY YARD.

Once a prominent shipbuilding yard for the US Navy, this facility now serves primarily as an administrative center and as a historic precinct used ceremonially as the "Quarterdeck of the Navy." Two military museums open to the public are located on the premises.

A Bit of History

In 1799 the first secretary of the Navy, Benjamin Stoddert, authorized this shipbuilding yard as the US Navy's first shore facility. The prominent architect Benjamin H. Latrobe was commissioned to design the complex. The Navy Yard expanded rapidly until the British occupation of Washington in 1814. At that time the yard's commandant, Capt. Thomas Tingey, ordered the facility burned down, to avoid its takeover by the enemy. The yard was rebuilt and continued ship production until the mid-1850s, when it increasingly turned to ordnance manufacture. By 1886 it had become known as the Naval Gun Factory. In both world wars its involvement in weaponry production necessitated expansion. The facility ceased operation in 1961.

Visit

🕐 *The grounds are open daily year-round. Visitors to the museums must call in advance for an appointment.* 😊 *A photo ID is required to enter the Navy Yard.*

Navy Museum
Entrance on 11th & O Sts.(weekdays), 6th & M Sts. (weekends). 🕐 *Open year-round Mon–Fri 9am–5pm; Sat-Sun by advance reservations only (by noon of the preceding Friday) 10am–5pm.* ✖ ♿ 🅿 ☏ *202-433-6897. www.history.navy.mil.*

Housed in a cavernous workshop of the former gun factory, this exhibit hall was opened in 1963. Its permanent displays of naval memorabilia, dioramas, ordnance and equipment interpret the history of the US Navy from the Revolutionary War through the space age. Among the highlights are an extensive collection of scale-model ships, including a 25ft-long, detailed model of a World War II landing craft (LSM). A number of gun mounts on display may be manipulated by visitors.

Permanently docked near the annex at Pier 2 is the **USS Barry**, a destroyer maintained for public display. The below-deck living and working quarters are open to the public.

ADDITIONAL SIGHTS IN DC

HILLWOOD ★★

4155 LINNEAN AVE. NW.
Ⓜ VAN NESS.

On a residential street above Rock Creek Park lies the 25-acre estate of Marjorie Merriweather Post (1887-1973), heiress to the Post cereals fortune. Administered by a private foundation, her mansion and grounds are open to the public and.

▶ **Orient Yourself:** The Metro lies .5mi from Hillwood. By bus: Take an L1 or L2 bus along Connecticut Ave. to Tilden St. (.5mi from Hillwood).
🅿 **Parking:** On-site parking is free.
🕐 **Organizing Your Time:** Allow 3hrs. First view an orientation video *(14min)* at the visitors center.

A Bit of History

A renowned businesswoman, hostess and philanthropist, Mrs. Post was also an avid collector. Though her columned brick mansion is somewhat unremarkable, its interior holds 18C and 19C French furnishings and the most extensive collection of **Russian decorative arts** ★★★ outside Russia.

Marjorie Post accompanied her third husband, Joseph E. Davies, to Moscow, where he served as ambassador from 1937 to 1938. In the late 1930s the Soviet government began selling art confiscated from the imperial family, aristocracy and Russian Orthodox church during the Revolution of 1917. The Davies purchased some of these treasures in the commission shops of Moscow and Leningrad.

Comprising 20 percent of her collection, the objects illustrate some 200 years of Russian decorative arts, from the reign of Peter the Great (1682-1725) to the days of the last Czar, Nicholas II (1868-1918), when jeweler Carl Fabergé created his fabulous Easter eggs.

Visit

🕐 *Open Feb–Dec Tue–Sat 10am–5pm.* 🐾 *Visit by self-guided tour (audio tapes available); guided tours of the mansion available.* 🕐 *Closed major holidays.* 💰 *$12. Garden tours available in spring and fall.* ✕ ♿ 🅿 ☎ *202-686-5807. www.hillwoodmuseum.org.*

Mansion
Hillwood boasts interior furnishings that reflect Mrs. Post's occupancy from 1955 to her death in 1973. The entry hall shows off Louis XV rock-crystal chandelier, Sèvres porcelain, portraits of Rus-

Hillwood Museum

Imperial Easter Egg (1895) by Carl Fabergé

sian royalty, and 18C French commodes of wood marquetry, bronze and marble. The octagonal **Russian Porcelain Room** is lined with cases containing dinner services commissioned by Catherine the Great (who reigned from 1762 to 1796) and produced in the Moscow factory established by the Englishman Francis Gardner. The oldest of the porcelains is a white pattern with pink rosettes, commissioned by Elizabeth I (daughter of Peter the Great) from the Imperial Porcelain Factory she established in 1744. Off the hall, the small **Icon Room**★★ contains the finest Fabergé pieces in the collection, including two of the more than 50 **imperial Easter eggs** commissioned by the Romanovs. The **diamond nuptial crown**, worn by Alexandra at her 1894 wedding to Nicholas II, is reputedly the only piece of Russian imperial regalia known to exist outside Russia. Occupy much of the first floor are the **French drawing room**, appointed in Mrs. Post's favorite style, Louis XVI; the **dining room**, featuring an inlaid-marble Florentine table with seating

for 30. The long pavilion was used as a movie theater and for square dancing, an activity Mrs. Post enjoyed. The **Russian Liturgical Gallery** contains Russian Orthodox robes brocaded with silver and gold threads and a 24-carat **gold chalice** commissioned by Catherine the Great.

The bedrooms on the second floor include an Adam-style guest room with blue and white Wedgwood jasperware, and Mrs. Post's own Louis XVI room.

Grounds

Gardens surrounding the mansion include an informal flower garden, a formal French parterre planted in boxwood, a rose garden encircling a pillar marking Mrs. Post's grave, a Japanese-style garden, and a flowering pet cemetery. In the wooded area south of the mansion is a log **dacha**, a replica of a Russian cottage. The **Adirondack building**, a wood cabin, displays the Native American basketry, rugs, pottery and silver objects that decorated Mrs. Post's retreat in the Adirondack Mountains of New York.

NATIONAL ZOOLOGICAL PARK★★

3001 CONNECTICUT AVE. NW.
Ⓜ WOODLEY PARK-ZOO OR CLEVELAND PARK.

With plants and landscaped environments an integral part of its concept, this "biopark" exhibits more than 2,000 wild animals and serves as a research institution devoted to the study, preservation and breeding of threatened species. One-fifth of the 400 species represented here are considered endangered.

▸ **Orient Yourself:** Use the accompanying map and take the zoo's main path, Olmstead Walk, which heads downhill from the visitor center; then follow Valley Trail back (⊙caution: it's a bit steeper, but has more shade). The Asia Trail, with its quarter-mile long path, showcases many animals that are new to the zoo.

Ⓟ **Parking:** There is a fee *($16 maximum)* for on-site parking.

🕐 **Organizing Your Time:** Allow at least 2hrs plus time for a meal.

Kids **Especially for Kids:** The Giant Pandas.

A Bit of History

Created in 1887 as the Department of Living Animals, the precursor of this zoo was located on the Mall and featured such indigenous American mammals as

bison, mule deer and lynx. In 1889 Congress appropriated funds for the creation of a true zoological park, to be administered by the Smithsonian Institution. A 166-acre tract above Rock Creek Park was purchased, and landscape architect

Frederick Law Olmsted laid out plans for the new zoo. Because of disagreement among zoo administrators, Olmsted's project was only minimally realized. Though it was an immediate success, the zoo was plagued with financial problems. Not until 1964, when appropriations for it became part of the Smithsonian Institution budget, was the zoo able to revamp and modernize its facilities.

Visit

Kids *Main entrance at Connecticut Ave.* *Grounds open Apr–Oct daily 6am–8pm; rest of the year daily 6am–6pm. Buildings open Apr–Oct daily 10am–6pm; rest of the year daily 10am–4:30pm.* *Closed Dec 25.* (fee) *☎202-673-4800. www.si.edu/natzoo.*

In recent years parts of Olmsted's original design have been implemented, and today **Olmsted Walk** forms a path through the zoo's state-of-the-art exhibits. The highlight of this walk is the newly expanded **Giant Panda Habitat**★★ and its popular inhabitants Tian Tian (b.1997) and Mei Xiang (b.1998), a breeding-age couple who produced their first offspring at the zoo in July 2005; their cub is named Tai Shan. The pair arrived in the US in 2000. The People's Republic of China receives $1 million per year for the loan of the pandas; these funds help preserve the wild panda population.

The zoo's oldest building (1906) now contains the **Think Tank**★, exhibits that focus on animal thought processes and communication skills. Here visitors may observe animal keepers working on symbolic language acquisition with resident orangutans, who commute between the Think Tank and the Great Ape House via the 0 line—vine-like cables suspended over the zoo's pathways some 20ft off the ground. Also on view along Olmsted Walk are large African ungulates (hippos, rhinos, giraffes and elephants) and an exhibit on great cats, which focuses on the biology and

conservation of lions and tigers. The Byzantine-style **Reptile Discovery Center** (1929) houses the world's largest lizard, the Komodo dragon, along with other reptiles and snakes.

The **Valley Trail** follows the wooded fringe of the zoo, where outdoor enclosures hold endangered Mexican wolves, birds, river otters, beavers, seals and sea lions. More than 40 species of waterfowl frequent the **Wetlands**, a natural setting of grasses and aquatic plants. The trail leads to the **Amazonia** exhibit, where a 15,000sq ft tropical forest habitat has

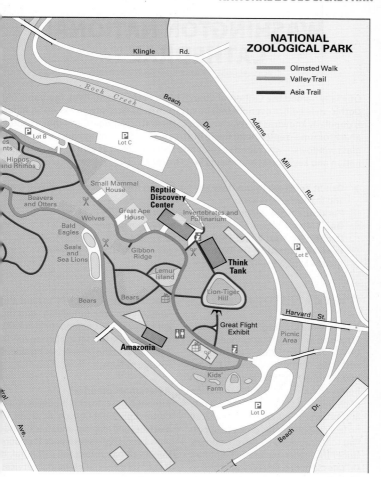

been re-created. On the ground level visitors explore life within the Amazon River system and learn how villagers cope with frequent floods. An aquarium here contains Amazon River fish; nearby, an Amazon field station illustrates how biologists study the region's varied flora and fauna. Upstairs lies a humid rain forest that sustains more than 350 plant species. The adjoining Science Gallery gives visitors the opportunity to see Smithsonian scientists at work.

Graced with waterfalls and groves of bamboo, the new six-acre **Asia Trail** (opened 2006) showcases red pandas, Asian otters, clouded leopards, fishing cats and sloth bears. Exhibits feature beekeeping, mushroom farming and other sustainable agriculture, as well as alternative fuel sources, such as biogas stoves, and job-creating conservation programs that improve the lives of Asia's villagers and animals. Zoogoers may interact with touch-screens at "decision stations" in the trail's two conservation plazas to solve environmental dilemmas facing scientists today.

WASHINGTON NATIONAL CATHEDRAL★★

MASSACHUSETTS AND WISCONSIN AVES. NW.

Officially named the Cathedral Church of St. Peter and St. Paul, the imposing Gothic-style edifice overlooking the city from its 57-acre site on Mount St. Alban is popularly known as the Washington Cathedral or National Cathedral. This 20C anachronism—replete with flying buttresses, vaulting, gargoyles and stained-glass windows—was raised to celebrate Christian faith as well as the American nation and key figures and events in its history.

▶ **Orient Yourself:** By bus: Take any no. 30s bus to the intersection of Wisconsin and Massachusetts aves.
Parking: On-site parking *(fee applies except on Sun)*.
Don't Miss: The panorama from the observation gallery.
Organizing Your Time: Allow 90min for a visit.
Especially for Kids: The Darth Vader sculpture on St. Peter's Tower.
Also See: US Naval Observatory.

A Bit of History

A Long Time Coming

In his plan for the capital, planner Pierre Charles L'Enfant proposed "a great church for national purposes," but the idea won little support, the new nation being committed to the separation of church and state. In 1893 Congress authorized the building but allocated no federal funds for the project; support had to be provided by private donors. Under the leadership of the Right Rev. Dr. Yates Satterlee, first Episcopal bishop of Washington, the foundation was able to purchase the Mount St. Alban site at the turn of the 19C. Satterlee insisted that the cathedral welcome all, regardless of faith or nationality, and that it be built in what he considered the only truly Christian architectural style—Gothic.

Construction

The foundation stone was laid by President Theodore Roosevelt in 1907, before a crowd of 10,000. Services have continued here every day since 1912, when the first service was celebrated. The cathedral, built primarily of Indiana limestone, was constructed by applying traditional techniques known to medieval European masons. Pneumatic tools and modern cranes accelerated the work. Thousands of people donated time, energy and money toward the construction, the furnishings and the landscaping. In a ceremony held in 1990, the final stone was set in place on the St. Paul Tower in the presence of President George H. Bush.

A National Cathedral

Although the cathedral is administered by the Episcopal Church, it strives to reach beyond religious and state boundaries. Every US president since Theodore Roosevelt has visited the cathedral. It has hosted special memorial services such as those for Vietnam War casualties, Iran hostages, Americans killed in the Persian Gulf War and victims of the September 2001 terrorist attacks. Several prominent figures are among the more than 100 Americans interred in the cathedral.

Visit

Open year-round Mon–Fri 10am–5:30pm (til 8pm May 31–Labor Day), Sat 10am–4:30pm, Sun 8am–6:30pm. Guided tours (30min) year-round Mon–Sat 10am–11:30am & 12:45pm–4pm (Sat 3:30pm), Sun 12:45pm–2:30pm. (fee except Sun) ☎202-364-6616. www.cathedral.org. Organ recitals Sun 5pm; carillon recitals Sat 12:30pm.

Washington National Cathedral, interior

S. Brimberg/Washington National Cathedral

Exterior

Measuring 514ft long from west facade to apse, the cathedral is among the world's 10 largest churches in size. Crowning the crossing, the **Gloria in Excelsis Tower**, with its 53-bell carillon, rises 301ft and dominates the skyline northwest of Washington.

The **west facade**, designed by Philip Hubert Frohman, is flanked by two identical towers dedicated to St. Peter *(left)* and St. Paul *(right)*. The carved tympanum above the central portal was designed by Frederick Hart, also known for his Vietnam Veterans Memo-

rial sculpture group on the Mall. The bronze gates of the central portal are decorated with scenes from the lives of Abraham and Moses, and a statue of Adam adorns the portal's *trumeau*, or central pillar. The centerpiece of the facade is the 26ft rose window—10,500 pieces of glass by stained-glass artist Rowan LeCompte.

Designed to carry rainwater away from the walls, the gargoyles and grotesques around the flying buttresses that support the vaulting of the nave reflect the whimsies that carvers were occasionally allowed to indulge. With binoculars, visitors can spot Kids a sculpture of Darth Vader from the film *Star Wars* on the St. Peter Tower.

Interior

The narthex, just inside the west entrance, features inlaid seals of the 50 states and the District of Columbia on its floor. The nave extends some 565ft to the high altar and has three levels: an arcade of pointed arches; the gallery, or triforium, which bears the state flags; and the upper section pierced with windows (the clerestory). The vaulted ceiling soars 102ft—about 10 stories. Bays honor Abraham Lincoln *(to the left of the entrance)* and George Washington *(to the right)*. Halfway down the right aisle *(over the 5th bay)*, the cathedral's most popular stained-glass window, the **Space Window**, commemorates the first manned lunar landing in 1969. A genuine moon rock is fitted in the center of the large red disc representing the moon. Just past the Space Window is the tomb of President Woodrow Wilson.

The four colossal pillars in the crossing provide support for the Gloria in Excelsis Tower. The pulpit, built of stone from England's Canterbury Cathedral, is still used every Sunday.

Above the high altar, the Jerusalem altar, is the **Ter Sanctus reredos**, a carved stone wall dominated by a representation of Christ in Majesty. To the left, note the Glastonbury Cathedra, a bishop's throne built of blocks from Glastonbury Abbey in England.

To the right of the choir, the War Memorial Chapel commemorates those who lost their lives for the nation. A statue of a young Jesus welcomes visitors to the Children's Chapel, which contains furnishings scaled down for youngsters.

Crypt

Access by the staircase on the north side of the choir. This vast underground labyrinth extends under the entire main floor. Of particular note are chapels dedicated to the birth (Bethlehem Chapel), death (St. Joseph's Chapel) and resurrection of Jesus (Resurrection Chapel).

Among Americans interred here are Helen Keller (1880-1968) and her teacher Anne Sullivan.

The crypt also houses the cathedral's visitor center.

Observation Gallery

7th floor. ◷*Open year-round daily 10am–4:30pm. Take either of the elevators in the narthex near the main entrance.* The gallery provides a **panorama** of Washington. The gallery's 70 windows also offer a bird's-eye view of the flying buttresses that support the nave. A slide show and a small exhibit illustrate the history of the cathedral.

Grounds

The landscaped 57-acre site on which the cathedral stands, also known as the Close, comprises three schools, a college for clergy and the **Bishop's Garden**, which provides a fragrant haven of herbs, flowers and boxwood.

THE KREEGER MUSEUM ★

2401 FOXHALL RD. NW.

Ensconced behind a high wall in a well-to-do neighborhood, this unadorned post-Modern mansion (1967, Philip Johnson) contains the formidable art collection of former residents David and Carmen Kreeger. Rife with 19C and 20C European paintings, the 200-piece collection includes African and 20C art.

▶ **Orient Yourself:** Drive north on Massachusetts Ave. to Nebraska Ave. At the circle, exit Nebraska Ave. to the west. Turn left onto Foxhall Rd.

A Bit of History

A Washingtonian, Kreeger made his fortune in the insurance industry. An avid collector, particularly of works by European Impressionists and post-Impressionists, he hired Philip Johnson to build a house that could function as a museum and performance venue. After her husband's death in 1990, Mrs. Kreeger vacated the house. In 1994 it was opened to the public as a museum.

The 24,000sq ft travertine dwelling comprises core modules of stacked cubes topped by barrel-vaulted ceilings. Most rooms have no doors. Designed as a concert hall and gallery, the Great Hall (22ft by 66ft) provides ample space for hanging art on its carpeted walls. Punctuated with floor-to-ceiling windows at each end, the hall opens onto a spacious terrace, the setting for outdoor sculpture.

Visit

Visit by guided tour (90min) only, year-round Tue–Fri 10:30am & 1:30pm; reservations required. Open Sat 10am– 4pm (no reservations needed). Closed Aug & major holidays. $8. 202-338-3552. www.kreegermuseum.org.

Tours focus on one or two selected works in each room to illustrate historic trends, schools of art or specific techniques. Of particular interest are early works by Cézanne (*The Blue Vase*, c.1882) and van Gogh (*Bouquet of Zinnias*, 1886) that do not resemble the styles for which the artists later became known.

First-floor galleries house 19C and 20C European art. Paintings and small sculptural works grace the Great Hall. Note Picasso's atypical *Café de la Rotonde* (1901). The dining room contains paintings by French Impressionists, including no less than nine by Monet. The works of Corot and Mondrian are highlights of the library; the landing showcases paintings by Picasso, Miró, Man Ray and others.

On the lower level, one gallery is devoted to large acrylic works representative of Abstract Expressionism and Color Field painting. An alcove contains African art, primarily large wooden masks.

Upstairs, the terrace features larger sculptures by Henry Moore, Jacques Lipchitz, Isamu Noguchi and others.

KENILWORTH AQUATIC GARDENS

ANACOSTIA AVE. AND DOUGLAS ST. NE.
DEANWOOD.

Located on tidal marshland along the eastern bank of the Anacostia River, this peaceful haven in northeast Washington comprises some 40 diked ponds devoted to the cultivation of water lilies, lotus and other aquatic plants.

▶ **Orient Yourself:** By Metro: Deanwood. By car: Drive northeast on New York Ave. From New York Ave. take 295 South. Exit Eastern Ave. and turn right on Douglas St. (2nd right after exiting freeway). Continue on Douglas St. to the gardens' entrance.

A Bit of History

Walter B. Shaw, a Civil War veteran, began the gardens in 1880 for his enjoyment. The lilies he grew multiplied so quickly that he began commercial cultivation. In the 1920s the gardens were popular for Sunday outings and were visited by presidents Wilson, Harding and Coolidge.

In the 1930s a dredging project proposed by the Army Corps of Engineers threatened the survival of the ponds. To save them, the Department of the

Interior purchased them in 1938. The 12-acre tract is currently administered by the National Park Service.

Visit

🕐*Open year-round daily 7am–4pm.* 🕐*Closed Jan 1, Thanksgiving Day & Dec 25.* ♿🅿 ☎*202-426-6905. www.nps.gov/ keaq.* 🌸*The blooms are most spectacular in the morning.*
Among the park's exotic flora are the **Victoria amazonica**, a water lily whose platter-shaped leaves grow as large as 6ft across, and the **East Indian Lotus**. In 1951 seeds for this rare plant were discovered in a dry lake bed in Manchuria, and were subsequently germinated by the Park Service. Believed to have been 350 to 575 years old, they are among the oldest viable seeds discovered to date. The ancient lotus plants can be viewed in the pond directly behind the visitor center. The Victoria lilies are located in a pond at the far western end of the gardens, near the Anacostia River.

NATIONAL ARBORETUM

3501 NEW YORK AVE. NE.

This federally owned 446-acre tract on the slopes of Mount Hamilton is one of the largest arboretums in the country. Established by Congress in 1927, the arboretum opened to the public in 1947, when some 15,000 azaleas were in bloom. Today its hills and valleys are covered in evergreens, wildflowers, flowering trees and shrubs.

▶ **Orient Yourself:** By car: From downtown, drive northeast on New York Ave. and enter the service road on the right after crossing Bladensburg Rd. Another entrance at 24th and R Sts. NE.

🕐 **Organizing Your Time:** Allow 2hrs. The arboretum is designed to be toured by car. Nine miles of paved roads lead past the various gardens, collections and designated parking areas along the route.

Visit

🕐*Open year-round daily 8am–5pm.* 🕐*Closed Dec 25.* ♿🅿 ☎*202-245-2726. www.usna.usda.gov.*

The **National Bonsai and Penjing Museum**★ (🕐*open daily 10am–3:30pm*) is renowned for its collection of Japanese, Chinese and North American bonsai. The 2-acre **Herb Garden** comprises a formal knot garden; a rose garden with

National Arboretum in Spring

NATIONAL ARBORETUM

Seasonal Highlights | Spring | Summer | Autumn

more than 80 varieties of "old" roses; and 10 specialty gardens, where herbs are grouped according to their uses throughout history. Atop a bluff stand the **National Capitol Columns**, which originally supported the east entrance portico of the Capitol prior to its expansion in the late 1950s. Pleasant stops along the drive include **Fern Valley**, the picturesque **Asian Valley** and the **Gotelli collection**, considered one of the finest groupings of dwarf conifers in the world.

NATIONAL MUSEUM OF HEALTH AND MEDICINE
WALTER REED ARMY MEDICAL CENTER
6900 GEORGIA AVE. NW.

Housed in an undistinguished building on the grounds of the Walter Reed Army Medical Center, renowned for its presidential patients, this small museum depicts medical progress through items ranging from Revolutionary War amputation implements to the medicinal leeches of modern microsurgery.

▶ **Orient Yourself:** By car: Drive north on 16th St.; take the first right after Aspen St. into the compound. At the circle, take the second right (14th St.). Turn right at stop sign. Museum is first building (no. 54) on the left.

A Bit of History

Begun during the Civil War by US Surgeon General William Hammond, the museum has advanced scientific knowledge through staff research conducted during wartime, epidemics and national tragedies such as the Lincoln and Garfield assassinations. As curator, Maj. **Walter Reed** (US Army surgeon 1851-1902) and his team identified the carrier of yellow fever, paving the way for the disease's control. In 1909 Maj. Frederick Russell successfully tested a vaccine for typhoid at the museum. Today the institution fosters public education through exhibits on contemporary health concerns, such as AIDS and heart disease.

Visit

🕐Open year-round daily 10am–5:30pm. 🗣Guided tours available second & fourth Sat 1pm. 🕐Closed Dec 25. ♿🅿 ☎202-782-2200. http://nmhm.washingtondc.museum. A floor plan is mounted on the wall near the gallery entrance. 😀Some exhibits are not for the fainthearted.

Highlights of the visit are photographs of injured Civil War soldiers taken before and after facial surgery, a large microscope collection dating from the late 16C to the 20C and such artifacts as the lead bullet that claimed Abraham Lincoln's life.

US NAVAL OBSERVATORY

3450 MASSACHUSETTS AVE. NW.

This naval facility is responsible for providing crucial astronomical and timing data to government agencies, the Navy and the country at large.

▶ **Orient Yourself:** By car: Drive north on Massachusetts Ave. past Embassy Row to visitors' gate at Observatory Circle.
🕐 **Parking:** Street parking available outside the entrance gate.
🕐 **Organizing Your Time:** Allow 2hrs. The tour is 90min and the video lasts 22min.

A Bit of History

Originally established in 1830 in Foggy Bottom, the observatory was the first true scientific agency in the country. With its 26in telescope, Asaph Hall discovered the two moons of Mars in 1877. To avoid the detrimental noise, light and vibrations of the Foggy Bottom area, the observatory was moved in 1893 to a more secluded location on the upper portion of Massachusetts Avenue. Noted architect Richard Morris Hunt designed the main buildings.

Since 1974 a white brick Victorian structure initially built on the observatory grounds as the superintendent's house has served as the official residence of the vice president of the US (⚓not open to the public).

Today the observatory is responsible for calculating the positions of the solar bodies, measuring the earth's rotation, and determining precise time—the accuracy of which is vital for navigation and communications on earth and in space.

Visit

Kids Entrance at South Gate. 🗣Visit by guided tour (90min) only, year-round selective Mon 8:30pm. 4- to 6-week advance reservations required: 🕐see instructions online. 😀A photo ID is required for entry. Tour involves walking in darkness on hilly grounds. 🕐Closed major holidays. No tours Jul 31–Sept 9. 🅿 ☎202-762-1489. www.usno.navy.mil. A video (22min) features the history of the observatory. Included on the tour is the **Master Clock** of the US, actually several rows of atomic clocks. Visitors are given an opportunity to view the sky (weather permitting) through a 12in Alvan Clark refractor telescope.

BASILICA OF THE NATIONAL SHRINE OF THE IMMACULATE CONCEPTION

4TH ST. AND MICHIGAN AVE. NE.

Ⓜ BROOKLAND CUA.

A 20C blend of Byzantine and Romanesque styles, this massive Roman Catholic church is the official national tribute to Mary, the Mother of Christ and the patroness of the US.

Official papal recognition of Mary as this country's patroness dates back to 1846, but it was not until 1914 that the plan for a national church for American Catholics was formulated, approved and designed. Construction of the crypt church began in 1920, and services have been held here since 1927.

Visit

🕐 Open Apr–Oct daily 7am–7pm. Rest of the year daily 7am–6pm. 🚶Guided tours (1hr) available. ✕&🅿 ☎ 202-526-8300. www.nationalshrine.com.
Constructed of brick, granite, tile and concrete, the shrine features the customary Latin cross design. Its dome is 108ft in diameter and 237ft in height to the summit of the cross. The **Knights' Bell Tower**—a gift from the Knights of Columbus—is surmounted by a 20ft gilded cross and stands 329ft high.

Inside, the church's nave rises 100ft and measures 58ft in width.

Among the richly adorned chapels in the **crypt**, note the Mary Altar (below the main altar) made of a block of golden Algerian onyx. The side chapels are dedicated to saints, martyrs, the Good Shepherd, Our Lady of Bistrica and Our Lady of Lourdes.

POPE JOHN PAUL II CULTURAL CENTER

3900 HAREWOOD RD. NE

Ⓜ BROOKLAND CUA.

Opened in 2001, this modern, 100,000sq ft facility designed by Leo A. Daly was built to provide a haven for exploring personal faith in the new millennium.

Visit

🕐 Open year-round Tue and Thu–Sat 10am–5pm, Sun noon–5pm. 🕐Closed Wed and major holidays. 💲$5 contribution requested. ✕&🅿 ☎202-635-5400. www.jp2cc.org.
The highlight of the main floor is the John Paul II Polish Heritage Room, which sheds light on Karol Joseph Wojtyla, the first non-Italian to be elected pope in 455 years. Among the keepsakes on view are a Tiffany clock, family photos, religious vestments, and downhill skis. Changing selections of art from the Vatican museums, accompanied by papal interpretation, occupy the second floor of the center. Ground-floor exhibits demand a high level of participation: interactive workstations, accessed by swiping a personal "smart card," cover everything from original sin to cloning. Visitors may also make virtual stained glass on a computer, collaborate on a song made from chimes or watch video-taped testimonials.

Upper Garden, Mount Vernon
©Mount Vernon Ladies' Association

EXCURSIONS

As the focus of this guide is Washington, DC, we have limited our selection of excursions to nearby sights whose histories are closely related to that of the capital. The five excursions described in the following pages are concentrated within 36 miles of Washington and are accessible by car or public transportation. The well-organized visitor can take in two or more excursions in the same day *(expect long entry lines at Mount Vernon during the spring and summer)*. **For longer excursions, the area offers a wealth of possibilities, including Baltimore** *(40mi from DC)* **and the vast Chesapeake Bay region in Maryland; and Manassas** *(31mi)*, **Fredericksburg** *(53mi)* **and Monticello** *(near Charlottesville—115mi)* **in Virginia.**

MOUNT VERNON★★★

MAP OPPOSITE

America's most visited historic estate, Mount Vernon sits on a grassy, shaded slope overlooking the Potomac River. Here, George Washington escaped the rigors of public office and enjoyed the life of a successful Virginia planter.

▶ **Orient Yourself:** Mount Vernon lies 16mi south of Washington. By car: Leave DC by the 14th St. Bridge, take Exit 11A (for National Airport) and continue south on the George Washington Memorial Parkway. By public transportation: Take Metro to Huntington station; then board bus no. 101 (Fairfax Connector) for Mount Vernon. **By Tourmobile:** Sightseeing buses run several times daily. By boat: see *Spirit of Mount Vernon* under Sightseeing Cruises in *Planning Your Trip*. At Mount Vernon, use the map of the estate distributed at the ticket booth. First watch the 18min film on Washington in the Ford Orientation Center.

🅿 **Parking:** There is plenty of free parking in the large on-site lot.

👁 **Don't Miss:** The slave quarters, Washington's tomb and the Pioneer Farm.

🕐 **Organizing Your Time:** Average round-trip driving time from downtown is 1hr. During peak season arrive early to avoid crowds; allow at least 3hrs for the mansion, grounds and new museum.

Kids **Especially for Kids:** River cruises from the wharf (see *Planning Your Trip*).

👁 **Also See:** Woodlawn Plantation, 3mi east of Mount Vernon.

A Bit of History

Family Heritage

The Mount Vernon property came into the Washington family in 1674 through a land grant from Lord Culpeper to John Washington, George's great-grandfather. The land passed through the hands of several descendants before Augustine Washington bought it from his sister in 1726.

In 1735 Augustine moved his family, which included three-year-old George, from Westmoreland County to the newly purchased Potomac property, then called Little Hunting Creek Plantation. The family spent four years here before again moving to a farm on the Rappahanock River. Records of the period, though sketchy, indicate that Augustine probably built a cottage near the location of the Mount Vernon mansion.

In 1740 Augustine deeded the Potomac property to his son Lawrence, George's elder half-brother. Lawrence renamed his 2,500-acre estate Mount Vernon, after a British admiral he had come to respect while serving in the Royal Navy. In 1743, when George was 11, his father died, and he came increasingly under the influence of his brother Lawrence.

Married to Anne Fairfax, the daughter of William Fairfax, one of Virginia's wealthiest landowners, Lawrence moved in prestigious circles. George, whose upbringing until that time had been more practical than formal, was exposed to genteel colonial society at Mount Vernon.

When Lawrence died in 1752, the 20-year-old George took over the management of Mount Vernon, leasing it from Lawrence's widow. Though he eventually became the nation's greatest hero and its first president, Washington considered farming the "most delectable" occupation.

The Gentleman Farmer

In 1759, after having distinguished himself in the French and Indian War, Washington married Martha Dandridge Custis, a widow with two children, John (Jacky) and Martha (Patsy). With his marriage to Martha, who owned some 15,000 acres in the Tidewater area near Williamsburg, Washington became one of Virginia's largest landowners. To accommodate his new family, Washington redecorated the simple 1.5-story farmhouse at Mount Vernon and added a full story to it. In 1761 his brother Lawrence's widow died,

Mount Vernon

making Washington the legal owner of the estate. Over the years he increased Mount Vernon's holdings to more than 8,000 acres, which were divided into five independent but adjoining farms and worked by some 300 slaves. Washington believed that farms should be self-sufficient, and to that end he constructed outbuildings for such activities as blacksmithing, shoemaking, weaving and fish salting.

Washington enjoyed entertaining at Mount Vernon and was active in the social life of nearby Alexandria, where he owned a small town house. In 1773 he began an ambitious enlargement of Mount Vernon, adding two-story additions to the north and south sides of the house, the piazza on the east, the cupola and the curving colonnades. The project took almost 15 years to complete.

The Public Years

In 1774 Washington was elected one of Virginia's delegates to the First Continental Congress meeting in Philadelphia to protest British injustices. A year later the Second Continental Congress unanimously voted him head of its military forces, a position that would keep him engaged in war and away from Mount Vernon until 1783.

Returning home from the Revolution, Washington set about rejuvenating his farms and finances, which had suffered during the war. His fortunes were further drained by an endless stream of house guests, many of them uninvited strangers. For the next six years Washington devoted himself to farming, experimenting with crop rotation and introducing new plant varieties. He took great pleasure in his wife's two grandchildren, Eleanor (Nelly) and George (Little Wash). The Washingtons brought the two children to live at Mount Vernon after their father, Martha's son John, was killed in the American Revolution.

From 1789 to 1797 Washington served as the country's first president. During his two terms, he managed to return to Mount Vernon on 15 occasions, sometimes for only a brief visit and at other times for several months. Refusing public demands that he serve a third term, Washington retired for a final time to Mount Vernon in March 1797.

The Final Years

The last two years of his life were lived once more as a planter. On December 14, 1799, having spent a snowy day overseeing work on the grounds, Washington contracted quinsy, an acute inflammation of the throat. Doctors administered gargles and bled him four times with leeches, but to no avail. A day later he passed away in his bed at the age of 67. His body was interred in the old family burial vault overlooking the river. Two years later, Martha Washington was buried beside her husband.

After Washington

After Martha's death the mansion passed to Bushrod Washington, a nephew and Supreme Court justice. He bequeathed it in turn to his nephew John Augustine Washington. When the latter's son, John Augustine Jr., came into possession of Mount Vernon in 1850, the estate was no longer agriculturally productive. Realizing the need to preserve the home and without the means to do so himself, John Washington sought to sell it either to the federal government or to the State of Virginia, but neither was in a position to buy it.

Instead, a woman in South Carolina, Ann Pamela Cunningham, began a grassroots effort to save the historic house. In 1853 she founded the Mount Vernon Ladies Assn. Through a public campaign, the association raised the $200,000 necessary to buy the estate. The association has owned and operated Mount Vernon since 1858.

Featuring interactive galleries and a state-of-the-art theater, the new **Donald W. Reynolds Museum and Education Center** was opened here in October 2006. The museum is filled with artifacts and documents that chronicle Washington's life. Some 11 videos are shown in the Education Center. Three life-size wax models of Washington at ages 19, 45 and 57 are the highlight of the exhibits.

The Mansion

🕐 *Open Apr–Aug daily 8am–5pm. Nov–Feb daily 9am–4pm. Rest of the year daily 9am–5pm.* 🎫*$13.* ✕ 🅿 ⅢⅢ ☎ *703-780-2000. www.mountvernon.org.*

The estate's main building is entered from the carriage side, opposite the river side, which boasts the well-known – columned piazza that is Mount Vernon's hallmark. The Georgian farmhouse is set off by a rust-red roof and curved colonnades connecting two flanking wings. A weathervane bearing the dove of peace tops its cupola. A facade of "rusticated board," a wood siding beveled and plastered with sand to resemble white stone, testifies to Washington's frugality; using real stone was much more expensive.

First Floor

The large **dining room**, or "new room," was the last addition to the house and is the most lavishly appointed. Here, as in the rest of the mansion, the decor is authentic to Washington's final years, and many of the furnishings belonged to him. Verdigris, a color favored by Washington, dominates the room and provides contrast to the ornate white woodwork around the Palladian windows and in the ceiling trim. The 21 side chairs are part of an original set made for this room by John Aitken of Philadelphia, who also crafted one of the mahogany sideboards. Washington characterized the ornate marble mantel, which was the gift of an Englishman, as "too elegant and costly…for my republican style of living."

The east-facing door in this room opens onto the piazza, which affords a pleasant **view**★ of the Potomac and the far Maryland shore. The center door in the piazza leads into the mansion's large central hall, whose pine paneling Washington had "grained" to resemble mahogany. Cross-ventilated from both the carriage and river sides, this hall was used for informal entertaining in the summer. On the south wall hangs a framed key to the Bastille prison in France, given to Washington by his French ally and friend, the Marquis de Lafayette.

Four rooms open off the hall. The small parlor used for informal family gatherings contains the harpsichord Washington ordered from England for his granddaughter, Nelly, who became an accomplished musician. Formal entertaining was done in the west parlor, which is painted in Prussian blue, a fashionable color at the time. A fine example of colonial Virginia architecture, the room retains its original ceiling molding, door and mantel pediments, and wall paneling. A number of portraits of family members hang here. The small dining room is appointed with richly glazed verdigris walls and mahogany furnishings. Over the mantel is an original **engraving** of the Washington family by Edward Savage. A bedroom opens off this room.

Second Floor

A heavy "grained" staircase leads to five bedrooms off a central hall. More lavishly decorated than Washington's simple bedroom, these guest chambers reflect Martha's tastes, with their worn, broad-planked floors and four-poster beds. So many guests visited the estate that Washington once called his home "a well resorted tavern, as scarcely any strangers who are going from north to south, or from south to north, do not spend a day or two at it."

The **master bedchamber** occupies a more private space in the south section. Simply furnished, this room contains the mahogany four-poster bed in which Washington died. The bedchamber also functioned as Martha Washington's office and contains the late-18C French desk at which she fulfilled her duties as an "old-fashioned Virginia house-keeper," as she called herself.

A narrow back staircase in this wing leads to Washington's own first-floor study. This large room contains many pieces intimately associated with him, including his desk and his presidential desk chair, which he brought back to Mount Vernon with him, and a terrestrial globe commissioned from a London manufacturer.

The two wings attached to the mansion by curving colonnades house a kitchen *(south)* and quarters for white servants *(north)*.

The Estate

Outbuildings

Twelve small dependencies are scattered along the lanes leading from both sides of the house. These structures re-create the operations of a self-sufficient estate, from the curing, spinning and laundry houses to the living quarters for overseers and slaves.

The stable at the south edge of the lower garden houses a fine example of an 18C coach. At the eastern edge of the upper garden, a small **museum**, built in 1928 and fully renovated in 1999, houses Washington memorabilia such as jewelry, china, swords and other personal items. It also displays a **bust of General Washington** executed at Mount Vernon by the French sculptor Jean Antoine Houdon.

Grounds

Today the estate comprises 40 acres of landscaped gardens and forests. The carriage entrance to the house is fronted by a sweeping bowling green bordered by stately trees. Several of the larger tulip poplars here were planted during Washington's lifetime. On the river side of the house, a deer park slopes to the Potomac. The upper garden on the north side of the bowling green is an ornamental flower garden, dominated by large boxwood hedges that date from Washington's day. The formal parterres are planted with annuals and perennials commonly found in 18C gardens. An imposing brick greenhouse, a reconstruction, forms the garden's north side. Opposite the upper garden, south of the bowling green, is the lower, or kitchen garden where a variety of fruits, berries and vegetables are grown.

Two different burial sites lie beyond the stables. George and Martha Washington were originally buried in the old family vault, a brick-fronted underground crypt. In the years following Washington's death, Congress proposed enshrining his remains in a crypt on the ground level of the Capitol. However, after years of complications and delays, his relatives decided against moving his remains. In 1831 they erected the present **tomb** for George and Martha Washington, building it of "Brick and upon a larger Scale," according to the wishes expressed in Washington's will. Beyond an iron grille, the couple's marble sarcophagi are visible within an open vault. Interred in the walls of the vault are 27 other family members. In front of the tomb are two marble obelisks in memory of Bushrod and John Augustine Washington, the 19C proprietors of Mount Vernon.

A path leads from the tomb to a shaded grove, where a small monument memorializes the slaves buried in unmarked graves at Mount Vernon.

Located near the wharf is a **pioneer farm** that features demonstrations of 18C animal husbandry, crop cultivation, brick making and timber transformation.

ALEXANDRIA★★

MAP P247

Situated just a few miles down the Potomac from the nation's capital, this enclave of historic homes and churches set along tree-shaded brick walks retains its colonial charm and an atmosphere of slow-paced Southern gentility. Alexandria's past is intimately bound with the founding of the country and with such preeminent Americans as George Washington, George Mason and Robert E. Lee.

- **Information:** Ramsay House Visitors Center, King and Fairfax Sts.; ☎703-838-4200; www.funside.com.
- ▶ **Orient Yourself:** Alexandria sits on the west bank of the Potomac River, 6mi southeast of Washington. By car: Leave Washington by the 14th St. Bridge, take Exit 11A (for National Airport), and go south on the George Washington Memorial Parkway. By public transportation: Take Metro to King Street Station; then board eastbound DASH bus no. AT 2 or AT 5.
- P **Parking:** One-day *(24hr)* parking permit available at Ramsay House Visitors Center (&*see information, above*).

A Bit of History

The Town Is Created

The area now called Old Town, Alexandria traces its beginnings to the early 1700s, when a tobacco warehouse on what is now Oronoco Street spawned a settlement. Scottish tobacco merchants and Virginia tobacco planters petitioned the Virginia General Assembly to establish a town. In 1748 the assembly did so, and named it after the Alexander family, upon whose land the town was sited. The town was laid out in the grid pattern characteristic of 18C urban planning. A public auction was held for sale of the 84 half-acre lots. Over a two-day period, 42 lots were purchased. To ensure the growth of the town, a dwelling had to be built within two years of land purchase.

A Prosperous Seaport

For the next quarter-century, Alexandria flourished as a colonial seaport and trading center. By 1763 the port had outgrown its space and was expanding westward. It also grew eastward as land was filled on the marshy Potomac shoreline around present-day Union Street. Growth ended with the Revolution in 1775. During the war Alexandria was a pivotal meeting point for such leaders as George Mason, whose plantation was in

Bird's-Eye View of Alexandria (1863)

Mariners' Museum, Newport News, VA

the area, and George Washington, who maintained a house in town and a plantation eight miles down the Potomac. The townspeople were divided during the Revolution: some were ardent patriots, while others resented the economic havoc war was playing with their lives. Battle threatened them only once, when British ships sailed up the Potomac, fired a few shots, then left. At the height of the war, in 1779, Alexandria was incorporated as a town.

Part of the New Capital

With the coming of peace, Alexandria's prosperity returned, and in 1789 the town's fortunes took a monumental turn when it was ceded by Virginia for the formation of the new federal city. Congress officially accepted it as part of the District in 1801. Alexandria's prospects were curtailed, however, by a congressional amendment that prohibited the construction of any federal buildings on the Virginia side of the river. Historians believe that this amendment was enacted at the instigation of President Washington, who owned Alexandria lands and feared allegations of favoritism. Nevertheless, the town had its heyday during the building of the new capital. Taverns, hostelries and businesses flourished, and the port became a major exporter of wheat, which had taken the place of tobacco as Virginia's cash crop.

In the early decades of the 1800s, Alexandria's fortunes declined as it lost trade to growing commercial centers in nearby Georgetown, Richmond and Baltimore. The town also incurred heavy debts in the building of the Alexandria Canal, which failed to stimulate the trade expected. Suffering economically from their association with the capital city and without representation in Congress, Alexandrians became disillusioned with their status as citizens of the nation's capital. In 1846 the County of Alexandria retroceded to Virginia, with whom it had always maintained strong social and political ties.

Civil War Years

From 1850 to 1860, with the coming of industrialization, a cotton gin and locomotive factory were built in town, and Alexandria once again thrived. Then federal troops moved in and occupied the town in 1861 for the duration of the Civil War, converting public buildings into Union hospitals and constructing a fort on Shooter's Hill, now topped by the granite tower of the George Washington Masonic National Memorial. During the Union occupation, Robert E. Lee, whose boyhood home still stands in Old Town, led the Confederate Army.

In 1870, soon after the war's end, Alexandria became an independent city, separate from the county of the same name (now called Arlington). Over the decades it spread west, annexing parts of the old county as it grew. Not until World War I did the town experience any real prosperity again, when the federal government constructed a torpedo factory on the waterfront.

During World War II Alexandria benefited from the growth that infected the entire metropolitan area. Today the city encompasses nearly 16sq mi, with a population of 111,000.

Elegant Enclave

In recent decades the Old Town quarter of the city has paid increasing attention to its architectural heritage, fostering an image of genteel provincialism. The city government carefully monitors the appearance of buildings in the historic district, which in 1969 was placed on the National Register of Historic Places.

Since the 1960s gentrification has overtaken what had been the working-class neighborhoods of the city. Professionals, lured by Alexandria's cachet, have bought and renovated the small colonials and elegant Georgians. Many now display the official metal plaques that designate buildings "of historic or architectural significance."

Today the city's waterfront is graced with parks, and restaurants and boutiques line King and Washington streets. At the foot of King Street, the **Torpedo Factory** has undergone a much-acclaimed urban renovation and now serves as an arts-and-crafts center, housing the shops and studios of visual artists.

Old Town ★★

Walking tour. Distance: 4mi. Map p247.

▶ *Begin at the corner of King and N. Fairfax Sts.*

Ramsay House Visitors Center

221 King St. ⏱Open year-round daily 9am–5pm. ⏱Closed Jan 1, Thanksgiving Day & Dec 25. ☎703-838-5005. www.funside.com.
The north portion of this colonial clapboard incorporates the remains of the oldest structure in Old Town. Built in 1724 by William Ramsay, a Scottish merchant, the small house was moved to Alexandria soon after the town's founding. It now functions as the official visitor and convention center.

▶ *Turn left on S. Fairfax St.*

Stabler-Leadbeater Apothecary Museum

105-107 S. Fairfax St. ⏱Open Apr–Oct Tue–Sat 10am–5pm, Sun–Mon 1pm–5pm. Rest of the year Wed–Sat 11am–4pm, Sun 1pm–4pm. ⏱Closed Jan 1, Thanksgiving Day & Dec 25. ⬤$4. 🅿 ☎703-838-3852. www.apothecarymuseum.org.
An apothecary from 1792 to 1933, this shop has been restored to its mid-19C appearance. Shelving, cases, glass bottles and equipment used for preparing medicines and remedies are from the original store, which served as a supplier of pharmaceuticals in the area.

▶ *Cross King St.*

Market Square

Now modernized and dominated by a steepled city hall (1873), this square has served as the city's focal point since the mid-18C. It has been the setting for historic gatherings, including Washington's drilling of his Revolutionary troops.

Carlyle House ★

121 N. Fairfax St. ⬤Visit by guided tour (45min) only, year-round Tue–Sat 10am–4pm, Sun noon–4pm. ⏱Closed Jan 1 & Dec 25. ⬤$4. ♿ ☎703-549-2997. www.carlylehouse.org.

Shops along Historic King Street
©Brigitta L. House/MICHELIN

Modeled after a Georgian manor house, this stone construction (1753) was built by John Carlyle, one of the Scottish entrepreneurs instrumental in founding Alexandria. Carlyle came to Virginia in 1741 as an agent for an English merchant, but he soon established his own trading concerns. He became a friend of George Washington, and a founding trustee of the town.

The mansion's hour of glory came in April 1755, when the British general Edward Braddock, en route to his ill-fated campaign against the French and Indians, headquartered himself here. During his stay he held the historic **Governors' Council**, at which five colonial governors met with Braddock in Carlyle House. He petitioned them for advice on military strategy and for financial support. The governors' contention that the colonists would refuse to provide funds to the British was an early sign of tension between England and the colonies.

When Carlyle died in 1780, his property passed to his heirs, but was eventually sold out of the family. In 1970 the Northern Virginia Regional Park Authority purchased the house and renovated it to its colonial appearance.

The two-story building, with a projecting central section and prominent quoins (or cornerstones), is topped by a hipped roof with two chimneys. Inside, the mansion is decorated in the style fashionable to its period. The popular tones of the day (verdigris, blue verditer and Prus-

Address Book

♿*For price ranges, see the Legend on the cover flap.*

WHERE TO STAY

Alexandria & Arlington Bed and Breakfast Network – ☎703-549-3415 or 888-549-3415. www.aabbn.com. The cobblestone streets of Alexandria make staying at a bed and breakfast particularly inviting. If you're looking to stay in the tranquil pockets of Northern Virginia, the Alexandria and Arlington Bed and Breakfast Network maintains a listing of private homes and bed and breakfasts available for short- and long-term rentals.

Morrison House – *116 S. Alfred St.* ✕♿🅿 ☎703-838-8000 *or* 866-834-6628. www.morrisonhouse.com. *45 rooms.* **$$$$** Built in the 1980s, Old Town Alexandria's finest hotel, a Kimpton property, maintains the appearance of a Federalist-era town-house while offering the service of an elite European inn. Furnished with period pieces and chandeliers, Morrison House features cozy four-poster beds against the backdrop of a decorative fireplace. At the hotel's dining spot, **The Grille**, American dishes draw on ingredients from area farms and artisans.

Almost Heaven Bed and Breakfast – *6339 Bracketts Crossing.* 🅿🛈 ☎703-921-9043. *3 rooms.* **$$$** Lodged in a lovely four-story home outfitted with antique furnishings and comfy bedding, Almost Heaven lives up to its name with a terrific location, amiable hosts and welcoming amenities. Each bedroom has its own private bath, and the property also features a pool, Jacuzzi and sauna.

WHERE TO EAT

Gadsby's Tavern – *138 N. Royal St.* ♿ ☎703-548-1288. www.gadsbystavern restaurant.com. **$$$ American**. One of the few remaining 18C dining establishments in the US, this tavern is aptly suited to the cobblestone streets of Old Town. Costumed servers and entertainers gad about the historic hostelry, as patrons dine by candlelight on colonial favorites such as fried oysters, Sally Lunn bread and George Washington's duck. The attached museum provides an intriguing glimpse into the history of the colonial port city.

La Bergerie – *218 N. Lee St.* ♿ ☎703-683-1007. www.labergerie.com. *No lunch Sun.* **$$$ French.** Housed in a historic brick warehouse near the river, elegant La Bergerie serves a tempting array of French dishes and Basque regional specialties. Crystal chandeliers sparkle above the comfortable dining room, where attentive servers monitor casual lunches and intimate dinners. Order a raspberry or hazelnut soufflé for dessert before diving into the savory roasted wild boar chop or pheasant breast stuffed with foie gras.

Majestic Café – *911 King St.* ♿ ☎703-837-9117. www.majesticcafe.com. *Closed Mon. No lunch Sat-Sun.* **$$ American.** The pink and blue neon signs that loom over colonial King Street join the 1700s and the 1930s in peculiar harmony. The Majestic Café serves up a tasty selection of stylish American favorites. Start off with the house-made chicken liver paté on toast points. Then move on to the home-style meatloaf, or roasted chicken with pan gravey, accompanied by a frosty glass of egg cream.

Stardust – *608 Montgomery St.* ♿ ☎703-548-9864. www.stardustrestaurant. com. **$$ Asian.** Guaranteeing "more atmosphere than the moon," Stardust is a whimsical departure from Alexandria's more traditional dining establishments. The menu successfully combines chef Pat Phatiphong's Thai expertise with far-reaching global influences. Oysters on the half shell are playfully doused with fruit pico de gallo, while a tasty traditional Asian roasted duck overflows with Chinese red wine sauce. Vegetarians can feast on a stir-fried bean cake made with peppers and jasmine rice, topped by hot chili soy sauce.

The Warehouse – *214 King St.* ♿ ☎703-683-6868. www.warehousebarandgrill. com. **$$ Cajun.** One of Old Town Alexandria's most well-loved casual eateries greets diners with hundreds of colorful, smiling caricatures of local personalities. Creole alligator stew and creamy she-crab soup usher in a Cajun-accented menu rich with meat and seafood dishes. A pleasingly old-fashioned caramel custard provides a rich finishing touch.

CALENDAR OF EVENTS

Listed below is a selection of Alexandria's popular annual events; some dates may vary each year. For more information contact the Alexandria Convention and Visitors Assn.☎ 703-838-4200 or www.funside.com. Unless otherwise indicated, the area code for all numbers is 703.

JAN-FEB
late Jan
Robert E. Lee Birthday Celebrations
Lee-Fendall House, Old Town
☎548-1789,
www.leefendallhouse.org

GEORGE WASHINGTON BIRTHDAY CELEBRATIONS (MID-FEB)
Birthnight Banquet and Ball
Gadsby's Tavern Museum
☎838-4242
Revolutionary War Encampment & Skirmish
Fort Ward Park, ☎838-4848
Parade
Old Town, ☎991-4474,
www.washingtonbirthday.net

MAR-APR
mid-Mar
St. Patrick's Day Parade King Street
☎237-2199,
www.ballyshaners.org
late Apr
Historic Garden Week Tour
Old Town, ☎804-644-7776,
www.vagardenweek.org

MAY-JUN
mid-May–early Jun
Armenian Festival
☎883-4686

late May
Memorial Day Jazz Festival
Fort Ward Park, ☎883-4686
early Jun
Civil War Camp Day
Fort Ward Park, ☎838-4848,
http://oha.alexandriava.gov
mid-Jun
Red Cross Waterfront Festival
Old Town, ☎549-8300,
www.waterfrontfestival.org

JUL-AUG
all summer
Doggie Happy Hour
☎549-6080,
www.doggiehappyhour.com
early Jul
USA & Alexandria Birthday Celebration
Oronoco Bay Park, ☎883-4686,
www.alexandriava.gov

SEPT-OCT
late Sept
Tour of Historic Homes
Old Town, ☎683-5544,
www.thetwig.org

NOV-DEC
mid-Nov
Historic Alexandria Antiques Show
Holiday Inn Hotel and Suites,
Old Town, ☎549-5811, www.historicalexandriafoundation.org
1st Sat, Dec
Scottish Christmas Walk
Old Town, ☎549-0111,
www.campagnacenter.org
mid-Dec
Historic Alexandria Candlelight Tours
Old Town, ☎838-4242,
http://oha.alexandriava.gov/

sian blue) predominate throughout the house. Note the fine woodwork cornices, pediments and paneling in the first-floor study and main parlor, the only two rooms that have retained their original architecture.
The second floor has bedrooms and an architectural exhibit room, where the restoration process is explained in captioned photographs and a section of the original rubble and mortar walls of the house is exposed. On the basement level is a servant's workroom containing various utensils of the day.
🙂 *A formal garden behind the house is laid out in parterres with brick walkways.*

Former Bank of Alexandria

133 N. Fairfax St. This restored brick Federal structure is the oldest building (1807) in Virginia that has been continually used as a bank. Carlyle's son-in-law, William Herbert, served as the bank's second president and a director. It is now a branch of BB&T.

▶ *Turn left on Cameron St.*

The row houses in the **300 block (A)** of Cameron Street, representative of the early- to mid-19C architecture of the area, house the kinds of storefront shops for which Old Town is known. No. 309 has a side courtyard and loggia.

Gadsby's Tavern Museum★

134 N. Royal St. ✏✎*Visit by guided tour (30min) only, Apr–Oct Tue–Sat 10am–5pm, Sun–Mon 1pm–5pm. Rest of the year Wed–Sat 11am–4pm, Sun 1pm–4pm.* ⏱ *Closed Jan 1, Thanksgiving Day & Dec 25.* ✆*$4.* ☎*703-838-4242. http://oha.alexandriava.gov/gadsby.*

This tavern is one of the most celebrated hostelries from the early days of the country. Functioning now as a museum and restaurant, it is actually two joined brick structures. The two-story Georgian-style tavern dates back to about 1785; the three-story Federal-style construction was built as a hotel in 1792 by John Wise, a local businessman. Englishman John Gadsby leased the larger building from Wise in 1796, and in 1802 Gadsby also took over the smaller one,

which he operated as a coffeehouse. The Federal-style building became the renowned Gadsby's Tavern. While the federal city was being built across the Potomac, Gadsby's Tavern frequently entertained its officialdom—the Jeffersons, the Adamses and George Washington, whose town house was just a block away at 508 Cameron Street. For years an annual gala celebrating Washington's birthday was held in Gadsby's ballroom.

The buildings functioned as a tavern until 1878. They were restored to their original appearance in 1975 and reopened in 1976. The ground floor of the Federal-style building is leased as a commercial restaurant (✆*see Address Book*). Much of the rest of the two buildings is devoted to a museum depicting the tavern as it appeared in Gadsby's day.

Visit – The first floor of the older building consists of an entrance hall and two public rooms. The larger room to the left is set as a dining room, with furnishings and food appropriate to the late 18C. The small dining room to the right contains a table set as it would have been for one of the private dinners that often took place here.

A large assembly hall dominates the second floor. Furnished with only a few chairs, this room was used by merchants to show their wares and by itinerant dentists to treat patients, as well as for social events.

Gadsby's famous **ballroom**, which occupies much of the second floor of

Carlyle House

R. Corbel/MICHELIN

ALEXANDRIA
OLD TOWN

the Federal building, was the scene of many elegant soirees. Its original paneling is now conserved in the Metropolitan Museum of Art in New York. A musicians' gallery is cantilevered out over the ballroom.

The canopied beds and pleasant decor of the two bedchambers on this floor contrast sharply with the spartan accommodations in the small third-floor bedrooms, where travelers sometimes slept two or three to a bed.

▶ *Return to Cameron St. and continue west.*

The modest clapboard building at **508 Cameron Street** is a recent reconstruction of the town house George Washington built as a convenient town office and lodging.

▶ *Turn right on North St. Asaph St.*

At the intersection with Queen Street, note **523 Queen Street** *(the second house from the corner)*, one of the small-

est houses in Old Town. Among the mid-19C clapboards in the 300 block of North St. Asaph Street is an example of a **flounder house** (no. 311). This vernacular architectural style, which dates from the first half of the 19C, derives its name from the flat, windowless side of the house, resembling the eyeless side of a flounder fish.

At the next intersection note Princess Street *(on the left)*, which has its original cobblestone paving. The cobbles often came across the Atlantic Ocean as ballast for ships.

▶ *Continue to the corner of Oronoco St. and turn left.*

Robert E. Lee's Boyhood Home★

607 Oronoco St. ⚫—⚬ *Not open to the public.* Constructed in 1795 by John Potts, a business acquaintance of George Washington, this Federal town house soon became the residence of William Fitzhugh, a close friend of Washington.

Here in 1804 Fitzhugh's daughter Mary married George Washington Parke Custis, Washington's ward and the squire of Arlington House.

In 1812 Revolutionary War hero Henry "Light-Horse Harry" Lee, a friend of Washington and father of Robert E. Lee, rented the house from the Fitzhughs, who were relatives of Henry Lee's second wife, Ann Hill Carter.

Soon after, Lee was wounded in a Baltimore riot. Virtually bankrupt save for his wife's income, he sailed to Barbados in the Caribbean, reputedly to recover his health. Six-year-old Robert never again saw his father, who died away from home five years later.

Widowed, Ann Carter Lee relied heavily on her youngest son, Robert. The family lived here until 1825, with the exception of a four-year hiatus, during which William Henry Fitzhugh was in residence and the Lees occupied a family property at 407 N. Washington Street.

Robert left his boyhood home in 1825 to become a cadet at West Point Military Academy. Unable to maintain a household without his help, Mrs. Lee moved to Georgetown.

The intersection of Oronoco and Washington streets is known as "Lee Corners" due to the cluster of Lee family residences. The Georgian building at 428 N. Washington Street was the home of Light-Horse Harry's brother, Edmund Jennings Lee, mayor of Alexandria from 1815 to 1818.

Lee-Fendall House

614 Oronoco St. (Enter on Washington St.) ◷*Open year-round Tue–Sat 10am–4pm, Sun 1pm–4pm.* ◷*Closed Thanksgiving Day & mid-Dec–Jan 1.* ◉*$4.* ▣ ☏*703-548-1789. www.leefendallhouse.org.*

This clapboard house was built in 1785 by Philip Richard Fendall, a distant Lee relative who bought the half-acre lot from Light-Horse Harry Lee. Fendall successively married three different Lee women, and members of the Lee family continually lived in the house until 1904. Today the house is decorated in early-19C style, with many authentic Lee pieces.

▶ *Continue down N. Washington St.*

Note the house at **no. 407**. Built by Charles Lee, another brother of Light-Horse Harry, this was the home in which young Robert E. Lee lived with his mother from 1817 to 1820.

Lloyd House

220 N. Washington St. John Wise, who established Gadsby's Tavern, built this late-Georgian brick edifice as his residence in 1797. In the early 19C a succession of prominent Alexandrians lived in the house, including Benjamin Hallowell, a Quaker schoolmaster who briefly tutored Robert E. Lee. In 1832 the house was purchased by John Lloyd, whose wife, Ann Lee Lloyd, was a first cousin of Robert E. Lee. The house remained in the Lloyd family until 1918. In 1976 it became part of the Alexandria library system.

Christ Church★

Corner of N. Washington and Cameron Sts. (Enter walled graveyard from Washington St.) ◷*Open year-round Mon–Sat 9am–4pm, Sun 2pm–4pm.* ◷*Closed major holidays.* ☛*Guided tours (20min) available.* ☺*As the church may be closed for private use, it is advisable to phone before visiting.* ♿ ☏*703-549-1450. www.historicchristchurch.org.*

Encircled by a high wall, the church grounds provide a haven where trees shade 18C grave markers. Both George Washington and Robert E. Lee worshiped in the brick and stone structure, with its pepperpot steeple. By tradition, presidents have come here to worship in Washington's pew on the Sunday nearest February 22, his birthday.

Construction of the church was completed in 1773. In its unadorned and luminous interior, a raised wineglass pulpit and a large Palladian window provide the focal point. Silver plaques mark the **pews** of Washington *(no. 60)* and Lee *(no. 46)*.

▶ *Return to Washington St., cross and walk down the 600 block of Cameron St.*

In 1811 the Georgian brick dwelling at **611 Cameron Street** was home to Light-Horse Harry Lee and his family, including his three-year-old son Robert E. Lee. Thomas, the final Lord Fairfax of Virginia, lived in the imposing Federal-style structure at **no. 607** in the 1830s.

▸ *Turn right on South St. Asaph St. and walk two blocks, past the intersection with King St. Turn right on Prince St.*

The large brick structure with Palladian windows, at the corner of Prince and Washington streets, is the **Federal District Courthouse** for Virginia's Eastern District. A number of nationally publicized trials, particularly involving Pentagon espionage, have been heard here. The statue (1889) (1) dominating the intersection of Washington and Prince streets commemorates Alexandria's Confederate dead.

▸ *Cross Washington St.*

The Lyceum

201 S. Washington St. ◷ *Open year-round Mon–Sat 10am–5pm, Sun 1pm–5pm.* ◷ *Closed Jan 1, Thanksgiving Day & Dec 24-25.* ♿ ▯ ☎ *703-838-4994. http://oha.alexandriava.gov/lyceum.*
In 1834 Benjamin Hallowell (♿ *see Lloyd House above*) interested his fellow citizens in founding a lyceum, or cultural center, and five years later this Greek Revival structure was built to house a library, lecture rooms and natural history exhibits. Many prominent 19C figures spoke here, including the orator Daniel Webster. After serving as a Civil War hospital, private home and office building, the building was restored in 1974. Today it houses a museum featuring changing exhibits on state and local history.

▸ *Continue one block south on Washington St., then turn left on Duke St. and continue one block to South St. Asaph St.*

Lafayette House

301 South St. Asaph St. ⊶ *Not open to the public.* Built about 1815 by a shipping agent, this three-story brick building, with an elegant double doorway topped by a fanlight and flanked by lunettes, is a fine example of a Federal-style town

house. In 1824 the Marquis de Lafayette stayed here during a state visit.

▸ *Continue down Duke St. two blocks to S. Royal St. Turn right and enter the brick gate marked no. 316.*

Old Presbyterian Meeting House

Between 300 block of S. Royal and S. Fairfax Sts. ◷ *Open year-round Mon–Fri 8:30am–4:30pm, Sun for services only.* ◷ *Closed major holidays.* ♿ ☎ *703-549-6670. www.opmh.org.*
Alexandria's Scottish immigrants established this church in 1772, contracting John Carlyle to oversee its building. It was the site of celebrations for Alexandria's Masons. In 1799, at Washington's death, the church bell tolled for four days, and his public funeral service was preached here. In 1835 lightning struck the steeple and the ensuing fire virtually destroyed the church. Within two years it was rebuilt.
The old flounder house manse inside the walled churchyard on the left was built in 1787. The graveyard beyond contains markers for John Carlyle and other prominent Alexandrians. The sarcophagus enclosed by a wrought-iron rail on the north commemorates an unknown soldier of the Revolution. *(The box beside the sarcophagus plays a videotape on the church's history.)*

▸ *From the church walk through the cemetery. Turn left (north) on S. Fairfax St., then turn right onto Prince St.*

Prince Street

The brick-paved 200 block of Prince Street is known as **Gentry Row**★, due to its dignified 18C structures. A fine example of this architectural period in Virginia, **no. 207** is believed to contain elements of a town house built by the George William Fairfaxes, Washington's close friends. At nos. 211 and 209 lived two of Washington's physicians, Dr. Elisha Cullen Dick and Dr. James Craik. The stuccoed, salmon Greek Revival **Athenaeum** (1852) on the corner was built as the Old Dominion Bank and now functions as a gallery for the Northern

Virginia Fine Arts Assn. (⏰*open year-round, call for hours;* ⏰*closed major holidays;* ☎*703-548-0035; http://oha. alexandriava.gov).*

The architecture changes abruptly along the cobbled 100 block of Prince Street. Known locally as **Captain's Row**★, the street may derive its name from the 18C sea captain John Harper, who owned land along the north side of the street. Many of the original houses were destroyed in an 1827 fire.

▸ *Turn left on S. Union St.*

On the corner *(6 King St.)* is an early-19C warehouse made of brick and stone. End your tour at the **Torpedo Factory**.

Additional Sights

George Washington Masonic National Memorial

101 Callahan Dr. Ⓜ *King Street.* ⏰*Open year-round daily 10am–4pm.* ⏰*Closed major holidays.* 🔗*Guided tours (1hr) available daily 10am, 11:30am, 1:30pm & 3pm.* ♿🅿 ☎*703-683-2007. www. gwmemorial.org.*

Crowning Shooter's Hill, this memorial to George Washington, the first master of Alexandria's Masonic Lodge, is a city landmark, at the western end of Old Town. The granite building, topped by a tiered tower, is modeled after one of the Seven Wonders of the World—the lighthouse on the island of Pharos near Alexandria, Egypt. Begun in 1923, the memorial was built over the course of 40 years.

Visitors enter **Memorial Hall**, dominated by a 17ft-high bronze **statue** of Washington. Two 46ft-long murals by artist Allyn Cox, who executed murals in the Capitol, depict Washington at the Masonic ceremony for the laying of the Capitol cornerstone, and with his fellow Masons at a religious service in Philadelphia's Christ Church.

The **Replica Room** *(down the hall to the left of Cox's cornerstone mural)* displays various Masonic articles associated with Washington, including the silver trowel and the Masonic apron he used while laying the Capitol cornerstone. The **Assembly Room** *(one floor below Memorial Hall)* has eight polished green granite columns that support the entire memorial. The 350-year-old Persian royal meshed rug measures 30ft by 50ft, supposedly the world's largest rug made on a single loom.

The seven-story tower houses a **museum** of Washington memorabilia, a library (⏰*open by appointment only)* and five small rooms, each devoted to a different order or type of Masonry, such as the Knights Templar and Grotto Masons. These chambers are decorated in the Persian, Egyptian, Hebraic and medieval motifs symbolic of the specific orders.

The top level opens onto an observation deck, with a **view** of Old Town.

Friendship Firehouse

107 S. Alfred St. ⏰*Open year-round Fri & Sat 10am–4pm, Sun 1pm–4pm.* ⏰*Closed*

George Washington Birthday Parade

Jan 1, Dec 25. ♿ ☎*703-838-3891. http:// oha.alexandriava.gov/friendship.*
Organized in 1774, the Friendship Fire Company lists among its honorary volunteers statesmen, governors and presidents, including George Washington. The current brick firehouse was completed in 1857. Though the company ceased fire fighting in the early 1870s, the Friendship Veterans Fire Engine Assn. maintains a ceremonial function.

Now the property of the city, the restored building features a first-floor exhibit room devoted to 18C and 19C fire-fighting equipment, including leather buckets, speaking trumpets and wheeled vehicles. The meeting room on the second floor displays memorabilia relating to the company's social role in the community.

ANNAPOLIS★

Set on the south bank of the Severn River, Annapolis, Maryland is known for its history and its harbor. The former dates back to 1649, when Virginia Puritans established Arundel Towne along the Severn. The latter shelters hundreds of yachts and sailboats tied up at City Dock, once home port for the Chesapeake Bay's oyster fleet.

🛈 **Information:** Annapolis & Anne Arundel County Conference & Visitors Bureau, 26 West St.; ☎410-280-0445; www.visitannapolis.org.

▶ **Orient Yourself:** Annapolis is located 36mi east of Washington. By car: Take US-50 East to Exit 24 (Rowe Blvd.); proceed on Rowe Blvd., crossing College Creek Bridge; stay in the right lane; Rowe will split into Northwest St.; look for signs to Visitor Center. By public transportation: Take the Metro to New Carrollton, then bus (infrequent) or taxi to downtown. Main Street is the historic city's hub.

🅿 **Parking:** Gotts Garage on Northwest St., next to Visitors Bureau.

🚢 **Don't Miss:** A boat cruise on the harbor (for cruise information, contact Visitors Bureau above).

Ⓚ **Especially for Kids:** The ship models at the US Naval Academy.

Annapolis Harbor

A Bit of History

Named in honor of England's Queen Anne, Annapolis became the seat of colonial government in 1695. Founding fathers laid out the new capital with the 1779 Georgian-style **State House**★ *(center of State Circle ☎410-974-3400; www.msa.md.gov/msa)*—which served as the US capitol between 1783 and 1784—occupying the highest point, while **St. Anne's Church** *(Church Circle ☎410-267-9333; www.stannes-annapolis.org)* was given the second-highest site. The rest of the town spread out on narrow streets from these structures, symbolizing the key positions of church and state. In the 18C Annapolis reigned as Maryland's premier port, as well as the colony's cultural capital.

Today the city's economy revolves around tourism, state government and the US Navy.

Sights

Hammond-Harwood House★★

19 Maryland Ave. ◗ Visit by guided tour (40min) only, Apr–Oct Tue–Sun noon–5pm (last tour 4pm). Rest of year, call for hours. ◉$6. ☎410-263-4683 ext. 16. www.hammondharwoodhouse.org.
This outstanding example of the Georgian style (1775), with its bowed wings,

US Naval Academy Cadets

DC Convention & Tourism Corp.

is the work of William Buckland. One of the country's first and foremost architects, Buckland emigrated from England in 1755. A joiner by trade, Buckland had a keen eye for detail, and the elaborately carved rose garlands above the entryway fanlight and the ornate woodwork and plaster ornamentation within are glorious proof of his skill. Inside, the tall arched window above the staircase is modeled on one found in London's Church of St. Martin's in the Field.

Chase-Lloyd House★

22 Maryland Ave. ◗ Visit by guided tour (20min) only, Mar–Dec Mon–Sat 2pm–4pm. ◉$2. ☎410-263-2723.
Built for Samuel Chase, a signer of the Declaration of Independence, this imposing three-story brick Georgian (1774, William Buckland) is best known for its **entrance hall** featuring a split, cantilevered staircase and a tall Palladian window. Only the first floor and the garden are open to the public as the rest of the house has served as a home for elderly women since 1890.

William Paca House

186 Prince George St. ◗ Visit by guided tour (45min) only, late Mar–Dec Mon–Sat 10am–5pm, Sun noon–5pm. Mid-Jan–mid-Mar Fri & Sat 10am–5pm, Sun noon–5pm. ◉$8. ☎ 410-267-7619. www.annapolis.org.
Patriot and signer of the Declaration of Independence, lawyer William Paca based his design of this brick town house (1765) on the Georgian principal of attaching wings to the main structure with short corridors called "hyphens." The **gardens** behind the house have been restored to their 18C appearance.

US Naval Academy★★

Armel-Leftwich Visitor Center, 52 King George St.; ☎410-293-8125. ◑Visitor Center open Mar–Dec daily 9am–5pm, rest of the year 9am–4pm; ◑closed Jan 1, Thanksgiving Day & Dec 25. ◗Guided tours available year-round; call for hours; ◉photo I.D. required; ◉$8. ✕◔☎410-293-8687. www.navyonline.com.
Midshipmen study to be officers in the US Navy and Marine Corps on a peaceful, 338-acre campus along the Severn River

and College Creek. In 1850 the five-year-old Naval School became the official undergraduate college for the US Navy. Today, competition is fierce to be one of the 4,000 midshipmen who gets a rigorous and free education at the academy. The guided tour around "the Yard," as the academy grounds are called, includes massive **Bancroft Hall**, the 1906 Beaux-Arts structure in the center of campus that covers 33 acres and boasts 5mi of corridors. Few buildings in Annapolis

rival the glorious gold-domed US Naval Academy **chapel**★★ (1908, Ernest Flagg), modeled after the Hotel des Invalides in Paris. In the chapel's eerily lit crypt, the remains of the nation's first naval hero, John Paul Jones, are interred in a black marble sarcophagus. After the tour, visit the Preble Hall **museum**, where you'll find a collection of ⟦Kids⟧**ship models**★★ made in England during the 17C and 18C, as well as other artifacts detailing the academy's history.

GUNSTON HALL★

This colonial Georgian estate was the home of **George Mason** (1725-92), a respected thinker whose writings influenced the course of the Revolution and the development of the young Republic.

▶ **Orient Yourself:** Gunston Hall lies 22mi south of Washington. By car: Follow directions to Woodlawn. Continue south on US-1 and follow signs.
🕐 **Organizing Your Time:** Average round-trip driving time from downtown: 1hr 30min. Allow 3hrs, including 11min film about Bill of Rights.

A Bit of History

During the Revolutionary period, George Mason wrote the **Virginia Declaration of Rights** (May 1776), which stated "that all men are by nature equally free and independent and have certain inherent rights…namely…pursuing and obtaining happiness…." Mason's friend Thomas Jefferson echoed this wording in the Declaration of Independence (july 1776). Mason opposed the original Constitution because it had no Bill of Rights and did not call for the immediate abolition of the slave trade. His opposition was influential in the adoption in 1791 of the first 10 amendments to the Constitution, commonly known are the Bill of Rights. A fourth-generation Virginian, Mason inherited considerable family landholdings when he was 10. In 1755 he began constructing Gunston Hall. He served as a county justice, member of the Virginia House of Burgesses and a delegate to the Constitutional Convention of 1787. Father of nine children, Mason died at his home in 1792. His estated remained in the family until 1866. After a succes-

sion of owners, it was deeded to the Commonwealth of Virginia.

Mansion

🔊 *Visit by guided tour (45min) only, year-round daily 9:30am–5pm.* 🕐*Closed Jan 1, Thanksgiving Day & Dec 25.* ⟨∞⟩*$8.* 🅿️ ☎️*703-550-9220. www.gunstonhall.org.* The unembellished brick facade is offset with quoins, or cornerstones, of local buff-colored Aquia sandstone. The carriage entrance features a pedimented

Bird's-Eye View of Gunston Hall

portico with a fanlight above the door. The river entrance portico is a semioctagonal porch with graceful ogee arches. The interior of the house is noteworthy for its mid-18C carved **woodwork** executed by English craftsman **William Buckland**, a carpenter-joiner who arrived in Virginia in 1755.

In the central hall, Buckland used pilasters, chair railings and a double arch offset with a pinecone finial. The Masons' bedroom opens off the left of the hall, and directly across from it is the **Chinese formal parlor**, the only surviving room in America featuring the scalloped Chinoiserie woodworking of the colonial period.

Grounds

Beyond the house on the south side is a small frame schoolhouse, a reconstruction of the one in which the nine Mason children were tutored. A gravel path connects the schoolhouse to the family **graveyard**, where 16 family members are buried. The two raised sarcophagi contain the remains of George Mason and his wife, Ann.

A double row of magnolias and cedars lines Magnolia Avenue, the carriage approach to the house. On the river side, an impressive boxwood allée leads through **formal gardens** to an overlook above a garden terrace. A mile-long walk through a wooded area leads to the river.

WOODLAWN ★

This gracious Federal-era estate reflects the refinement of its original owners, Lawrence Lewis and Nelly Custis Lewis. Favored relatives of George Washington, whose own Mount Vernon lies only three miles away, the Lewises brought to their home many of the furnishings and memorabilia of the original Washington estate when they moved into the completed north wing in 1802.

▶ **Orient Yourself:** Woodlawn lies 19mi south of Washington. By car: Follow directions to Mount Vernon. Continue 3mi west on Rte. 235 and follow the signs to Woodlawn. By public transportation: Take the Metro to Huntington station and transfer to a 9A (Fort Belvoir) bus to Woodlawn.

🕐 **Organizing Your Time:** Average round-trip driving time from downtown: 1hr 30min. Allow 2hrs for a visit.

A Bit of History

In 1797 Lawrence Lewis, Washington's nephew, came to Mount Vernon to serve as his uncle's personal secretary. There he met **Eleanor** (Nelly) **Parke Custis**, the granddaughter the Washingtons had raised. After a quiet courtship, Nelly and Lewis were married in 1799. Washington ceded a 2,000-acre tract west of Mount Vernon to them on which to build their home. Washington died less than a year after the wedding; in 1802 Martha Washington died, the year in which the Lewises moved into the completed north wing of Woodlawn.

When Lawrence died in 1839, Nelly went to live with her son. In 1846 Woodlawn was offered for sale, and was subsequently owned by businessmen, private owners and a foundation. In 1957 the estate became the property of the National Trust for Historic Preservation.

Visit

Both houses: 🚶 *visit by guided tour (35min each) only, Mar–Dec Tue–Sun 10am–5pm, every 30min.* 🕐 *Closed Thanksgiving Day & Dec 25.* 💰 *$13 for both houses (💰$7.50 Woodlawn).* 🅿 ☎*703-780-4000. www.woodlawn1805.org.*

Mansion

Prominent architect Dr. William Thornton was involved in the construction of the house. The structure has a two-story central core with symmetrical one-story wings that are connected to the main house by hyphens.

Decorated as it might have been during the Lewises' lifetime, the house contains furnishings that belonged to the family, including several from Mount Vernon. Opening off the center hall are a parlor and living room. Adept musicians, Nelly and her daughters often gave performances on the harp and piano that still dominate the parlor. The fire screen was embroidered by Nelly.

Off the living room the master bedroom holds personal items of the Lewises.

The one-story hyphens connected to the center house were kitchen and work areas in the Lewises' day. They now hold a reception room *(south side)* and an educational space *(north side)*, which were added at the turn of the 19C. The two wings connected to the hyphens are used as administrative offices.

The second floor contains four bedrooms and a linen room, all of which open off a central hall.

The **grounds** are graced with large trees and boxwoods. The parterred garden is noted for its roses.

Pope-Leighey House

This small, L-shaped house in a wooded setting is one of the few publicly accessible examples of what the 20C's most eminent American-born architect, **Frank Lloyd Wright** (1867-1959), called his "Usonian" architecture—functional, simply designed homes affordable to middle-class Americans.

Built in 1941 for Loren Pope, a journalist in nearby Falls Church, Virginia, the 1,200sq ft, five-room house cost roughly $7,000. The Leigheys bought the house from the Popes five years later. When it was threatened with demolition because of highway construction in 1964, Mrs. Leighey donated it to the National Trust for Historic Preservation, which moved it to its current site.

The house contains the furniture that Wright designed for it and is built only of cypress, brick, glass and concrete, following the Wright tenet to use as few materials as possible.

Woodlawn, West Front

National Trust for Historic Preservation

Food Stand along the Mall
©Brigitta L. House/MICHELIN

WHERE TO STAY

Party lines aside, the city's range of accommodations is sure to please both discerning diplomats and budget-minded backpackers. Swank boutique hotels, charming guest houses and the city's grande-dame luxury establishments provide sanctuary to the thousands of families, journalists, politicians and international visitors who come to the capital each year. Most hotels are located in the Downtown and Georgetown areas, while less-expensive rooms can be found in the Dupont Circle and Adams Morgan neighborhoods.

The properties listed below were selected for their ambience, location and/or value for money. Prices reflect the average cost for a standard double room (two people) in high season (not including any applicable city or state taxes). Room prices may be considerably lower in off-season, and many hotels offer discounted weekend rates. The presence of a swimming pool is indicated by the ⌁ symbol. The presence of a full-service spa is indicated by the Spa symbol.

$$$$$	over $350
$$$$	$250-$350
$$$	$175-$250
$$	$100-$175
$	less than $100

ADAMS MORGAN

$$ Kalorama Guest House – *1854 Mintwood Pl. NW.* &. ☎*202-667-6369. www.kaloramaguesthouse.com. 28 rooms.* Nestled in culturally diverse Adams Morgan, this charming assortment of Victorian townhouses pampers visitors with homey comforts, such as afternoon sherry and tasty continental breakfast selections. Rooms are sparse and simple, tinged with Victorian flair that mirrors the neighborhood.

CAPITOL HILL

$$$$ Hotel George – *15 E St. NW.* ✗&ℙ ☎*202-347-4200 or 800-576-8331. www.hotelgeorge.com. 149 rooms.* Washington's hippest hotel stormed onto the hotel scene in 1998 to the chagrin of hotel traditionalists and to the delight of style-hungry liberals. With vibrant colors and contemporary artistic tributes to the first US president, Hotel George's vogue minimalist interior and its proximity to Union Station have made it a staple of business and leisure travelers and celebrity guests.

$$$$ Phoenix Park Hotel – *520 N. Capitol St. NW.* ✗&ℙ ☎*202-638-6900 or 800-824-5419. www.phoenixpark hotel.com. 149 rooms.* Situated between Union Station and the US Capitol, Phoenix Park pairs a convenient location with generous amenities and live Irish entertainment. The welcoming exterior harkens back to an 18C Irish manor, while the lively downstairs pub draws a steady crowd of Capitol Hill staffers.

$$$ Doolittle Guest House – *506 E. Capitol St.* ℙ ☎*202-546-6622. www. doolittlehouse.com. 3 rooms.* Situated on a quiet, tree-lined street, this 1866 Victorian stands four blocks from the US Capitol. From here, guests can walk to the Smithsonian museums. Three antique-appointed guest rooms and a library stocked with magazines and newspapers make for a comfortable night's stay. Breakfasts are prepared with local organic produce.

$$$ Washington Court Hotel – *525 New Jersey Ave. NW.* ✗&ℙ ☎*202-628-2100 or 800-321-3010. www.washington courthotel.com. 267 rooms.* Luxurious suites offer an unparalleled view of the Capitol dome in this charming Capitol Hill hotel. The Washington Court provides easy access to DC's monuments, attractions and popular eateries.

DOWNTOWN

$$$$$ Hay-Adams – *6th & H Sts. NW.* ✗&ℙ☎*202-638-6600 or 800-853-6807. www.hayadams.com. 145 rooms.* With a view of the Executive Mansion from its location across Lafayette Square, the Hay-Adams is closer to the White House than any of Washington's grande-dame hotels. Steeped in Washington lore, this elaborate, Renaissance-inspired beauty repeatedly houses world leaders and discerning travelers.

$$$$ Morrison-Clark Inn – *1015 L St. NW.* ✕⚪🅿 ☎*202-898-1200 or 800-222-8474. www.morrisonclark.com. 54 rooms.* This turn-of-the-19C mansion seems misplaced in downtown's business district. Past the antiques-filled parlor, with lace curtains and burgundy wall coverings are three styles of accommodations. Choose from neutral-toned Neoclassical, opulent Victorian and country-style distressed woods and wicker. The restaurant's Southern-style specialties make it a national favorite.

$$$$ Renaissance Mayflower Hotel – *1127 Connecticut Ave. NW.* ✕⚪🅿 ☎*202-347-3000 or 800-228-7697. www.renaissancemayflower.com. 657 rooms.* A perennial favorite of frequent visitors, the Mayflower flaunts the splendor of Washington's golden age along busy Connecticut Avenue. The lobby of this luxury hotel is graced with Federalist furniture and gilded accents, while the guest rooms recollect the genteel elegance of a distant era with their marble bathrooms and antique furniture.

$$$$ St. Regis Washington, DC – *923 16th St. NW.* ✕⚪🅿 ☎*202-638-2626 or 877-787-3447. www.stregis.com. 193 rooms.* The St. Regis looms over Washington's thriving business district with an air of distinction. Since Calvin Coolidge cut the ribbon for the hotel's grand opening, every president has stopped by this hotel, which frequently hosts royal guests. The hotel will debut its renovated look in the fall of 2007.

$$$$ Willard InterContinental – *1401 Pennsylvania Ave. NW.* ✕⚪🅿 ☎*202-628-9100 or 888-424-6835. www.washington.intercontinental.com. 332 rooms.* A bastion of Washington tradition, the Willard towers over Pennsylvania Avenue. Inside, the dreamy Beaux-Arts lobby recalls an earlier age of opulence and political mystique with its grand columns and glittering chandeliers. The Round Robin Bar has served many a president mint juleps and potent brandies. Rooms sport a tasteful, antique-drenched decor, with views of the Washington skyline.

$$ Channel Inn Hotel – *650 Water St. NW.* ✕⚪🅿⌧ ☎*202-554-2400 or 800-368-5668. www.channelinn.com. 100 rooms.* Billed as Washington, DC's only waterfront hotel, Channel Inn offers comfortable, affordable rooms with views of Washington Marina. Seafood restaurants and DC's fresh-fish market neighbor the property. Airy rooms offer full amenities and balconies from which to watch the sailboats and river cruise ships glide past.

$$ Henley Park Hotel – *926 Massachusetts Ave. NW.* ✕⚪🅿 ☎*202-638-5200 or 800-222-8474. www.henleypark.com. 96 rooms.* This hotel's Tudor-style exterior and meticulously restored rooms reflect the classic elegance of Washington's earlier days. Gargoyles and lead windows guard the entrance to this charming property.

$$ Hotel Washington – *515 15th St. NW.* ✕⚪🅿 ☎*202-638-5900 or 800-424-9540. www.hotelwashington.com. 345 rooms.* Sporting one of the best views of Washington atop its rooftop terrace, this hotel sits a mere block and a half from the White House. Luxuriously appointed bedrooms feature marble bathrooms and spectacular views of historic Pennsylvania Avenue.

$$ The Madison – *15th & M Sts. NW.* ✕⚪🅿 ☎*202-862-1600 or 866-563-9792. www.themadisondc.com. 353 rooms.* Perhaps best known for its collection of antiques, The Madison proudly markets itself as "Washington's Correct Address." Located just a few blocks from the White House, the hotel

View of the White House from the Hay-Adams Hotel

DC Convention & Tourism Corp.

offers guest rooms appointed with custom-made furnishings that reflect Williamsburg and English-Regency styles.

DUPONT CIRCLE

$$$$ Jefferson Hotel – *Closed for renovation until fall 2008. 1200 16th St. NW.* ✗♿🅿 ☏*202-347-2200. www. thejeffersonhotel.com. 100 rooms.* Built as a grand private residence in 1923, the Jefferson dazzles with its established reputation and classic exterior. A cheery courtyard leads into an inviting lobby with tasteful furnishings. The hotel will welcome guests after its renovation.

$$$$ Hotel Palomar – *2121 P St. NW.* ✗♿🅿🛇 ☏*202-448-1800. www. hotelpalomar-dc.com. 335 rooms.* This modern, 10-story property bustles, especially late afternoons when patrons enjoy complimentary wine and hors' d'oeuvres in the sleek lobby. Guest rooms are large, sporting contemporary furnishings, colorful wall art and high-tech gadgets. The full-service, on-site restaurant, **Urbana ($$$)**, serves up primarily Northern Italian dishes.

$$ Hotel Tabard Inn – *1739 N St. NW.* ☏*202-785-1277. www.tabardinn.com. 40 rooms.* A Dupont Circle institution, this hotel radiates character with its scarlet walls, twisting staircases, stained-glass lamps and heavy antique furnishings. Rooms vary in size and decor; some share bathrooms. The plush couches and overstuffed chairs in the lounge are great places to unwind over cocktails. The restaurant's acclaimed contemporary fare can be savored in the simple dining room or on an enclosed patio. A continental breakfast is included in the room tab.

$$ Jurys Washington – *1500 New Hampshire Ave. NW.* ✗♿🅿 ☏*202-483-6000. www.jurysdoyle.com. 314 rooms.* Flanking Washington's Dupont Circle, the Jurys hotel is well-situated. Spacious guest rooms boast technological amenities and business comforts such as voice mail and a trouser press. Along the circle, Jurys' restaurant and bar reflect the hotel's Irish ownership, complementing the cosmopolitan spirit of the neighborhood.

FOGGY BOTTOM

$$$$$ Ritz Carlton – *1150 22nd St. NW.* ✗♿🅿 ☏*202-835-0500 or 800-241-3333. www.ritzcarlton.com. 300 rooms.* This luxury Washington hotel, part of an international group of high-end properties, brings sought-after amenities to the West End. The wood-paneled lobby features comfortable seating and a fireplace. Bathed in rose tones, the elegant rooms show off sumptuous bedding, heavy draperies and high-tech business perks. Guests enjoy privileges at the Sports Club/LA fitness center.

What you should know about Washington, DC hotels:

- Quoted rates do not include the city's substantial **hotel tax** of 14.50 percent. For example, with a quoted room rate of $139, you will actually pay $159 for that night's stay.

- Rate categories shown should be taken as a general guideline only. **Rates** can be higher or lower depending on season, day of the week and volume of advance reservations.

- Guest **parking** will cost, on average, from $15 to $30 per day.

- For **price-shopping** and to find available rooms during the high season, consider using a rooms broker like Hotel Discounts (*www.hoteldiscount. com*), Expedia Travel (*www.expedia.com*), Capitol Reservations (*www.washingtonhotelsdc.com*) or Quikbook (*www.quikbook.com*).

- **Pet owners** should contact hotels directly or peruse www.petswelcome. com for a list of establishments that are dog- and cat-friendly.

- In-room **telephone charges** can range from 50¢ to as much as $2 for local calls. Some establishments will charge as much as four to five times the usual rate for long-distance calls. Even using a long-distance calling card can sometimes incur connection fees. When checking in, be sure to ask the price for local calls and connection fees for toll-free numbers. When in doubt, use your cell (mobile) phone or, as a last resort, the pay phones off the lobby.

$$$$ The Fairmont Hotel – *2401 M St. NW.* ✕♿🅿🏊 ☎*202-429-2400 or 800-257-7544. www.fairmont.com. 415 rooms*. The great outdoors reigns at the Fairmont, as sunlight pours through the glassy atriums where trees flourish. Ample guest rooms are clothed in elegant furnishings and sunny hues; posh executive suites are tailored to suit business travelers and to accommodate small meetings. Located on the fringes of Georgetown, the Fairmont provides easy access to shops and restaurants.

$$$$ The Watergate Hotel – *2650 Virginia Ave. NW.* ✕♿🅿🏊 ☎*202-965-2300 or 800-289-1555. www.watergate hotel.com. 250 rooms*. Few Washington hotels are as cloaked in scandal as the Watergate, but management has restored dignity to the riverside property. The complex offers stunning river views and easy access to the Kennedy Center and Georgetown. Rooms are simple yet tasteful, and the rooftop bar serves an enticing summer martini.

$$$ Hotel Lombardy – *2019 Pennsylvania Ave. NW.* ✕♿🅿 ☎*202-828-2600 or 800-424-5486. www.hotellombardy.com. 136 rooms*. Restored to reflect its original 1929 character, Hotel Lombardy is located just four blocks from the White House in the center of Washington's business district. Luxurious bedding complements the densely woven oriental rugs and sleek chrome bath fixtures. Technological amenities coexist with the quaint ambience of this bastion of traditional DC hospitality.

$$$ The Melrose Hotel – *2430 Pennsylvania Ave. NW.* ✕♿🅿 ☎*202-955-6400 or 800-635-7673. www.melrosehotel. com. 240 rooms*. Sporting a catchy new name and fresh look, the Melrose reopened its doors in Foggy Bottom after an extensive remodeling project. The rooms bespeak flawless elegance, while nightly rates have not raced to catch up. Located within walking distance of the Kennedy Center and Georgetown, the hotel's sunny, cheery rooms are a Washington bargain.

GEORGETOWN

$$$$$ Four Seasons – *2800 Pennsylvania Ave. NW.* ✕♿🅿🏊 ☎*202-342-0444 or 800-819-5053. www.fourseasons.com. 211 rooms*. With an unassuming brick exterior, this upscale hotel earns its distinguished marks with luxurious furnishings and impeccable service. Original art adorns the walls of the roomy suites, complementing the flavor of surrounding Georgetown. Guests can also take advantage of the state-of-the-art fitness center and spa.

$$$$ The Latham Hotel – *3000 M St. NW.* ✕♿🅿 ☎*202-726-5000 or 888-587-2377. www.thelatham.com. 142 rooms*. With a primo Georgetown location that houses Citronelle, one of Washington's most revered restaurants, the Latham's comfy guest rooms and rambling suites readily impress. The hotel boasts elegantly appointed guest rooms with generous amenities, and eight unique, two-story carriage suites.

$$$ Georgetown Inn – *1310 Wisconsin Ave. NW.* ✕♿🅿 ☎*202-333-8900 or 888-587-2388. www.georgetown collection.com. 96 rooms*. Combining European elegance and colonial charm, the Georgetown Inn sits along bustling Wisconsin Avenue in the heart of Georgetown's tony shops and restaurants. Luxurious marble bathrooms and heavenly four-poster beds lend an air of regal warmth to a hotel that has housed the Duke and Duchess of Windsor during past visits to Washington, DC.

$$$ Georgetown Suites – *1111 30th St. NW.* ♿🅿 ☎*202-298-7800 or 800-348-7203. www.georgetownsuites.com. 219 rooms*. Perfect for families and long-term visitors, this all-suite hotel is just minutes from historic Georgetown's shops and restaurants. The spacious suites come equipped with kitchenettes and generous amenities.

$$$ Hotel Monticello of Georgetown – *1075 Thomas Jefferson St. NW.* ✕♿ ☎*202-337-0900 or 800-388-2410. www.monticellohotel.com. 40 rooms*. The Hotel Monticello's cozy, sunny suites brim with European charm and Georgetown sophistication. Just footsteps from the historic C & O Canal and lively Wisconsin Avenue, the Monticello's bright, ample rooms provide an excellent base for exploring Georgetown.

WHERE TO EAT

Dine alongside famous politicians or conduct your own "external investigation" at establishments owned by political pundits. Search out the best chili-cheeseburger in town or "make a deal" in the hush-hush wood-paneled interiors of not-so-politically-correct steakhouses. Visitors to the nation's capital can sample the same delicacies enjoyed by some of the world's most visible leaders—from old-fashioned barbecue to red Thai curry prawns and lamb vindaloo. A city for the people, Washington, DC boasts restaurants that typify the variety of tastes and pleasures of the nation it represents.

The venues listed below were selected for their ambience, location and/or value for money. Rates indicate the average cost of an appetizer, an entrée and dessert for one person (not including tax, gratuity or beverages). Most restaurants are open daily—except where noted—and accept major credit cards. Call for information on reservations and opening hours.

$$$$	over $75
$$$	$50-$75
$$	$25-$50
$	less than $25

ADAMS MORGAN

$$ Mama Ayesha's – *1967 Calvert St. NW.* ☎*202-232-5431.* *www.mamaayeshas.com.* **Lebanese.** This cozy Middle Eastern eatery emanates a welcoming air of family camaraderie. Start with one a variety of hummus or stuffed grape leaves before feasting on couscous smothered by seasoned vegetables or kabobs. Bigger appetites will be whetted by the daunting baked lamb shank. Dinners conclude with a cup of sweet Arabian coffee and decadent baklava.

$ Lauriol Plaza – *1835 18th St. NW.* ☎*202-387-0035. www.lauriolplaza.com.* **Mexican.** One of Adams Morgan's most popular eateries, Lauriol Plaza keeps pitchers of margaritas flowing freely during happy hour. Fabulous fajitas and other Tex-Mex mainstays are joined by Puerto Rican and Latin American selections on the extensive menu. With ample outdoor dining, Lauriol Plaza sizzles on summer evenings.

$ Saigonnais – *2307 18th St. NW.* ☎*202-232-5300. www.dcnet.com/saigonnais.* **Vietnamese.** Located in the heart of Adams Morgan, Saigonnais tantalizes with aromatic Indochine creations. Stylish and simple, the spring rolls are crisp and flavorful, while the assembly-required, pork-filled crepe rolls offer a challenging prelude to the lemongrass chicken and other generous dishes.

CAPITOL HILL

$$$ Bistro Bis – *15 E St. NW.* ☎*202-661-2700. www.bistrobis.com.* **French.** Located in the stylish Hotel George, this decisively French bistro swarms with political figures. Washington celebrities hover around the zinc bar and nestle into cozy leather booths, while three dining levels complement the contemporary offerings. Worth trying: chef Jeffrey Buben's monkfish marseillaise and seared sea scallops provençale.

$$ Capitol City Brewing Company – *2 Massachusetts Ave. NW.* ☎*202-842-2337; also 1100 New York Ave. NW.* ☎*202-628-2222. www.capcitybrew.com.* **Pub.** Casual and comfortable, the District's oldest microbreweries serve up simple bar tastes in two restored historic buildings. Beer fans can try a Sampler of all four in-house brewery blends. Servers promptly bring soft, warm pretzels for patrons to munch on while perusing the menu. Giant sandwiches and ample salads rejuvenate after a day of sightseeing. For dessert, share the massive Monumental Brownie.

$$ Tortilla Coast – *400 First St. SE.* ♿ ☎*202-546-6768. www.tortillacoast.com.* **TexMex.** Wayward Texans have found their way to Tortilla Coast for potent margaritas and spicy tastes of home since 1988. Cleanse your palate with the Stars and Stripes margarita, a blend of traditional and strawberry margaritas

What you should know about Washington, DC restaurants:

Smoking is not allowed in Washington, DC restaurants or bars. Although **jackets** may not be required, gentlemen might feel more comfortable wearing one in the more expensive restaurants. **Reservations** are highly recommended. Gratuities are generally not included on the bill; a tip of 15 to 20 percent is considered standard.

laced with Blue Curacao. Spinach and mushroom enchiladas and soft tacos satisfy vegetarians, while southwestern flavors shine through in the hickory barbecue chicken fajitas.

$$ White Tiger – *301 Massachusetts Ave. NE. No lunch Sat.* ☎*202-546-5900. www.whitetigerdc.com.* **Indian.** Just footsteps from Union Station, the tropical decor and Raji mystique of White Tiger seem a far cry from the nearby steak houses. The menu weighs heavily on lighter, northern Indian fare, with impeccable tandoori chicken or lamb dishes and savory naan bread. Outdoor seating makes this restaurant a favorite of Capitol Hill employees.

DOWNTOWN

$$$ Butterfield 9 – *600 14th St. NW.* ☎*202-289-8810. www.butterfield9. com.* **American.** Butterfield 9 evokes the subtle glamour of black-and-white Hollywood. Its creative American menu skillfully combines retro and modern flavors. Start with chervil and ricotta gnocchi or a roasted beet gateau with blue-cheese fondue. From there, move on to a traditional steak or poached Artic char, before savoring baked Alaska with rum raisin ice cream for dessert.

$$$ The Caucus Room – *401 9th St. NW.* ☎*202-393-1300. www.thecaucus room.com.* **American.** This restaurant is the consummate Washington steak house, where power players disappear into the dark wooded interior to down a tender steak and a glass of merlot. Truly a bipartisan venture, The Caucus Room is partially owned by Republican Haley Barbour and Democrat Tom Boggs, and boasts a colorful William Woodward mural of a jovial donkey and elephant amicably enjoying a lavish feast. Generous portions and impeccable service justify the high prices.

$$$ Oceanaire – *1201 F St. NW.* ☎*202-347-2277. www.theoceanaire.com.* **Seafood.** This seafood restaurant offers over two dozen fresh catch options each day in a rambling downtown setting. Chef Rob Klink features two menus each day, to accommodate fresh arrivals. Start with the regional favorite Maryland blue crab soup or zesty oysters Rockefeller before moving on to the peppery cioppino. Nostalgia triumphs for dessert: fresh-baked Toll House cookies and frosty glasses of milk have been eagerly received by discerning Washington diners.

$$$ Rasika – *633 D St. NW. Closed Sun.* ☎*202-637-1222. www.rasikarestaurant. com.* **Indian.** This new (2005) DC hot spot pulls diners in with its sophisticated setting and contemporary Indian cuisine, served as small plates. Start with a pomegranate marguerita, then order the much-talked-about appetizer *palat chaat* (crisp baby spinach) with sweet yogurt, tamarind and date chutney. For your main course, try the wild boar chop or the signature black cod.

$$$ 701 – *701 Pennsylvania Ave. NW.* ☎*202-393-0701. www.701restaurant. com.* **Contemporary.** Tucked behind the Navy Memorial, 701 recalls the elegance of an upscale supper club, with its piano music and vast selection of vodkas and caviar. The fresh fish selections are dramatic preludes to performances at the nearby Shakespeare Theatre. For elegance at an affordable

TenPenh

Fredde Lieberman/Simone Ink

price, try the pre-theater menus, or stop by for dessert after the performance.

$$$ TenPenh – *1001 Pennsylvania Ave. NW. ☎202-393-4500. www.tenpenh. com.* **Asian.** The sumptuous decor and notable flavors of one of Washington, DC's most popular Asian restaurants resulted from a three-week shopping and tasting journey to South Asia. Begin with the Thai-style coconut and chicken soup with portobello mushrooms before moving on to the macadamia and sambal halibut or the red Thai curry prawns. Wash it down with sake or ginger limeade.

$$$ Vidalia – *1990 M St. NW. ☎202-659-1990. www.vidaliadc.com.* **Southern.** With upscale versions of shrimp and grits and chicken and dumplings, Vidalia is an oasis of Southern comfort food in Washington's bustling business district. Vidalia's sunny yellow walls match the warm cornbread and refreshing lemonade that accent a summer lunch. Try the signature roasted Vidalia onion in season, and close your meal with sticky pecan pie paired with bourbon-laced ice cream.

$$ Café Atlantico – *405 8th St. NW. ☎202-393-0812. www.cafeatlantico. com.* **Latin American.** Café Atlantico is widely considered conservative Washington's most daring restaurant. Chef Katsuya Fukushima tastefully modifies Nuevo Latino flavors to suit DC's conservative and liberal taste buds. Updated versions of Brazilian classics, such as *feijao tropeiro* (black beans, pork, white rice) are suitably paired

with refreshing rum-based mojitos or cachaça-inspired caipirinhas.

$$ DC Coast – *1401 K St. NW. www.dccoast.com. ☎202-216-5988.* **Contemporary.** A towering bronze mermaid sculpture greets hungry locals at this hot downtown restaurant. Housed in an Art Deco-era bank, the contemporary dining room features lantern-style chandeliers, oversized oval mirrors and spiral-shaped booths. Chef Jeff Tunks' tri-coastal specialties (Mid-Atlantic, Gulf and West) include mushroom-crusted halibut with truffled potatoes, and grilled beef tenderloin with fingerling potato cake and sautéed rapini.

$$ Zaytinya – *701 9th St. NW. ☎202-638-0800. www.zaytinya.com.* **Mediterranean.** This very popular restaurant near the National Portrait Museum draws DC-ites to its large, whitewashed dining levels, accented with Aegean blues. The *mezze*-based menu offers Greek, Turkish and Lebanese seafood, meat, and vegetarian options, accompanied by puffy pita bread and oil. Try the skewered lamb (Adana Kebab Tike), the swordfish, and the falafel, to sample each option. The muscat-soaked apricots make a great ending to your meal.

$ Nooshi – *1120 19th St. St. NW. ☎202-293-3138. www.nooshidc.com.* **Asian.** Nooshi features sushi on its menu, fusing Malaysian, Japanese, Indonesian, Thai and Chinese variations of noodles. Select from udon, ramen, egg, chow fun, and then select a preparation style—the frenzied cooks do the rest. The savory satays and chicken-coconut soup are worthy introductions to a quick, simple meal.

DUPONT CIRCLE

$$$$ Restaurant Nora – *2132 Florida Ave. NW. ☎202-462-5143. www. noras.com.* **Contemporary.** America's first certified organic restaurant, Nora is housed in an updated 19C grocery store off Dupont Circle. Nora Pouillon's menu features delights such as chilled corn soup with

Sean Cannon

Zaytinya Restaurant

Clyde's of Georgetown

grilled shrimp, and pan-seared Maine lobster with Cuban black-bean ragoût. DC diners have praised her innovative organic creations for 20-plus years. Nora's sister restaurant, Asia Nora, *(2213 M St. NW ☎202-797-4860; www. noras.com)* boasts an intriguing Asian influence.

$$ Kramerbooks & Afterwords Cafe – *1517 Connecticut Ave. NW. ☎202-387-1462. www.kramers.com.* **International.** A longtime favorite with literature lovers and cafe-goers, this Dupont Circle institution combines a well-stocked bookstore with a bar and restaurant. Entrées range from filet mignon or Moroccan lamb to seared sushi tuna or Thai-steamed mussels. There's a changing selection of microbrewery draft beers. If you're in the mood for simply kaffeeklatsching, the coffee and dessert menu is extensive.

$ Pizzeria Paradiso – *2029 P St. NW. ☎202-223-1245. www.eatyourpizza.com.* **Pizza.** Tucked inside a tiny row house near Dupont Circle, Pizzeria Paradiso serves up one of the best pizzas in the nation's capital. Delicate crust and fresh ingredients are the key. The exceptional crust soaks in a rich, smoky flavor from the wood-burning oven, as the fresh mozzarella melts over a bed of thinly sliced roma tomatoes.

FOGGY BOTTOM

$$$ Kinkead's – *2000 Pennsylvania Ave. NW. ☎202-296-7700. www.kinkead.*

com. **Seafood.** Chef Bob Kinkead's innovative combination of sauces and ingredients makes his award-winning American brasserie one of the premier seafood restaurants in the city. Choices from his daily changing menu may include pepita crusted salmon with crab, shrimp, corn and chile ragoût.

GEORGETOWN

$$$ 1789 Restaurant – *1226 36th St. NW. ☎202-965-1789. www.1789restaurant.com.* **American.** This Washington fine-dining legend is named for the year in which nearby Georgetown University was founded. Its country-inn setting and seasonal American menu have assured its longevity. Though the chef is new, a few long-time favorites remain on the menu, namely, the signature rack of lamb, oyster stew and Nantucket scallops.

$$ Bangkok Bistro – *3251 Prospect St. NW. ☎202-337-2424. www.bangkok bistrodc.com.* **Thai.** The smooth lines and soothing violet and green colors of this eaterie garnered an award from Architectural Digest. With its outdoor cafe and garden seating, the restaurant draws a summer dining crowd, while the fiery Thai flavors sizzle all year long. Bangkok Bistro eschews potent chiles for subtler flavors in its best dishes.

$$ Cafe Deluxe – *3228 Wisconsin Ave. NW. ☎202-686-2233. www.cafe deluxe.com.* **American.** With the feel of a trendy brasserie, Cafe Deluxe eases patrons into a menu of traditional comfort foods. Dark booths provide a relaxing backdrop for the grilled meatloaf with Creole sauce, while the contrasting Art Deco decor prompts the spontaneous ordering of new renditions on old cocktails such as sour-apple martinis. The cafe placates vegetarian patrons with generous salads and pizzas smothered with vegetables and cheese.

$$ Clyde's of Georgetown – *3236 M St. NW.* ☎*202-333-9180. www.clydes.com.* **American.** With several locations in the Washington metropolitan area, cheery, saloon-like Clyde's has burgeoned into a Washington legend. Casual diners can opt for traditional burgers, sandwiches and chili, while patrons with greater expectations can select from a lengthy list of fashionable martinis and fresh seafood catches.

$$ Old Europe – *2434 Wisconsin Ave. NW.* ☎*202-333-7600. www.old-europe. com.* **German.** One of Washington's only German restaurants, Old Europe draws a healthy contingent of beer and schnitzel lovers who find solace in few other locales. The walls are covered, as anticipated, with steins and wooden crests that create a perpetual air of Oktoberfest. Satisfying, hearty dishes are served up in a quick, friendly and unpretentious manner.

$$ Old Glory – *3139 M St. NW.* ☎*202-337-3406. www.oldglorybbq.com.* **Barbecue.** Don't miss this fun, lively barbecue joint perched on the busy Georgetown corner of M Street and Wisconsin Avenue. Settle into a booth, and a server will promptly arrive to powerfully "brand" your table with a purposeful slap of an iron stamp. Each table comes equipped with six regionally inspired sauces to suit patrons' preferences. Mosey up to the lavish hickory bar, which boasts the largest selection of bourbons in DC.

$ Rocklands – *2418 Wisconsin Ave. NW.* ☎*202-333-2558. www.rocklands.com.* **Barbecue.** For an inexpensive meal in Georgetown, follow the sweet smell of hickory smoke up Wisconsin Avenue to Rocklands. Traditional barbecue staples, from ribs and pulled pork to jalapeño cornbread, are deftly handled here. If you're shopping for something a little different, try the smoky grilled swordfish or the salmon sandwich.

U STREET

$ Ben's Chili Bowl – *1213 U St. NW.* ☎*202-667-0909. www.benschilibowl. com.* **Chili.** Ben's is common meeting ground for DC's traditional African-American community and young urban dwellers; sloppy chili dogs, thick milkshakes and fries loaded with cheese and bacon have proven to be universal pleasers in this Washington dining landmark. The interior retains the nostalgic charm of a 1950s diner, while modern business lunchers swivel around on the barstools during their power lunches.

WHITE HOUSE AREA

$$ Georgia Brown's – *950 15th St. NW.* ☎*202-393-4499. www.gbrowns. com.* **Southern.** This well-appointed restaurant has pushed Dixie cooking to new heights by combining standard Southern ingredients in unusual ways and presenting them with a decidedly artistic flair. For starters, try the she-crab soup or the fried catfish fingers. Entrées include "head-on" shrimp with spicy sausage and creamy grits, and Southern-fried chicken.

$$ McCormick & Schmick's – *1652 K St. NW.* ☎*202-861-2233. www.mccormick andschmicks.com.* **Seafood.** This upscale (but not pricey) restaurant, with a score of establishments nationwide, is renowned for its exceptionally fresh and varied seafood. The menu typically features a dozen kinds of shellfish from both coasts as well as a wide array of fish. Request menu items grilled or sautéed to your taste.

WOODLEY PARK

$$ Lebanese Taverna – *2641 Connecticut Ave. NW.* ☎*202-265-8681. www. lebanesetaverna.com.* **Lebanese.** One of the most popular restaurants in Woodley Park, this taverna teems with young professionals and outdoor-cafe enthusiasts. Large groups can begin with a savory array of *mezza*—a spread of hors d'oeuvres, paired with the warm, soft pita bread that emerges from the wood-burning ovens. The juicy rotisserie chicken and lemony chicken *shish taouk* are tasty and satisfying.

ENTERTAINMENT

Just 15 years ago, Washington was not equated with a lively night scene, with the exception of U Street and perhaps Adams Morgan. Downtown DC pretty much closed up at night, save for the scant restaurant trade. But today, the capital city boasts a wide array of options for entertainment, especially after-dark. Classical music-lovers, club-goers, jazz enthusiasts and dance fans can find almost every venue here, from concert halls to mega-dance floors to intimate lounges. And not just in DC, but in Georgetown, Tysons Corner and areas nearby as well.

Performing Arts

Washington provides visitors with a great diversity of performing-arts offerings year-round. Highly respected dance, symphony and opera performances are held primarily at the Kennedy Center. Located in Vienna, Virginia, just 30 minutes from Washington, **Wolf Trap** is the country's only national park dedicated to the performing arts. Visitors can enjoy a relaxing dinner under the stars on the grounds or bring a picnic for concerts, dance, jazz, opera and other performances from late May to early September. In the DC area, several dozen live-performance **theaters** mount a variety of stage productions performed by traveling Broadway companies and acclaimed regional and local groups. DC's main theater district centers on E Street between 7th and 15th Streets NW (the National, Warner, Ford's and Shakespeare theaters), while the Arena Stage along the southwest waterfront presents classic and contemporary drama in its three theaters. Catering largely to DC's African-American community is the Lin-

Music and Dance
Below is a selection of the area's venues and performing arts organizations:

Classical Music

Folger Consort	Folger Shakespeare Library	Oct–May	202-544-7077 707-5502	folger.edu
Juilliard Quartet	Call for locations	Oct–Dec	202-397-7328 707-5503	julliardstring-quartet.org
National Gallery Orchestra	National Gallery of Art	Oct–Jun	202-842-6941	nga.gov
National Symphony Orchestra	Kennedy Center Wolf Trap Park	Sept–Jun Jun–Sept	202-467-4600 877-965-3872	national symphony.org
Washington Opera	Kennedy Center	Sept–Jun	202-295-2400	dc-opera.org
Washington Symphony	Various locations	Year-round	202-546-9797	washington symphony.org.
Wolf Trap Opera Company	Wolf Trap Park	May–Sept	703-255-1900	wolftrap.org

Dance

	Venue	Season	☎	www
Carla & Company (and other troupes)	Dance Place	Year-round	202-269-1600	danceplace.org
Washington Ballet	Multiple Locations	Sept–May	202-362-3606	washington ballet.org

Theaters and Companies

Curtain Up, an online theater magazine, provides descriptions, reviews and schedules of plays currently being performed: www.curtainup.com.

Theaters	Address	☎	www
African Continuum Theatre Company	3523 12th St. NE	202-529-5764	africancontinuumtheatre.com
American Century Theater	2700 S. Lang St., Arlington, VA	703-553-8782	americancentury.org
Arena Stage	6th St. & Maine Ave. SW	202-488-3300	arena-stage.org
Church Street Theater	1742 Church St. NW	202-265-3767	smart.net/~esm/
Eisenhower Theater	Kennedy Center	202-467-4600	kennedy-center.org
Folger Theatre	Folger Shakespeare Library	202-544-7077	folger.edu
GALA Hispanic Theatre	3333 14th St. NW	202-234-7174	galatheatre.org
Horizons Theatre	3700 S. Four Mile Rd., Arlington, VA	703-391-2929	horizonstheatre.org
Le Neon	1611 N. Kent St., Rosslyn, VA	703-243-6366	dcmdva-arts.org
Lincoln Theatre	1215 U St. NW	202-328-6000	thelincolntheatre.org
National Theatre	1321 Pennsylvania Ave. NW	202-628-6161	nationaltheatre.org
Shakespeare Theatre	450 7th St. NW	202-547-1122	shakespearedc.org
Signature Theatre	4200 Campbell Ave., Arlington, VA	703-820-9771	sig-online.org
Studio Theatre	1501 14th St. NW	202-332-3300	studiotheatre.org
Sylvan Theatre	Washington Monument grounds	202-619-7222	
Teatro de la Luna	4020 Georgia Ave. NW	202-882-6227	teatrodelaluna.org
Warner Theatre	13th & E Sts. NW	202-783-4000	warnertheatre.com
Washington Stage Guild	1901 14th St. NW	240-582-0050	www.stageguild.org
West End Dinner Theatre	4615 Duke St., Alexandria, VA	703-370-2500	
Woolly Mammoth Theater Company	641 D St. NW	202-393-3939	woollymammoth.net
Long-Running Performance			
Shear Madness	Kennedy Center	202-467-4600	shearmadness.com

coln Theatre on U Street. Popular rock and alternative **music** are performed at intimate and large-scale nightclubs as well as at stadiums and other large venues throughout DC, northern Virginia and neighboring Maryland. Area bookstores, coffeehouses and other locations host **public readings** or talks by both established and up-and-coming authors throughout the year.

For a detailed listing of events, consult the *Washington City Paper (distributed Thursday), Washingtonian* magazine, the "Weekend" supplements in the Friday edition of the *Washington Post* and in the Thursday edition of the *Washington Times,* or the free publications listed in this guide under *Planning Your Trip.*

TICKETS

As some of the more popular events sell out months in advance, it is advisable to buy tickets early. Full-price tickets can be purchased directly from the venue's box office or from one of the brokers listed below; a service charge of 10% or more may be added to the ticket price. Ticket brokers sometimes have tickets available when the box office is sold out, but expect to pay a substantial service fee. Hotel concierges may also be able to help secure tickets.

Tickets.com (☎888-223-6000; www.tickets.com) takes phone and online reservations for selected events and sights in DC and environs. Major credit cards are accepted. The service charge added to the price of each ticket varies, depending upon the event. Tickets may be purchased in person at various Olsson's Books & Records locations throughout the DC area (www.olssons.com). These locations only accept cash for ticket purchases.

Ticketmaster (☎202-397-7328 or 800-551-7328; www.ticketmaster.com) outlets are conveniently located throughout the area; call or check online for locations. Major credit cards are accepted. A convenience charge is added to the ticket price.

TICKETplace offers tickets for selected events on the day of the show at half price, plus a service charge of 12% of the full face-value of the ticket. Purchases must be made in person (major credit cards only) from the box office at 407 7th St. NW (◐open year-round Tue–Fri 11am–6pm, Sat 10am–5pm; ☎202-842-5387; www.cultural-alliance.org).

Nightlife

TYSONS CORNER

eCitie Restaurant & Bar
8300 Tyco Rd. ☎703-760-9000. www.eciticafe.com.
Housed in a former warehouse, eCiti quickly became the toast of the Northern Virginia tech quarter. Designed to satisfy the thousands of young professionals who work in burgeoning Tysons Corner, eCitie has also become popular with Washington, DC, residents and workers. Though better known for its nightlife scene, eCitie serves up affordable weekly specials in its award-winning restaurant. Free salsa lessons and occasional dance exhibitions round out the offerings.

ADAMS MORGAN

Habana Village
1834 Columbia Rd., NW. ☎202-462-6310. www.habanavillage.com.
Forget the embargo on Cuba; Habana Village does its best to re-create the island in DC. Sultry and sexy characterize all three stories of the club, where women never pay cover charges, and even shrinking violets move from the wall to dance the salsa, rumba and bolero. There's live music on weekends, when bartenders pour mojitos by the hundreds.

Madam's Organ
2461 18th St. NW. ☎202-667-5370. www.madamsorgan.com.
"Sorry, we're open" reads the mural outside, just below a busty redhead's boldly painted portrait. The bright colors and brazen sarcasm of Madam's Organ have made it one of the most familiar sites in DC. Inside, it's just as quirky. Take the stairs up to Big Daddy's Love Lounge & Pick-Up Joint, but beware…it's aptly named.

Chief Ike's Mambo Room
1725 Columbia Rd. NW. ☎202-332-2211. www.chiefikes.com.
Not much Mambo about it—George Stephanopoulos made frequent visits to this Adams Morgan haunt, setting off an invasion of preppie Capitol Hill staffers. Chief Ike's packs a big crowd on weekend nights, but the kitschy bar spills out onto a roomy terrace for fresh air and less harried conversation.

DUPONT CIRCLE

18th Street Lounge
1212 18th St. NW. ☎ 202-466-3922.

Adams Morgan

Celebrity residents and visitors are often spotted in the 18th Street Lounge, one of Dupont Circle's most coveted places for nightlife. Bouncers stand guard over the beautiful property—a historic mansion that was once home to Teddy Roosevelt—and maintain a strict admissions policy. Leave the jeans, sneakers and ballcaps at home, though; if you want to experience the ESL (as it's known to locals), you've got to project a level of "cool."

MCCXXIII

223 Connecticut Ave. NW.
☎*202-822-1800. www.1223.com.*
This is a place for those who like rubbing elbows with the rich and famous. Located in the heart of Dupont, MCCXXIII adds a touch of elegance to the Circle's entertainment options. SPANK is the new top-floor VIP level. *No sneakers, flip flops, ballcaps or athletic wear.*

Dragonfly

1215 Connecticut Ave. NW. ☎*202-331-1775. www.dragonflysushibar.com.*
Dragonfly filled a void in Washington, providing a cosmopolitan, trendy, yet unique nightlife option with its extensive sushi menu and liquor to match. The decor within is surreal, yet minimalist—Bruce Lee footage races across the whitewashed walls, while music trickles out from the dance floor.

Gazuza

1629 Connecticut Ave. NW.
☎ *202-667-5500.*
Sleek furnishings and outside seating overlooking busy Connecticut Avenue have placed Gazuza on the Washington nightlife map. The chic ambience and enviable property don't engender a sense of exclusivity, though; Gazuza's Dupont Circle location attracts a healthy mix of revelers seeking house music and trendy martinis.

DOWNTOWN

Ozio

1813 M St. NW. ☎ *202-822-6000. www.oziodc.com.*
Marketing itself as a "cigar and martini lounge," Ozio paints a tempting picture of urban chic to Washington's international crowd. It's got the martini menu and lingering cigar smells to match, though the splashy murals and muted walls detract from its loungy qualities.

Platinum Club

915 F St. NW. ☎ *202-393-3555. www.platinumclubdc.com.*
If you're looking for a place to dance, its hard to beat Platinum Club. Three

dance floors pulse with music (house, R&B, hip hop, and reggae) and a fourth floor is dedicated as a VIP lounge. People of all ages crowd into the club on weekends, finding solace in the music of their choice. There are drink specials before midnight and 3am closings on Friday and Saturday.

GEORGETOWN

Blues Alley

1073 Wisconsin Ave. NW. ☎ 202-337-4141. www.bluesalley.com.
Few Washington nightlife places have enjoyed the success and notoriety of Georgetown's Blues Alley, which has been praised by *New York Times* critics and Dizzy Gillespie alike. Since it opened in 1965, Blues Alley has touted itself as "DC's Best Jazz Supper Club" and is worthy of the distinction; some of the biggest names in jazz have played and recorded albums here.

Sequoia

Washington Harbour, 3000 K St. NW. ☎ 202-944-4200. www.arkrestaurants.com.
Yachts and sporty racing boats sidle up to the Georgetown waterfront on warm summer evenings to enjoy the dockside night scene. A constant stream of music wafts from the docked boats into the bar, where DC's "bold and beautiful" down beer and margaritas in the two-level glass-front restaurant.

Paper Moon

1073 31st St. NW. ☎202-965-6666. www.papermoon-dc.com.
A sleek international crowd flocks to this Tuscan villa-inspired restaurant that morphs into a lively dance party on weekend nights. Playing largely house and international music, Paper Moon bursts with nearby Georgetown and George Washington University students and internationals who make their home in DC.

Third Edition

1218 Wisconsin Ave. NW. ☎ 202-333-3700. www.thethirdedition.com.
This Georgetown mainstay served as the backdrop for the 1985 movie *St. Elmo's Fire* and has hosted many a beleaguered college student since it opened in 1969. On Wednesday through Saturday nights, a dance party erupts on the upper level, leaving the mellow downstairs beer-sippers and game-watchers in the wake of pop and rock classics. In the summertime, a lively Tiki Bar opens to offer one of Georgetown's few opportunities for outdoor nightlife away from the riverfront.

U STREET

Bohemian Caverns

2001 11th St. NW. ☎ 202-299-0801. www.bohemiancaverns.com.
One of DC's best jazz spots in the days of Duke Ellington, Bohemian Caverns

U Street Mural

DC Convention & Tourism Corp.

reopened fairly recently with a fresh new look and a pleasing lineup of performers. Three levels were added above ground. An upscale restaurant occupies the main level, while live music trickles up from the refurbished caverns below. The second level holds a lounge, Club 2001.

The Black Cat
1811 14th St. NW. ☎ 202-667-7960.
www.blackcatdc.com.

Live-music lovers flock to The Black Cat for a sneak preview of some of rock's rising stars. With an ample space that can hold 550 fans, The Black Cat is readily packed with pierced and tattooed punk- and alternative-music fiends. The familiar U Street haunt is co-owned by former Nirvana drummer and current Foo Fighter Dave Grohl.

SHOPPING

Visitors to Washington can find everything from specialty shops and boutiques in Georgetown to established department stores situated in and around Downtown. Scattered throughout the city are several enclosed malls featuring multilevel arcades and offering a wide selection of shops, restaurants and movie theaters. Some of the more exclusive malls (Willard Collection, Mazza Gallerie) house boutiques of internationally renowned designers. Galleries, antique shops and bookstores can be found in the neighborhoods of Adams Morgan, Dupont Circle and around Eastern Market on Capitol Hill. Fashionable Connecticut Avenue from K Street to Dupont Circle presents fine shops and specialty stores. In Old Town Alexandria, visitors can find an array of gift and antique shops and galleries.

DOWNTOWN AND VICINITY			
Department Stores			
	Address	☎	**www**
Macy's Metro Center	12th & G Sts. NW	202-628-6661	macys.com
Filene's Basement	1133 Connecticut Ave. NW	202-872-8430	filenesbasement.com
Shopping Malls			
La Promenade, L'Enfant Plaza	480 L'Enfant Plaza, One level below L'Enfant hotel Lobby	202-485-3300	
Pavilion at the Old Post Office	1100 Pennsylvania Ave. NW	202-289-4224	oldpostofficedc.com
Shops at National Place	1331 Pennsylvania Ave. NW	202-662-1250	
Union Station	Massachusetts Ave. & 1st St. NE	202-289-1908	unionstationdc.com
Specialty Shops and Trademark Stores			
ApartmentZero	406 7th St. NW	202-628-4067	apartmentzero.com
Pua Naturally	444 7th St. NW	202-347-4543	pua-naturally.com.

Downtown Specialty Shops and Trademark Stores (continued)			
ESPN Zone	555 12th St. NW	202-783-3776	espnzone.com
Hard Rock Cafe	999 E St. NW	202-737-7625	hardrockcafe.com
Political Americana	1331 Pennsylvania Ave. NW	202-737-7730	politicalamericana. com

CONNECTICUT AVENUE/ DUPONT CIRCLE

Specialty Shops and Designer Boutiques

	Address	☎	www
Betsy Fisher	1224 Connecticut Ave. NW	202-785-1975	betsyfisher.com
Burberry	1155 Connecticut Ave. NW	202-463-3000	burberry.com
Montblanc	1006 Connecticut Ave. NW	202-466-5001	montblanc.com
Rizik's	1100 Connecticut Ave. NW	202-223-4050	riziks.com
Commander Salamander	1420 Wisconsin Ave. NW	202-337-2265	

Bookstores

Kramerbooks & Afterwords Cafe	1517 Connecticut Ave. NW	202-387-1400	kramers.com
Politics & Prose	5015 Connecticut Ave. NW	202-364-1919	politics-prose.com

GEORGETOWN

Shopping Malls

	Address	☎	www
Georgetown Park	3222 M St. NW	202-298-5577	shopsatgeorgetownpark. com

Specialty Shops and Designer Boutiques

Coach	3259 M St. NW	202-333-3005	coach.com
BCBG Max Azria	3210 M St. NW	202-333-2224	bcbg.com
Banana Republic	3200 M St. NW	202-333-2554	bananarepublic.com
Betsey Johnson	1319 Wisconsin Ave. NW	202-338-4090	betseyjohnson.com
Benetton	1200 Wisconsin Ave. NW	202-625-0443	benetton.com
French Connection	1229 Wisconsin Ave. NW	202-965-4690	frenchconnection.com
MAC Cosmetics	3067 M St. NW	202-944-9771	maccosmetics.com
Restoration Hardware	1222 Wisconsin Ave. NW	202-625-2771	restorationhardware.com
Steve Madden Shoes	3109 M St. NW	202-342-6195	stevemadden.com
Patagonia	1048 Wisconsin Ave. NW	202-333-1776	patagonia.com

MARYLAND			
Shopping Malls			
	Address	☎	**www**
Chevy Chase Pavilion	5335 Wisconsin Ave. NW	202-686-5335	ccpavilion.com
Mazza Gallerie	5300 Wisconsin Ave. NW	202-966-6114	mazzagallerie.com
Montgomery Mall	7101 Democracy Blvd., Bethesda	301-469-6025	westfield.com/ montgomery
White Flint Mall	11301 Rockville Pike	301-468-5777	shopwhiteflint.com
Specialty shops and designer boutiques			
Cartier	5471 Wisconsin Ave.	301-654-5858	cartier.com
MicMac Bis	5454 Wisconsin Ave. NW	301-654-8686	
Saks Fifth Avenue Women's Store	5555 Wisconsin Ave.	301-657-9000	saksfifthavenue.com
Jandel Furs	5510 Wisconsin Ave.	301-652-2250	
Tiffany & Co.	5481 Wisconsin Ave.	301-657-8777	tiffany.com
Lord & Taylor.	5255 Western Ave	202-362-9600	lordandtaylor.com

VIRGINIA			
Shopping Malls			
	Address	☎	**www**
Ballston Common	4238 Wilson Blvd., Arlington	703-243-8088	ballston-common.com
Fashion Centre at Pentagon City	I-395 at S. Hayes St., Arlington	703-415-2400	simon.com
Tysons Galleria	2001 International Dr., McLean	703-827-7700	tysonsgalleria.com
Landmark Mall	5801 Duke St., Alexandria	703-354-8405	landmarkmall.com
Springfield Mall	I-95 South, Springfield	703-971-3600	springfieldmall.com
Tysons Corner Center	1961 Chain Bridge Rd., McLean	703-893-9400	shoptysons.com

Museum Shops		
	☎	**www**
Arthur M. Sackler Gallery	202-633-4880	asia.si.edu
Corcoran Gallery of Art	202-639-1791	corcoran.org
Decatur House	202-842-1856	decaturhouse.org
Folger Shakespeare Library	202-675-0364	folger.edu

Museum Shops (continued)		
	☎	www
Freer Gallery of Art	202-633-4880	asia.si.edu
Hillwood Museum	202-686-8500	hillwoodmuseum.org
Hirshhorn Museum	202-357-1429	hirshhorn.si.edu
Library of Congress	202-707-8000	loc.gov
National Air & Space Museum	202-357-1387	nasm.si.edu
National Building Museum	202-272-7706	nbm.org
National Gallery of Art	202-842-6002	nga.gov
National Museum of African Art	202-786-2147	nmafa.si.edu
Smithsonian American Art Museum	202-633-7970	americanart.si.edu
National Museum of Natural History	202-633-1000	mnh.si.edu
National Portrait Gallery	202-275-1738	npg.si.edu
National Postal Museum	202-633-9849	si.edu/postal
Renwick Gallery	202-633-7970	americanart.si.edu
Lyceum (Alexandria)	703-838-4994	oha.alexandriava.gov/lyceum

Spas			
	Address	☎	www
Celadon	1180 F St. NW	202-347-3333	celadonspa.com
Red Door Spa	5225 Wisconsin Ave. NW Chevy Chase, MD	202-363-1627 202-362-9890	reddoorsalon.com
Spa at the Mandarin Oriental Hotel	1330 Maryland Ave. SW	202-787-6100	mandarinoriental.com
Georgetown Aveda	1325 Wisconsin Ave. NW	202-965-1325	aveda.com
Bluemercury	3059 M St. NW Georgetown 1619 Connecticut Ave. NW	202-965-1300 202-462-1300	bluemercury.com
Jacques Dessange	5410 Wisconsin Ave Chevy Chase, MD	301-913-9373	jacques-dessange.com

SPORTS AND FITNESS

Spectator Sports

Tickets for sporting events such as those in the charts below can usually be purchased at the venue itself or through Ticketmaster (☎ 202-432-7328 for DC, ☎ 410-481-7328 for Baltimore, ☎ 703-573-7328 for Virginia; www.ticketmaster.com). When games are sold out, you can sometimes get tickets through a ticket agency (see the Yellow Pages of the phone directory).

Where to Get a Workout

The **National Capitol YMCA** is open only to YMCA members and guests of members (1711 Rhode Island Ave. NW ☎ 202-862-9622; www.national capitalymca.org). The **fitness centers** listed opposite allow nonmembers to use their facilities (weight rooms, aerobics classes and pool, if available) for a nominal daily fee ($10–$25). Members of IHRSA should ask if they are entitled to a lower daily fee.

Professional Sports			
Sport/Team	Season	Venue	☎ Information/Tickets
◎ Baseball (AL) **Washington Nationals**	Apr–Sept	RFK Stadium E. Capitol & 22nd Sts. SE	Info: 202-675-6287 Tickets: 407-839-3900 www.nationals.mlb.com
◎ Football (NFL) **Washington Redskins**	Sept–Dec	FedEx Field Landover, MD	Tickets: 301-276-6050 www.redskins.com
◎ Hockey (NHL) **Washington Capitals**	Oct–Apr	Verizon Center 7th & F Sts. NW	Tickets: 202-432-7328 www.capsitals.nhl.com
◎ Basketball (NBA) **Washington Wizards**	Nov–Apr	Verizon Center 7th & F Sts. NW	Info: 202-661-5000 Tickets: 202-661-5050 www.nba.com/wizards
◎ Basketball (WNBA) **Washington Mystics**	May–Aug	Verizon Center 7th & F Sts. NW	Info: 202-266-2200 Tickets: 877-324-6671 www.washingtonmystics.com

Horse Racing			
Racetrack	Season	Event	☎ Information
Laurel Park	Oct–Mar Jun–Aug	Thoroughbred racing	301-725-0400 www.marylandracing.com
Pimlico	Mar–Oct 3rd Sat/May	Thoroughbred racing Preakness Stakes	410-542-9400 www.marylandracing.com
Rosecroft Raceway	Year-round	Harness races	301-567-4000 www.rosecroft.com
Charles Town Races	Year-round	Thoroughbred racing	800-795-7001 www.ctownraces.com

Polo			
Venue	Season	Event	☏ Information
Lincoln Memorial Polo Field	Jun–Oct Wednesdays 5pm Saturdays 1pm	local tournaments	☏301-972-7288 www.gopolo.com www.americascupof polo.com

Fitness Centers			
City Fitness	3525 Connecticut Ave. NW	☏202-537-0539	www.fitphysique.org
Tenley Sport and Health	4000 Wisconsin Ave. NW	☏202-362-8000	www.sportandhealth.com
Washington Sports Club	214 D St. SE 1211 Connecticut Ave. NW 3222 M St. NW 1990 K St. NW	☏202-547-2255 ☏202-296-7733 ☏202-338-0911 ☏202-466-6500	www.mysportsclub.com

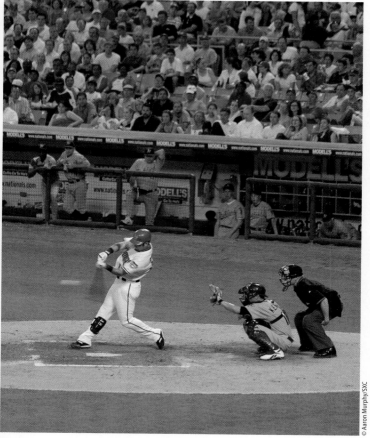

© Aaron Murphy/SXC

The Washington Nationals baseball team faces off against the Oakland Athletics

A

B

C

INDEX

INDEX

WHERE TO EAT

MAPS AND PLANS

LIST OF MAPS

COMPANION PUBLICATIONS

North America Road Atlas

◆ A geographically organized atlas with extensive detailed coverage of the USA, Canada and Mexico. Includes 246 city maps, distance chart, state and provincial driving requirements and a climate chart.
◆ Comprehensive city and town index
◆ Easy-to-follow "Go-to" pointers

Map 583 Northeastern USA/Eastern Canada

◆ Large-format map providing detailed road systems and including driving distances, interstate rest stops, border crossings and interchanges.
◆ Comprehensive city and town index
◆ Scale 1:2,400,000 (1 inch = approx. 38 miles)

Map 761 USA Road Map

◆ Covers the principal US road network and presents shaded relief detail of the overall physiography of the land.
◆ Features state flags with statistical data and state tourism office telephone numbers
◆ Scale 1:3,450,000

Regional Road Atlas

◆ Measuring a slim 4.5: x 10", and only fractions of an inch thick, Michelin's regional road atlases can actually fit in your glove box, your purse, or anywhere you need. They are a convenient alternative to large, cumbersome road maps and you'll never have to worry about folding them up.
◆ Clear, colorful and easy to read cartography
◆ Detailed city maps are indexed alphabetically in the back of the book.
◆ Washington, DC is included in the Mid-Atlantic USA Regional Road Atlas.

Regional Road Atlas + Travel Guide

◆ For the traveler who wants to know more about what to do along the way, without sacrificing portability, Michelin's Road Atlas + Travel Guide series is the perfect solution. You get the same great Michelin mapping from the road atlases, paired with charming hotel and restaurant selections, scenic tours, fabulous color photos and much, much more!
◆ Washington, DC is included in the Mid-Atlantic USA Regional Road Atlas + Travel Guide.

LEGEND

★★★ **Highly recommended**
★★ **Recommended**
★ **Interesting**

Sight symbols

➡ ▬▬▬ Walking tour with departure point and direction

✝ ♱	Church, chapel	☀ ☀ Panorama – View
✡	Synagogue	▬ Building described
AZ B	Map co-ordinates locating sights	☐ Other building
■ ▲	Other points of interest	▪ Small building
▪	Statue, monument	⚓ Lighthouse
⊙	Fountain	⊞⊞ Cemetery described – Other

All maps are oriented north, unless otherwise indicated by a directional arrow.

Other symbols

🛣 Interstate Highway   🛣 US Highway   ⑤⑤ Other Route

▬●▬	Highway, interchange	🛈 Visitor information
▬▬	Toll road, bridge	✚ Hospital
⊐ ---	Tunnel with ramp	🎁 Gift shop
⟶	One way street	🚻 ✗ Restrooms – Restaurant
▬▬ ⟜⟜	Pedestrian street – Steps	↕ ⤴ Elevator – Escalator
✈ Ⓜ	Airport – Subway station	🅿 ✉ Parking – Post Office
🚆 🚌	Train station – Bus station	▬□▬ Railroad passenger station
⛴	Ferry: cars and passengers	—·—·— Gate
⛴	Ferry: passengers only	▶ Golf course – Stadium
🎠	Sight of special interest for children	⚓ Harbor cruise

Abbreviations and special symbols

🏳 🏳 **Embassy:** described – mentioned   🌳🌳 Japanese cherry trees

Michelin Apa Publications Ltd

A joint venture between Michelin and Langenscheidt

Suite 6, Tulip House, 70 Borough High Street, London SE1 1XF, United Kingdom

No part of this publication may be reproduced in any form
without the prior permission of the publisher.

© 2007 Michelin Apa Publications Ltd
ISBN 978-1-906261-11-5
Printed: September 2007
Printed and bound in Germany